DUKE ELLINGTON'S SYMPHONIC VISIONS

ADVISORY BOARD

David Evans, General Editor
Barry Jean Ancelet
Edward A. Berlin
Joyce J. Bolden
Rob Bowman
Curtis Ellison
William Ferris
John Edward Hasse
Kip Lornell
Bill Malone
Eddie S. Meadows
Manuel H. Peña
Wayne D. Shirley
Robert Walser

DUKE ELLINGTON'S SYMPHONIC VISIONS

LUCA BRAGALINI

PREFACE BY ALOMA BARDI
FOREWORD BY DAVID SCHIFF

UNIVERSITY PRESS OF MISSISSIPPI / JACKSON

The University Press of Mississippi is the scholarly publishing agency of
the Mississippi Institutions of Higher Learning: Alcorn State University,
Delta State University, Jackson State University, Mississippi State University,
Mississippi University for Women, Mississippi Valley State University,
University of Mississippi, and University of Southern Mississippi.

www.upress.state.ms.us

The University Press of Mississippi is a member
of the Association of University Presses.

The English language edition of this book was published in collaboration
with the International Center for American Music.

Any discriminatory or derogatory language or hate speech regarding race,
ethnicity, religion, sex, gender, class, national origin, age, or disability
that has been retained or appears in elided form is in no way an endorsement
of the use of such language outside a scholarly context.

Original publication in Italian. *Dalla Scala a Harlem. I sogni sinfonici di Duke Ellington.*
© 2018 EDT Srl, Turin, Italy. All rights reserved.
Translation copyright © 2025 by University Press of Mississippi
All rights reserved
Manufactured in the United States of America

∞

Publisher: University Press of Mississippi, Jackson, USA
Authorized GPSR Safety Representative: Easy Access System Europe -
Mustamäe tee 50, 10621 Tallinn, Estonia, gpsr.requests@easproject.com

Library of Congress Cataloging-in-Publication Data

Names: Bragalini, Luca author | Schiff, David writer of foreword | Bardi, Aloma writer of preface
Title: Duke Ellington's symphonic visions / Luca Bragalini, David Schiff, Aloma Bardi.
Other titles: American made music series
Description: Jackson : University Press of Mississippi, 2025. |
Series: American made music series | Includes bibliographical references and index.
Identifiers: LCCN 2025035949 (print) | LCCN 2025035950 (ebook) |
ISBN 9781496858207 hardback | ISBN 9781496860156 trade paperback | ISBN 9781496860163 epub | ISBN
9781496860170 epub | ISBN 9781496860187 pdf | ISBN 9781496860194 pdf
Subjects: LCSH: Ellington, Duke, 1899–1974—Criticism and interpretation |
Orchestral music—History and criticism | African American jazz musicians |
African American composers | Jazz—History and criticism | Jazz musicians
Classification: LCC ML410.E44 B73 2025 (print) | LCC ML410.E44 (ebook) |
DDC 782.42165092—dc23/eng/20250905
LC record available at https://lccn.loc.gov/2025035949
LC ebook record available at https://lccn.loc.gov/2025035950

British Library Cataloging-in-Publication Data available

CONTENTS

Note of Acknowledgment vii
Preface ix
    ALOMA BARDI
Foreword xi
    DAVID SCHIFF
Introduction: For Symphony Orchestra and Jazz Band 3

1. **LA SCALA, PART I:** Condemned to Oblivion 7
2. **NEW WORLD A-COMIN':** Proud to Be on the Air 24
3. **HARLEM:** Sounds from the Air Shaft 55
4. **NIGHT CREATURE; THE GOLDEN BROOM AND THE GREEN APPLE:**
    Visions in Blue 93
5. **LA SCALA, PART II:** Fathers, Sons, and the Blues 122
6. **THREE BLACK KINGS:** A Tribute to Black History 148
7. **CELEBRATION:** The Score Forgotten
    on the Bottom of the River 167

Notes 187
Bibliography 239
Index of Works and Titles 255
Index of Names 263

NOTE OF ACKNOWLEDGMENT

Over long years of research, many individuals have contributed to the making of this book. While apologizing to those whose names, due to this author's unforgivable oversight, are not listed below, gratitude is expressed to:

the numerous Ellington collectors around the world, from South Africa to Sweden, who generously opened their archives, especially Steven Lasker, Sjef Hoesmit, Bjorn Andresen, Lance Travis, Geoff Smith, Liborio Pusateri, Luciano Massagli, and Vittorio Castelli;

maestro Mario Marzi of La Scala, who facilitated the research at the La Scala Archives in Milan, and Canadian cultural activist Ted O'Reilly, whose mediation with Ron Collier's widow was pivotal to the discovery of *Celebration*;

Edie Shaw, daughter of photographer and filmmaker Sam Shaw, who combed through his archives and uncovered valuable information for understanding the third movement of *Three Black Kings*;

the musicians who offered their expertise for some transcriptions, Marco Marzi for the chapters on *La Scala* and Bruno Cesselli for the examples in chapter 4;

all those who assisted this writer in his various investigations, whether they led to Spanish churches searching for Nativity mosaics (Pedro Cervantes), to identify Latin rhythms (Edu Hebling), or to recover old Polish television footage (Valeria Tiganik);

Walter Scotti, Pierantonio Peron, and the others who patiently read the first drafts of this text, providing useful suggestions;

the Symphony Orchestra of the Marrucino Theatre of Chieti, Italy, the SIdMA Jazz Orchestra with soloists Bepi D'Amato and Paolo Birro, and conductor Bruno Tommaso who enthusiastically recorded the music complementing this book, accessible on the ICAMus channels.

my family, friends, colleagues, and conservatory students, who supported me in this demanding task, especially in the most trying moments; among them, Laura Bonessa stands out, having repeatedly prevented me from throwing in the towel.

For this edition of the book in English, the contribution of the International Center for American Music and its team of experts has been decisive, particularly the accurate and highly competent scholarly supervision and editing work of ICAMus director Aloma Bardi, to whom I extend my utmost respect.

The English manuscript was also read with great attention by musicologists and Ellingtonians experts, who provided invaluable suggestions; among them, I wish to thank Lewis Porter, Andrew Homzy, the late Barbara Heyman, David Schiff, Alexandra Monchick, and Bill Doggett.

Luca Bragalini, Milan, Italy, August 25, 2025

This book is dedicated to all Ellington collectors and enthusiasts around the world, especially to friends Liborio Pusateri and Luciano Massagli; without their generosity, this monograph would stand on much weaker foundations.

PREFACE

ALOMA BARDI

It is with great pleasure and pride that ICAMus-The International Center for American Music presents to the English-speaking and international readers Professor Luca Bragalini's book on Duke Ellington's symphonic compositions, an important, fascinating subject matter that never before has been so thoroughly explored in monographic format.

Duke Ellington's Symphonic Visions has a true international nature and stature, as it is founded on original research conducted on firsthand, previously unexplored sources on both sides of the Atlantic Ocean. The Italian side of the theme is for instance a field of compelling discoveries, shaping the chapter on *La Scala*. Professor Bragalini's exploration of the profound connections between the symphonic Ellington and the Harlem Renaissance is equally innovative. The entire book combines in a creative fashion different disciplines—musicology, music history, social history, photography, art, politics—for a resulting kaleidoscopic look at its subject.

Luca Bragalini's book delves into a topic that has been traditionally regarded as border territory within a musical and musicological context that separates jazz and classical music. The symphonic Ellington had long remained a neglected and misunderstood object of prejudice, a destiny shared with other cases of unique American composers who occupied borderlands between genres and styles, the first and foremost of whom has been of course George Gershwin.

It has been meaningful to work on the English edition of this book in 2024 in conjunction with the Ellingtonian year of celebrations worldwide, when the fiftieth anniversary of Duke Ellington's death has been honored with initiatives and events. At a time of renewed interest in Ellington's life and music, the content and approach of the publications that have appeared in recent years—from *Duke Ellington Studies*, edited by John Howland, 2017, to *Duke Ellington: The Notes the World Was Not Ready to Hear*, by Karen S. Barbera with Randall Keith Horton, 2022—continue to overlook his symphonic output, or at the most to devote occasional attention to it, yet never in an organic perspective—a trend that reconfirms the novelty of Luca Bragalini's musicological study.

Duke Ellington's Symphonic Visions, the result of Luca Bragalini's many years of research, addresses the English-language readers in an adapted and revised edition based on the book published by EDT in Italy in 2018, *Dalla Scala a Harlem: I sogni sinfonici di Duke Ellington* [*From La Scala to Harlem: Duke Ellington's Symphonic Visions*]. In the English text, based on Professor Bragalini's original Italian text, translated by Dr. Brent Waterhouse under the scholarly supervision of ICAMus and Aloma Bardi, who worked in close association with the author, the University Press of Mississippi edition of Luca Bragalini's book can now meet the large audience it was meant for. We wish to express our most sincere appreciation to the publisher for believing in this research and supporting this project, which we trust will contribute to a more comprehensive knowledge of the unique Ellington experience.

ALOMA BARDI—ICAMus-The International Center for American Music
The ICAMus Studio, Ann Arbor, MI, USA
Curator, American Music Center/Centro di Documentazione sulla Musica Americana, Palazzo della Musica, Prato, Italy
October 31, 2024

FOREWORD

DAVID SCHIFF

Much of what passes for jazz history is really just folklore—tales repeated and repeated until they assume the appearance of truth. The creators of these stories were often promoters, record collectors, or enthusiasts more interested in celebrating the art form than in seeking answers to hard questions—or even asking those questions. These tasks require the instincts and training of a true historian like Luca Bragalini.

Bragalini is a historian/detective. He notices barely visible clues and follows up unpromising leads—and solves many mysteries. A good example of his discoveries, just one of many in this book, appears in his groundbreaking research on Duke Ellington's piano concerto, *New World a-Comin'*, which premiered in Carnegie Hall on December 11, 1943. Like many of the other extended works that Professor Bragalini analyzes in this book, *New World* was greeted with a critical skepticism. Six months before its premiere, John Hammond, the most influential producer of jazz concerts and recordings of all time, had dismissed Ellington's *Black, Brown and Beige* as pretentious non-jazz: "It was unfortunate that Duke saw fit to tamper with the blues form in order to produce music of greater 'significance.'" Even though Hammond was a political progressive, he ignored the political implications of Ellington's grandest piece, or, worse, implied, by placing "significance" in scare quotes, that Ellington had no business engaging with serious themes. While Aaron Copland was honored for musical compositions with political themes such as *Fanfare for the Common Man* and *A Lincoln Portrait*, both of which premiered in 1942, Ellington, whether as a representative of jazz or as an African American, was deemed incapable of such expression. The idea that Ellington should have stuck to a three-minute format and danceable "hot" music has somehow persisted among jazz critics down to the present day.

Not surprisingly, then, few white critics took the title *New World a-Comin'*, the sequel to *Black, Brown and Beige*, seriously. Ellington's title honored the book *New World A-Coming: Inside Black America* by Roi Ottley, published in 1943. Ottley presented a detailed analysis of Harlem's history and social institutions at a time of crisis. Harlem, "the nerve center of advancing black America," was decimated by the economic collapse of the Great Depression. As the United States prepared for the Second World War, any hope that the war effort would improve the condition of African Americans was dispelled by the barring of Black workers from defense industries. In July 1941, six months before Pearl Harbor, a meeting of Black leaders with President Roosevelt and the threat of a march on Washington led the president to proclaim "the first presidential order affecting Negroes directly since Lincoln's day," which created a Committee on Fair Employment Practices. Immediately opposed by white labor unions and southern white supremacists, the work of the committee had little effect. The United States soon found itself fighting a war against racism in Europe with a racially segregated army and few effective measures to improve conditions. A. Philip Randolph, head of the NAACP, asked, "How can we fight for democracy in Burma, a country we have not seen, when we don't have democracy in Birmingham, a city we have seen?" Protests, both peaceful and otherwise, soon followed, and the African American political leaders presented the president with an "Eight Point Program" for racial justice that appears in full in Ottley's book (253).

In borrowing Ottley's title, therefore, Ellington was endorsing the book's political agenda, but as was his usual practice, he never said so explicitly in public, and a few years after the war, in a very different political climate, he gave the impression that he was not really familiar with the contents of the book. Could this be true?

Enter Luca Bragalini, historian/detective. Sensing that there must be evidence of a connection between Ellington and Ottley, he turned not to the obvious sources in the jazz literature but to the annals of New York's progressive radio station at the time, WMCA. There, he discovered that a radio series named after Ottley's book was aired on WMCA every Sunday afternoon for two years beginning in March 1944. Unlike the programming of the national networks, this series dealt directly with racial injustice. The spoken credits to the show stated that its "musical theme was by Duke Ellington" and, indeed, as Bragalini discovered, that theme was drawn from Ellington's *New World a-Comin'*.

As a historian, Prof. Bragalini here accomplishes far more than just nailing down a detail in Ellington's biography. He is opening a window, hardly ever seen in so-called jazz history, to the very specific way that Ellington's music interacted with the political consciousness of the Harlem community, and once he opens that window, he fills in the picture with an illuminating account of the context.

Every page of this book is full of similar discoveries that challenge and overturn so many of the myths and misunderstandings that still surround Ellington's music and, in particular, his symphonic music. Reading through Professor Bragalini's discoveries, we feel that a new Ellingtonian world is now within our view.

DUKE ELLINGTON'S SYMPHONIC VISIONS

INTRODUCTION

FOR SYMPHONY ORCHESTRA AND JAZZ BAND

1963 was a year that shook the world. It was the time of Kennedy's assassination and the birth of Beatlemania; the race to space and a scandal involving British War Secretary John Profumo (who shared a lover with a Soviet agent); the Cold War, which seemed to ease slightly, and the one in Vietnam, which worsened dramatically. This was the year that saw Martin Luther King Jr.'s massive March on Washington and his famous speech, "I Have a Dream." It was also the year in which one of Duke Ellington's personal dreams came true with the recording of the Reprise LP *The Symphonic Ellington*.

Certainly, seen alongside these momentous historical upheavals, Duke's album did not attract a large amount of attention. Put more bluntly, no one noticed, not even within the more restricted boundaries of the microcosm of jazz. And yet that very album represented a belief Ellington had stubbornly pursued for many years: the idea that bringing together symphonic music and jazz in a single score could lead to excellent results.

Unfortunately, all of Ellington's efforts were met with a simple, collective shrug. Both worlds, classical music and jazz (with their respective recording executives, impresarios, critics, and fans) refused to collaborate. The upshot is that only two LPs of his symphonic jazz were actually released; one posthumous work was poorly completed by its orchestrators; and one (never recorded) score was forgotten along the way. One must furthermore note that some of the pieces included in the two LPs were older compositions, which only made their way onto an album after suffering refusals for years (the symphonic version of *New World A-Comin'* arrived in the recording studio two decades late). Clearly, this part of Ellington's output was welcomed somewhat halfheartedly.

Over the following pages, these compositions, often seen as secondary, will be brought into the limelight, thanks in part to the previously unreleased symphonic music that was recorded in order to accompany this book.

The Duke was not the first nor the last jazz musician to seek the best of both worlds. Signs of classical music coming together with syncopated music had been in the newspapers ever since the first half of the Roaring Twenties, when the father of symphonic jazz, Paul Whiteman, launched a series of concerts titled "An Experiment in Modern Music." In 1924, this project showcased Gershwin's brilliant *Rhapsody in Blue*, and works by other American composers were performed in the following editions.[1] These were mainly classical musicians who dabbled in jazz (or, better yet, symphonic jazz). All things considered, they did little more than enlarge the ranks of those who, as of the late nineteenth century, had enlivened their scores with ragtime syncopation and colored them with blue notes.[2]

Ellington, on the contrary, was a jazzman who, halfway through his career, decided to approach the symphony orchestra, which had fascinated him ever since his earliest years with the Washingtonians.[3] Following in the footsteps of his mentor James Price Johnson (a ragtime pianist who, as of the second half of the twenties, dedicated himself to symphonic jazz), Ellington set out down a path also treaded by musicians such as John Lewis (with his 1961 ballet *Original Sin*, balanced between jazz, baroque music, and late Romantic Era orchestration) and Gerry Mulligan (in late works including his forgotten masterpiece *Octet for Sea Cliff*), among many others.[4]

A number of eminent scholars have investigated the reasons that led these jazzmen to approach classical music. In his volume *Ellington Uptown*, John Howland, taking up writings by historian Lawrence Levine, suggests that a desire to fill the gap between art music and pop explains the interest shown by some jazz composers toward classical music.[5]

In *The Power of Black Music*, Samuel Floyd turns to the concept of "signifyin(g)," proposed to interpret African American literature by intellectual Henry Louis Gates Jr. in his essay *The Signifying Monkey*. Floyd maintains that Black American musicians had always appropriated elements from other traditions, often transforming them through the distorting lens of irony into something personal.[6] This critical perspective, which has some elements in common with the theory of the "mastery of form" conceived by Houston A. Baker Jr. in his *Modernism and the Harlem Renaissance* and adapted by Paul Allen Anderson in *Deep River: Music and Memory in Harlem Renaissance Thought*, represents, according to the latter, a subversive strategy involving a false assimilation of classical music in African American scores.[7]

A tension between Black and white, or a striving for a double cultural citizenship, inspired the concept of "double consciousness." Introduced by

W.E.B. Du Bois in the early twentieth century in his essential *The Souls of Black Folk*, this idea is still at work in many writings by eminent musicologists, such as the volume by Catherine Parsons Smith, *William Grant Still: A Study in Contradictions*.[8]

A less widespread model, which could however provide much food for thought, comes from what 1950s sociology identified as the figure of the "negro [sic] gentleman." In his recent volume *John Lewis and the Challenge of "Real" Black Music*, musicologist Christopher Coady has employed this model to grasp the meaning of the music of the Modern Jazz Quartet, balanced between baroque and bebop.[9]

Lastly, a further branch of theory that can be applied only to a few musicians (among whom is Duke Ellington) locates the driving force that led some jazzmen to approach classical music within the dictates of the Harlem Renaissance.[10]

These critical approaches overlap at some points but also diverge. Ellington's work, and his symphonic output in particular, has lent itself to many of these contrasting readings. Scholars often tend to avoid contradictions, fearing they might hinder the fluidity of their theses. And yet artists are often contradictory, especially jazzmen interested in classical music (and above all, Black ones with an inclination toward white music . . .). Ellington certainly showed a good many incongruities: he wrote odes to Blackness and yet portrayed a comic-book Africa; he was a Black cultural hero and yet refused to take part in the March on Washington; he expressed his aversion to the use of string instruments in jazz to the periodical *DownBeat* while, in the meantime, asking Luther Henderson to orchestrate *New World A-Comin'* and *Harlem* for symphony orchestra.[11]

We could thus approach the Duke's prismatic music from a good many points of view, basing ourselves on a range of theories. Nevertheless, seeing this specific branch of his production through the lens of the Harlem Renaissance seemed to be the most suitable approach to put it into focus. His links with this world of Harlem leaders, artists, and intellectuals are indeed deeper than has been maintained until the present.

And so, since we will show that the brightest beacon that guided Ellington toward symphonic music consisted in his firm beliefs in the principles of the Black Renaissance, this same light was chosen to orient our research. Not only will it help us explore the content of this unique trunk full of scores, but it will also bring out the most hidden (and often non-musical) meanings concealed under those staves. In other words, once we have inspected this particular treasure chest, by turning to disciplines other than musicology, we will attempt to discuss the most precious part of its content, concealed until present in its false bottom.[12]

LA SCALA, PART I
CONDEMNED TO OBLIVION

PROLOGUE

The long voyage that awaits us will cover a quarter-century of Duke Ellington's career, investigating seven symphonic works conceived in various parts of the world and recorded in studios in Europe and America. Throughout this journey, music will be intertwined with the history of African American cultural movements, sociology will cross paths with art history, and music analysis will come together with a reading of Black American literature.

And yet in this first chapter, the reader will find no trace of such broad perspectives. On the contrary, the story will be set in a fog-beset Milan in the early sixties, which may seem provincial to many. While European cities may have been perceived some time ago as far-off and exotic, the internet has now brought latitudes dramatically closer (Milan and Manila are not all that distant anymore), making the exotic less mysterious and therefore less appealing.

Nevertheless, this initial forty-eight-hour focus on a single episode in the Duke's life, which doesn't even take pains to begin our narration in a conventional chronological order, will act as a springboard, allowing us to dive, later on, into unexplored seas.

While venturing into this seemingly bizarre first chapter, which stubbornly insists on reconstructing an episode that may seem secondary, giving voice to a composition accused by some of being mediocre, our readers are asked—not without some embarrassment—to become archivists. That is to say, they must be willing to accompany the author while flipping through newspapers of the time, interviewing obscure characters (no more than footnotes in music history), and tracking down unpublished documents.

They must be willing to eavesdrop on rehearsals in a recording studio, jotting down the slightest details in their notebooks.

They must be willing to wait before admiring this magnificent composition and prepared to analyze only one small (and apparently insignificant) fragment under the microscope, trusting that this initial survey will point toward a broader story.

And so, now wearing our lab coats, let us put our eyes up to the lens.

FEBRUARY 20-21, 1963, ITALY

The prominent national newspaper *Il Corriere della Sera* billed as "The Event of the Year" two concerts given by Duke Ellington's orchestra, due to take place on those two days. These were in fact the only dates scheduled in Italy during his European tour that, after beginning in London on January 9, would come to its conclusion in Paris on March 2.

After playing at Zurich's Kongresshaus the previous evening, Ellington arrived in Milan by train on February 20 and was accompanied to the luxurious Hotel Palace; the orchestra, as was customary at the time, would be accommodated elsewhere, at the Hotel Duomo.[1]

In the eyes of the local press, what made the two concerts particularly significant, above and beyond trumpeter Cootie Williams's return to the ranks of the orchestra after many years of absence ("Cootie Williams, the Prodigal Son" was the headline run by *Il Giorno* on February 21), was the fact that the venue for Ellington's performance was the prestigious Verdi Hall at the Milan Conservatory, an institution named after the opera composer. The headline "Ellington at the Conservatory" appeared in the *Corriere della Sera* (February 21, 1963), reiterated by *La Notte* as "Duke at the Conservatory" (February 20 to 21, 1963), while *Il Giorno* (February 21, 1963) joined in the chorus with "Ellington at the Conservatory." Based on these articles, it seems that the two concerts were taken as a sign that a certain cultural ground had been conquered. Classical music had decided to open its doors to jazz, meaning that the latter had by now reached adulthood, casting off its childhood clothes: "Jazz now wears a tie. The great Negro musician due to play in the main hall of the music conservatory named after Giuseppe Verdi" is how the *Corriere d'Informazione* put it on February 19 and 20, 1963.

The two thousand seats, all sold out for both evenings, foreshadowed the huge acclaim given to Ellington by those attending the concerts, followed by unanimous critical praise.² Nevertheless, describing the event as a cultural watershed might have been no more than a projection of the press's own expectations, and those syncopated music–loving journalists may have actually made quite a blunder. I was told by Licia Sirch, archivist at the Verdi Conservatory in Milan, that the main hall was regularly rented without the institution itself necessarily participating in terms of sponsorship or promotion of a given event.³ Otherwise, the same symbolic weight would have been given to other jazz concerts that took place in the same setting, such as the live concerts given by Roland Kirk or the Mitchell-Ruff Trio, held at the same venue in 1963.⁴ Even though Ellington's orchestra was "finally welcomed in our most renowned concert halls," this did not necessarily mean, according to my research, that it had earned any particular laurels.⁵

THE "ITALIAN SUITE"

One of the many admirers who thronged to the Conservatory was a physician named Tano Ponzoni, who, with rather adventuresome methods, had managed to be received by Ellington at the Hotel Palace on the afternoon of February 21. During his brief meeting with Ponzoni, Ellington mentioned a composition of his that was due to be recorded with the orchestra of the Teatro alla Scala.⁶ He was referring to the piece released a few months later on the Reprise LP *The Symphonic Ellington* under the title *La Scala, She Too Pretty to Be Blue*. This work, which brought together one of the greatest jazz composers in history and one of the world's most prestigious symphony orchestras, should have been recognized by the press (more so than the concerts given at Verdi Hall) as a crucial and long-awaited milestone, a crowning cultural achievement in the relations between jazz and classical music.

Yet the city's journalists remained almost completely silent as to the joint effort made by a few musicians from Ellington's big band and a considerable number of members of the La Scala orchestra on the afternoon of Thursday, February 21, 1963, at the Regson Recording Studios.

Even the specialized press made no mention of this extraordinary rendezvous, only giving coverage to the concerts held at the Verdi Conservatory. For example, the March issue of the magazine *Musica Jazz*, whose cover bore a photo of the bandleader at the Conservatory, included a lengthy piece titled "Ellington Refuses to Grow Old: The Triumphal Duke at the Milan Conservatory." However, the only articles providing more explicit information about the recording session were written by Vittorio Franchini and Daniele Ionio, the two critics present in the studio.⁷

So these were the only voices heard murmuring, in February 1963, about an *Italian Suite* (as his fans had baptized the composition that Ellington later decided to call *La Scala*). They were drowned out, however, by the commotion raised by other press services, all intent on putting the spotlight on the two concerts at the Conservatory. My question thus became: Why on earth did Ellington's collaboration with this prestigious orchestra go almost completely unnoticed?

Convinced that the answer was to be found in the enormous Scala Archives, on November 22, 2005, I boldly set out toward the theater to meet its two experts[8] who had agreed to assist me in a research project that would presumably require a number of days. Actually, a few hours of excavation sufficed to unearth something completely unforeseen, which provided an equally astonishing answer to my question.

CONDEMNED TO OBLIVION

Our research began in the Music Archive, but here it led to nothing: no manuscripts, no scores, not a single orchestral part. All our hopes rested in the Microfilm Service. Contracts, press reviews, playbills, photos, notebooks, any sort of memorabilia that could eventually have been brought together in a PDF file. All this would have breathed life into an event that seemed not to have aroused the curiosity of journalists in 1963 nor of historians in the decades to come.[9]

Quite a surprise was in store for us. Out of all the binders,[10] not one file could be gleaned. The archivists began to doubt that the recording itself even existed. I immediately showed them the CD and assured them that they could easily find a copy at the music shop on the corner, so we went on with our work. Nor in all the other binders[11] was a trace to be found.

One of the archivists, Giuseppe Busetta, somewhat alarmed, promptly made a request to the person responsible for La Scala's General Archive, Lorenzo Lemoni. The two of them, astounded that the least scrap of information couldn't be found, flipped through yet more binders.[12] We were still left in the dark. After taking a very close look at the paychecks for the members of the orchestra, we even learned that no recording activity had been documented for February 21, as though that afternoon had been struck out of the history books.

We made further attempts over the next few days, but they failed just as dismally. In the end, the Archives sent me an official communication that reads as follows: "As you have seen, no reference to the aforementioned recording has been conserved at the Teatro alla Scala."[13]

Not only did our thorough examination of those archives prove to be fruitless in solving the puzzle of the "media blackout" surrounding the recording of *La Scala*, it made the pieces even more difficult to put back together. The complete lack of evidence made the whole thing seem like a job for a private investigator rather than a musicologist. The only path that remained involved tracking down any of Ellington's fans who were still alive and may have been present at the event in order to interview them, relying on their memories to reconstruct that day, which seemed to have disappeared. The same method could then be used with the orchestral musicians.

The only two starting points for the second and equally challenging part of the investigation were the list of La Scala musicians who took part in the session and the fact that only two photos were taken of the event, in which these same musicians are portrayed.[14]

When my search began, over forty years had passed since February 21, 1963. And yet what seemed to be an impossible undertaking led to unexpected results: I was indeed able to establish contact with many members of the orchestra, who turned out to be perfectly willing to give interviews. Cellist Ennio Miori finally provided an answer to my first question. He recalled that day quite clearly and also remembered an artistic panel made up of musicians from the orchestra who debated whether or not it was appropriate to release the recording with Ellington under the brand name of the Teatro alla Scala. In the end, the commission deemed the recording not worthy of this prestigious sponsorship.[15] So, the reason that nothing came out in the media was that the theater had withdrawn its support. The press office at La Scala wouldn't have set its wheels in motion for an event in which the theater as a whole was no longer involved.

The same fact explains the scarce number of photos: the theater's official photographer was not summoned to the recording session.[16] The upshot of all this is that no documentation whatsoever can now be found at the Scala Archives.

The absence of Ellington's name in the archives is perhaps, as the picture gradually became clearer, the most significant and eloquent detail. It points toward something quite similar to a condemnation of memory (*damnatio memoriae*) that, regrettably, unlike the ones inflicted in antiquity on Caligula or Nero, worked all too well. The interview granted to me by Franco Tabarelli, flautist and additional member of the orchestra at the time and later responsible for the Scala Music Archive, was particularly illuminating in this sense.

Tabarelli explained to me that in those days, jazz was widely banned, even for conservatory students, who "were forbidden to play popular music, with jazz being absolutely out of the question."[17] The committee's decision to withdraw the orchestra's support from Ellington must therefore be seen against this particular cultural background.[18]

A different case, involving Luciano Chailly, might shed further light on the distaste for jazz shown by classical institutions at the time. It also rules out the hypothesis of a racial issue, which had no role in our story. In 1960, Chailly composed the ballet *Ghosts at the Grand Hotel* to a libretto by Dino Buzzati. One of the ballet's scenes was set in a cabaret, and Chailly had written music in a jazz style. The passages in question were, however, expunged from the ballet, as requested by the theater's management on account of their being disrespectful.

Chailly later wrote, "Our supposed lack of respect, naturally, had to do with jazz; a monster, or at the very least an inferior breed. It was out of the question (as dictated by etiquette at the time) to celebrate a morganatic marriage between jazz and this historically blue-blooded orchestra."[19]

Having zoomed out from Ellington's *La Scala* to embrace a wider view of the cultural scenario in Italy during the sixties, we are now able to understand and perhaps justify the orchestral musicians' reluctance to grant the theater's aegis to a jazz record. Even so, no less than fifty-one of these same musicians wound up alongside Ellington in a recording studio on that Thursday afternoon in 1963. And for some of them, it was a fairly important occasion.

Flautist Bruno Cavallo considered it "an honor to record with the Duke."[20] Violinist Franco Fantini remembers that day in some detail and even recalls Ellington's gestures as a conductor, describing them as "very gentlemanly."[21]

Others, probably somewhat removed from the world of jazz, didn't show the same degree of enthusiasm. Violist Armando Burattin, during my interview with him, often compared the afternoon with Ellington to the popular music recording sessions he used to accept due to the high fees that were paid for them.[22] Horn player Michelangelo Mojoli as well, even though his brother was the outstanding jazz saxophonist Franco Mojoli, maintained that the episode surrounding *La Scala* "wasn't a very exceptional musical experience."[23]

THE COLLECTIVE AMNESIA STARTS TO WAVER: NEW PHOTOS COME TO LIGHT

Few photos testify to Ellington's encounter with the La Scala orchestra. This scarcity of iconographic material is all the more desolating when compared to the dozens and dozens of photos taken at the two evening concerts at the Conservatory, or again, to the bandleader's abundantly photographed arrival at Milano Centrale.

A more extended reconnaissance was thus urgently required. A greater amount of photographic material would surely have stimulated the memories of the orchestral musicians I interviewed, helping them reconstruct the recording studio environment and offer opinions as to the technical equipment used, perhaps even solving one major conundrum: if the Teatro alla Scala did not organize the recording session, who took care of everything? Booking the facility, coordinating the symphony orchestra, deciding on compensation, contacting Ellington and a few of his men to make sure they found their way to the studio?

The only shots published were taken by two men: Davide Mosconi, whose photos appeared in *Jazzland*, and Studio Giancolombo, whose shots accompanied the article written by Vittorio Franchini and, years later, appeared in the two issues of *Musica Jazz*.[24]

But the ghosts of our story began to materialize when Susanna Colombo, Gian Battista Colombo's daughter and curator of the Giancolombo Archive, phoned to tell me that she had found twenty photos gathered together and labeled by her father's agency "Ellington in Milan—February 1963." Fortunately, these were not additional shots of the concerts held at the Conservatory but actually contained the much sought-after images of the recording session with the orchestra. What's more, they were excellent photos aesthetically speaking as well. This was to be expected given that Giancolombo was among the country's leading photoreporting agencies in the postwar period, and Colombo himself was one of the top four professionals in the field.[25]

After this discovery, I resumed my interviews with the orchestral musicians, who, upon viewing these unpublished documents, were more readily able to recall the details of that day. New protagonists thus emerged.

Recognizing bassoonist Oreste Canfora, portrayed arm in arm with Ellington, the musicians remembered who had invited them to participate in the session.[26] Working within the La Scala orchestra, Canfora was unofficially responsible for recruiting musicians who were willing to take part in popular music (and, on rare occasions, jazz) sessions.[27]

At a later date, our bassoonist apparently contacted an organization that would have taken care of the rest. But what organization could have taken this upon itself, certain that La Scala wanted no responsibility in the matter?

The photos rediscovered at the Giancolombo Archive, after protracted scrutiny, provided an answer to this question and even made it possible to identify the man who planned it all: Giuseppe Giannini, a senior manager at the Compagnia Generale del Disco. The record company CGD was the Italian franchisee of Reprise, the label that eventually released the record. In charge of the CGD-Internazionale branch, Giannini was given the task of organizing the session, thanks, among other things, to his excellent English. Proud of being given this job (a photo of that day with Ellington could be seen hanging in his office for his entire career), he deemed it appropriate to call a photoreporting agency with which he often collaborated: Giancolombo.[28]

These shots turned out to be valuable in yet another sense: once the musicians recognized who was sitting next to them at the music stands, it became possible to draft a list of those who participated in the session held on February 21, 1963.[29] (See table 1.1 in the appendix to this chapter.)

Table 1.1 is no mere inventory of names: it is a source that, if correctly read, may well add something to our story. For example, by comparing this list with the ensemble's complete 1963 register, we learn, not without bitterness, that the official first chairs declined to participate in the session, owing to the cultural scenario described above.[30]

STUDIO ZANIBELLI, MILAN. THURSDAY, FEBRUARY 21, 1963, 5:00 P.M.

In 1949, a leftist independent center managed by the Bertacchi Cooperative was established at 57 Via Ludovico il Moro; one of its halls often hosted music and dance soirées. Later, in the early sixties, the premises were purchased by two brothers, Carlo and Umberto Zanibelli, who decided to set up a recording studio, which officially operated as of 1962.

Studio Zanibelli became a reference point for the city, with many leading figures in popular music recording songs here. While this book was being written, the recording studio was still in business. Known as Officine Meccaniche as of 1998, when it passed into the hands of Mauro Pagani, it has welcomed many pop stars and a few outstanding jazz musicians on the national and international scene, such as John McLaughlin and Jim Hall.

Not without some apprehension, I visited the establishment in December 2005, hoping to obtain information about the recording session for *La Scala*. Mauro Pagani, accompanied by head engineer Tommaso Colliva, showed me the main hall where the session was held in addition to the recording equipment used on that occasion, explaining their technical characteristics in detail.[31] There can be no doubt that on February 22, 1963, Ellington found himself in a highly professional context, at least as far as the recording studio was concerned.[32] Tellingly, when Ellington needed to rehearse in Milan again (and to record the session on tape), he chose Studio Zanibelli.[33]

Another strong point was the recording technician. It is highly likely that the sound engineer for *La Scala* was Kurt Grieder. My interviews with

Milan's most prominent professionals working in this field in the sixties not only unanimously pointed toward this Swiss man as Studio Zanibelli's sound technician but also described him as a man with a huge amount of expertise and technical skill. A colorful character, often in trouble with women and at times heavily in debt, Grieder had an infallible musical ear and knew his equipment to perfection.[34]

Yet the scarce amount of time available (from 5:00 to 8:00 p.m.), the lack of enthusiasm shown by some members of the orchestra toward the recording (which hadn't received the theater's sponsorship), and some degree of naïveté shown by Ellington himself while planning it all compromised rather seriously the quality of the recording. And as though that was not enough, some of the Duke's men seemed to do their best to undermine things.

For the afternoon of February 22, among his ensemble, Ellington had chosen drummer Sam Woodyard, bassist Ernie Shepard, himself at the piano, and two soloists: Paul Gonsalves on the tenor sax and Ray Nance playing the trumpet. The latter two arrived late, with Nance showing up visibly drunk. All of the orchestral musicians recalled their embarrassment over his behavior; with a bottle of hard liquor under his chair, he attempted a few solos that didn't turn out too well. Violist Armando Burattin's way of putting it was that Nance seemed to have difficulty "finding inspiration." Even Ellington's fans who came to the studio that day remember the trumpeter as being unable to get his bearings well enough to participate; Daniele Ionio wrote in *Jazzland* that he was seen "at 5:20 p.m., perfectly calm as he walked out of Rinascente [a department store located in Piazza Duomo, quite far from the recording studio] with a bottle of cognac."[35]

Additional problems, from a technical point of view, concerned how to capture the sound of the soloists, who risked being drowned out by the orchestra. A fan present in the studio recalls that the panels used to isolate the strings were ineffective; with little time available, the sound engineers improvised a couple of solutions but weren't able to achieve excellent results.[36] In the end, Ellington decided to overdub the solos at a later date in the United States.[37]

Perhaps not overly convinced while listening to the Studio Zanibelli recordings, the Duke ultimately opted for not two but four soloists: in addition to Paul Gonsalves, he later summoned trombonist Lawrence Brown and clarinetist Russell Procope. The sound of the trumpet was to remain but played by a different musician: Ray Nance was replaced by Cootie Williams. Asking Nance to pass the baton may have been intended as punishment for his slack behavior, but as such, it does not seem to have worked. Nance's unprofessional conduct continued, forcing Ellington to dismiss him in the fall of that same year.[38]

Owing to the way events unfolded that day in Milan, Ellington had no choice but to leave the studio with no more than the recording of the orchestral background, lacking the crucial contribution of his own soloists. This partially explains some of the orchestral musicians' low opinion of that work: what they heard of *La Scala* seems like an anonymous series of homophonic chords with no thematic invention nor timbral or rhythmic flair, which in any case was all that Ellington succeeded in getting down on tape that afternoon.

According to direct testimony, upon seeing Ellington at an impasse, Billy Strayhorn suggested overdubbing as a possible expedient.[39] Be this as it may, Strayhorn's contribution to *La Scala* came to an end with this excellent piece of advice; indeed, the Duke's right-hand man took no part in orchestrating the work and all the less in composing parts of it. From this point of view, *La Scala* stands out as the only one of Ellington's symphonic works that he entirely orchestrated himself, unlike, as we shall see in the following chapters, his other scores in this genre.

Nevertheless, since Ellington was late (and the score was completed directly in Milan, at the Hotel Palace), he was, in all likelihood, assisted in the final phases of the orchestration by the man who would quickly write out the single parts as soon as the score was complete. This was a man who had wrongly been forgotten by jazz historians in Italy well before 1963: Piero Rizza, who materialized in one of the photos that surfaced during my research.[40]

Born in Genoa in 1907, Rizza was a saxophonist, clarinetist, and arranger accomplished enough for Sam Wooding's great all-Black orchestra, which passed through Milan in February 1930, to engage him. A leading figure in Italian jazz for at least two decades, at the end of the fifties, Rizza left the country and headed to Florida to follow his wife, who had made a name for herself in show business thanks to a number involving trained dogs! And so, everyone completely forgot about a musician who was "among the best in European jazz between the two wars." He died alone at the Giuseppe Verdi Foundation retirement home for musicians on July 20, 1998, aged ninety-two.

Rizza had met Duke Ellington in 1932 at the Lafayette Theatre in Harlem. From that moment on, the two stayed in contact for the rest of their lives, and in February 1963 in Milan, it was none other than this Italian jazzman who looked after a few details of the orchestration, and above all, writing out the single parts of *La Scala*.[41]

Ex. 1.1. *La Scala*, Introduction, take 3 (Reprise).

But let us return to the complications that came up during the session by focusing on some additional unfortunate events that a close examination of the tapes inevitably brought to light: the recorded music, indeed, bears the signs of a few mishaps. The entire work will not be analyzed here (this being reserved for chapter 5), but a closer look at some passages may enlighten us as to what went wrong during those three hours.

Three takes were recorded during the session, of which the third became the master take, i.e., the one released by the label Reprise on *The Symphonic Ellington*.[42] The Introduction, as heard on the album, follows a twelve-bar blues form and is given to the piano, accompanied as of m. 9 by the double bass and drums (ex. 1.1).

Ellington had actually foreseen not one but two blues choruses. The first, a piano solo played *rubato* and lacking the swing articulation in the eighth notes, was to reach m. 8; then, as of m. 9, where the double bass and drums were to enter, it was to continue *a tempo* and with a swing inflection. The arrangement used in these last four bars (the resolution of the first chorus) would then have continued for all twelve measures of the following chorus (ex. 1.2). The entire Introduction is shown in example 1.1.

But something went wrong. When the musicians reached the third measure of the second chorus, a Larsen effect came from one of the microphones and the squealing noise irreparably damaged the recording. Takes 1 and 2, what's more, could not be used due to the orchestra's imprecise entry. Not much time had been allotted for the session and it was quickly running out, so Ellington chose to drastically amputate his work: The Introduction ultimately released is an assemblage of the first ten measures of the first chorus and the last two of the second, as can be confirmed by listening to the record and comparing it with example 1.1.

Ex. 1.2. *La Scala*, Introduction, take 3.

Examining the tapes, we furthermore learn that parts were not given to some of the musicians, including Sam Woodyard (Ellington didn't habitually write out drum parts), double bassist Ernie Shepard, and—among the orchestral musicians—the harpist and the percussionists.

The two soloists, Ray Nance and Paul Gonsalves, probably didn't even have a formal outline to follow (bearing in mind that the structure of *La Scala*, as we shall see later on, is relatively complex). What's more, in a few passages, the arrangement took shape directly in the recording studio. All of this can be inferred from a close inspection of the D-minor blues section, which is noticeably different in all three takes (ex. 1.3 and ex. 1.4).

In take 1, Shepard responds to the phrase played by the bassoon and contrabassoon, re-proposing it; the classical percussions follow the same rhythmic pattern. The orchestration is rather clumsy and overly dense: no rests were left for the soloist (who, in the Reprise LP, became trumpeter Cootie Williams) to intervene.

In take 2, this section becomes much more discrete, somewhat nocturnal: the classical percussions are eliminated, Ellington introduces some pointillist coloring at the piano, and Shepard's double bass phrases no longer simply duplicate the melody played by the bassoon and contrabassoon but are developed in their own right.

Ex. 1.3. *La Scala*, blues section in D minor, bassoon and contrabassoon riff.

Ex. 1.4. *La Scala*, blues section in D minor (take 3).

And yet this take is the one that, at this point, contains the most errors made by the orchestra: Ellington was forced to discard it. Which is a shame, considering it's the only one where the contrabassoon plays each phrase correctly.

Take 3, the one that was ultimately released, sounds rather like a judgment of Solomon pronounced on the two previous arrangements. Nevertheless, it's also the one with the most blemishes.

The contrabassoon makes a mistake in the fourth repetition of the riff (mm. 6–7), the classical percussionist plays hesitantly (or perhaps was recorded from too far away), and above all, double bassist Ernie Shepard forgets the modulation and, for the first two bars of the passage in question, keeps playing in F major, the key of the previous section.

Some responsibility for these flaws and for the few moments in which the classical orchestra seems to be somewhat at a loss must be given to Ellington himself. Over forty years of experience acting as his own orchestra's bandleader, he had perfected a practice that his men knew down to the last detail. For example, it was par for the course for him to go into the recording studio and change the arrangement then and there or else play a part at the piano so that one section of the orchestra could repeat it; come what may, his big band would have backed him up without missing a step.

The Teatro alla Scala Orchestra, understandably, could in no way have been accustomed to these methods, extremely rare as they were in classical milieus. Nor can we overlook, as mentioned earlier, the behavior shown by Ray Nance, some of the orchestral musicians' lack of enthusiasm, and a range of unexpected technical obstacles that not even a sound engineer such as Kurt Grieder could have overcome in fewer than three hours.

In any case, Ellington had no time for second thoughts. He grabbed the tapes with only the orchestral parts recorded on them, stuck them under his arm, and hastened over to the Giuseppe Verdi Conservatory, where he was to carry on with his busy schedule by giving an evening concert. Equally urgent matters awaited the members of the orchestra: that evening at the theater, they were due to play the opening performance of *Madama Butterfly* conducted by Gianandrea Gavazzeni.

Ellington's live concert, as we know, was a success. Similar acclaim was given to the orchestral musicians who, according to Eugenio Montale, the recipient of the Nobel Prize in literature in later years and then music critic for the *Corriere della Sera*, gave "a stupendous interpretation of Puccini."[43] And so, each of the two worlds that had so fleetingly encountered one another was drawn back into its own orbit.

UNRELEASED AND YET UNRECOGNIZED

Like a magnet surrounded by iron dust, *La Scala* attracted an unbelievable mishmash of errors, misunderstandings, and neglect; inaccuracies even cropped up concerning the title of the work itself. The fifth edition of the Ellington discography, compiled by W. E. Timner, indicates it as *La Scala, She Too Pretty to Be True*.[44] The technician charged by Reprise with preparing the master in the United States wrote it down as *La Scala, She Too Pretty to Be Blues*.[45] Actually, as can be gleaned from the ASCAP copyright obtained in 1964, the correct subtitle is *She Too Pretty to Be Blue*.[46]

Yet another blunder that, counted alongside everything else that went wrong with *La Scala*, seems to suggest that only some kind of damnation could be responsible for the fate met with by such an unfortunate piece. And, as though this were not enough, further punishment was inflicted on it by a sentence that still today has not been lifted: it has never been recognized as the only previously unreleased work on the LP *The Symphonic Ellington* but has wrongly had to share this honor with *Non-Violent Integration*.

The album released by Reprise consists of four pieces: *Night Creature*, *Harlem* (symphonic version), *La Scala*, and *Non-Violent Integration*, all officially recorded here for the first time on LP. Nonetheless, the first two had already been conceived in a symphonic version in the early fifties and were performed live (and broadcast over the radio) various times prior to 1963. *La Scala* and *Non-Violent Integration*, instead, appear to have been written for the occasion. And yet a closer look at the manuscripts and a few of Ellington's recordings dating to the forties forces us to retract this recognition in the case of the second piece.

The composition of *Non-Violent Integration* indeed began in 1947 with a piece titled *Boogie Bop Blue*, a score written in Ellington's hand that also includes orchestral parts.[47] A big band version similar to the autograph score was recorded in October 1947 as *Boogie Bop Blues* and, in December of the same year, another simplified version titled *Basso Profundo* was performed at Carnegie Hall. Sometime later, *Boogie Bop Blue* was given yet another name, *Grand Slam Jam*. This latter elaboration, orchestrated by Calvin Jackson (one of the arrangers who worked with Ellington in the late forties), was played by the Philadelphia Orchestra on July 25, 1949.

The Duke referred to it as a "little thing" he had put together for the occasion; in 1963, this same "little thing" was transformed once again, reincarnated as *Non-Violent Integration*.[48]

The scores that emerged in the wake of *Boogie Bop Blue* are all quite similar, meaning that none of them can be considered an original composition.[49] The only authentically new feature of *Non-Violent Integration* would seem to be the first blues theme, which opens the recording; introduced by the piano accompanied by the double bass and drums, it is used for the first two choruses (of which the second includes variations), not nearly enough to consider the piece a true novelty![50] In any case, all uncertainty would vanish if we took the trouble to compare the melody in question with a sketch signed by both Ellington and Johnny Hodges titled *Who Struck John?* The first theme of this blues, recorded on June 9, 1947, and never taken up thereafter (neither live nor in a recording studio), reappeared in an identical form, including the *acciaccaturas*, sixteen years later in *Non-Violent Integration* (ex. 1.5).

Non Violent Integration

Piano — Duke Ellington

Ex. 1.5. *Non-Violent Integration*, first theme.

And so, *La Scala*, a work whose ink was still wet, so much so that it was completed during the hours immediately preceding the studio session, now stands out as the only previously unreleased piece on the entire LP.[51] Above and beyond its status as the premiere recording, however, it is an exquisite sketch whose charm is so intimate and demure as to never have attracted much attention.

Truth be told, not much interest has been shown toward the piece itself in this chapter either, entirely dedicated as it has been to the historical facts alone. It would surely have been premature to unveil this Cinderella's full beauty in these opening pages or hint at the huge significance it had for Ellington. In the same vein, it would have been reckless to attempt to provide answers to the various queries the preceding paragraphs will no doubt have raised, such as: "What in the world could have driven Ellington, who in 1963 was at the peak of his career, to record this work with the Teatro alla Scala Orchestra, in spite of all this dreadful adversity?"

The proper place for these reflections will be the fifth stop along our journey, organized into seven chapters in which the Duke's other symphonic works will be examined; only at the end of these meanderings will we be able to come back to *La Scala*. Now, it is time for us to leave the beaten path and go down toward the valley: from that vantage point, we may realize what an imposing mountain lies before us.

APPENDIX

List of La Scala musicians who took part in the session and their respective roles. Regson Recording Studios, February 21, 1963.

Flutes: Bruno Cavallo (1), Aldo Garavini, Giuseppe Rocca
Oboes: Francesco Ranzani (1), Alfredo Panciroli
English horn: Alfonso Fededegni
Clarinets: Paolo Del Pistoia (1), Mario Moretti, Miles Turolla

Bass clarinet: Stefano Monti
Bassoon: Renato Musi
Contrabassoon: Oreste Canfora
Horns: Michele Berrino (1), Michelangelo Mojoli, Alberto Moretti, Adolfo Strappo
Percussion: Angelo Abruzzi, Domenico Renzetti
Harp: Lidia Borri Mottola (added from the Rai Orchestra)
First violins: Franco Fantini (1), Battistino Bacchetta, Giovanni Braghiroli, Walter Falcomer, Mariano Frigo, Edgardo Macchinizzi, Gianni Porzio, Giuseppe Volpato
Second violins: Roberto Bortoluzzi (1), Ferruccio de Poli, Vittorio Ernini, Benedetto Focarino, Luigi Govi, Aldo Nardo, Giacomo Pogliani, Michele Seccia-Pesce
Violas: Armando Burattin (1), Adriano Bertozzi, Alcide Carpana, Domenico Righetti, Renato Romano, Marcello Turio
Cellos: Mario Gusella (1), Walter Caletti, Umberto Galli, Genunzio Ghetti, Ennio Miori, Luigi Veccia
Double basses: Carlo Capriata (1), Luigi del Carmine, Luigi Gramatica, Franco Scotto

NEW WORLD A-COMIN'
PROUD TO BE ON THE AIR

"... BEFORE BLACK WAS BEAUTIFUL"

Ellington is now seventy-one years old, elderly, and tired. Within a few months, his doctor will diagnose him with hepatic cancer; two years later, he passes away. But today is July 2, 1970, and the Duke is in surprisingly good shape, ready to give us a lesson in jazz history from the studios of the French broadcaster ORTS, illustrated by a dozen or so of his own compositions played at the piano.

Ellington's incisive comments act as preludes, or postludes, to these pieces. Some are brief reflections on technical matters or meditations on the very concept of jazz history; others are dedications to the leading members of his orchestra or are intended to portray the historical and geographical context that gave birth to a certain piece.

One pointed remark, however, stands out from all the others. Not much more than an asterisk placed at the end of "Black Beauty," the Duke's observation is "written in 1928, before black was beautiful." As concise as a haiku, this comment exudes (African American) sarcasm, which is only emphasized by the lack of expression on Ellington's face. Perhaps he meant to deliver it like a fencing lunge: this was no time to be witty. Or again, it may have been his way of hitting two birds with one stone: those who had always labeled him as a political moderate uninterested in his people's collective fate and the new "black is beautiful" generation that, apparently, may have woken up a bit too late.[1]

In the session shot in Paris, this brief piece, somehow reminiscent of Schubert, is followed by the longest work for piano in Ellington's entire output: *New World A-Comin'*. The composer presents this piece as being one movement from his *First Sacred Concert* and dedicates a brief statement to it, imbued with spiritual and religious elements: "*New World A-Comin'* is a place in the distant future, where there would be no war, no greed, no nonbelievers, no categorization, where love is unconditional and no pronoun is good enough for God."

In both compositions, a vibrant political conception with militant overtones is matched by a serene utopian-spiritual inspiration. Or so it would seem. And yet the history of *New World A-Comin'*, as we shall see shortly, has much more to tell us, and it is no coincidence that this piece and "Black Beauty" wound up side by side in the final edited version of the documentary.[2]

1965: THE BIRTH OF A RITUAL

According to the indications provided by Ellington in the video, the origins of *New World A-Comin'* were in the premiere of his *First Sacred Concert*, dated September 16, 1965. So let's turn the clock back one year and visit San Francisco's Grace Cathedral, packed with an audience of over two thousand people listening to this work (along with other compositions by Ellington and spirituals sung by the Herman McCoy Choir), one of whose movements was *New World A-Comin'*, played by the composer at the piano. Ellington, captured by the cameras of local broadcaster KQED, played a shorter version of *New World A-Comin'* than the one featured in the 1970 video: in the cathedral, dressed in a pure white suit, he dedicated four minutes to this composition, while in France, it lasts nine. The performance of the *First Sacred Concert*, held on December 26, 1965, at New York's Fifth Avenue Presbyterian Church, appeared on an RCA LP released the following year under the title *Concert of Sacred Music*; here, *New World A-Comin'* appears as the work's seventh movement and once again comes to eight and a half minutes.[3]

Inquiring into the future vicissitudes of this fragment of the *Concert*, which took on a life of its own, we learn that Ellington continued to play it in a state of communion with his instrument until the end of his days. Its last performance, of which an unreleased recording exists, dates to July 21, 1973. Probably during a break at Waldameer's Rainbow Gardens (Pennsylvania), the Duke enjoyed himself by improvising melodies, harmonic progressions, and robust walkin' basses, with a segment of *New World A-Comin'* appearing in the midst of this maelstrom. An interesting tidbit for collectors: this latter version is not overly significant from a musical point of view, unlike the extraordinary display seen one year earlier at the prestigious setting of the Whitney Museum of American Art, which was included in the Impulse CD *Duke Ellington Live at the Whitney*.[4]

Another remarkable version, along with the one in the 1970 Paris video, played with great conviction, appeared in a recital held in France at the Château de Goutelas in Marcoux on February 25, 1966. Critic Eddie Lambert has described this as "the finest recorded performance" of *New World A-Comin'*; Ellington himself dedicated a paragraph of his autobiography to this experience, and in 1971, he elaborated on his memories of it, composing a five-movement work titled *Goutelas Suite*.[5]

Consulting the Ellington discographies, however, we soon discover that this piano piece was not originally conceived as a movement of the *First Sacred Concert*. Ellington had publicly performed the first version of *New World A-Comin'* for piano solo at the MOMA in New York a good three years before the sacred concert: a live recording dated January 4, 1962, indeed includes an early reading of this version that still contains a few uncertainties.[6] Only by listening to some unreleased tapes of his performances, however, do we find out that in 1965, this work was (at least) two decades old.

On Thursday, April 12, 1945, the thirty-second president of the United States, Franklin Delano Roosevelt, died. The Department of the Treasury canceled its traditional Saturday evening program and asked Ellington to play something appropriate. From New York's 400 Restaurant, the bandleader conducted some of his most moving compositions, a spiritual and a dedicated melody ("Chant for F. D. Roosevelt," a sort of prelude to "Come Sunday"); he then continued by playing at the piano—"for the president who was a friend of the Negroes" (according to the ABC host's introductory remarks)—the lyrical first theme of *New World A-Comin'*, omitting the other sections and rounding off the concert with a gospel cadenza.[7]

Even without going into an in-depth analysis, simply listening to the recordings suggests that these performances were not improvised; *New World A-Comin'* gives some interpretational leeway (mainly regarding the choice of tempo) but nothing more. Significantly, the piece lasts around eight or nine minutes on all occasions.[8] These documents unquestionably indicate that the composition certainly dates to a period prior to the sacred concert, but even so, 1965 marked a crucial turning point. From the *First Sacred Concert* onward, all of Ellington's spoken introductions identically repeat the same utopian phrase he recited in the French broadcasting studio in 1970: "*New*

World A-Comin' is a place in the distant future, where there are no wars, no greed, no categorization, no nonbelievers."

This is the light in which the work was presented in the program for the *First Sacred Concert*. When the concert was recorded three months later, by speaking with Stanley Dance, who was responsible for the liner notes, Ellington ensured that those words would reach all those who purchased the record.[9] Later, the Duke felt compelled to repeat this story, concert after concert, passing it down like a grandfather to the younger generations, always in an identical form. This same declaration appeared verbatim in the *Words of the Week* column of the African American magazine *Jet*'s January 1967 issue, and in 1973, only a few weeks before his death, Ellington consigned it to a passage of his autobiography.[10]

From this point of view, 1965 was a watershed year. From this point on, the Duke clearly intended to recount exactly what *New World A-Comin'* was, and in so doing, he followed a specific ritual; before this date, in his improvised introductions, he took pains to tell us what *New World A-Comin'* was not. This latter approach is even more steeped in meaning, as we shall shortly see.

For now, let's continue along our path backward through time, which began in the seventies (with the recording of the *First Sacred Concert*) and continued through the midsixties (with a second stop consisting in the piano performances), ultimately leading to a green valley in Philadelphia's Fairmount Park. It was the summer of 1949.

ROBIN HOOD DELL, 1949

In 1929, in one of the meadows found in Fairmount Park, still today one of the world's largest municipal parks, an amphitheater with ten thousand seats was built, named Robin Hood Dell. Managed by a cooperative of musicians from the Philadelphia Orchestra, as of 1930, it became the venue for this ensemble's summer concerts; over the next two decades, figures such as Leopold Stokowski, Eugene Ormandy, Fritz Reiner, and Dimitri Mitropoulos appeared on the podium alongside world-famous soloists including Arthur Rubinstein, Jascha Heifetz, and Claudio Arrau (to mention only a few of the more illustrious names). The African American community was represented by its opera stars: Paul Robeson (who was regularly invited), Marian Anderson, Todd Duncan, and Anne Brown (the latter two being the singers who debuted Porgy and Bess in Gershwin's 1935 opera).

Despite these celebrity appearances, attendance flagged in 1948, and the following year, the Philadelphia Orchestra turned to jazz to recuperate, inviting Sarah Vaughan and Duke Ellington.[11] Vaughan would perform with both orchestras, and so would the Duke. On Monday, July 25, 1949, with Russ Case on the podium, Ellington performed *New World A-Comin'* at the piano in the form of a concerto grosso, with an arrangement that combined the resources of the two ensembles.[12]

It was Ellington's first time with a symphony orchestra.[13] And he was certainly not mistaken to try; on the contrary, the audience of thirteen thousand (one thousand more than the concert that inaugurated the first season in 1930) and the positive response coming from critics encouraged the Duke, reassuring him as to the value of *New World A-Comin'* and at the same time stimulating him to experiment with other combinations of classical music and jazz.[14]

This open-air summer concert sparked an interest in symphonic music that remained with Ellington for the rest of his life. For now, however, let us simply zoom in on one of the protagonists of this story: *New World A-Comin'* as a concerto grosso.

On June 20, 1951, the symphonic version of this work reappeared at New York's Lewisohn Stadium as part of a fundraising concert for cancer research. In the second part of this live event, Ellington's big band played alongside sixty-three musicians of the NBC Symphony. The performance of *New World A-Comin'* without a conductor (and with Ellington at the piano) left some displeased.[15] The concert, given four years later at Carnegie Hall, featuring the Symphony of the Air (formerly the NBC Symphony) with Ellington on the conductor's podium and Don Shirley at the piano, was instead triumphal.[16]

One of the many intellectuals whose company Ellington cultivated, Donald Shirley was a Jamaican American who obtained three PhDs (in music, psychology, and liturgical art) and was fluent in eight languages. In the fifties and the sixties, he was particularly close to the bandleader. A classical virtuoso, he performed in the world's most prestigious halls, including La Scala, where, in 1965, he played in a ballet titled *Gershwiniana* whose ballerinas included the great Carla Fracci.[17]

He was also a competent jazz musician: two Cadence LPs, dating to the same period as his live performance with Ellington, *Tonal Expressions* and *Piano Perspective*, demonstrate his familiarity with the standards. Not unlike George Shearing a few years later in his *The Shearing Piano* (Capitol, 1957), Shirley introduced elements of classical music into Broadway songs: in "My Funny Valentine" and "The Man I Love," he pays his respects to Bach's counterpoint, while "I Cover the Waterfront" owes much to Ravel and Debussy, and "Secret Love" incorporates elements of the Late Romantic chamber tradition. Without forgetting his tribute to Ellington, "I Let a Song Go Out

Ex. 2.1. *New World A-Comin'*, cadenza.

of My Heart" contains a deft and not in the least contrived citation of "Don't Get Around Much Anymore."

According to the author of the liner notes accompanying the album that contains this tribute, "Duke Ellington recently gave a concert at Carnegie Hall. He wrote a piano concerto for Don to perform."[18] While this is clearly an allusion to *New World A-Comin'*, the information is incorrect. The critic most likely heard it from Shirley himself, which would be in line with a certain haughtiness shown by this musician on other occasions. He was, in fact, prone to overestimating himself and displayed hostility toward some of his fellow musicians, Ellington as a composer in particular, whom he deeply envied during his entire life.[19] One explanation for these feelings could be that Shirley himself had written a fair number of symphonic works (on the border between the world of classical music and African American jazz and spiritual traditions), just like Ellington, but without obtaining the same success.

Ironically, the most prominent occasion in the first part of this pianist's career arrived on March 16, 1955, and he owed it to no other than the disparaged composer of *New World A-Comin'*. One must say that Shirley played his cards quite well and, being a solid virtuoso, in some instances he made quite an impression, for example, in the improvised cadenzas, above all, the last one, which led to thunderous applause.[20] And yet, in a few crucial aspects of the solo passages, Shirley seems to have missed the mark compared to Ellington's performances. In particular, the physical impact habitually given to a few passages by the Duke does not come across.

Example 2.1 is revealing. While Shirley interprets these bars like a Late Romantic cadenza, for Ellington, they are lashes of sound historically rooted in 1920s Harlem stride piano. And, truth be told, his limited knowledge of ragtime performance practice was exactly what got our classical virtuoso into trouble: the following secondary theme (ex. 2.2), entirely in the spirit of music by Eubie Blake or James P. Johnson, is pure ragtime.

Ex. 2.2. *New World A-Comin'*, ragtime theme.

The Duke's left hand does justice to the theme's origins in "syncopated music," using a percussive articulation for the chromatic figure and thus giving the theme a strong propulsive drive. This is precisely what Shirley failed to do. Ellington, with some degree of malice, later noted this shortcoming shown by Shirley, who, even though he was well used to playing Liszt and Rachmaninov, didn't seem to be up to a simple ragtime lick.[21]

Of course, we must note that these defects are part of a valuable performance, taken as a whole; still, the Duke significantly never again left the solo part in the hands of another pianist.[22]

The concert, as mentioned above, was a huge success and acted as a springboard for the orchestral future of *New World A-Comin'*, so much so that only one year later, Ellington, probably entirely convinced of his creation's value, began musing on the idea of recording it. On July 10, 1956, he asked for the technical equipment required for a live recording with the New Haven Symphony. Listening to those tapes, it is clear that the nine thousand people who attended this concert at the Yale Bowl were treated to a high-quality performance; in particular, the more lyrical orchestral passages were performed with great poise. And yet, no record was released.[23] This was the beginning of a protracted ordeal, largely made up of rejections coming from recording companies who weren't in the least interested in the classical sector of the Duke's output.[24]

Other performances followed, sometimes changing the instrumental forces involved (such as the one given on July 23, 1957, with the Buffalo Philharmonic Orchestra and only the rhythmic section of Ellington's big band), until the idea of recording it came to the fore once again in 1963.[25] Some sources indicate that Ellington had come to the decision of recording *New World A-Comin'* that winter during his European tour, adding it to the other pieces expected to appear on *The Symphonic Ellington*. But this proved to be yet another fruitless attempt.[26]

Many other live performances followed, some with renowned orchestras such as the New York Philharmonic (July 31, 1965), the Los Angeles

Symphony Orchestra (August 23, 1966), and the London Philharmonic, which invited Ellington as a piano soloist to the prestigious Royal Albert Hall (February 19, 1967), but an official recording simply didn't seem to be in the works.[27] Not until spring 1970 did Decca decide to endorse Ellington's symphonic compositions, producing the LP *Orchestral Works*.

Erich Kunzel, conducting the Cincinnati Symphony Orchestra, recorded *New World A-Comin'* introduced by a "poetic commentary" by Ellington; this was the same utopian phrase to which the Duke's audiences had been accustomed since 1965, the same narration that he recited in front of the Los Angeles Symphony and even felt it necessary to include in the recording. After those words, we hear the first theme of a piece that, from its earliest symphonic version dating to 1949, had to wait more than two decades and swallow quite a few bitter pills along the way before being canonized by a recording and finally finding rest![28]

It is highly likely that Luther Henderson also had reason to celebrate in the spring of 1970. Henderson was indeed the one who, twenty-one years earlier, following Ellington's indications, drafted the symphonic version of *New World A-Comin'*.

LUTHER HENDERSON

Born in 1919 in Kansas City, Missouri, Luther Henderson spent his early childhood in Langston, Oklahoma. His parents were music lovers: Florence was an accomplished pianist and Luther Sr. conducted the Henderson Quartet, an a cappella group. Both parents worked as schoolteachers and, in order to further their careers, the family moved in 1923 to New York, settling in the well-to-do area of Harlem known as Sugar Hill.[29] Just a few blocks away, at 381 Edgecombe Avenue to be precise, some years later, in 1931, a bourgeois African American family would move in. There were five family members: two paternal grandparents, an aunt, a separated father, and a young grandson; the latter, whose name was Mercer, was the same age as Luther and eventually wound up in the same high school. It was Mercer Ellington.

And so, the Duke's son and Luther became friends, scampering around the streets of Sugar Hill together and both cultivating their passion for music. Mercer concentrated on the trumpet while his friend played the piano, even though both showed an inclination toward composition and arrangement. Not by chance, in due course, both entered the renowned Juilliard School of Music.

Luther began attending courses here in 1937 and finished his studies in 1942. That very year, his close relations with the Ellington family began to bear fruit: a few of the young man's compositions were published by the Duke's newly born publishing house, Tempo Music (directed by his sister Ruth). In July 1942, his orchestra even recorded a song co-composed by Mercer and Luther, "A Slip of the Lip." A piece with jive elements sung by Ray Nance, it enjoyed a certain amount of success and stayed in the group's repertoire until 1944.[30]

From 1944 to 1946, Luther was busy writing arrangements for the United States Navy's big band but also found the time to keep cultivating his relationship with Ellington. He brought a handful of scores of standards (including "Stardust") to the bandleader's attention, some of which were performed live. The Duke showed further trust in him in 1946, when he set him to work alongside Billy Strayhorn on orchestrating the musical *Beggar's Holiday*; as was the case with other musical theater works by Ellington, the show was a flop and closed after only sixteen repeat performances. All the same, this occasion marked the beginning of a collaboration between Ellington's right-hand man and Henderson.

The two later joined forces for other theater productions: a staging of the musical *Cabin in the Sky* by Vernon Duke and John Latouche, arranged for two pianos and given summer performances in 1953, and *Rose-Colored Glasses*, composed by both Strayhorn and Henderson in 1954. In the early fifties, Strayhorn even considered the idea of completely breaking away from Ellington and establishing a creative team with Henderson.[31]

Meanwhile, in 1949, Luther demonstrated his thorough knowledge of both big band and orchestral writing to the Duke by arranging *New World A-Comin'* as a concerto grosso. On July 25, 1949, in Robin Hood Dale, Luther became, in Ellington's own words, his "classical arm," and this was the crucial role that Henderson was to play in Ellingtonia in the years to come. Indeed, he was the man the Duke turned to in 1951 for the symphony orchestration of *Harlem* and in 1955 for the suite *Night Creature*. The symphonic adaptation of the posthumous ballet *Three Black Kings* was once again Henderson's work.

Surely enough, during the fifties, Henderson grew to be known as one of the most competent figures working in the musical panorama, distinguishing himself in two areas in particular: as an orchestrator of musicals (during his entire career, he contributed to over fifty productions) and a pianist with expertise in accompanying and arranging pop-jazz songs. Ellington and Strayhorn helped him make a name for himself in this area as well.[32] They were the ones who introduced him to their friend Lena Horne, whose musical director Luther became for three years. In no time at all, throngs of singers, including celebrities such as Carmen McRae, Diahann Carroll, and Carol Haney, wanted him by their side; Haney then introduced him to the world of television, bringing him to the *Ed Sullivan Show*, and Henderson began to write scores for the small screen as well.

The first two LPs he recorded as a bandleader, *Clap Hands!* and *The Greatest Sound Around*, both released by Columbia in 1959, show him at the head of a pop orchestra interpreting a handful of songs. Scores such as "On the Sunny Side of the Street," "The Honey Song," "Sometimes I'm Happy" (with its creative combinations of timbres), or "Lover Come Back to Me" (with its inspired counterpoint in the strings) fully confirm that the Duke had bet his money on the right horse.

One year earlier, Henderson had written marvelous arrangements of a few pieces from *Stepping into Swing Society* by his friend Mercer, with whom he had been collaborating in the recording studio for over a decade. In 1947, indeed, he began recording as a pianist in the ensembles led by his friend, which brought together, in the Duke's words, "the greatest young talent."[33]

Henderson remained close to Ellington for his entire life, happy to accept a few odd jobs for the Duke. Even the humblest, such as editing the latter's pieces published by Tempo Music or writing for minor recording sessions (such as the one held in 1969 that led to an LP included with *Reader's Digest*), or the most gratifying, such as completing *Three Black Kings*, the Maestro's last great uncompleted work.[34] It was not an easy collaboration, not even at the outset. At the 1949 performance with the Philadelphia Orchestra, neither Henderson nor Calvin Jackson was publicly recognized for their work as orchestrators (the former for *New World A-Comin'* and the latter for *Grand Slam Jam*); not one playbill nor program contains their names. Nevertheless, on this occasion, the two friends—Luther and Calvin had known each other for over ten years, both part of Mercer's inner circle—simply shrugged their shoulders. "Working for Ellington is gratifying enough in itself," they may well have thought. Perhaps they also bore in mind their friendship with Mercer, the nights spent racing around in the Ford that Daddy Ellington had given to his son in 1938, and the gratitude that they both (above all, Henderson) owed to the Duke.[35]

Be this as it may, when Ellington's ego continued to dominate the credits for the following live symphonic concerts, Henderson began to feel resentful. Not even at the 1955 Carnegie Hall concert was any recognition given to his work: "I went down to Carnegie Hall before the concert to see if my name was in the program, it was not. . . . I didn't like him for that. Which was very hard on me. Because I loved the Duke."[36] One year later, the Duke, in an interview, showed no signs of repentance and, in one sense, laid it on even thicker: "Writing for the symphony orchestra is a technique." It's something that can be done by mere technicians, Ellington seems to be suggesting, not much more than a task for schoolchildren, to be carried out, moreover, following his own guidelines: "I make a six-line score and give it to Luther and let him to do it . . . with suggestions, you know . . . I mean, these things are good as they are."[37]

All the expertise required by the art of orchestration considered as mere technique, or worse, a task to be doled out to hirelings; a rather merciless sentence! In any case, one thing is sure: Luther Henderson knew that "technique" quite well, and a close look at the staves of the final score, as we shall soon see, will allow us to recognize his mastery. First, however, we'll have to ask another question: Which score of *New World A-Comin'* did the Duke provide to his arranger? The answer compels us to take one last step in our trip backward in time, reaching the "year one" of this composition; more precisely, December 11, 1943, when Ellington presented his new work to the audience at Carnegie Hall. This time, *New World A-Comin'* is for big band and concertante piano.

DECEMBER 11, 1943: YEAR ONE

Half of Manhattan was in bed with the flu, and the gusts of icy wind blowing that Saturday afternoon left those who were spared from the virus with little desire to go out. In any case, the war was weighing heavily on everyone and there weren't all that many good reasons to spend a night on the town or at a concert. And yet, a week before Ellington's performance, three thousand tickets had been sold, with Carnegie Hall only having 2,729 seats!

The Duke had made an appearance here at the beginning of the year as well. On January 23, he presented his new composition, *Black, Brown and Beige*, which did not meet with much enthusiasm overall and even got a few negative reviews. For his second visit to this famous venue, the new piece on the program was *New World A-Comin'*. A few newspapers, including the *Pittsburgh Courier* and the *New York Times*, expressed rather high expectations for this premiere, and the concert was indeed a success: the music was performed splendidly by the orchestra, even though trombonist Juan Tizol was not present due to a serious case of pneumonia. The newborn score, however, like *Black, Brown and Beige* earlier that same year, did not win over all of its listeners. Praise was lavished on it by Barry Ulanov, Ellington's biographer, who wrote, "*New World* consists of a series of florid piano passages, in and out of tempo, amplified with great tonal beauty by the orchestra, rich in its chord structure, in its soft, sensuous mood." The critic writing for the *New York Times* fundamentally agreed: "The episodes of *New*

World A-Comin', bound together by elaborate cadenzas for the piano . . . were well-contrasted, tuneful, and led to a rousing finale of especially optimistic nature." *Variety* was less enthusiastic: "[A]n unpretentious but pleasant slice of Ellington," as was *DownBeat*: "I dislike *New World A-Comin'*, not as music, because it was very attractive, but because it didn't go any further along [compared to *Black, Brown and Beige*]." The *New York Amsterdam News* was rather dissatisfied: "[I]t was spotty, although the theme has infinite possibilities if developed further."[38]

Ellington had gotten to work on composing this piece only a few weeks before its debut. In his autobiography, he recalls having completed the score during an engagement at New York's Capitol Theatre, which would mean between October 14 and November 11, 1943.[39] It is nevertheless possible that, when he wrote his memoirs in the early seventies, some of the Duke's more distant recollections were slightly out of focus. Journalist Richard Boyer, at any rate, wrote a brief portrait of Ellington in 1944, only a few months after the work was born. In his article, which appeared in *The New Yorker* and was based on his conversations with the orchestra while on tour, he informs us that Ellington wrote "most" of *New World A-Comin'* while traveling by train from Ohio to Pennsylvania; the band may have made this journey in late November, once their stay at the Capitol Theatre was over.[40]

Ellington thus worked on the manuscript in the fall of 1943. This document is highly interesting because its staves contain both the big band arrangement and a few indications as to a possible orchestration. Three different handwritings can be distinguished on these sheets of music belonging to Ellington, copyist Tom Whaley, and Luther Henderson. For example, it was the latter who wrote "*swinging strings?!!*" in the margin beside one passage.[41] Ellington, while drafting the score for big band, had already discussed the piece with his collaborators and imagined his *New World A-Comin'* played by the string section of a symphony orchestra.

For now, however, let us return to our seats at Carnegie Hall to better appreciate the stirring beauty of a work that only a few were able to truly understand.

IN THE CUTTING ROOM

A succession of contrasting themes with distinct melodic and rhythmic contours, often in different tonalities (introduced without modulations) and each having a specific mood: this kind of process has much in common with film editing and is used in many of Ellington's scores. Diversity is paramount here, while juxtaposition never leads to incoherence because a fine weft of

Ex. 2.3. *New World A-Comin'*, first theme.

Ex. 2.4. *New World A-Comin'*, vamp (toward the second theme).

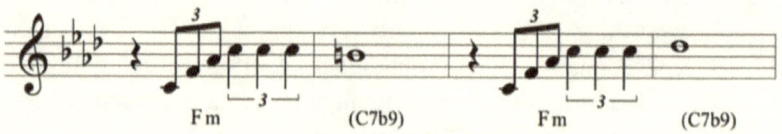

Ex. 2.5. *New World A-Comin'*, second theme.

silver threads, interlaced with the technique of motivic development, binds together the themes of the entire tapestry. The structure seems to dissolve, and yet observing its patterns from a distance, the shapes clearly emerge. *New World A-Comin'* is one of the manifestos of this poetics; a paradigmatic example of a compositional technique that, for Ellington, was perhaps no simple process but a specific vision of the world. The work has three main themes, which alternate with secondary episodes and brief transitions in a continuous dialogue between the piano and the orchestra.[42]

The first theme is nostalgic, and according to David Schiff, its atmosphere is similar to both Strayhorn's ballad "Something to Live For" and the first movement of Howard Hanson's Symphony No. 2, "Romantic."[43] First stated by the reed instruments, it unfolds diatonically in C major, but a poignant modulation to the minor subdominant in m. 4 immediately perturbs this assertive tonal milieu and introduces a melancholic note. This is the only theme presented by the big band (the others being introduced by the piano) and is the one that turns up most frequently in the score, appearing in various tonalities (ex. 2.3).

An ostinato that clearly introduces the tonality of F minor directs us toward the second theme; this is a two-bar vamp for piano and double bass that, with no changes, underpins the entire episode (ex. 2.4).

The second theme then makes its entrance, expanding upward with an arpeggio ending on three repeated notes; then, in m. 2, the melody falls back

Ex. 2.6. *New World A-Comin'*, third theme.

Ex. 2.7. *New World A-Comin'*, vamp that opens the third theme.

on a poignant blue note (ex. 2.5). The melancholy suggested by the impressionistic first theme has now given way to a more dramatic effect, bleakly underscored by Ellington's percussive touch on the piano.

The third theme, in the new tonality of F major, introduces a change of tone: chromaticism, not found in the first two, now pervades the entire melody. Here, the tragic expression of the minor theme is overturned, giving way to a farcical atmosphere worthy of an opera buffa (ex. 2.6). Chromaticism plays a key role in Ellington's entire production, at least as of 1928, acting as a device to express anguish or pain and thus taking up an age-old semantic tradition. Nonetheless, the Duke also lent other meanings to it, evoking heartrending love or beguiling seduction, as in "Prelude to a Kiss" or "Chromatic Love Affair," but also the lighter "affects" implied by a playful irony or *divertissement*. The latter category includes examples such as "Dancers in Love," "Purple Gazelle," and "Latin American Sunshine," as well as the theme currently being discussed. This is, put briefly, the Scherzo of *New World A-Comin'*, a bitterly playful one, as comes out in the tension between the melody and the chords that sustain it.

These three themes, once extracted from the alternation of various secondary episodes and the abrupt transitions from one to the next and put into an orderly sequence, show an extraordinary coherence even in their contrast. Each of them, in fact, develops one or more ideas found in the previous one, as can be seen in examples 2.7 through 2.9.

The third theme is introduced by a vamp that shows a close affinity to the ostinato associated with the second theme (ex. 2.4 and 2.7). Melodically speaking, both begin with an eighth-note triplet (ex. 2.5 and 2.6) and proceed by creating dissonances with the underlying harmony.

Instead, the first theme, on more than one occasion poised between major and minor thanks to modal borrowing, is followed by the second, which,

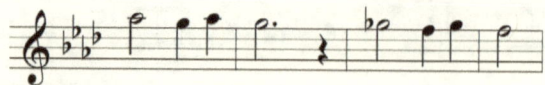

Ex. 2.8. *New World A-Comin'*, transition episode.

Ex. 2.9. *New World A-Comin'*: a) Ellington's melody; b) Henderson's countermelody.

while being in a minor key, comes to a conclusion in the relative major, thus showing two tonal areas. Ellington, however, would never have set them out in this linear and all too predictable narration, which, among other things, would have given way to a story told in a single long take.

Ellington, instead, counts on an approach to musical form linked to film editing: each theme is placed between passages that create brusque and rapid shifts between different episodes. This is what happens in the lively excursus into a piano rag in C major (ex. 2.2) that abruptly arrives after the melancholic theme in F minor. Nonetheless, upon closer look, in addition to creating startling surprises, these episodes reveal a second function: they act as an indispensable binding force. The repeated notes, for example, do not simply characterize the second theme without having anything more to say but also reemerge in both cadences (ex. 2.1), revolving not by chance around C natural, the same note as the beginning of the theme in a minor key. The development of the chromatic element that marks the last theme is even more sophisticated; before this exposition, the figure had made an appearance in no fewer than three secondary episodes, one of which is the brass melody in the bars providing a transition (ex. 2.8) leading to the second theme.

In the carousel of materials found in *New World A-Comin'*, Ellington also inserted a clarinet cadenza played by classically oriented Jimmy Hamilton who, at Carnegie Hall, expressed his own musical background with occasional references to Debussy's *Prélude à l'après-midi d'un faune*. This section in D minor then passes the baton to a piano solo for Ellington, who continues with the second theme in this same tonality.

After the concert held on December 11, 1943, this latter idea no longer convinced the Duke, who eliminated the cadenza in the revised version dating to 1945. This was the year Ellington recorded the work on a V-Disc (Victory Disc), a record intended for American soldiers at war. Indeed, the disc, recorded for the armed forces on June 16, 1945, became a central moment in the evolution of *New World A-Comin'*: it was what Luther Henderson used as a starting point for his symphonic orchestration.[44] Furthermore, the V-Disc (released in October 1946) is the last document bearing witness to the big band version of this work: as of the late forties, Ellington made every effort to present it in its concerto grosso version or, beginning in the sixties, as a piano solo.

From a certain point of view, this demonstrates the quality of Henderson's work; despite the disparaging attitude shown by the Duke, his orchestrator wrote an arrangement that, over the long journey from the premiere in 1949 to the official recording in 1970, was a great source of satisfaction for Ellington. A few passages show its mastery. For example, the light coloring given to the opening theme: even with considerable resources available, the arranger assigned the melody (previously played by the reed instruments) to an evocative combination of horns and bassoons in unison, nuanced by slight touches of an English horn, two clarinets and a bass clarinet; below this, pianissimo, a timpani tremolo on the tonic.[45]

When, as of m. 9, the theme passes to the strings and two trumpets in the low register (all in unison), the arranger makes room for a countermelody in the horns that, while lasting only one bar, is highly elegant. Henderson's expertise comes across at its best in these unexpected counterpoints; in this sense, the line that arises in the strings after the piano's first solo appearance is so poignant that it seems to be the theme, not the chromatic motif that Ellington had written (ex. 2.9).

Even the most discrete and apparently conventional touches are subtly refined, such as the expressive pizzicato upbeat in the strings during the exposition of the sorrowful second theme, like a stroke of Indian ink that makes this desolate landscape all the more sinister.

Now that we've had a taste of this work and given all due merit to Luther Henderson, let's rewind the tapes one last time and take our seats among the audience at Carnegie Hall. This time, it won't be to listen to the music but to hear what Ellington has to say about his *New World A-Comin'*, just a few words stated without too much prior thought before sitting down on the piano bench.

2.
"I'VE NEVER READ THAT BOOK!"

"And now a new attempt, one inspired by a great writer, who wrote a great book. The book, or rather the writer, is Roi Ottley, who wrote *New World A-Coming* [applause]. He's here tonight and I hope that he won't be disappointed. We didn't try to really do a parallel to the story, or describe what he said in words by doing it in a musical strain. What we did was accepted the title as possibility and, very optimistically, anticipated this better condition. And so, with the title, just as it is, we have a very, we hope a very contented feeling in *New World A-Comin'*."

In this introduction, given off the top of his head with some uncertainty, the Duke seems slightly embarrassed. Perfectly used to charming his audiences with flippant remarks and visionary descriptions of his own compositions, he is now at a loss. The ironic understatement in "he's here tonight and I hope that he won't be disappointed" doesn't seem to come across; the audience doesn't react. More importantly, however, he doesn't say a word about the author of the book, who was African American, nor its content. Quite the contrary: he seems to take his distance so as to avoid the issue. "We didn't try to really do a parallel to the story"; there's no "parallel to the story," as Ellington used to say. This was his expression, which had a number of variations for works intended to translate a story or place into sound, at times using specific descriptive codes. The suite *Black, Brown and Beige* (1943) is a "tone parallel to the history of the Negro in America"; *Harlem* (1951) is a "tone parallel to Harlem." *New World A-Comin'* is not. So, the Duke candidly informs us that all he took from the book was its title, as a phrase capable of instilling hope. That's all.

Nevertheless, some affinity with Roi Ottley could still be detected in 1943, even if only faintly: On November 13, the *Pittsburgh Courier* presented Ellington's latest work as being inspired by his bestseller, and on December 5, a photo portraying the composer and the author together was printed in the Sunday edition of the *New York Times*.[46] Two years later, when the V-Disc was made, the bandleader reiterated (in his spoken presentation included in the recording) that "we didn't try so much to properly describe the book and what is said in it, as much as to try to describe the realization and anticipation of the beautiful things to come." The text has now become a simple pretext, and any links with Ottley have become weaker. From that point on, no further references to the work's primary source of inspiration would appear.

When Ellington played *New World A-Comin'* with symphony orchestras, he would give the work's "classical" résumé to the host so that the audience would learn which other prestigious ensembles had performed it; when it was interpreted for piano solo, he would either refrain from introducing it or amuse his listeners with a witty remark (as in the case of his 1962 recital at the MOMA, when he noted that it was the first time he performed the work all on his own).

Later still, from 1965 until the end, as mentioned above, the work would be presented each time through a ritual consisting in well-calibrated words, phrases designed to highlight the utopian-spiritual content of this piece that had recently become part of the *First Sacred Concert*. For years and years, even the slightest contact between the composition and the book was painstakingly avoided: Ottley definitively disappeared.[47] Who knows, maybe Ellington really was only attracted to the title, as he had openly confessed, seeing in that expression a utopian ideal or at least a sense of optimism toward the future. That is what he implied at Carnegie Hall, and that is what we find in the presentations of his old age.

Be this as it may, from the nineteenth century to the present day, African American culture has been fascinated by utopian ideals. Utopian socialism, which, in the United States, had led not only white utopian communities (such as the one in New Harmony, Indiana) but also African American ones to be created, is perhaps the primary manifestation of this ideal; one must, however, turn to Black literature to see it at its most vibrant.[48]

Imperium in Imperio, written by Baptist preacher and activist Sutton Griggs in 1899, tells of a secret African American state and its shadow government within the white empire. Five years later, Edward Johnson, in *Light Ahead for the Negro*, went even further in his imagination: the Black protagonist, after falling asleep for a century, wakes up in 2006 to find himself in a utopian society; he eventually marries a white woman. George Schuyler considered a preemptive approach in the vicious satire of his *Black No More* (1931): a scientist invents a machine that turns Black people white.

Later on, Black science fiction narratives in the sixties and seventies would find some of their roots in this utopian literature dating to the early decades of the century. Writers such as Samuel Delany, Octavia Butler, and Charles Saunders now proposed their vision of worlds founded on superior ideals of harmony, peace, and justice. As Saunders wrote: "Just as our ancestors sang their songs in a strange land when they were kidnapped and sold from Africa, we must, now and in the future, continue to sing our songs under strange stars!" This, put very briefly, is the Afrofuturist message launched by jazz musician Sun Ra when he resolutely affirmed that "[o]uter space is a pleasant place, a place where you can be free!"[49]

Ellington—who, over his career, would write (and sing!) "Moon Maiden" (1969) and, earlier, "Blutopia" (1944), whose *A Drum Is a Woman* (1957) would include a "Ballet of the Flying Saucers," who would title one of his LPs *Blues in Orbit* (1959), and who would die having already written the program for a composition titled *The Race for Space*—with *New World A-Comin'* may have wanted to show how deeply he shared this faith in a utopia projected into the "distant future"; a faith expressed in a nutshell by the title of Ottley's book. Book titles, however, like film trailers, may not succeed in reflecting the content of the work in question and may not even attempt to do so. In Ottley's case, truth be told, the title is not all that misleading: the second chapter is called *Passage to Utopia*, the last one lends its title to the entire book, and other passages also convey the idea that "[the author] has performed a distinguished service for the better world, toward which some individuals are striving," as noted in the *New York Times* (November 12, 1943). But Ottley also has different things to say. Quite different. Much more of a pragmatist than an idealist, he was more concerned with imminent events than with the distant future. Ottley had no wish to let his imagination soar into interstellar space. Intent on staying right where he was, he wanted to change things here and now, in the streets of Harlem, during the war.

One gnawing doubt remains: What if the Duke never wanted to tell us anything about the book simply because he hadn't read it? The evidence seems to point toward this strange hypothesis, and an audio interview given by Ellington to journalist Carter Harman would turn it from mere conjecture into a tenable thesis. On that occasion, answering a question about *New World A-Comin'*, Ellington dryly said, "I've never read that book!" A moment later, he repeated those same blunt words. Harman, in 1956, didn't ask for any further clarification. But today, perhaps we ought to do just that.

A DUKE IN THE MIDST OF HIS PAPERS

Brent Hayes Edwards might turn up his nose at the thought that Ellington composed a piece inspired by a literary work without having a good familiarity with the source, and what's more, without even having taken the time to read it. In his essay "The Literary Ellington," this scholar shows that literary elements lie at the root of many of Ellington's creations.[50] *Suite Thursday* (1960) and *Such Sweet Thunder* (1957) are respectively based on John Steinbeck's novel *Sweet Thursday* and various works by Shakespeare. Ellington and Strayhorn read the Bard's complete works and furthermore consulted some leading authorities of the time. The fact that the movements "Sonnet for Caesar," "Sonnet to Hank Cinq," "Sonnet for Sister Kate," and "Sonnet in Search of a Moor" have a structure with fourteen musical phrases with ten notes each, a musical translation of the Shakespearian sonnet and its strophe made of fourteen iambic pentameters, confirms that Ellington not only read Shakespeare but studied his works in depth.

With a pencil in his hand, ready to take notes, the Duke engaged in readings that provided the inspiration for his last two sacred concerts. He carefully read *Forward Day by Day*, a periodical dedicated to biblical hermeneutics that he received by mail from 1968 to 1973, and underlined the passages of the Holy Scriptures concerning music. One project that floundered involved adapting *Mine Boy* by South African novelist Peter Abrahams. To all this, one must add Ellington's own writings: poems, musical verses, articles for periodicals, texts that he narrated and recorded, a sizeable autobiography, and—above all—various tales that acted as programs for many of his compositions. The latter category includes *Harlem*, *The Golden Broom and the Green Apple*, and *Celebration* (to mention only a few works that will be dealt with in the following chapters), all examples of a tendency he had shown as of the late twenties and that led him to write almost forty pages of narrative text for his first suite, *Black, Brown and Beige* (1943).

And then there's *New World A-Comin'*. A work that would debut at Carnegie Hall (arousing the curiosity of dozens of newspapers); a work that saw the composer himself perform as a soloist (after the concerts of the thirties and the early forties, played by his orchestra); a work that later became his first symphonic composition; a work, like many others, based on a book. And this really was the only time that Ellington didn't even bother to flip through the text? There seems to be something wrong here.

A remark by his son Mercer makes the knot even harder to unravel: "There was nothing in the book that was new to Ellington, but he considered it well researched and capably written."[51] This makes it perfectly clear that Ellington had read *New World A-Coming*; he may have even studied it. What he found in those pages, on the one hand, stimulated him so highly that he wrote a major composition that is inextricably tied to it, and on the other, brought him such turmoil that he felt forced to take his distance from it. What kind of book could have been so thorny?

"NEW WORLD A-COMING" AND ITS AUTHOR

Vincent Lushington "Roi" Ottley was born in Harlem in 1906 to parents of Caribbean origin.[52] His middle-class family, who lived in a beautiful house on famed Strivers' Row, would certainly have approved of the boys their son spent time with: Adam Clayton Powell Jr. (who would be elected to

Congress), Frankie Steele (who would become a famous medical doctor), W. C. Handy Jr. (son of the legendary "Father of the Blues"), and Thomas Fats Waller (who would shortly be recognized as a masterful jazz pianist). This bunch of friends used to call themselves the "Young Thinkers," and at twenty years old, Roi proved to have not only a brain but also a body that was in excellent shape: the awards he won in athletics gained him a scholarship at St. Bonaventure University.[53]

An avid reader, he soon switched to journalism and attended the University of Michigan, but the racist environment he found on campus got the better of him. As a young man, he left school. His dreams were not shattered, however; on the contrary, a few conferences given by Black intellectual James Weldon Johnson spurred him on, and in the middle of the Great Depression, without a degree, he became a columnist for the *New York Amsterdam News*. With his *Hectic Harlem*, in no time, he was one of the city's most fashionable journalists. A few years later, he even became head of the Harlem branch of the Federal Writers' Project; this Popular Front initiative had brought together a handful of writers led by Ottley and given them the task of documenting African American experience in New York. He thus guided the efforts of many of the twentieth century's most illustrious African American writers (Ralph Ellison, Richard Wright, Dorothy West, and Claude McKay, to mention only a few).[54] The fruit of their research, as we shall soon find out, directly concerns our current topic.

The House Un-American Activities Committee eventually shut down the project, but Ottley managed to stay on his feet and, still feeling the enthusiasm, was able to get his first book published by the important editor Houghton Mifflin: the first edition's fifty thousand copies sold made it his greatest success, gaining him the American Life Houghton Mifflin Prize and the Ainsworth Award.

The following years go beyond the scope of our investigation. As briefly as possible: Ottley published three more books (including *The Lonely Warrior*, a biography of the editor of *The Chicago Defender* and still today cited in its field) and made further achievements in journalism, eventually working for white newspapers as well, such as the *Chicago Tribune*. He died of a heart attack in 1960. Nevertheless, we must dwell on at least the first year of his career after *New World A-Coming* was published. Ottley developed a strong interest in war journalism, which had already nourished a few chapters of his bestseller. In 1944, he became a captain and, in his two years of activity as a war correspondent, traveled over sixty thousand miles in Europe, Africa, and the Middle East, documenting the conflict from an African American perspective for *P.M. News* and the *Pittsburgh Courier*.

And so, while the (few) Black correspondents were forbidden to take photos of the desolate condition of African American troops or inform public opinion of racist discrimination (Black nurses could only care for German soldiers!), Ottley began to vocally denounce all of this, and what's more, he did so in the white newspaper *P.M.*[55] Let's return, however, to 1943 and take a closer look at his book. What is *New World A-Coming* about? African American social history, above all, during the two most recent decades. It is made up of twenty-three chapters, many of which are set in Harlem, the "Capital of Black America"; "The Negro Pitches His Tent!" sings the praises of Harlem as cultural capital; "How Colored Is Harlem" brings out the neighborhood's various ethnicities (Mexican, Puerto Rican, Philippine, Chinese, Japanese); "Springtime in Harlem" is dedicated to the explosion of culture seen in the twenties; "The Slum-Shocked" is a condemnation of the ghetto's corrupt police; and "The Cafe-au-Lait Society" mocks the super-rich living in Harlem. Many cultural heroes from this part of Manhattan come into the spotlight. A few appear in the chapters "The Apostles of Race" and, above all, "Who Are the Negro's Leaders?" and a more focused biographical look is given to some who were most closely tied to Harlem: Father Divine ("I Talked with God"), Marcus Garvey ("Up, You Mighty Race"), boxer Joe Louis ("Joe Louis and His People") and his friend Adam Clayton Jr. ("Glamour Boy").

Other parts of the volume have a more national scope and greater historical depth (such as "Passage to Utopia" on slavery and the Reconstruction period). The last five chapters are dedicated to Black soldiers on the battlefield with the outcry, "The enemy is taking advantage of American racism to win the war!"

The book was well received by critics: "Roi Ottley is at his best" (*New Republic*, September 6, 1943); "he has portrayed well what the Negro thinks" (*Social Forces*, December 1943); "a tragic and stormy picture with that extra accuracy, that deep understanding and intense feeling give a trained, observant reporter" (*Book Week*, August 15, 1943). Ottley's former collaborators at the Federal Writers' Project were less inclined to heap praise on it. In no uncertain terms, they maintained that a considerable amount of the text owed much to their research in the thirties. When the project came to an end, Ottley apparently took home numerous boxes full of sheets of paper. Ellison didn't hesitate to brand a few chapters as sensationalistic, and historian John Hope Franklin had even stronger doubts. It may be that Ellison's low opinion of Ottley, interested solely in "the bar, the bed, and the table," and, above all, the strict rules that Ottley imposed on all of them during their collaboration, made their opinions somewhat less than objective. Nevertheless, any indirect contribution coming from these intellectuals, from our current point of view, could only give additional value to the work brought together under the title *New World A-Coming*.

When the Duke leafed through this book, what probably arose in him, chapter after chapter, were increasingly contradictory feelings, leaving him torn between agreement with those ideas and discomfort for how overtly, even unabashedly, they were expressed. What truly led him to feign indifference toward this bestseller was not, therefore, its content (even though the description of the Communist Party as the association that "did more than any other" for Blacks may have given him some reason to worry) but the trenchant tone running through the entire text.[56] Ottley was no radical, but in his first book, he used some very strong words. "His [the African American's] rumblings for equality in every phase of American life will reverberate into a mighty roar in the days to come. For the Negro feels that the day for talking quietly has past [*sic*]" (344). Or again: "Negroes are no longer in a mood to be placated by pious double-talk" (236).

His idea of the struggle for civil rights had nothing to do with tactful negotiations; it was closer to the resolute action taken by Paul Robeson who, in a theater in the South, interrupted the concert to deliver an exhortation against segregation that made the white audience's hair stand on end (240). Nor can we forget that this was 1943, the year the country was shaken by racial conflict. Rioting was seen in forty-seven cities (including Harlem, which counted six deaths at the end of the uprising), political temperatures were high, and Ottley, while standing against any kind of violent action, was fully determined not to keep his voice down.

The extremely moderate Duke, who always refused to become openly involved in the sphere of politics, not to mention militancy, had no other choice but to see this fascinating book as having the two faces of Janus: he openly admired one of them, to the point of dedicating a composition to it (the utopian-optimistic one expressed by the title), while not even glancing at the other, or at least not in public (the one standing for firm political engagement).

THE DUKE'S BRAND OF POLITICS: MASKS AND TROMBONES

Don George, who wrote the lyrics for "I'm Beginning to See the Light," was a close friend of Ellington's as of 1943. At the same moment as the Duke was working on *New World A-Comin'*, George, who didn't miss a set of the Duke's show at the Capitol Theatre, enquired into his ideas on politics. First, he tried to goad him into taking a stance by reminding him of the miserable conditions of Black Americans, then he carefully took aim and threw the dart.

"How come you never say anything?" Ellington serenely replied: "Don, at the Capitol Theatre, people come and pay seventy-five cents to see me. They're not paying to see a politician. They come here to be entertained, not politicized."[57]

When, twenty years later, comedian Dick Gregory asked Ellington to participate in the March on Washington along with Lena Horne, Sidney Poitier, and Sammy Davis Jr., his cryptic answer was: "I'm not a marcher, I'm a lover." Not even the conditions offered by Bob Kennedy, who guaranteed the group of artists a private jet and full protection, were enough to change the Duke's mind, and he declined the offer with a flimsy excuse: "I'd love to go, but I've got sore feet. I can't walk that far." He later summed up his feelings by confessing to George: "I'd never get involved in anything like that."[58]

And yet this attitude, vaguely portrayed by his lyricist friend, seems to contrast with the sincere interest in social issues shown by Ellington's compositions from the twenties to the end of his career. This vein is perhaps best represented by the musical revue *Jump for Joy*. Written in 1941 along with a team of fifteen writers (both white and Black), the show was intended, in Ellington's words, "to correct the race situation in the U.S.A. through a form of theatrical propaganda"; the all-Black cast, "well aware of its controversial impact," along with the show's biting satire, aimed at excluding the figure of Uncle Tom from American theaters once and for all.[59]

Then, in 1946, came the *Deep South Suite*, which ridiculed racist stereotypes about African Americans; one year later, the mixed cast of *Beggar's Holiday* added a new piece to the puzzle; again, the opera *My People* (1963) contains one movement dedicated to Martin Luther King Jr.'s struggle in Alabama, explicitly titled "King Fit the Battle of Alabam." Picking another card at random from this rather large deck, we might come up with the soundtrack of the film *Change of Mind*, the story of a Black man who receives a transplant of a white man's brain. The film dates to 1970, the same year in which our long journey began, with the television documentary where Ellington noted that his "Black Beauty" had already said everything there was to say, four decades before the slogan "black is beautiful" became popular; certainly, he had said so with music, not by giving speeches from a soapbox. And this is exactly how, in the elusiveness and ambiguity of musical discourse, that is, Ellington's political thought comes across at its best. "You can say anything you want on the trombone, but you gotta be careful with words," the Duke once explained to Richard Boyer, who was surprised to see that Ellington's collection of African American history books had "heavily underlined" the passages on slave uprisings. *Who would have expected this from the good-natured Duke?*—who, in public, used to wear "a grin as wide as possible"—the journalist must have thought.[60]

"What we could not say openly we expressed in music" was what the bandleader confessed to the music magazine *Rhythm* in 1931, and he insisted on the idea forty years later when writing about *Jump for Joy* in his memoirs: "I think a statement of social protest in the theater should be made without saying it."[61]

The path chosen by the Duke inevitably led to an oblique, elusive, or enigmatic form of expression; the protest found in some of his works is indeed so ambiguous that, on a few occasions, it has been misinterpreted. For example, the grotesque vein that runs through the *Deep South Suite* caught a few critics (including James Lincoln Collier) off guard so badly that they were unable to understand its true satirical content.

And so, the cocktail is complete. Here's the recipe. One part consists of Ellington hiding behind "a grin as wide as possible" to avoid thorny questions (such as being directly linked to an all too openly political book). One part consists of African American culture's tendency to freely express itself only in music ("It is only in his music that the Negro in America has been able to tell his story," James Baldwin has written). One part consists of the Duke's strategy of conveying things without saying them (which, according to Graham Lock, is one of the guiding principles of Ellington's aesthetics).[62] The overall result, much more than a simple drink, is an explosive mixture that has wreaked havoc on our ability to analyze Ellington's political thought.

This cocktail got us all so tipsy that we hurriedly wrote off the Duke as an artist only blandly interested in civic participation. That's why we believed in the fairy tale of a composer with an inclination toward literature who dedicated an entire score to a politically engaged book without even taking the time to read it. We got hoodwinked.

This is what we learn from the folder titled "Edward (Duke) Kennedy Ellington 100-hq-434443" that the Federal Bureau of Investigation opened in the spring of 1938 and closed with details of his Russian tour in 1971, thirty-three years later! Even without taking into account the "Second Red Scare" that affected the country in the postwar years, this folder allows us to measure the considerable weight that political engagement had in his life. All we have to do is flip through the first few pages and underline a passage or two:

[page 1]
On May 13, 1938, Ellington endorsed the All-Harlem Youth Conference, an association that ten years later would be classified by the Un-American Activities Committee as "among the more conspicuous Communist-front groups."

[page 2]

On June 27, 1943, he participated in the Tribute to Negro Servicemen, sponsoring the National Negro Congress, later investigated as a communist association, one of whose founders was Roi Ottley.

On October 24, 1943, he played at the Golden Gate Ballroom to support Benjamin J. Davis Jr., the Communist Party's candidate for New York's Town Council. [African American Ben Davis won this election and the following one, staying in office until 1949.]

[page 3]

A reliable source dating to January 1944 tells us that Ellington sent 1,500 fundraising letters for the National Committee to Abolish the Poll Tax. [The committee, which fought against this particular restriction on voting rights (a campaign that would only be won twenty years later), was considered by the California Un-American Activities Commission to be "among the communist front organizations for racial agitation."]

In April 1944, he participated in the Tribute to Fats Waller sponsored by American Youth for Democracy, which became a "tremendous, spontaneous demonstration of inter-racial unity." [This phrase, part of the dossier, was certainly not intended as praise for the event, considering that American Youth for Democracy was later targeted by the Department of Justice as a communist organization.]

[page 4]

In 1947, he performed in a fundraiser for the National Council for American-Soviet Friendship. [The organization was branded as communist by Executive Order 9835, signed that very year by President Truman; known as the Loyalty Order, it was designed to eliminate communist influence from the American government.]

The dossier continues with a copious list of further investigations reaching the early seventies, even though it is mainly focused on the late thirties and the following decade.

Ellington, however, had already been on the move for some time when the FBI opened its investigation. In 1931, he played at a concert organized by the National Association for the Advancement of Colored People to raise funds for the Scottsboro Boys.[63] One year later, playing the piano in Benny Carter's orchestra, he stood for the same cause in a charity concert organized by the well-known manager John Hammond. On January 21, 1931, he performed for the Urban League. On February 22, 1933, he donated his own pay to the Brooklyn Home for Aged Colored People.[64]

Even in the period in which he was monitored by the FBI to a lesser degree, i.e., the fifties and, above all, the sixties, the Duke was active. For example, in 1951, he played for the NAACP and raised the considerable sum of $16,000; with a jump cut to the next decade, we find him performing on August 20, 1963, at the Stars of Freedom Rally promoted by the Southern Christian Leadership Conference; five days later, he was in the spotlight once again at a charity concert for the March on Washington with leading political figures, including socialist unionist Asa Philip Randolph, giving speeches on the same stage.[65]

The links between Ellington and the (African) American left also emerge in a field of studies in which much work remains to be done concerning the participation of Blacks (above all, those living in Harlem) in the cultural program of the American Popular Front.

Beginning in the midthirties, trade unions, anti-fascist groups expressing their solidarity with the Spanish people, Ethiopians and Chinese, political refugees having escaped from Nazi regimes, and a considerable portion of the (white and Black) left gave birth to the Popular Front, whose impact on American society was felt, above all, in terms of culture. Orson Welles, John Hammond, Paul Robeson, Langston Hughes, and Richard Wright (to mention only a few figures close to Ellington) were part of this intelligentsia. The Harlem branch of the Front, which partially relied on the Communist party and its Black member Benjamin Davis, had brought together in the National Negro Congress no fewer than 585 organizations, eventually counting over one million members.

Jazz played its part. A few record producers joined in this movement, first and foremost John Hammond, but also Norman Granz and Eric Bernay; the latter, who founded Keynote Records, had been the editor of the Marxist periodical *The New Masses*. Many musicians themselves felt close to these ideas. A long string of jazzmen played at the events organized by the Popular Front: swing artists such as Count Basie, Benny Carter, Benny Goodman, Artie Shaw, Fletcher Henderson, Cab Calloway, Chick Webb, and Billie Holiday, as well as emerging bebop musicians such as Dizzy Gillespie and Charlie Parker.

A special place in this list belongs to Duke Ellington, who was one of the most active. He played, for example, an important part in getting Benjamin Davis elected, both the first time in 1943 (as noted by the FBI) and the second in 1945, and his progressive musical *Jump for Joy* became one of the Popular Front's most significant theatrical productions, along with Marc Blitzstein's *The Cradle Will Rock* and Harold Rome's *Pins and Needles* (both written in 1937).[66]

In a nutshell: with his "love you madly mask," Ellington pulled the wool over our eyes!

The expression "love you madly mask" (coined by David Schiff) refers to the way the bandleader presented himself to audiences: "You are very beautiful, very sweet, very gracious, very generous . . . and we love you madly!" All of this amounted to an excessively mannered ceremony that brought a smile to its listeners' lips as soon as, after the umpteenth superlative, they got the joke. Putting on this act, which, for Ellington, was a very serious affair, was something he did offstage as well: over his entire life, the Duke wore the costume of a benign and moderate character, a costume used to camouflage the man (and activist) Edward Kennedy Ellington. If anyone tried to peek behind the curtain (in particular, anyone white), Ellington would have satisfied their curiosity with a few lies.

He pulled it off with Don George, who must have been rather gullible to believe that Ellington wasn't interested in Martin Luther King Jr.'s March on Washington (as we now know, he played in two fundraising concerts in New York during that same week in August 1963, while at the same time, his *My People*, with a movement dedicated to King, was playing in Chicago).

He pulled it off with John Hammond, the manager who didn't notice Ellington's militancy in the Popular Front and thus accused him in an article published in 1935 of "shut[ting] his eyes to the abuses being heaped upon his race" and "he has never shown any desire of aligning himself with forces that are seeking to remove the causes of these disgraceful conditions."[67]

He even pulled it off with the FBI. The agency, probably appeased by a few public statements in which he distanced himself from the left, backed off. The FBI dossier in fact includes the following testimony by Ellington, dating to 1950: "I've never been interested in politics in my whole life . . . the only communism I know is that of Jesus Christ." The folder also contains an article written by the composer, titled *No Red Songs for Me* and published by the *New Leader*; in this piece, published that same year, Ellington stated quite clearly that he wanted nothing to do with communism.[68]

The Duke's astuteness made it even easier for him to cover up the political content of many of his works, content that was already elusive in itself, entrusted, as mentioned above, "to the trombone" instead of explicit declarations. And so, this cover-up eventually extended to *New World A-Comin'*, whose "red" roots, cut off long before, became even more undetectable in the age of McCarthyism.

Recently, issue no. 228 of the *Socialist Review* (March 1999) gave due credit to the political commitment that Ellington poured into his music. Perhaps, however, as far as *New World A-Comin'* is concerned, we could have grasped the piece's inextricable links with Ottley and the underlying ideology if we had only turned to the people who were directly concerned, i.e., Harlemites in the forties. It would have been enough to ask them a simple question: "Do you know *New World A-Comin'*?" Few would have replied that they'd read Ottley's book. A somewhat larger number would have said that they were aware of Ellington's composition. The largest percentage, instead, would have no doubt answered: "Sure I know *New World A-Comin'*! I tune in every Sunday."

"NEW WORLD A-COMING": PROUD TO BE ON THE AIR

Today is March 5, 1944. It's Sunday at 3:03 p.m. A listener tunes his radio to New York broadcaster WMCA to follow the first episode of a new show: *New World A-Coming*, a broadcast that will make Harlem proud for the next two years. Ottley's book has indeed become a radio series.

Helen Straus was impressed by the book and, as of its opening pages, sensed that it could be transposed. Helen and her husband Nathan had purchased WMCA a few months earlier and, progressives as they were, decided along with the City-Wide Citizens' Committee on Harlem, a left-wing interracial committee, to give voice to those pages. The idea was to give the book's content a theatrical form, assigning the dialogues to actors.

The great African American actor and activist Canada Lee was chosen as the narrator. Beginning in the midthirties, American radio stations had already hosted a few productions dealing with Blacks. In 1935, *A Harlem Family* spoke of the difficulties faced by an African American family during the Depression (the program was written, directed, and interpreted by Blacks); in 1941, *Freedom's People* highlighted the contribution to music made by Black artists (conceived by African American Ambrose Caliver, one of the show's guests was Paul Robeson); between 1942 and 1944, a few broadcasts had brought to light the efforts made by Black soldiers: *For My People* (1942), *Fighting Men* (1943), *Men Behind the Gun* (1943), *Something About Joe* (1943), and *Dorie Got a Medal* (1944).[69]

But none of these programs had as great an impact as *New World A-Coming*, which represented, according to the author of the study *Broadcasting Freedom*, Barbara Dianne Savage, "an extraordinary divergence from national radio's timid and cautious approach to discussions about racial inequality."[70] Basing its work on the chapters of Ottley's book, the independent network WMCA denounced the abuse suffered by Black soldiers both on the front line and at home, exposed the racist ideology of segregation, and discussed Black people's aspirations and the importance of their contribution to American society.[71]

Some of the episodes were dedicated to music. The fourth, "The Negro in Entertainment" (March 26, 1944), featuring jazz pianist Hazel Scott, portrayed the difficulties faced by a young musician trying to be accepted in the white world of classical music. Even in this first episode dedicated to music, the stance taken by the program was reflected by a focus on social criticism instead of merely aesthetic issues. This was the perspective from which episode number seventeen, "The Story of Negro Music" (June 25, 1944), was also conceived: the energy of African rhythm, the pathos of spirituals, the seduction of blues, and then "jazz Negro knowledge" influenced American music in its entirety. To demonstrate this, it ended with an outstanding performance of "I Got Rhythm." George Gershwin's song was played by a host of "the nation's greatest jazzmen": Art Tatum, Roy Eldridge, Charlie Shavers, Edmond Hall, Ben Webster, Al Casey, Slam Stewart, Benny Morton, and Vic Dickenson. Earlier, Billie Holiday had performed "Fine and Mellow," showing the appeal of city blues. "Music at War" (the episode aired on October 20, 1944) begins by stating that "you will hear songs old and new . . . songs expecting the hope of the extension of democracy, not only abroad, but right here in America too" and continues with a portrait of the United States Coast Guard Quartet, an ensemble made up of two Black and two white Coast Guard bands.

"A Tribute to Handy" (November 19, 1944) is a theatrical biography of the "Father of the Blues" that does not shy away from giving examples of racial discrimination. The interview with the seventy-one-year-old composer underlines the universality of the blues language, whose message has found listeners in every part of the world. At the end of the first season, the press was enthusiastic about what the *New York Times* described as "a public invitation to decent thinking."

The second season opened on October 8, 1944, with a few particularly flattering reviews: "A hard hitting show that is certain to create a furor" (*Daily News*), "It's a powerful and important program" (*Billboard*), "It's a straight from the shoulder approach to the problem of racial prejudice and intolerance" (*Variety*), and even though it was only aired in New York, it aroused the interest of the *Pittsburgh Courier*, whose comment was, "[T]he show was being handled without the old embellishments of Uncle Tom."[72]

Meanwhile, the Duke kept saying he was unaware of the content of Ottley's book, content that had reached half the nation and all of Harlem. But Ellington didn't limit himself to associating his composition with one of the most radical radio broadcasts in American history; he also provided that program, "Straight from the Shoulder," with its theme song. "A new world is a-coming with the sweep and fury of the Resurrection," Canada Lee declares with a voice made of granite; every Sunday, for a few years, this catchphrase resounded on the air, broadcast by the WMCA, and the motto was sustained by accompanying music. This music is a transition episode taken from Ellington's *New World A-Comin'* (ex. 2.8). For his contribution, the Duke was included in the end credits, read over an elaboration of the theme song whose atmosphere resembles that of "Mood Indigo"; over those notes, the speaker names the arranger and the conductor and concludes by saying, "Musical theme composed by Duke Ellington."[73]

This theme did not simply act as a curtain, rising and falling at the beginning and the end of each episode, but was, at times, heard within the narrations themselves: in the first episode, it provides a comment to a scene in which Black soldiers are thrown out of a cinema theater in New Jersey; in the second ("The Negro Fascism and Democracy," March 12, 1944), it closes the reading of a little girl's essay on the freedom the war could have brought; and in the episode "Music at War," it appears at the end of the performance of "When the Saints Go Marching In."

It was not, however, the only fragment of Ellington's *New World A-Comin'* heard in this broadcast. The third theme of the composition, the Scherzo (ex. 2.6), is also found in some episodes, including one sequence conceived for the premiere: a group of African American soldiers walks into a segregated cafeteria in Virginia, with the (re-elaborated) third theme providing a counterpoint to the narration.[74]

In 1941, Ellington participated in the broadcast *The Negro and National Defense* promoted by the African American association The National Urban League (NUL). That same year, he showed his support for actor and activist Canada Lee, celebrated in a radio broadcast for his theatrical successes: Lee had interpreted the protagonist of *Native Son* (*Fear*) in the theater adaptation of Richard Wright's book with the same name, gaining praise from all critics. That *Salute to Canada Lee* brought together various politically engaged Black cultural heroes (such as Bill Robinson and Joe Louis), as well as some of the more outstanding members of the Popular Front, including Paul Robeson and Richard Wright (who participated in the broadcast externally), in addition to Ellington and Lee themselves.

Probably, however, the Duke thought that he could do more. So, when his actor friend became involved in the *New World A-Comin'* project, Ellington felt it appropriate to add a contribution of his own.[75] A few parts of his work inspired by Ottley's content probably seemed to be the most suitable tribute. And yet Ellington was convinced that this sort of manifest involvement would have led to some kind of hassle: being Black, a left-wing activist, and a star loved by huge audiences were three things that didn't go together, or at least not in open daylight. So the Duke put a great deal of effort into elaborating a strategy to throw everyone off track, and once he had put on his "love you madly mask," he sat down and introduced his piece by telling the tale that . . .

HARLEM
SOUNDS FROM THE AIR SHAFT

A DUKE IN THE OVAL OFFICE

During his years at the White House, President Lyndon Johnson received Ellington no fewer than seven times. Eisenhower, the old general with a soft spot for "Mood Indigo," also welcomed him with open arms. Nixon went as far as playing "Happy Birthday" for him on the piano the day he turned seventy.[1]

This informal atmosphere, which was to last for two decades, may well have been established during the very first meeting between Ellington and an American head of state. On April 29, 1950, Harry Truman welcomed the Duke into his private office and, once he had dismissed his bodyguard, created such a relaxed environment that Ellington later recalled the scene with a unique image: "We were a couple of cats in a billiard parlor." During this visit, set for 12:30 p.m. (wedged in between the president's 12:15 meeting with the secretary of Agriculture and the one held at 12:45 with the vice president of the National Bank of Commerce in New Orleans), the Maestro gave the most important man in the country the manuscript score of his latest suite: *Harlem*.[2] This was a work conceived by Ellington in both symphonic and jazz orchestra versions, and judging by a photo that portrays Ellington and Harry Truman poring over the score together, we might have reason to believe that the manuscript score in question was the one for big band.[3] This is precisely the form in which the work was debuted on January 21, 1951, at the Metropolitan Opera House of New York, as part of a benefit concert whose proceeds would go to the NAACP; the event was intended to raise awareness among Americans of the issue of segregation. Ellington invited the president and his daughter Margaret, who was a competent opera singer, but no one from the White House showed up nor was heard from.[4]

The following year, the Duke tried to invite the president to another of his live concerts but didn't meet with any success this time either.[5] Probably, he assumed that Truman's love for music—the president being an amateur pianist—was strong enough to convince him to come. The Duke was under the wrong impression: The head of state only loved classical music and detested all contemporary genres (to which he referred with the expression "modern noise"). Truman's record collection contained 680 albums; not one of them was by Ellington.[6]

"HARLEM" ON A TRANSATLANTIC

The October 20, 1950, issue of *DownBeat* contains an interesting piece of news in American music: the radio broadcaster WNBC had just commissioned a *Portrait of New York* to be written by six different musicians. A single work in a number of movements, entirely dedicated to Manhattan, it was to be composed by Skitch Henderson, who was to portray the outskirts, Vernon Duke, who was entrusted with Central Park, Sigmund Romberg, who would have described Broadway, Don Gillis, whose work would be inspired by the subways, and Ellington, who was naturally requested to represent the ghetto in Harlem. And while negotiations to determine the identity of the sixth composer were still underway (Aaron Copland and Leonard Bernstein were on the list), a TV premiere and a recording produced by Victor had already been planned.[7] The project never came to fruition, and *Harlem* was the only piece of the mosaic to see the light of day.

The original idea did not clarify whether the great Arturo Toscanini, who had been conducting the NBC Orchestra since 1937, would have honored this score by performing it himself or whether each composer would have taken up the baton for their own movement.[8] At a time when some degree of uncertainty still surrounded the project, the Duke seems to have suggested that Toscanini himself had commissioned the score from him (and would later have conducted it). Like a seed, this anecdote was planted into the Ellington literature in 1951, later blossoming and growing into a sturdy oak tree. Actually, the entire story has no ascertainable roots: no evidence confirms that Toscanini was ever directly involved in the "Portrait of New York" project, and he himself never conducted "Harlem."[9] In his autobiography, Ellington was careful not to write anything questionable, stating that "Harlem" had been requested by the NBC Symphony "during the time when

Maestro Arturo Toscanini was its conductor"; in the meantime, however, the rumor, picked up by fans and family members (in 1989 his sister Ruth, during an interview given late in her life, said that she was proud that the commission had come from Toscanini), turned into the truth.[10]

In any case, whether conducted by a prestigious baton or not, Ellington was certain that the work, when completed, would be performed by the NBC Orchestra, and so he set down to work on it. Once again, his autobiography suggests the spatial and temporal coordinates of the creative act: "On our return on the *Île-de-France* I wrote 'Harlem.'"[11] This passage is a snapshot of his journey back to the United States by sea after a three-month European tour, in which his orchestra was engaged from April 4 to June 20, 1950 (and in the middle of which, from May 5 to 25, the band also appeared in Italy).

Biographer David Palmquist has recently shown that, after preparing their boarding passes, Ellington and his musicians didn't travel on the *Île de France* but on the transatlantic SS *De Grasse*. The orchestra (except for Ray Nance, who flew with Air France) set sail from the port of Cherbourg on June 21 and docked in New York on June 30.[12] In any event, regardless of these details, it would seem that the Duke wrote the suite during that lapse of time in his first-class cabin (the members of the orchestra traveled in second class). Actually, while he may well have completed it during that week, perhaps writing it all down on manuscript paper, he most certainly didn't compose it from scratch; this piece had been buzzing around in his mind for at least a year . . .

THE BIRTH OF "HARLEM" IN TWO TON'S LIVING ROOM AND KING KONG'S JUNGLE

The University of Wisconsin, after awarding him an honorary degree in music in 1971, organized a Duke Ellington Week one year later; from July 17 to 21, the members of his band held workshops and the Duke was scheduled to give two masterclasses.[13] For the one that took place on July 20, attended by a crowd of fans in the university's auditorium at 2:00 p.m., Ellington asked an old friend to give him a hand at the piano: Richard Baker.[14]

Nicknamed "Two Ton" (on account of his weight), Baker was a talented entertainer from Chicago who had been very popular in the forties. A radio and TV star, he delighted children with programs specially designed for them and enchanted adults as a remarkably gifted pianist. He was a staunch admirer of the Duke: the January 1941 issue of *DownBeat* hailed him as "the number one Ellington fan" around, and Baker dedicated a few compositions to him ("The Duke's Back Again" and "The Duke Tunes

Up") and recorded some of his pieces, including an appealing version of "Dancers in Love" (1947).

In 1949, Baker met his idol in Chicago. Ellington had traveled there for his first engagement at the Blue Note. From that point on, the two of them stayed in touch, and about a quarter of a century later, Baker was invited to play the piano at the University of Wisconsin during its Duke Ellington Week.[15] In the auditorium, he gave an inspired performance of "Dancers in Love," but first he thought he would play around with the audience a bit, accompanying at the piano an extremely rare performance given by the Duke as a singer. The song they chose for the number was "I'm Afraid," which hadn't been in Ellington's repertoire for at least twenty years. Never much of a crooner, he couldn't remember the lyrics that Don George had written in 1949. Two Ton scolded him: "You wrote it!" The crowd enjoyed their comedy sketch. But then suddenly, taking his hands off the keyboard and turning toward the audience, Baker oddly remarked, "We have a tape of you singing this thing at home!"[16] *A recording featuring Ellington as a singer! He must be pulling our leg!* everyone must have thought. The university professors may have written it off as a quip intended to show everyone, perhaps even brag about it, what a close bond there was between Baker and the great composer. But what our entertainer said was no joke; he was perfectly serious. And he was telling the truth. Two Ton Baker had indeed recorded a tape of his hero the very first time they met in Chicago, which was in March 1949.

As mentioned above, the Duke Ellington Orchestra was engaged at the Blue Note from the 14th to the 27th of that month. One of those evenings, most likely after one of their two days off (either the 15th or the 22nd), Baker invited the bandleader to a party at his home. The Duke entertained the guests at the piano (and at the electric piano), beginning with no other than a version sung by himself of "I'm Afraid" and continuing with well-known pieces such as "Rockin' in Rhythm," older compositions like "Creole Rhapsody" (only playing the third theme), the sublime "Mystery Song" (that he dusted off after setting it aside for many years), and a hilarious improvised number that he sang with an excellent Italian accent (even though he had not yet performed in Italy)! At one point in the recording, we hear him pass from "Fantazm," a recent piece of his with a Latin feel, to an apparently rhapsodic or improvised moment. Baker's guests didn't seem to appreciate this unknown piece and started chattering more loudly; luckily for us, however, not loudly enough to cover those three minutes of music, some of which Ellington would later baptize as *Harlem*.[17] A healthy portion of the score, coming to roughly the first half of the suite, was in the composer's head well before the NBC commission arrived.

The tape proves that the Duke, even though he hadn't yet gone to the trouble of writing anything down, had planned out every detail.[18] Listening to this recording while following the score, indeed, one realizes that the part between m. 9 of the A section until the end of D1 had been meticulously composed.[19] Even a few of the more rhapsodic passages in the suite, such as the clarinet's two rapid chromatic scales in sextuplets at the beginning of section A1, had already been defined.[20] There are indeed very few differences with the score, the most interesting being the theme Ellington later gave to the baritone sax (section B2): this piano version does not have a Latin character (as in the final draft) but is in the style of a ballad and not introduced by the ostinato that in the score is (erroneously) indicated as a "bolero" (sections B and B1).[21]

In the end, the only sections that are missing are the one that opens the suite, a significant blues episode, and, as previously indicated, the spiritual. It is highly likely that the commission from NBC stimulated Ellington to write both the sacred theme and the blues, which he presumably composed on the transatlantic ship in June 1950. Nevertheless, a further investigation of Ellington's (micro)cosm would seem to suggest that other fragments of *Harlem* may also have resulted from a period of compositional development that began even earlier than 1949.

To embark on our voyage and search for the work's origin, we will, however, have to leave the safe haven of incontrovertible evidence (such as the tape recorded by Baker) and sail through an open sea of hypotheses, trying to steer clear of mere conjecture. Our first destination will be the work's very beginning, i.e., the nine opening bars that Ellington failed to play at Two Ton's party. Let us, therefore, cast anchor just off a sinister island, an atoll inhabited by monstrous apes by day and crazy Russian aristocrats by night.

King Kong cost a pretty penny: over $10 million today. This was a considerable amount of money, especially for a producer such as RKO that didn't have the same financial resources as the major studios. The film was a huge success at the box office, setting a new record for the highest-grossing opening weekend in 1932. There was, however, no way that producers and directors Merian C. Cooper and Ernest B. Schoedsack and executive producer David O. Selznick could have foreseen this, and while working on the film, they devised a strategy to cut down on costs: they would use the same set and the same actors to shoot two films at the same time, *King Kong* by day and *The Most Dangerous Game* by night. The soundtracks of the two films, once again following the rationale of working a double shift, were also written by the same composer, Max Steiner.

Ex. 3.1. *The Most Dangerous Game*, opening theme.

This Viennese composer, who took piano lessons from Johannes Brahms as a child and studied with Gustav Mahler as a young man, wrote two scores that had an enormous influence on the history of cinema: both soundtracks, indeed, make abundant use of extradiegetic musical comments and are skillfully interwoven with leitmotifs.[22] The first score Steiner completed was for *The Most Dangerous Game*, so hastily composed that the ink only dried two weeks before the film was released in movie theaters (on September 9, 1932) because Steiner had to step in and replace the music written by W. Franke Harling, whose work was deemed unsatisfactory.[23]

The sinister plot of *The Most Dangerous Game* involves Zaroff, a Russian aristocrat who owns a castle on an island in the middle of nowhere and has a passion for a unique sport: he organizes manhunts. Right from the opening credits, the music portrays this ominous atmosphere with a solitary horn call: only two notes, to which the orchestra responds ruthlessly with heavy quarter-note chords and a menacing chromatic profile (ex. 3.1).[24]

The reference to the hunt is clear: not by chance, in the scene where Zaroff pursues his human prey, the crazy aristocrat plays this interval on a makeshift horn as a call for his hounds.[25] Both the descending minor third (which continues to echo throughout the entire score) and the orchestra's response are surprisingly similar to the opening bars of *Harlem*.[26] The resemblances concern the solo instrument that states the motif (a brass instrument, in both instances), the tempo, the interval in question, and the orchestra's response.

The reader may legitimately feel some doubt, finding this analogy somewhat contrived and not seeing any kind of plausible relationship between the two works. I myself raised this same objection when Ellington collector and expert Steven Lasker pointed out that there was a possible relationship between Steiner's soundtrack and *Harlem*.[27] How could we possibly know if the bandleader, busy as he was during the early thirties, went to see this particular horror film? And even if he did, what would give us the right to say that he paid enough attention to the soundtrack to be able to elaborate (or unconsciously dig up) a passage from it many years later?

The answer to both questions is found in a short article published by the *Pittsburgh Courier* on January 26, 1935, titled "Duke Ellington, Who Goes to the Movies Between the Shows, Wrote Song Hit 'Solitude' Three Years Ago." The piece, written by Frank Marshall Davis, informs us that "when that Joel McCrea–Robert Armstrong sensation, *The Most Dangerous Game*, appeared, Duke worked a theater where it played. Every day during the entire week, he sat in the audience to see it over and over. Yet he was most impressed with the music as synchronized by Max Steiner, which he considers the best he has ever seen and heard."[28]

A close comparison between the passages found in both compositions, obviously, brings out a few differences, beginning with the tonality: in Steiner, it is minor, and the interval lies between the major sixth degree of the scale and the tonic (giving the passage a Dorian flavor), while in Ellington, it is major, and the descending minor third motif emphasizes a blue note. The two notes written by Steiner, in the end, seem to evoke (in addition to the hunting call) Zaroff's past with a fragment of a melody from Mother Russia, unlike Ellington's opening, which clearly refers to the world of the African American.[29] And yet, despite all this, it is entirely plausible to maintain that Steiner's motif resurfaced in the Duke's memory and was elaborated a few years later.

Yet another fragment does not correspond to the account provided by the Duke in his autobiography: the Coda (section Y).[30] It may have been written on the transatlantic ship, but not by Ellington. Those ten bars are the handiwork of passenger William Strayhorn, who traveled with the orchestra during that tour.[31] When the Duke's right-hand man was asked about the role he played in *Harlem*, he replied reservedly, confessing that he was not involved in composing the work "other than maybe discussing it with [Ellington]."[32] Nevertheless, the manuscripts, recently studied by musicologist Walter van de Leur, are at odds with Strayhorn's modesty.[33]

THE FOUNDATIONS OF THE GHETTO

Ellington laid the first bricks of his construction in the late forties, but the planning had been underway since the previous decade. It is difficult to assign a date to one curious manuscript written in Ellington's hand, but it may reasonably have been drafted in the late thirties: twenty-nine pages without one single note. The Duke, indeed, felt a compelling desire to write something else, a narration alternating prose and poetry that would act as the scaffolding for an ambitious project that had been tormenting him since at least 1930 and that, under continuously changing names, remained in progress for the next thirteen years. His idea involved a composition in a number of movements that would retrace the epic journey made by the African people from ancient times to Harlem.

In 1930, when the outline did not even have a name, it was intended to cover Black history starting from no less than Ancient Egypt; in 1934, it was nicknamed "Ellington's Opera," and its path would have led from the African jungle to Harlem; four years later, some journalists were informed of an *African Suite* in five movements that described the same journey. In 1941, the draft was rebaptized *Boola*, and in a similar way, would have told the extraordinary tale of an African slave from a life in chains to freedom and ultimately finding a place in the modern Black ghetto in New York. This was the point reached by Ellington's work in progress when he decided to draft the manuscript mentioned above. But the idea refused to leave him. Meanwhile, sometime around 1942, his notes were transcribed in a fair copy and extended to thirty-three typewritten pages. This latter working version was finally set to music under the title *Black, Brown and Beige*, Ellington's first important suite, and the score was performed at Carnegie Hall on January 23, 1943.[34]

The typewritten outline, which now rests in a folder at the Smithsonian Institution, unveils this work's deepest meaning.[35] From our current viewpoint, the most interesting movement is *Beige*, the one dedicated to Harlem.[36]

"Harlem, black metropolis!" writes Ellington. "But did it ever speak to them of what you *really* are?" This is clearly a rhetorical question: the Duke knew perfectly well that the photograph of the ghetto taken by white men was not quite in focus, and he had no doubt that being in Harlem was not all fun and games ("It can't be true / That all you do / Is dance and sing / and moan!"). This belief becomes firmer with a second rhetorical question that takes the form of a delightful quatrain in alternate rhyme: "Did it say to them / That all your striving / To take the rightful place with men / Was more than jazz and jiving?"

The program notes printed for the debut of *Black, Brown and Beige* also underline the fact that Harlemites are above all "rich in education"; in his own presentation at Carnegie Hall, the Duke introduced the movement *Beige* by specifying that Blacks, who may not have any food on the table or anywhere to sleep, are nevertheless "rich in education."[37] Another piece of the manuscript that wound up in the program notes (and, later, in his autobiography) portrays New York's ghetto as a community that, in spite of its weaker spots from a moral point of view, has always had "less cabarets than churches." Once again, using the expression "more churches than cabarets" some years later, Ellington would introduce *Harlem*.

The music of *Black, Brown and Beige* fully respects this multifaceted portrait of the life of the Black community in which there is a time for jazz, but there is also, above all, a time for spirituals ("Come Sunday"), in which there is room for works songs ("Work Song") but also a sophisticated waltz that alludes to the Black intelligentsia living in uptown Harlem ("Sugar Hill Penthouse").

As we shall shortly see, *Harlem*, too, was charged with transforming its composer's penchant for narrative *topoi* into music—for example, the phrase "more churches than cabarets," which led to one of Ellington's most admirable spirituals.[38]

All the same, in the first half of the thirties, while the Duke was still meditating on the project that eventually led to *Black, Brown and Beige* and later *Harlem*, his mentor had already written a symphony dedicated to "black Manhattan" and seen it performed with a certain degree of success. In the winter of 1930, J. P. Johnson, the pianist who had been the young Ellington's guru (and whose piano roll of "Carolina Shout" was so important for him), had begun work on his *Harlem Symphony*. The score was completed in the summer of 1932.[39] The first of many works dedicated to the Black community of New York (including the ballet *Manhattan Street Scene* and the unsuccessful opera *De Organizer* with a libretto by Langston Hughes), this symphony premiered at the Lafayette Theatre on November 21, 1937, on an extremely important occasion: the double debut performance of the American Negro Ballet and the New York Negro Symphony Orchestra.

Ellington, busy on tour in Florida, was not able to attend (nor could he listen to the piece, broadcast by the local radio station WOR), but it is highly likely that he learned about the work from the enthusiastic reviews that appeared in the press; even the great intellectual James Weldon Johnson went out of his way to write about it, describing the concert as "an epochal event in the cultural history of the American Negro."[40] The symphony was also performed at the Brooklyn Museum in 1939 (on three different occasions) and at Carnegie Hall in 1940, once again in Manhattan (at the Heckscher Theater) in 1942 and in a triumphal concert yet again at Carnegie Hall in 1945.[41] To come straight to the point, Ellington couldn't have been unaware of this work, and above all, its narrative intentions, with a descriptive program that resembles *Harlem* far too closely to be a coincidence.

Just like Ellington's suite, Johnson's symphony portrays a stroll through Harlem proceeding from south to north. Both tours make a stop in the Latin area that the two composers thought they would render with a rumba.[42] Then they carry on, following parallel paths through the streets where the cabarets were found: here, Johnson reworked his "Innovation," an old ragtime dating to 1917, while Ellington wrote a new jazz blues. At the center of his suite, Johnson placed his own version of the belief that in Harlem, "there are more churches than cabarets," writing a vibrant spiritual titled "Baptist Mission." This is an arrangement that, through a reinterpretation of the classics "I Want Jesus to Walk With Me" and "Let My People Go," depicts a Baptist congregation increasingly caught up in the ecstasy of its rite, as can be seen in the *crescendo* from the initial *piano* to the paroxysmal finale.[43] In a similar vein, Ellington conceived a gradual surge in the development of his spiritual, relying, however, more on counterpoint than dynamics.

It must be pointed out that from a purely musical point of view, the Duke didn't borrow a single bar of the *Harlem Symphony* written by the more elderly composer. Nonetheless, it is plausible that, on a conceptual level, Johnson offered him more than one point from which to take his cue.

It is also certain that, well before the idea of an extended work dedicated to Harlem slowly took shape in his mind, the ghetto had already been portrayed by the Duke in a series of single, minute compositions tailored to fit within the space of a three-minute 78 rpm record. His catalog eventually included over two dozen of these small Harlemite numbers.

HERE IT IS...

Ellington had not yet been to "Black Manhattan," but during the years of his youth in Washington, it captivated him from afar: "Harlem, to our minds, did indeed have the world's most glamorous atmosphere. We had to go there."[44] And so he did.

In February and April 1923, the Duke and his fellow Washingtonians Sonny Greer and Otto Hardwick played in New York under bandleader Wilbur Sweatman, a bizarre vaudeville musician known for being able to play three clarinets at the same time. Apparently, he was disappointed with his pianist, and after a few gigs at the Lafayette Theatre, the three of them wound up unemployed; in April, they went home, downcast and penniless.[45] But a fire had been lit in his heart: the longing Ellington felt for Harlem became positively feverish when the young musician had the chance to experience those "Arabian nights" (as he himself picturesquely defined them) firsthand. And so, not in the least discouraged after this initial cold shower, the Duke went back to storm Black Manhattan three months later.

In July, he returned, appearing as a pianist in the ensemble led by banjoist Elmer Snowden, which was engaged at the Exclusive Club in Harlem. This was the group with which he was to set foot inside a recording studio for the first time. In the end, Victor Talking Machine Company decided not to release the recording, but nevertheless, Ellington had found a place in showbiz, and as soon as he had established himself in Harlem (where he had rented a room in the house owned by choreographer Leonard Harper at 2067 Seventh Avenue), he began to portray it with fervent passion and unwavering precision.[46] In 1926, during the session that produced the masterpiece "East St. Louis Toodle-Oo," Ellington recorded "Harlem Nights," and even if Vocalion opted not to release it, that same year came to an end with a double tribute to Black Manhattan: "Immigration Blues" and "Parlor Social Stomp."

The first piece's title is a reference to the Great Migration, the foremost event in the creation of the Black ghetto in New York. Stretching from the late nineteenth century to the fifties, Black migration from the rural South toward the urban North brought tens of thousands of people to New York and, in particular, to Manhattan, whose African American population increased by 24,000 inhabitants between 1900 and 1910. At the time, Harlem was still the second-largest Black community in America, only overcoming Washington in the twenties. In that decade, no fewer than 73,000 African Americans lived in North Manhattan; very few of them were originally from New York, while most of this mass of humanity was made up of migrants who had left behind the racism and poverty seen in Virginia, North Carolina, South Carolina, and Georgia. Or, at least, so they thought.[47]

"Immigration Blues" narrates all this by unfolding two themes. While the first suggests the folklore of the "Old South" with coarse, muted brass instruments, the second is a blues theme that, given to the more sophisticated saxophones, leads us into the fully urban setting. The second composition, "Parlor Social Stomp," is instead a wild ragtime that lets us into one of the rituals performed in Harlem in the twenties: the rent party. With rents sky-high (a three-room apartment came to forty-one dollars per month in 1927, much more than anywhere else in New York), Blacks devised a way to scrape together some cash to cover this expense, which swallowed up about half of their salaries. Tantalizing invitation cards—one of which reads: "Hey! Hey! Come on boys and girls. Let's shake that thing. Where? At Hot Poppa Sam's West 134th Street, three flights up. Jelly Roll Smith at the piano. Saturday night ... Hey! Hey!"—promised that there would be good whiskey to drink and delicious food, including tripe stew, pigs' feet, cabbage, and potato salad. Nor would there be any lack of good music, usually played by a pianist, who made sure that the night would include wild dancing. In exchange, guests were asked for a modest "admission fee," anywhere from ten cents to a dollar; the change that was gathered was then used to partially take care of the rent.[48]

Those parties are amply portrayed in the literature of the Roaring Twenties (by both white writers such as Carl Van Vechten and Black ones like Wallace

Thurman), which contains many a colorful depiction. One of the most evocative accounts comes to us, however, from the infallible memory of one of the party's habitués, the great pianist Willie "the Lion" Smith, who described the speckled mixture of humanity that thronged to these events: "You would see all kinds of people making the party scene; formally dressed society folks from downtown, policemen, painters, carpenters, mechanics, truckmen in their working clothes, gamblers, lesbians, and entertainers of all kinds."[49]

All of this made a deep impact on Ellington, and what happened, in Bessie Smith's words, "up in Harlem every Saturday night," inspired him to write three pieces: "Parlor Social Stomp," "Saturday Night Function," which deploys the same dialectics as "Immigration Blues," with one folk and one urban blues theme, and the swinging "Rent Party Blues," that relays all of the lightheartedness of those nights.[50] And, perhaps, "Harlem Flat Blues" could be another variation on the same theme.

These musical sketches of working-class "happenings" and the vision of immigration phenomena that accompany them are crucial for us here because this is where Ellington began his thorough study of New York's Black community. The Duke indeed put a great deal of effort into rendering Harlem's dances: we find the stomp, danced at the Cotton Club, to which he dedicated two different compositions with the same title ("Cotton Club Stomp"); the refined dicty glide ("Dicty Glide"); the strut that was popular at the Savoy Ballroom ("Savoy Strut"); and the uptown shim sham ("Sugar Hill Shim Sham [You Ain't in Harlem Now]"). Put briefly, this was his "Harlem Rhythm," his "Uptown Downbeat."

Or again, like a scrupulous topographer who is also a passionate anthropologist, Ellington traced out a path down Seventh Avenue ("I'm Slappin' Seventh Avenue with the Sole of My Shoe"), inviting us all to follow him ("Drop Me Off in Harlem") and keep our ears perked because this "Blue Harlem" would no doubt ring its bells ("Blue Bells of Harlem") and reverberate ("Echoes of Harlem"), perhaps amplified by the ventilation system ("Harlem Air Shaft"), and even make its own voice heard ("Harlem Speaks").

Taken as a whole, all these works make up an immense polyptych of Black Manhattan. Then again, as Andrew Berish has shown, borrowing the concept of "audiotopia" from Josh Kun, music has the potential capacity to re-create places.[51] Important reflections on this topic are also found in Leonard B. Meyer's *Emotion and Meaning in Music*,[52] and yet our fundamental question here is slightly different: Could Ellington have chosen these titles with no programmatic intent whatsoever?

Our hypothesis is propped up by the Duke himself, who in "My Hunt for Song Titles," an article published in 1933 in the English periodical *Rhythm*, solemnly declared, "I think jazz is a serious thing, I must be serious in my choice of song titles." A bit further on, he specifies that "every one of my song titles is taken from, and naturally principally from, the life of Harlem."[53] Furthermore, a few of the works in his Harlem catalog have a descriptive program that he revealed in spoken and written presentations. One example is the story underlying "Harlem Air Shaft," whose music is intended to portray the synesthesia of sounds and smells flowing through ventilation shafts.[54]

Table 3.1 is a catalog of all the Duke's *Harlems*. It is intended to demonstrate that the suite he completed in 1950 is only the tip of the iceberg, evidence of the compelling need he felt for a quarter of a century to make tributes to the ghetto.[55] A quick glance at the right-hand column, which shows the dates the pieces were recorded, brings to light a curious piece of information: all these compositions were written between the second half of the twenties and the late thirties. Why did Ellington compose all his variations on the theme during this lapse of time? And what led him to let a complete silence fall over Black Manhattan, only to come back to it ten years later with the suite?

Answering these questions will delay us for a few more pages before we can take our places at the Metropolitan Opera House in New York for the premiere of *Harlem*; the knowledge we will gain, however, will, at the very least, give us a privileged seat from which to enjoy the work.

Table 3.1. Catalog of Ellington's pieces dedicated to Harlem.

Title	Year of recording
"Parlor Social Stomp"	1926
"A Night in Harlem"	1926 (unreleased)
"Immigration Blues"	1926
"East St. Louis Toodle-Oo" ("Harlem Twist")	1927/28
"Saturday Night Function"	1929
"Rent Party Blues"	1929
"Harlem Flat Blues"	1929
"Dicty Glide"	1929
"Cotton Club Stomp"	1929
"Cotton Club Stomp 2"	1930
"Jungle Nights in Harlem"	1930
"Blue Harlem (Send Me)"	1932

"Clouds in My Heart" ("Harlem Romance")	1932
"Drop Me Off in Harlem"	1933
"Harlem Speaks"	1933
"Merry Go Round" ("142nd Street and Lenox Avenue" / "Cotton Club Shim Sham")	1933
"Harlem Rhythm"	1934
"Echoes of Harlem"	1936
"Uptown Downbeat"	1936
"Harmony in Harlem" ("Have Some")	1937
"Sugar Hill Shim Sham" ("You Ain't in Harlem Now")	1937
"Blue Bells of Harlem" ("Christmas Bells of Harlem")	1938
"Boys from Harlem"	1938
"I'm Slappin' Seventh Avenue with the Sole of My Shoe"	1938
"Savoy Strut"	1939
"Harlem Air Shaft" ("Rumpus in Richmond")	1940
Harlem Suite	1951

HARLEMANIA JUNGLE

In 1974, scholar Floyd Henderson wrote an article for the New York Folklore Society titled "The Image of New York City in American Popular Music: 1880–1970."[56] The result of his research, complete with percentage estimates and charts, is quite clear: the Big Apple had a significant presence in the collective imagination of American music as of the Roaring Twenties and reached its peak during the following decade. And, while the compositions of the early twentieth century mainly dealt with Broadway, the focus soon shifted to Harlem: as of the thirties, the Black ghetto became the location of virtually all songs about New York.[57]

A New Yorker of the time would have used one single word to sum all of this up: "Harlemania." During the years in question, this term cropped up as the title of a short film produced by Vitaphone and three different songs (one of which was recorded by Ellington, among others), and it describes the fascination that was widely felt for Black Manhattan.[58] Harlem found its way into the titles of novels (from *Home to Harlem* to *Nigger Heaven*), films (from *Harlem in Heaven* to *Dark Manhattan*), theater pieces (from *Harlem to Sugar Hill*) and hundreds of songs situated somewhere between pop and jazz.[59] Listening to these songs is the best way to have a clear idea of Harlem's image: here, the ghetto comes across as an earthly paradise with delicious food and promiscuous sex, a carefree El Dorado or, again, from a more American point of view, a gigantic amusement park with an extravagant jazz club at its center. Put briefly, in Cole Porter's words, this was a place where all "eat, sleep, and make love" ("The Happy Heaven of Harlem"); a place where all people do is "dance when the day breaks," as we are told by Hoagy Carmichael ("Old Man Harlem"), inhabited by a local community of fun-loving people who did their best to greet visitors with open arms, as Cab Calloway reassures us in "Harlem Hospitality." This welcoming behavior was intended, above all, for whites, who loved to venture into the Black ghetto and take a look around, following Van Vechten's advice ("Go Harlem"), perhaps accompanied by a beautiful woman dressed in "ermines and pearls" ("The Lady Is a Tramp").[60] This is perhaps only natural, given that what they found waiting for them was an exotic and utterly irresistible Harlem. A bit of spare change was enough for a taxi ride that led them inside a fascinating and somewhat sinister African jungle, one with huge pots of boiling water, cannibals with their noses pierced with bones and gorgeous Black (but obviously light-skinned) women dressed in grass skirts.

Ellington's entire output concerning Black Manhattan falls within this scenario, which offers us an overview of the period during which he wrote his pieces. His blues pieces and swinging compositions dating to the twenties and the thirties are the offspring of this trend, dictated by popular music, to which Ellington adhered. Or rather, to which he made a considerable contribution. For example, "African" Harlem (as of the 1910s, the ghetto earned itself the nicknames "The Jungle" and "Little Africa") is a subject that Ellington repeatedly portrayed in unequivocal hues. Obsessive ostinatos in the low register, shady minor keys, very few chords (two, or at times, only one harmony that appears as a drone), and penetrating timbres (such as muted brass instruments) clearly indicate that the "Echoes of Harlem" or the "Echoes of the Jungle" stem from the same imaginary landscape: the Black jungle and Harlem coincide with one another.[61]

In "Echoes of the Jungle" (1931), African colors (an allusion to primitivism intended!) appear over a minor blues background, with the clarinet playing a chromatic scale in the chalumeau register, followed by strident glissandos on the banjo and a menacing growl coming from the trombone with a plunger mute. The topical moment of "Echoes of Harlem" (1936) is the first theme, so much so that the second theme (which Ellington borrowed from "Blue Mood," 1932) received gradually less room over the years, even disappearing in the versions dating to Ellington's final period. Over this first section, Ellington outlines a somber ostinato in F minor, above which Cootie Williams's trumpet lets out ominous growls.

In a nutshell, all the nights at the Cotton Club were, borrowing the title of another of the Duke's works, "Jungle Nights in Harlem" (1930). Critic Barry Ulanov was perfectly right when he noted that "all of Duke's jungle nights have been spent in Harlem"; here, Harlem/Little Africa is once again in the limelight, with chromatic ostinatos in the low register, minor tonalities, muted brass instruments with a tendency to growl, and chromatic scales in the clarinet that, as though insisting on the idea, J. P. Johnson took up one year later in his "Go Harlem."[62]

All things considered, Ellington's Harlem is the one found in pop music: full of rhythm and dance, and enticingly exotic. What a bizarre contradiction! The very same person who, in the early forties, ranted against the cliché of a Harlem that only had earthly pleasure to offer just finished drafting his umpteenth piece based on an inventory of musical stereotypes.[63] The Duke scrupulously avoided focusing on other aspects of the neighborhood. For example, he omitted the fact that in the twenties, Harlem began to be transformed into a slum and that it would definitively sink into poverty when the Great Depression arrived.

Journalist Konrad Bercovici reported that the ghetto was "overcrowded, underfed, with children crippled with rickets and scurvy" as early as 1924, and one year later, Winthrop Lane wrote a piece titled "The Grim Side of Harlem" that portrayed a situation no less desperate. The *New York Herald Tribune* defined this community as "the poorest, the unhealthiest, the unhappiest" and, furthermore, "the most crowded single large section of New York."[64] In reality, things were even more serious: Harlem was the most heavily populated Black ghetto in the entire country, with more than three times the number of inhabitants per acre than Philadelphia, the country's second-largest Black district.[65]

And so, already having to deal with rampant juvenile delinquency, widespread prostitution, and a mortality rate 42 percent higher than anywhere else in New York, Black Manhattan entered the decade of the Great Depression. In spite of the reforms contained in the New Deal, ten thousand families lived in cellars infested with rats; tuberculosis was only one of the problems faced by a community that sooner or later would explode. And, surely enough, it did. In March 1935, a racial conflict left fifty-seven wounded and severely damaged several blocks; in August 1943, an even more violent uprising saw six deaths (all Blacks), 189 wounded and damage from vandalism amounting to roughly $5 million.[66]

Now, as the *New York Times* wrote, this "unhonored and unsung Harlem" found no place in Ellington's compositions.[67] And, while it is comprehensible that the Duke's audiences would not be attracted to this sort of scenario, it is more difficult to understand why he refused to give a voice to the other, opposite Black Manhattan, that is, the upper Harlem inhabited by a Black bourgeoisie that represented the *crème de la crème* of the African American intelligentsia; a Harlem that Ellington knew quite well because he lived in the area and spent a great deal of time there.

In 1930, the Duke found accommodation in a spacious three-bedroom apartment at 381 Edgecombe Avenue.[68] This neighborhood is known as Sugar Hill, the elegant suburb north of Harlem along the A line of the subway ("You must take the 'A' Train / To go to Sugar Hill way up in Harlem," "Take the 'A' Train") and was inhabited not only by "brown sugar lassies" (Langston Hughes, *Harlem Sweeties*) but also by Manhattan's Black elite. Rent was sky-high, as denounced by Harlem writer Claude McKay, but for those who could afford to live on the hill that, both geographically and socially, overlooked the entire valley, money was not an issue.[69] "Harlem's most talked-about men and women" (*Ebony*, November 1946) were willing to pay whatever it took to have their hardwood floors, electric fridges, superbly tiled bathrooms, luxurious lobbies, elevators, and uniformed doormen (as indicated in the *New York Post*, March 28, 1935).[70]

The tallest building of this citadel, the fourteen-story apartment block located at 409 Edgecombe Avenue, was also its most prestigious. In the thirties and forties, it was home to public figures such as intellectual W. E. B. Du Bois; painter Aaron Douglas; the first Black member of the Supreme Court, Thurgood Marshall; composer Clarence Cameron White; and the secretary of the NAACP, Walter White. Ellington lived only a few steps away from this collection of illustrious personalities. The buildings at the foot of the hill, the Paul Laurence Dunbar Apartments, were only slightly less impressive and equally sought-after. Financed by the son of John D. Rockefeller, this complex, containing 551 apartments, won first prize from the American Institute of Architects in 1927 and soon became home to celebrities including Paul Robeson, Fletcher Henderson, and Bill Robinson, to mention only a few names in show business. The three blocks between 138th and 139th Streets, planned by the famous architect Stanford White in the 1890s, also fall within the loftier part of the neighborhood and became a mecca for New York's most prominent Blacks. "Strivers' Row" is how the lower classes living in the ghetto sarcastically defined this area and its social climbers who, according to Reverend Adam Clayton Powell Jr., had "a protocol more rigid than that of the Court of St. James."[71] Last but not least, another highly attractive area was found north of Sugar Hill. Apartments in buildings in American Gothic style found in the upper part of St. Nicholas Avenue sold like hotcakes to those who could afford them. This is the very spot, at 935 St. Nicholas Avenue, to which Ellington moved in 1939, living in apartment 4A until 1961.[72]

The Duke wrote the *Harlem* suite while living in this extraordinarily chic Black Manhattan.[73] And yet, as mentioned above, Ellington did not portray the Harlem inhabited by subtle intellectuals and refined aristocrats. "Sugar Hill Shim Sham (You Ain't in Harlem Now)" is a lively swing composed with Rex Stewart, which, however, has very little to do with that world. The only music dating to this period that alludes to New York's black elite is "Sugar Hill Penthouse," which truly does give the impression of seeing the African American bourgeoisie dancing to this charming waltz on their top floors. This piece, however, which made its way into *Black, Brown and Beige*, was written by Strayhorn.[74]

Lastly, the protagonists of another setting not filmed by the Duke's camera would have revealed a deeply religious ghetto tenaciously anchored to the church. The African American church played a crucial role in Harlem's development: in the 1910s, New York's most prominent Black religious institutions (including Bethel African Methodist Episcopal Church, "Mother Zion" Church, and St. Philip's Protestant Episcopal Church) moved to North Manhattan, investing dizzying amounts of money in real estate. For example, in 1911, St. Philip's came up with no less than $640,000 to purchase ten buildings on 135th Street, the most important transaction in the city's history involving African Americans.[75] This policy continued over the following years, and as of the twenties, all the central places of worship were found in Harlem: in 1926, this 150-block ghetto counted 140 churches.[76] In the thirties, according to James Weldon Johnson, the number rose to 160, not including a host of unofficial churches, some of which had picturesque denominations such as the Temple of Luxor or The Metaphysical Church of Divine Investigation.[77] Put briefly, the church truly was, as defined by George Haynes in the issue of *Survey Graphic* dedicated to Harlem, "the most resourceful and the most characteristic organized force in the life of the Negroes of the Northern cities." The reason for this is that, as James Weldon Johnson has observed, it did not simply meet the community's religious needs but also provided recreational activities and promoted mutualist initiatives. It was a space for socialization with the neighborhood's inhabitants, the place where one might well find one's soulmate.[78] Furthermore, during the Great Depression, Harlem's Black churches showed a vibrant tendency toward socialism, intervening to fight injustice through the direct actions taken by a few politically engaged ministers, such as Ethelred Brown or the more well-known Adam Clayton Powells, father and son.[79]

One possible allusion to this is found in "Immigration Blues," with its introduction based on a plagal cadence and its first theme, sixteen bars long, that might bring to mind a spiritual.[80] In this sense, the fleeting moment condensed into four of the twelve bars that make up the introduction to "Harlem Air Shaft" is clearer, while extremely short-lived: between the first four bars in A flat major and the last four in E major, Ellington inserts four in C major where the saxophones imitate a church organ, fully in line with the composition's descriptive program mentioned above ("people praying").[81] Apart from these brief passages, however, nothing else is found in the Duke's Harlem sketchbook.[82]

Only with the *Harlem* suite did he offer us, without reserve, all that he had previously withheld, probably in deference to the fashion imposed by Harlemania. In the meantime, a decade had gone by, during which time Black Manhattan—also disappearing from the music scene in America—did not seem to interest him.

Let us attempt to shine some light on the causes of this reversal. Or, rather, a flash. The period between the two great racial revolts seen in New York's Black ghetto (1935 to 1943) also marked, according to Sara Blair, the author of *Harlem Crossroads: Black Writers and the Photograph in the Twentieth Century*, "a moment of an explosive phenomenon, the so-called Leica revolution: The development of high-quality, portable 35 mm hand-held cameras, roll film, and lightweight flash equipment that enabled rapid and sequential shooting under uncontrolled or quickly changing conditions."[83] Leaving its heavier equipment behind in the studio, photography went out onto the streets, now giving Americans an unfiltered vision of what was happening in the world, in their country, and in the ghettos of the cities of the North.[84] These were the years of *Life* magazine, which, thanks to the informative, even eloquent shots taken by its photographers, only one and a half years after it was born (1936), reached seventeen million readers; this was the period when the genre of documentary photography definitively established itself in America.[85]

Harlem, as Blair points out, soon became a highly appealing testing ground for photojournalism.[86] Images of police vans packed with injured African Americans or shattered shop windows provided vivid descriptions of the tumult that took place in 1935, which no written article could have narrated as effectively. The photos documenting the 1943 revolt were even more powerful, exposing a situation that had spun dramatically out of control: cars burning in the streets, demonstrators whose faces were covered in blood, gutted and ransacked shops.[87] Moreover, photojournalism did not stop with capturing on film the most explicitly tragic moments of life in the ghetto but also took great pains to narrate its equally distressing daily life, which appears in the photo essays by Aaron Siskind and Helen Levitt, both white, the former in particular with his compilation *Harlem Document*.[88]

Shortly after, as of the midforties, African American masters of photography also contributed. In 1948, *Life* published Gordon Parks's shocking piece, "Harlem Gang Leader," with its violent images of young bodies riddled with bullets; Roy DeCarava published *The Sweet Flypaper of Life* (1955), his photo essay on Black Manhattan.[89] The portraits of Black bourgeois families in stiff postures and children wearing their Sunday best, shot in the twenties by Black photographers such as James Van Der Zee in their studios, now disappeared, replaced by iconographies of minors abandoned in desolate streets littered with garbage.[90] Essentially, photography opened the eyes of public opinion to the Harlem that nobody wanted to see. In only a few years, the safaris in Little Africa no longer fascinated voyeurs from downtown.

In African American society, the other arts soon followed the path set out by the masters of the Leica. William Johnson's disturbing oil painting titled *Moon over Harlem* (1943–44) represents a violent clash between policemen and demonstrators during the 1943 uprising. In this painting, one figure taking part in the scuffle, covered in blood, is wearing a smoking jacket: this character is not the product of the artist's imagination but indisputable evidence of how deeply photography had shaken people's consciences. Johnson's work was, in fact, based on two shots that appeared in different newspapers in August 1943, which immortalized three Black adolescents who, after plundering a clothing store, wore smoking jackets. In the late thirties, Jacob Lawrence also painted a poverty-racked ghetto drowning in alcohol and defaced by petty crime, often finding his inspiration in photojournalism.[91] In much the same way, literature also contributed to dismantling the image of exotic Harlem. Roi Ottley dedicated most of the chapters of his *New World A-Coming* (1943) to the New York ghetto, denouncing its dysfunctionality; Ann Petry in *The Street* (1946) held a magnifying glass to 116th Street, which she describes as being paved with "bags of garbage, old shoes, newspapers." This is the same metropolitan jungle that, some years later, Chester Himes described in unreserved language in his series of hardboiled novels featuring Harlem policemen Coffin Ed Johnson and Gravedigger Jones.[92]

The flashes had lit up Harlem. And surely enough, this dazzling light itself cast the neighborhood, no longer seen as enticing, into a long and sinister darkness, like the one portrayed by Black painter Charles Alston in his *Harlem Night* (1948). Darkness and silence: music, which played no part in this painful exposure, had no more songs about Black Manhattan.[93] Thus, it was not the Great Depression that struck the deeply distressed ghetto out of the songbooks (and out of the inventory compiled above of Ellington's pieces) but the belated awakening brought about by photography (and, later, art and literature).

Then, in 1951, *Harlem* appeared, like a *vox clamantis in deserto*, breaking the long silence.[94] With this suite, the Duke gave musical consistency to the three-dimensional idea of Black Manhattan that, in the twenties and the thirties, he couldn't resolve to portray. This suite gave him the chance, paraphrasing the words of the manuscript discussed above, to focus his lens or rather to insert a wide-angle lens capable of portraying the community as a whole. So with *Harlem*, Ellington brought music in step with literature and photography; that microcosm, described in a stream of consciousness by Gordon Parks as a tangle of churches and cabarets and immortalized by his colleague Roy DeCarava "in the schools, bars, stores, libraries, beauty parlors, churches" became stereoscopic for Ellington as well; his suite shattered all remaining one-dimensional images of Harlem, creating one of the most multifaceted prisms found in African American music.[95]

HARLEM ON STAGE

On January 21, 1951, a throng of three thousand six hundred spectators filled all the tiers of the Met, with 250 of the Duke's die-hard fans standing up so as not to miss out on the concert. The front row was filled with show business stars such as W. C. Handy, Lena Horne, and Ethel Waters, along with authorities including the mayor of New York, Vincent Impellitteri, and the senior members of the NAACP (which received the proceeds totaling $16,000), African American civil rights activist Arthur Spingarn, and the national secretary Walter White.[96]

This is the occasion in which *Harlem* was presented to the public, who greeted it with the same heartfelt enthusiasm that was expressed by critics. The February 23, 1951, issue of *DownBeat* described the suite as one of the high points of the evening; in 1952, the same periodical dedicated an entire issue to the bandleader's twenty-five-year career, and Ellington, in an article written by himself, ranked the live concert at the Metropolitan Opera House ninth in his personal hit parade.[97] Truth be told, the performance was not extraordinary: many passages were played in somewhat slow tempos, above all, the Latin section, which lacks the necessary rhythmic drive; furthermore, the fast blues chorus, found at letter M of the score, puts some strain on the reed instruments.[98]

An impeccable reading was instead given by the orchestra in Columbia's recording studios on December 7, 1951. The fame enjoyed by *Harlem* is due, above all, to the formidable performance captured on this album, which doesn't have the slightest flaw.[99] Equally satisfying performances soon followed, such as the live recording made on March 25, 1952, at the Civic Auditorium in Seattle, released by Victor (even though the timpani played by Louie Bellson at measure 15 weighed down the martial theme), or again, the one heard in Washington on April 20, 1955, the overseas concert held in London on February 20, 1964, and all the way up to the Duke's latest years, such as the performance given in Alexandria on April 28, 1972.

There were, however, a few stumbles along the way. In the *Harlem* heard in the Great Paris Concert (1964, Atlantic), double bassist Ernie Shepard fumbles the groove in the Latin section, thus creating problems for the reeds; the live recording made in San Diego on November 16, 1966, is spoiled by a number of poorly performed passages.

And while the Duke was playing the big band version of his suite for audiences on either side of the Atlantic, a new *Harlem* made its way into Ellington's catalog as of June 20, 1951; that Wednesday, nine thousand people flocked to New York's Lewisohn Stadium to hear the symphonic version of the suite. After the intermission, the sixty-three members of the NBC Symphony Orchestra joined Ellington's ensemble in a performance of the work as it had originally been conceived for the *Portrait of New York* project.[100]

The orchestration was once again entrusted to Luther Henderson, whose score of *New World A-Comin'*, prepared two years earlier, had satisfied Ellington. In the piano concerto, Henderson included daring and well-calibrated combinations of timbres and added significant countermelodies; in *Harlem*, he kept to a more conventional orchestration. Nevertheless, a few passages take on additional value in the symphonic version: for example, the ones that tend toward a grandioso expression, such as measures 3–6 of section A1, in which the suite's opening motif is stated by the entire orchestra and thus takes on greater weight.[101] From the point of view of timbre as well, a few of his choices enhance the score, such as the sorrowful theme in D minor played by the clarinet in section O1. Here, the pizzicato in the double basses and cellos, along with the pianissimo chords in the violas and the violins, creates an atmosphere that is even more moving than the one in the version for jazz orchestra.[102]

This score, as well, like the one for big band, was at times performed in a less than satisfactory way. In an important concert at Carnegie Hall held on March 16, 1955, the double basses of the Symphony of the Air botched the groove of the Latin theme, and Ellington's ensemble was not in excellent shape, either. Even the straightforward spiritual theme does not come across well right from the simple triadic beginning of the melody in the trombone.[103] An unreleased tape recorded in New Haven on October 7, 1956, with the New Haven Symphony Orchestra, bears witness to a highly successful performance, so much so that Ellington meditated on releasing it.[104]

Nevertheless, the Duke had to wait until 1963 to see the symphonic version of *Harlem* on LP; the performance dates to January 31, when Ellington, engaged in a European tour, united his men with the symphonic ensemble of the orchestra of Paris in the luxurious Salle Wagram. The recording wound up on the Reprise label's album *The Symphonic Ellington*, which contains what is perhaps the best *Harlem* of all recordings now available. Listening to the unreleased tapes of the rehearsals, however, one realizes that the Duke went to great pains to give the right polish to his black Manhattan. Problems arose as of the opening measures, where the orchestra seemed to have difficulty following Ellington's gestures while conducting the rubato parts, the double basses repeatedly got stuck in the Latin groove, and a virtuoso passage for the reeds and the woodwind section caused some trouble for the orchestral musicians.[105]

Seven years later, on May 28, 1970, the Duke recorded this score once again. Without his band, however. This time, the piece was recorded by the Cincinnati Symphony Orchestra alone, conducted by Erich Kunzel, and this version of *Harlem* is featured on the Decca LP *Orchestral Works*.[106] On this occasion, Ellington played the piano, which had never been included in either the big band or symphony versions. Admittedly, the timbre of the piano adds very little, even giving a somewhat impoverished black-and-white rendering of a few colorful passages such as the blues chorus in section J, originally played by the saxophones.[107] At times, one notes the absence of Ellington's musicians; the score (prepared by conductor Maurice Peress, among others) attempts to overcome this absence by giving the solo themes from the 1963 recording to a range of instruments; one example lies in the opening motto, which Ellington conceived for Ray Nance's trumpet, but which, in this score, echoes across various staves.[108]

In any case, whether for orchestra or big band, performed accurately or with a few slips, *Harlem* won over all its audiences, becoming the suite played most often in Ellington's entire career.[109]

The time has now come to explore the inner workings of the piece, embarking on a real tour of New York's Black ghetto; this stroll through the chords and the melodies of *Harlem* will soon turn into an initiatory journey. Our trip, that is, will reveal another side of the Black Mecca, which we have not as yet discussed and which is perhaps the innermost heart of the entire suite. We will be guided by the Duke in person, hoping that for the man who for over twenty years—in his detailed program notes, lengthy live presentations, and spoken introductions in recording studios—took audiences across the world for a walk through his neighborhood, one more stroll won't be too much of a burden.

A TOUR OF *HARLEM*

The audience that listened to the premiere of *Harlem* at the Met on January 21, 1951, was given, as a guide to the work, program notes drafted by critic Leonard Feather, who acted without doubt upon Ellington's indications. According to this booklet, "The Harlem depicted here, originally stretching from 110th to 145th Streets but now encompassing outer fringes from 96th to 160th, is a metropolis within a metropolis, imitated by every Negro community in the world."[110]

In his live presentation dated March 25, 1952 (captured on a Victor album), Ellington provided further details as to the topography in question, noting that the home stadiums of the Giants and the Yankees are located just to the north; later, in an unreleased tape dated July 10, 1956, the bandleader added further elements, specifying that the borders of the ghetto he had described were "founded on the South by the rumba belt," referring to the Latin area, "on the East by the very fashionable East River" and "on the West by the historic Hudson River." Four years later, the Duke clarified that the piece was a sort of tour from south to north from 110th Street up to 145th, and in 1964, speaking from the WNEW television studios in New York, he gave us yet another clue, saying that our way through Harlem would lead us up Seventh Avenue.[111]

Ellington's suite thus seems not to be an abstract or metaphorical projection but a detailed topographic reconstruction of North Manhattan. Not in the least absolute music, it does not settle for allusions; on the contrary, it even spells out two syllables quite clearly: "Har-lem."

The program printed for the premiere indeed concludes by observing that "the first two notes of Ray Nance's trumpet, introducing the first theme, are the notes that say "Harlem." On every occasion, Ellington insisted on the explicitly descriptive nature of this interval (played first by Ray Nance, then by Cootie Williams as of 1964, and toward the end of the Duke's career, occasionally by Johnny Coles). A descending minor third, this is a motivic cell that not only refers to the Black community by establishing the mood of the blues (the trumpet, indeed, plays the blue third and then, when the cell appears for a second time, the blue seventh). Skillfully elaborated and supported by expansive orchestrations, it also offers us a thrilling bird's-eye view of Harlem or perhaps an aerial panning shot; it is as though the camera that filmed the beginning of *West Side Story* (a few years ahead of time) had been located a bit to the right and a bit farther north.[112]

Ellington essentially illustrates the borders of the ghetto, as described in the program, with one single interval; this motivic cell periodically alternates with a brief chromatic motif initially given to the clarinet, then to the strings, and lastly to the baritone sax, a very small idea that gives melodic variety to the opening part of the suite. Once this sort of introduction has come to a close, we step down onto the ground and, on foot, begin the actual tour, starting from what the Duke identified in his various explanations as the "rumba border," that is, El Barrio.

From the late nineteenth century to the end of the thirties, another wave of migration swept across the island of Manhattan. At the same time that many Blacks were arriving from the Deep South, a multitude of Caribbeans reached New York. Over this lapse of time, 150,000 left the archipelago, headed for the United States: roughly half of them settled in the Big Apple, in particular in Harlem, which became one-fifth Caribbean. And, while the African American laborers from the South were all but warmly greeted by their brothers from New York, these foreigners, largely mixed-race, found themselves confronted by both factions of the Black community. The *Saturday Evening Post* described them as overly inclined to "make a lot of noise about their rights," and the African American *New York Age* went to even less trouble to beat around the bush, labeling them as undesired, even dangerous foreigners. One thing is certain: this proud community, which included radical intellectuals, competent professionals and respected businessmen, redrew the map of American music, spreading new sounds across the country from a specific base of operations: El Barrio.[113]

The area of Manhattan between 96th and 125th Streets, bordering to the west with Fifth Avenue and to the east with East River Drive, became home to various Cuban and Puerto Rican musicians who left their mark on jazz as well, in particular as of the midtwenties. Names such as Rafael Hernández, Manuel Jiménez, Vicente Sigler, Alberto Socarrás, and Don Azpiazú became well-known in that part of the ghetto, which soon filled up with Latin clubs including the famous San José Theater and Campoamor. The community also had its own radio program, hosted by Julio Roque and broadcast on WABC.[114]

Ex. 3.2. *Harlem*, sections B, B1, B2, double bass Latin groove.

Ex. 3.3. Rumba clave.

Meanwhile, on May 13, 1930, Victor made a recording that led to a boom of Latin music in the United States: "The Peanut Vendor," a rumba foxtrot (according to the label of the 78) recorded by Don Azpiazú's Havana Casino Orchestra with the voice of Antonio Machín. Soon a nationwide hit, it gave birth to the rumba craze, a trend that gave way to other Latin genres a few years later.[115]

Ellington was well acquainted with this world, which, during the same years he was writing *Harlem*, led to "cubop," a mixture of bebop as played by Charlie Parker and Dizzy Gillespie and the Cuban tradition as defined by Machito, Chano Pozo, and Mario Bauzá. Actually, as of the early twenties, the Duke was well-informed about what was happening in Spanish Harlem. He played with double bassist Ralph Escudero at the Lafayette Theatre in 1923, and the same year, he heard violinist Angelina Rivera (a member of his future banjoist Fred Guy's band) live and was so impressed that he mentioned her half a century later in his memoirs. As early as 1928, Ellington's piano performances suggest that the Latin-style Rafael Hernández taught to the masters of stride piano in Harlem (in particular, Luckey Roberts) was familiar to him (as can be heard in the second theme of "Swampy River"); he had certainly also listened to the recordings made by Alberto Socarrás, who played the flute for Clarence Williams and Cab Calloway, without forgetting that trombonist Juan Tizol, beginning in 1929, played in the Duke's band for fifteen years. Furthermore, the numerous Latin pieces he recorded before *Harlem* (many of which were composed by Tizol), of which more were to come after 1951, show how close Ellington was to the music played in El Barrio.[116]

In his own suite, Ellington decided to portray Spanish Harlem with a rumba—or at least this is what the bandleader tells us in his introductions (and wrote in the score). But the music says something else. The ostinato in the double basses (playing in unison with the cellos, both pizzicato) that supports a lyrical theme in the baritone sax follows a 3–2 clave rhythm used in the *danzón*, not the rumba (ex. 3.2).

The rhythmic formula of the rumba, indeed, has a specific profile with which Ellington, in *Harlem*, seems not to be acquainted (ex. 3.3).

Another Latin theme appears in the E and F sections, but here as well, the rhythmic clave, which lasts a single measure, does not allow us to classify this passage as a rumba; it is perhaps closer to a mambo for reasons including the percussions, which emulate the bongos (as is suggested in the score).

In other words, Ellington, unconcerned with philology, only truly aims at rendering the color of Spanish Harlem.[117] Meanwhile, the harmonic structure and phrasing in the trombones inform us that we are moving away from East Harlem: in the sixteen measures of the F section, Ellington inserts a blues, making room for it after the first four measures. To bring this progression even more clearly into view, Ellington gives the tenor sax a twelve-bar solo while the trombones newly propose their riff, linked to the blues scale. It is almost as though one scene was fading out while another faded in: while we still hear the rhythm of El Barrio, a jazz-like blues can already be heard coming from a cabaret in Central Harlem. The blues indeed arrives accompanied by swing (section G), followed by another twelve-bar fragment over a pedal point in which, for the last time, the Latin rhythms appear (section H). From here on, we leave El Barrio behind us while crossing Lenox Avenue, headed north.

The program notes for the 1951 debut indicate that our path would have woven between Small's Paradise, the Savoy Ballroom, and the Apollo Theater. It almost seems like we are inside the famous map of Harlem's cabarets drawn by African American caricaturist E. Simms Campbell in 1932, which displays the best-known high spots (as the Duke defined them in his presentation on March 25, 1952) located between 132nd and 138th Streets.

This area of Harlem, packed with luxurious clubs reserved for a white clientele (such as the Cotton Club or Connie's Inn), clubs for homosexuals (including Clam House and the Hamilton Club), and integrated cabarets (among which are Small's Paradise and the Nest Club), is depicted by Ellington with a blues that passes through four tonalities along the circle of fifths from F to A flat, giving the idea of a continuous movement.[118] Exactly when the blues is restated in A flat (section M), Ellington deploys a daring harmonic gesture. In the first four measures, while the walkin' double bass follows the chords of a blues (i.e., Ab7), he inserts two diminished scales one semitone apart, given to the reeds and the strings (ex. 3.4): one begins on D and the other on D flat (ultimately coming together with the first on a B natural, the augmented ninth of the tonality).[119]

Ex. 3.4. *Harlem*, section M, reeds and strings melody.

Ex. 3.5. *Harlem*, section P1, bass clarinet.

Ex. 3.6. *Harlem*, section Q, spiritual theme, upper stave: bass clarinet counterpoint, lower stave: trombone theme.

The two octatonic melodies, alternating tones, and semitones cover almost the entire chromatic spectrum; this strong tension is partially resolved by the repetition of a similar ascending figure in measure 5; this time, indeed, it is on a simple D flat major scale, which fits (almost) perfectly over the subdominant of a blues in A flat. Then a brief reference to the Harlem motto appears, leading us out of the carefree mood of the ghetto's glittering nightlife. Here, a solo clarinet leads us by the hand in D minor. We are now in the middle of a somber funeral procession.

The booklet distributed at the Met didn't mention that the suite sketched out a funeral, among other things; the bandleader personally tells us so, however, beginning in the sixties. From that point on, in fact, with every live introduction, he made sure to invite the audience to "imagine a funeral." The Duke's fans can't have had too much trouble seeing one in their mind's eye, given the descriptive strength of this part of the work. The horns proceeding in thirds (along with the alto and tenor saxophones) follow the coffin with descending quarter-note steps from A flat to G, F, and E in a one-measure cell repeated for the entire section; around it, we hear immobile open fifths in the strings.

This type of movement in the horns is an age-old symbol of pain in the history of music, but here we also have a dramatic clash between the A flat in the first horn and the A natural played by a concertante clarinet and other orchestral parts in long notes. The grief becomes unbearable when, in the last measures of section P, the brass instruments also enter, growling, and the dynamics increase; then, while an iridescent tremolo appears in the strings, making the scene even more metaphysical, the tortuous chromatic motif that we heard at the beginning of the suite appears only once, as though to remind us that the death took place in Harlem.[120] Finally, with a skillful anticlimax, all the instruments fall silent except for one single voice, a whispered lament in the bass clarinet that lasts two measures (ex. 3.5).

We might still be in D minor, but Ellington has something else in store for those who wish to follow him through his Harlem. Indeed, while maintaining a religious atmosphere, the Duke decided that the sorrow would be followed by the dignified rejoicing of a spiritual in the relative major tonality.[121]

Over the notes of one of the most inspired passages in his boundless production, we are accompanied to a place that, this time, cannot be pinpointed on a map of New York, a place where the deepest meaning of this suite will be unveiled. There is a preacher; it's the trombone, which delivers its sermon in a plain pentatonic melody. This admonishment, pronounced as though in a falsetto over the backdrop of a bare eight-measure progression that comes to a close with a plagal cadence, has a single counterpoint in the bass clarinet; meanwhile, the double basses and the timpani play open fifths, making a stern comment in stop-time (ex. 3.6).[122] "Let us imagine," Ellington seems to be saying to us, "that it's Sunday and we see people going to church."

The congregation is now joined along its path by the clarinet, which takes it upon itself to restate the theme, while the bass clarinet and the trombone converse.[123] In the following section, another clarinet and a trumpet join the back of the procession in one of the most astonishing contrapuntal essays in Ellingtonia.[124] Then, in section S, the scene abruptly changes.[125] With no modulation, we find ourselves in A minor; the dynamics go from *piano* to *fortissimo*, the brass plays a coarse shake, and the strings and reeds take up a descending riff with a shuffle accompaniment by the drums. This new atmosphere is not in the least religious; one could even say that it is highly profane.

The Duke took some time to explain this sudden change of direction: only in 1964, speaking at the WNEW television studios in New York, did he inform us that "in contrast, on the other side of the street, we see a real 'hip chick' standing on the corner, stopping traffic," as though to say: this too is part of Harlem.

But the faithful, while perhaps tempted, do not waver; the religious theme appears again, in F major, this time played by the reeds that introduce slight glissandos, giving it a gospel flavor.[126] By now, the procession has reached the church and the entire congregation is present. Ellington renders this idea by passing from counterpoint to a homophonic chordal writing: brought together in a choir, the brass section, playing *mezzo piano* (and in the new key of A flat major), takes up the spiritual theme. It is a compellingly beautiful moment.[127] The Duke, after a long transition section, then offers these fervent believers from Black Manhattan, once again, the pentatonic theme as a majestic finale: here, the spiritual is played by the entire orchestra, like a jubilant fanfare.[128]

Put briefly, the entire second half of the score is intended to depict, in great detail, Harlem's religiousness, and, through the eyes of the community, Ellington relays his own spirituality. The three sacred concerts of his old age are indeed only the tip of the iceberg compared to the substantial religious production on which he worked in the twenties.[129]

Above and beyond these three imposing scores for jazz orchestra and choir, we find a few compositions, to name only a few: "Black and Tan Fantasy" (1927), a blues preceded and followed by an English hymn and a funeral march; the moving "Hymn of Sorrow" (1934) from the short film *Symphony in Black*; "Come Sunday," the theme inserted in the suite *Black, Brown and Beige* (1943); the neglected spiritual "Sunswept Sunday" (1959), admirably arranged for a chamber ensemble and merged into the soundtrack for *Anatomy of a Murder*; "Mahalia" (1961), originally from the *Girl's Suite* but revisited in greater detail in 1970 for the *New Orleans Suite* under the title "Portrait of Mahalia Jackson," a twofold tribute to the great gospel singer with whom he made a recording in 1958; "The Shepherd Who Watches over the Night Flock" (1966), initially conceived for jazz trio but then included in the *Second Sacred Concert*; and "Martin Luther King" (1974–75), the last movement of a posthumous symphonic ballet completed by Luther Henderson.

And then there is a certain tendency shown by Ellington, as musicologist Mark Tucker has acutely observed, toward lending a "quasi-religious" mood even to a few pop songs.[130] His close relation with Father Norman O'Connor and, above all, the Reverend John Garcia Gensel (the second dedicatee of "The Shepherd") are further clues indicating an interest in religion that lasted all his life and that in his works, as of the thirties, was mainly expressed by the spiritual, as confirmed by the glorious sacred theme of *Harlem*.[131]

For Ellington, however, this long-standing African American tradition was not only the materialization in sound of an intimate part of the human soul; his repeated and convincing tributes to these hymns of sorrow were, for him, a precious chance to show how close he was to one of the most vibrant cultural movements in the entire history of the Black ghetto: the Harlem Renaissance.

THE DUKE, FROM THE RENAISSANCE TO THE VICTORIAN AGE

"The day of 'aunties,' 'uncles,' 'mammies,' 'Uncle Tom,' and 'Sambo' is gone."[132] Thus wrote a Black philosophy professor in an essay dating to 1925 that banned the stereotypes that had afflicted African Americans for centuries with no room for appeal. This intellectual, whose name was Alain Locke, spoke for many: the New York *Crusader* had cried out that the "old Negro" with "his abject crawling and pleading" would soon have to leave because, as *The Call* avowed, "the time of cringing is over."[133]

The "old Negro," rough and embarrassing, was to make way for the lofty "new Negro." This new figure's entrance onto the American cultural scene is discussed in the aforementioned article written by Locke, titled *Enter the New Negro* and published in the single issue of *Survey Graphic* focused on Harlem, which established that Black Manhattan would become the "Mecca of the New Negro." During those same months, the same essay was republished in a voluminous anthology edited by Locke himself: *The New Negro*. The Bible of this new credo, it was embellished with illustrations by Aaron Douglas and Winold Reiss and wove together poetry, politics, literary essays, and fiction. Young writers such as Langston Hughes and Countee Cullen, along with old-school intellectuals including W. E. B. Du Bois and James Weldon Johnson, signed this manifesto, which was a key piece of what would be known as the "Harlem Renaissance."[134]

Primarily a literary movement, it could rely on capable and enterprising editors such as Jessie Fauset and especially Charles Johnson: African American fiction, essays, and, above all, poetry skyrocketed after two decades of stagnation, tied to a few, albeit highly eminent, names (Charles W. Chesnutt, Laurence Dunbar, Weldon Johnson, and Du Bois). This modern generation of "new Negroes," dignified, authoritative, and proud of their African roots, aimed at achieving excellent results in the arts, which would act as a trampoline and help them become integrated into white American society. In the words of Weldon Johnson, "[N]othing can go farther to destroy race prejudice than the recognition of the Negro as a creator and contributor to American civilization."[135] This was a battle whose main weapon was the copyright (to paraphrase the acute expression coined by David Levering Lewis, which perfectly sums up the entire Harlem Renaissance: "civil rights with copyright"); strategically, it was based on the idea sustained by Du Bois, according to whom Black art had to have a propagandistic intent.¹³⁶

Ellington, with his refined manners and the fruit of a middle-class education, along with his awareness of Black history, self-assuredness, and ambition, has often been associated with this Harlem movement. Mark Tucker, who wrote an important essay titled "The Renaissance Education of Duke Ellington," is the scholar who has provided the most evidence for this claim, seeing Ellington's youth in Washington as the education of a man who in the twenties "came to embody the ideals of the New Negro artist in his dignified manner and cultivated persona."¹³⁷

But the Duke may have been more deeply tied to this school of thought than imagined hereto. For example, no attention has ever been given to his relationships with the painters of the Harlem Renaissance, the many artists who took part in this cultural revolution (Aaron Douglas, Palmer Hayden, Archibald John Motley Jr., William Johnson, Malvin Gray Johnson, and Winold Reiss, alongside sculptors such as Augusta Savage, Richmond Barthé, Meta Vaux Warrick Fuller and Sargent Claude Johnson), indeed, fully adhered to the tenets of the "new Negro."¹³⁸

One of the most influential masters, deeply engaged in teaching as well, was Charles Alston. After gaining a fine arts degree from Columbia University, in the midthirties, he opened a studio at 306 West 141 Street; this Harlem atelier became a gathering place for the most eminent figures of the Harlem Renaissance (regularly frequented by Alain Locke, Claude McKay, Langston Hughes, Wallace Thurman, and Carl Van Vechten) and for young artists such as Jacob Lawrence and Romare Bearden, who made a name for themselves thanks to Alston. The guest welcomed most warmly, however, was most likely Duke Ellington, a habitué at "306."

Alston loved jazz, to which he dedicated various paintings, and in particular, the Duke, whom he portrayed in at least a hundred caricatures (which did not, however, satisfy Alston because of their strong resemblance to Warner Oland, the film actor cast as Charlie Chan!). For the bandleader, he also designed the album cover for the Columbia recording of *Black, Brown and Beige*.

Ellington (who called the artist by his nickname, Spinky), and even more so, his sister Ruth, bought many of Alston's works, sustaining him in his career.¹³⁹ What's more, a twist of fate complicated matters. Doctor Arthur Logan (the hypochondriacal Duke's personal physician) had a sister who married Alston, and this entire cultural elite often met in the salon of activist Bessye J. Bearden, whose son was the famous painter Romare and who also became Alston's aunt; Alston's mother's second husband was Harry Bearden, Romare's uncle.¹⁴⁰ Ellington was thus also acquainted with the work of the latter and purchased one of his first works; in exchange, Romare (who also composed a few jazz pieces, including "Seabreeze," recorded by Dizzy Gillespie) made repeated tributes to the Duke with a series of collages, a technique in which he excelled.[141]

In spite of all this, it is highly likely that the bandleader would have come into contact with the world of Harlem Renaissance painters even without these intricate relationships worthy of a historical novel. Ellington, who never forgot his studies as an illustrator at the Armstrong Technical High School, painted during his entire lifetime; painting also stimulated his musical production and its highly colorful titles, and the synesthetic Duke perceived Harry Carney's D's as being dark blue and Johnny Hodges's G's as light blue.[142]

It was, however, with music, understandably, that Ellington succeeded in most fully showing his loyalty to the movement. The Renaissance intelligentsia had a very clear idea about what kind of music was most appropriate for its voice to sing. And it was not jazz. Syncopated music, indeed, did not have the aloofness required by the "new Negro": *Opportunity*, which even wrote that the glorious musical *Shuffle Along* "did not enthuse," paid almost no attention to jazz whatsoever; an entirely similar attitude was shown by *The Crisis* and *The Age*; *The Messenger* proved to be more broadminded but significantly turned to white journalist W. Astor Morgan for a piece on blues; New York's *Amsterdam News* once dismissed this "aborted instrumentation" as "the chop-suey of the musical world," and on another occasion, described jazz in apocalyptic terms, comparing it to a drug that "is killing some people."[143]

The leaders of the Harlem Renaissance firmly believed that the decorous tradition of the spiritual was the only kind of music that could elevate their race. Not Broadway spirituals, vulgarized by their proximity to pop songs, not the (only apparently) authentic ones, whose main purpose was to satisfy the white man's thirst for primitivism, but concert spirituals. Locke's volume *The Negro and His Music* and the monumental (and unjustly neglected) study by Maud Cuney-Hare titled *Negro Musicians and Their Music*, both published in 1936, are vibrant tributes to Black classical composers (including Harry Burleigh, Nathaniel Dett, William Dawson, Florence Price, and William Grant Still) and Black opera voices (such as Paul Robeson and Roland Hayes). The former based their symphonies on sacred African American melodies, and the latter conceived programs in which "Deep River" and "Listen to the Lambs" were sung alongside Lieder by Schubert and Schumann.[144]

Renaissance figures had words of praise for these artists, who, showing ability and courage, challenged the whites on their own turf and mastered classical music without denying their own Black roots.[145] This is what the symphonic spiritual is all about, and it is also what the spiritual that animates Ellington's *Harlem* is all about. In the end, the majority of the Duke's religious production, in particular the symphonic works, is an echo of the Renaissance. This movement, even though it reached its peak during the Prohibition era, continued influencing African American culture even in the postwar years, to the extent that scholar Jon Michael Spencer, in his *The New Negroes and Their Music: The Success of the Harlem Renaissance*, has demonstrated that some of the oldest dreams of the Renaissance finally came to fruition in the decades following the Great Depression.[146]

As late as 1949, Locke described the movement's unstoppable progress in one of the last issues of *Opportunity*, while the January 7, 1950, issue of the *Pittsburgh Courier* set out a (provisional) evaluation. This African American newspaper praised the positive results of the Harlem Renaissance, mentioning the names of those responsible for its successes; Duke Ellington, who during those very months was putting the final touches on his portrait of Black Manhattan, is included in the list. Moreover, it was not only the spiritual presented as a concerto grosso in *Harlem* that earned the Duke the admiration of the Renaissance intellectuals (even though he was a jazz musician).[147] A few passages in his presentations of the suite confirm that Ellington was a true "new Negro," down to the bone.

When *Nigger Heaven*, a novel written by the white author Carl Van Vechten, was published in 1926, a substantial portion of the African American press inveighed against it. Many maintained that it had simplistically (and metonymically) condensed Black Manhattan into a single, enormous cabaret. Particularly indignant comments appeared in *The Crisis* (December 26, 1926) in an article by Du Bois, who in no uncertain terms pointed out to Van Vechten that "the average colored man in Harlem is an everyday laborer, attending church."[148]

The motto "more churches than cabarets"—which Ellington included in the aforementioned typewritten manuscript for *Black, Brown and Beige*, referring to the section on Harlem, and that roughly a decade later he reused in all his presentations of *Harlem*—unmistakably corresponds to the thought of one of the fathers of the Harlem Renaissance.[149] With *Harlem*, the Duke not only gave substance to the concept of the "art spiritual," a term that Du Bois himself was one of the first to employ, but, with the same conviction as this great intellectual, showed that he also felt the need to rid Harlem of its stereotypes.

For many years, with his repertoire of pieces dedicated to the New York ghetto, Ellington followed in the footsteps of certain travel literature that had given birth to novels such as *Nigger Heaven* and *Home to Harlem*, which both indicated the locations of gambling houses and cabarets in the ghetto. On the pages of these books (and on the sheets of Ellington's scores), the variegated

Black community seems to be crushed under the weight of clichés. With *Harlem*, the Duke turned over a new leaf; or rather, he wrote the story over from the beginning, charting a course for a completely different voyage. Here, yet again, his words perfectly match those of the founders of the Renaissance.

James Weldon Johnson, in his essay *Black Manhattan* (1930), dismantled the idea of Harlem as a place that "never sleeps and that the inhabitants thereof jazz through existence," stating that most of its inhabitants are "ordinary, hard-working people."[150] In an interview given in 1964, Ellington, protesting the sensationalistic hype that generally went along with descriptions of the ghetto, informed the journalist that Harlem "is a place where, well, nice quiet people live, and they live a very conservative life."[151] This vision, so close to the one expressed by Weldon Johnson, also appears in the suite. His Harlem is, as Ellington notes in his 1964 London presentation, "like every other place in the world, some happy people, some blue, some are pretty well-off, some are not too well-off."

Ellington took all the emphasis, all the exclamation points, out of his narration of Black Manhattan; his music portrays a many-hued community in which there are prostitutes and believers, jazz clubs and funerals, blacks from the West Indies and, in the background, the great patriarchs of the Black Renaissance. Once again, the repeated references to Black beauty in his introductions to this suite amount to an act of loyalty toward the movement: "[N]ice people live in Harlem," the Duke proudly stated when presenting this work at the WNEW television studios in 1964; in 1970, he used even stronger words on the Decca album *Poetic Commentary*: "[E]xceptionally handsome people lived there"; in a 1972 concert in Virginia, he took pains to repeat that Black Manhattan is "a community of extremely handsome people."

This proud awareness of African American beauty had been introduced by the manifesto *The New Negro* where it was celebrated by poets such as Countee Cullen (*To a Brown Girl*), Lewis Alexander (*Enchantment*), and Langston Hughes (*I Too*); the latter turned *black beauty* into the key expression of some of his most well-received poems. And, while painter Charles Alston set out the features of this beauty in *Girl in a Red Dress* (a true symbol of the Renaissance) and Sargent Johnson gave shape to it in his sculptures (confessing that he wanted to "show the beauty"), Ellington gave voice to this concept in a series of works that goes from "Black Beauty" (1928) to "The Green Apple" in *The Golden Broom and the Green Apple* (1965), without forgetting the spiritual in *Harlem*. Precisely, the "untarnishable beauty" of the suite's central melody is what will give us the strength required to bring our long pilgrimage through Harlem to its conclusion, reaching a final destination that is actually quite far from the limits of the ghetto.[152]

3.
THE OLD WORLD: LONDON, 1900

The British musical scene is in ferment over an oratorio written by a young composer just out of the Royal College of Music: *Hiawatha*, the trilogy that Samuel Coleridge-Taylor presented, in its entirety, on March 22, 1900, in the prestigious setting of the Royal Albert Hall. For this twenty-five-year-old musician, it was the beginning of a brilliant career: *Hiawatha* became the most-loved English oratorio of the time.

The score contains a quotation of the spiritual "Nobody Knows the Trouble I've Seen" that Coleridge-Taylor had heard performed by the African American Fisk Jubilee Singers during their tour in England. He was furthermore acquainted with the eminent African American poet Paul Laurence Dunbar, who had come to London for a few readings. *Seven African Romances* (1897), for voice and piano, marked the beginning of their collaboration. Our young Englishman's interest in Black culture was perfectly comprehensible: This composer, immortalized in photos showing him frozen in a rigid Victorian pose, was the son of an African from Sierra Leone.[153]

News of this African British composer's career soon made its way to America's Black community, which took him as a model: as an African, he had succeeded in having his own classical music performed in Europe's sumptuous concert halls! Washington's African Americans, however, didn't simply praise him; they also founded the Samuel Coleridge-Taylor Choral Society. This all-Black ensemble debuted on April 23, 1903, with *Hiawatha*; the press immediately grasped the importance of this historic concert, above all, in terms of social progress. And so, the Society's members took a chance: they invited Coleridge-Taylor to Washington to personally conduct them. Their only fear was that racism might have discouraged their guest from coming. A succinct letter from London, dated September 14, 1904, mingling English understatement with African pride, put the Washingtonians at ease: "As for prejudice, I am well prepared for it."[154]

The concerts were set for November 16 and 17, 1904. The wait was agonizing; on November 12, the *Washington Bee* reported that all people were talking about was the concert by Samuel Coleridge-Taylor. When the moment finally arrived, the "magnetic conductor" (*Washington Post*, November 17, 1904) gave a magnificent performance, changing the history of African American culture from that very podium.

This experience in America gave Coleridge-Taylor the opportunity to come into close contact with the two leading Black intellectuals of the time: Du Bois (whose *The Souls of Black Folk* he defined as "the greatest book he had ever read" and with whom he corresponded regularly for the rest of his life) and Booker T. Washington (who didn't hesitate to write a preface for the collection *Twenty-Four Negro Melodies* [1905], published in the United States by Oliver Ditson). This Black leader defined Coleridge-Taylor as "the most cultivated musician of his race" and added, "It is especially gratifying that [he] should seek to give permanence to the folk-songs of his people by giving them a new interpretation and an added dignity."[155]

Coleridge-Taylor's African American musical production increased exponentially after his first tour in the United States and was soon fueled by two further visits in 1906 and 1910. Spirituals were what captivated him more than anything else: his version of "Deep River" (contained in the *Twenty-Four Negro Melodies*) established this melody as a classic in its genre.[156]

When, on September 1, 1912, Coleridge-Taylor died prematurely, Harry Burleigh, Du Bois, Roland Hayes, and many other prominent figures in African American culture organized a memorial concert held in Boston on January 13, 1913, to bid farewell to the man who had done so much in promoting Black musical culture in classical milieus.[157] The spirituals written by Harry Burleigh (also known as "the American Coleridge-Taylor"), Nathaniel Dett, William Dawson, and William Grant Still (who considered Coleridge-Taylor his hero and who, as a boy, imitated him even in his haircut!), along with many others, owe much to the sacred melodies arranged and composed by him; so much that he may be counted among the fathers of a Renaissance that, after beginning in London in the late nineteenth century, spread to Washington in the first decade of the following century and fully flourished in Harlem in the Roaring Twenties.[158]

When Coleridge-Taylor performed in Washington, Ellington was still a boy, reluctantly taking dreary piano lessons at Mrs. Clinkscales's house. Still, in the years to come, the Duke would certainly have had the chance to hear his music. In the capital city, Coleridge-Taylor's name was on everyone's lips for years; in 1922, he appeared in Marcus Garvey's magazine *Negro World*, in 1923, in *Opportunity*, and in 1925, *The Crisis* put him on the front cover; in the 1925 anthology *The New Negro*, Georgia Douglas Johnson dedicated a poem to him.[159] Later still, in the thirties, while the works of the father of "sorrow songs" were being performed in concerts given by the Chicago Symphony Orchestra, the two aforementioned volumes published in 1936, *The Negro and His Music* by Locke and *Negro Musicians and Their Music* by Maud Cuney-Hare, set aside entire chapters for him.[160]

Ellington, who, furthermore, may have heard Coleridge-Taylor's music in the sumptuous pageant *The Star of Ethiopia* (which he probably saw in Washington in 1915), thus had innumerable chances to learn about Coleridge-Taylor's idea of the dignified spiritual.[161]

On one occasion, Ellington described New York's Black ghetto as an air shaft.[162] A cramped space between the walls of two skyscrapers, with barely enough room for light and air. And yet, for Ellington, it had no boundaries. In the end, this is what Harlem is about: a simple air shaft transformed by the Duke's imagination into a space so immense it was able to accommodate the past and future of African American history.

4

NIGHT CREATURE; THE GOLDEN BROOM AND THE GREEN APPLE
VISIONS IN BLUE

CITY WITCHES AND FANATIC BOOGEYMEN

"They told us it was necessary for me to emcee. I didn't know the first thing about how to emcee and the thought of it had me half scared to death. Then there we were on the stage, and I opened my mouth and nothing came out."[1]

It is hard to believe that Duke Ellington made this confession. In the spring of 1929, the man we know as a gifted raconteur, whose riveting presentations can be heard on countless albums, was standing in front of a microphone at Broadway's Palace Theater and couldn't utter a sound.[2] The truth is, we're dealing with two Ellingtons here. The first, an unassuming bandleader, was reluctant to step up to the microphone, as is clear in his live recordings up to the early forties.[3] The second, who burst onto the scene in the postwar years, was an unrestrained showman, an extroverted and jaunty storyteller light years away from that young man at the Palace Theater, frozen with embarrassment.

This second Duke charmed his audiences until the end of his days with delightful presentations that stemmed from his lively and abundant imagination.[4] To better entice his listeners, at times he spoke nonsense, like in his introduction to "Angu" (1963), which went like this: "Not quite (t)angu but almost blue." Or he might rely on a single neologism to capture their attention, such as the irresistible expression coined for tip-tap dancer Bunny Briggs, who interpreted the leading role in "David Danced Before the Lord" (1965): the Duke introduced him as "the most super-leviathanic-rhythmaturgically-syncopated-tapstamaticianist."[5]

For other compositions, he made up stories with a fully developed plot. The psychedelic program of "The Little Purple Flower" (1968) is a mini-screenplay, just a couple of pages long. Included in the recording, it flashes by quickly: A flower, picked in the country, is brought into town, where it goes to medical school and eventually becomes a celebrity.

A full-blown script ties together the pieces contained in *A Drum Is a Woman* (1956), an imaginative allegory of the history of jazz. Partially narrated by the composer himself, it also makes room for a love story between Caribee Joe and Madame Zajj (a female personification of jazz) and a ballet of flying saucers.

The Duke once gave an equally extravagant explanation of his "The Tattooed Bride" (1948) to an audience at Carnegie Hall. A bride's body is entirely covered in tattoos with the shape of the letter W, and "You know—remarks the bandleader—if you take a pencil and write a W you get the sound of *za-zu-za-za* . . . So, you know, just like . . . [four instruments each play the figure, one after the other]. That's the way we rehearsed it. So we've taken that musical figure and, by repetition, present it to you now as 'The Tattooed Bride.'"[6]

These brief sketches are not simple divertissements, evidence of Ellington's rapid evolution from a timid presenter to an intrepid entertainer, but true programs that provide us with interesting keys with which to interpret his work. He himself confessed in more than one interview that many of his pieces are underpinned by a narrative. This is particularly true of his large-scale works that broadly portray places (such as the previously discussed *Harlem* suite) or, more often, stage dramas with female leads.

Barry Ulanov was one of the first scholars to comment on this in a 1960 essay titled "The Ellington Programme." He noted, "On stage Duke introduces each 'major work' with a vagabond syntax that makes one wonder why he bothers. But if one listens carefully, both to the worlds and music, one discovers why."[7]

Nine years later, it was Mercer, the composer's son, who said to Stanley Dance, "In the extended works, I think his music tends more toward narrative . . . . He always has his verbal explanation of what is taking place, as with *The Golden Broom and the Green Apple*."[8] Mercer Ellington, not by chance, was referring to a symphonic work dating to 1965, whose program is crucial in understanding the music itself (and the compositional procedures underlying it). The narration, straight out of the theater of the absurd, is perhaps the zaniest of all the Duke's tales. After illustrating it live for years and making a studio recording of it in 1970, Ellington set down this "modern allegory in three stanzas" in his autobiography:

Stanza I: "The Golden Broom"

The Golden Broom is a reflection of the haze we enjoy in the spin of today's whirl, as our luxuriously appointed vehicle (designed originally for the Beautiful Rich City Witch) dashes through space with its vacuum jet stream magnetizing the golden gleam of material security.

Stanza II: "The Green Apple"

As we relax graciously, we love thinking that in spite of how far we have gone to acquire our position of advantage, we still have our Green Apple (naturally grown and owed by the Poverty Strick' Country Chick), the symbol of our potential, our virtues, our God-made and untouched purity.

Stanza III: "The Handsome Traffic Policeman"

In the third movement, we may find the symbol of ourselves in the very Handsome Traffic Cop, flashing his reds, greens and ambers as he stomps his authority around the intersection, where the paths of the Beautiful Rich City Witch with her Golden Broom and the Poverty Strick' Country Chick with her Green Apple will sooner or later converge . . . and the decision has to be made. With only one ticket left in our book, which of the two ladies gets the ticket? (The reason that the Handsome Traffic Cop's book is so depleted and down to one ticket is that all the more desirable ladies prefer to commit their violations at his intersection).[9]

The program for another symphonic work composed ten years earlier, *Night Creature*, also draws on extremely vivid imagery. This three-movement suite portrays nocturnal beings far more eccentric than the surreal *Personnages dans la nuit* painted from the forties through to his latest years by Joan Miró, whom Ellington had met in France and to whom he dedicated a blues.[10]

For the March 16, 1955, premiere, the bandleader decided to provide the Carnegie Hall audience with program notes that were fairly brief but sufficiently clear. These notes explain that the three movements are nocturnal scenes whose respective protagonists are a blind insect, a fearsome monster, and a fascinating queen of the night.[11]

In his subsequent live performances, the Duke almost always offered a verbal narration. Here, his descriptions were more minute. And more visionary.[12] The most precise account is found, once again, in *Music Is My Mistress*: the first tableau is titled "Blind Bug" and portrays the wild dance of an insect that "because he is the king of the night creatures he must dance"; the last, "Dazzling Creature," depicts a breathtaking queen of the night whose song passes through three keys. Her vocal prowess is so arousing that, at a snap of her fingers, "everybody scrambles to be in place, wailing and winging into the most overindulged form of up-and-outness."[13]

And yet the central movement, "Stalking Monster," is where we reach the peak of Ellington's imagination. It's the middle of the night, and we are facing a monster anyone would be afraid to meet. When radio host Patti Cavern asked for further details about this creature, Ellington, who had no intention of making such an ineffable vision overly concrete, shrugged her off by saying, "One of the ones, like, don't open the door or something ugly will jump out and bite you." In the end, he didn't waste too many words because he was actually interested in concluding his introduction with the following startling revelation: "When we meet him, I'm sure we shall find that he too does the boogie-woogie."[14]

It starts out like a tale by Edgar Allan Poe, but the ending is completely unexpected. Could this be a parody? If the creature had explicitly danced, perhaps it would. But this is not the case. The ambiguous narrative sketches out a dreamlike landscape with two protagonists: ourselves (like in all dreams), as we know perfectly well how to behave on a dance floor, and a monster, who—perhaps to reassure us—soon lets us know that he loves dancing as much as we do. In any case, our happy-go-lucky ogre (or boogeyman) doesn't necessarily have to dance to prove it because, for goodness' sake, boogie-woogie fans understand one another in the blink of an eye![15] Breton and Bukowski put together couldn't have done any better. And the music for this "Stalking Monster," as we shall soon find out, marvelously communicates this taste for the grotesque permeated with wry humor.

The programs for *Night Creature* and *The Golden Broom and the Green Apple* deploy some of the topoi that inhabited Ellington's imagination. The first is entirely dictated by the idea of dance: from the Blind Bug's ballet (nimble like the fireflies in the "Lightning Bugs and Frogs" movement of the *Queen's Suite*) to the Stalking Monster's boogie-woogie, and lastly, the allusion to a wild dance when the queen of the night snaps her fingers in the third movement.[16] The Duke's interest in dance as a narrative element for a program surfaces in many other compositions, such as the sublime "Dancers in Love" from the *Perfume Suite* (1944) or "Red Garter" from the *Toot Suite* (1959), where striptease artists do a shake dance. Within his symphonic output, it appears in his last completed creation, *Celebration*.[17] The figure of the "Sophisticated Lady" also emerges repeatedly: our provocative "Dazzling Creature" is every bit as enchanting as the Beautiful Rich City Witch in *The Golden Broom and the Green Apple*.

The three stanzas of the 1965 work are actually a rich anthology containing some of the Duke's favorite inventions. We find a Green Apple, uncontaminated like an "African Flower," which reappears with similar symbolism in the "Sonnet of the Apple" found in the *Second Sacred Concert* (1968); we find some metaphorical traffic that Ellington later took up in the comedy *The Jaywalker* (1967) (whose pieces include "Traffic Cop," "Traffic Extensions," "The B.O. of Traffic") and in "The Biggest and Busiest Intersection" of the *Second Sacred Concert*, at least as crowded as the one where we find the Handsome Traffic Cop, in turn, a figure he had already used in *A Drum Is a Woman* (1956). Lastly, another of the Duke's much-loved themes emerges: the contrast between the virginity and pureness of the countryside—which, as we shall see, can geographically expand, covering the Black Mother's entire jungle—and the modern city, home to corruption and temptation. The Country Chick with her green apple and the City Witch with her luxurious golden broom are symbols of this opposition, which Ellington, at times, brought together in a single character. For example, the young lady in "Monologue" (1951, for narrator and clarinet trio) is transformed from a simple, innocent countrywoman into a *femme fatale* (even more charming than the "hip chick" we previously encountered in *Harlem*); the "Little Purple Flower" mentioned above, too, when uprooted and brought downtown, takes a turn for the worse.

Put briefly, above and beyond their seemingly peyote-inspired programs, the themes that emerge in these two symphonic works also appear in a conspicuous amount of Ellington's output, and therefore, they will be discussed together in this chapter. A close look at the music itself will furthermore reveal that other common threads tie the two scores together; one particularly strong one will force us to pass through Harlem once again before reaching, as promised, our final destination, the Teatro della Scala in Milan.

4.
"OPEN LETTER TO DUKE"

"I walked into the hall just as the concert was starting, and was shocked to see that it was two-thirds empty.... It was sad to reflect that this attraction could not fit the hall even, when, just last Saturday, Brubeck, Baker, and Mulligan completely packed it twice." With chagrin, Leonard Feather was forced to inform the readers of *Melody Maker* that *Excursions in Jazz*, a concert held at Carnegie Hall on Wednesday, March 16, 1955, was unable to attract a large audience.[18] That evening, the Symphony of the Air (formerly the NBC Symphony) came together with the Duke Ellington Orchestra in a program made up of compositions by Don Gillis and the Duke himself. The two composers were expected to conduct their own works.

The evening got off on the wrong foot. Gillis presented a few of his works, conducting the orchestra that, until one year earlier, had been guided by Arturo Toscanini. His music, a sort of light classical music with jazz overtones, didn't win anyone over.[19] Feather, with heavy sarcasm, went so far as to write that Gillis used dominant seventh chords pretty much everywhere in his pieces because he "must have heard once that C E G B flat constituted a jazz chord, which is frankly as pathetic as a one-legged man's dependence on a crutch."[20] In the second part of the concert, things went much better. Ellington conducted the two ensembles, which joined forces in playing the world premiere of the concerto grosso commissioned by Don Gillis: *Night Creature*. The program was completed by the symphonic versions of *New World A-Comin'* and *Harlem*.

While rather small, the audience included various celebrities from the world of music, such as Lena Horne, her husband Lennie Hayton (who was an outstanding arranger), and a jazz genius who, on this occasion, worked as a critic for *Metronome*: Charles Mingus. He gave almost no consideration to Gillis's works, dismissing them simply by saying that "nothing happened during the first half of the concert. Obviously the composer hates jazz." But he also had harsh words for his idol. The man to whom he later dedicated *Open Letter to Duke* was accused of not putting any real effort into composing these pieces. And yet this "tired" Duke's *Night Creature* was praised even by the unforgiving Mingus, who recognized the value of this score.[21]

And so, while Gillis's attempt to combine classical music and jazz failed miserably, Ellington, according to the *New York Times*, proved that "[a] symphony orchestra and a jazz band can be thrown together on the same stage and induced to make exciting music."[22] Furthermore, the performance of *Night Creature* at Carnegie Hall was very good; excellent, considering it was a debut.[23] Compared to the 1963 studio recording (and the score published by G. Schirmer), the work had a somewhat different profile that evening in New York.

The man responsible for the orchestration was once again Luther Henderson, and once again, after *New World A-Comin'* and *Harlem*, his hard work was not recognized in the credits on the playbill.[24] Nevertheless, half a century later, at eighty years of age, he confessed to Peter Lavezzoli, the author of *The King of All, Sir Duke*, how satisfied he was for the trust Ellington placed in him: "[In *Night Creature*] Duke gave me the freedom to choose which instruments in the symphony orchestra would assume certain parts." He also clarified the origins in jazz of those nocturnal creatures, which, according to Henderson, represented "an evolution of the basic jungle sound."[25]

Henderson was the one who decided to begin with a bucolic four-measure introduction, given to the woodwinds and pizzicato strings. The album version, instead, begins directly with the theme; moreover, while in the Carnegie Hall performance, the symphony orchestra presents the melody of "Blind Bug," in *The Symphonic Ellington*, the piano does so.

In the third movement, the differences with the studio recording become more significant: above and beyond the longer introduction given to the percussion instruments and the double bass, the main theme has a different number of measures and is stated twice by the oboe in the Carnegie Hall version, unlike the album in which the same melody is played first by the oboe, then by the baritone sax (Harry Carney), and a third time by the trumpet with a plunger mute (Cootie Williams).

But the most substantial divergence is in the central movement: there are no solos. The sublime improvisations by Ray Nance on the violin, the brief trumpet excursions by Cootie Williams, and the elegant phrases added by Johnny Hodges and Lawrence Brown had not yet found their way into the score.[26] And so, in this form, *Night Creature* went on tour.

"NIGHT CREATURE" ON THE ROAD

On July 10, 1956, the New Haven Symphony Orchestra played on the same stage as Ellington's big band, with the Duke on the podium. The performance wasn't particularly brilliant, spoiled by discontinuities in tempo and rapid surges in dynamics. What's more, the orchestra made a few slips, for example, messing up a contrapuntal moment during the first movement after the theme appears in the woodwinds and fumbling the break at the end of the score.[27] Apparently, Ellington's strict diet, which allowed him to lose thirty pounds, had an adverse effect on his gestures as a conductor . . .

"As I was conducting the third movement of *Night Creature* that night, I suddenly realized my pants were falling down. And holding to my pants to keep them from falling down . . . I had to maneuver them back into position before turning to face the audience for my bow. The musicians in the symphony continued to laugh long after I had left the stage." In any case, more worried about the lavish dishes he was forced to relinquish than his conducting standards, the prosaic Duke noted in his autobiography that "looking back, I feel I had a pretty good run for my money."[28]

A few days later, on July 25, the work was heard in Ohio, played by the Cleveland Pops Orchestra. The form of the second movement was adjusted here, with a significant number of measures removed. The performance was satisfactory in spite of a few blemishes, including the final break, which would turn out to be many orchestras' Achilles' heel.[29] The Duke presented this work again with the same ensemble on June 28, 1961, now leaving the baton in Louis Lane's hands.

This time, other formal and expressive devices were tested. For example, the "Blind Bug" movement begins directly with the piano (as would ultimately be the case on the album), and then the bucolic introduction heard at Carnegie Hall reappears, condensed, however, into two measures. "Stalking Monster," clearly the part of the work that troubled Ellington the most, goes through other changes: the form heard at Carnegie Hall now returns (with the sixteen-measure piano theme restated halfway through the movement) with a blues chorus added to the section in 12/8.[30]

Meanwhile, the Duke was busy promoting his new creation, which had not yet been officially recorded, on the *Negro Digest*. The November 1961 issue, whose front cover featured the bandleader, included an article written by the Duke himself in which he explained that, as regards *Night Creature*, "the main purpose of it was to try to make the symphony, which I believe we did very successfully."[31] And indeed, the rhythmic drive of swing is palpable throughout the performance given by the National Symphony Orchestra, conducted by Gunther Schuller, on May 31, 1962.

Everything went smoothly in Washington: listening to the unreleased tapes, one has the impression of an extraordinary attention toward dynamics and a technical mastery even in the more difficult passages. By now, the form seems to have taken its definitive shape and the revisions are more discrete, the most significant appearing in "Stalking Monster": greater prominence was now given to an ironic passage consisting in four chromatically descending notes heard over various octaves, which now appears in various places in the score.[32]

So it seems that *Night Creature* had successfully completed its trial phase after being on tour for seven years. But no record label seemed interested in releasing it. Feather had been convinced of the quality of this work since its debut in 1955; according to him, *Harlem, New World A-Comin'* and *Night Creature* were already perfectly ready to be considered as "the most extraordinary and important LP ever created by a jazz composer."³³ But Capitol Records wasn't in the least attracted to the idea; producer Dave Dexter didn't care much for these classically oriented works. In 1955, Ellington switched to Columbia, but he still couldn't manage to make any progress. This label was not willing to come up with the funds required to call an ensemble consisting of at least one hundred musicians into the recording studio.³⁴ The bandleader, who had unsuccessfully tried to convince journalist Carter Harman to give *Night Creature* some space in the cover article he was preparing for the August 1956 issue of *Time*, had to wait for an enlightened artistic director of a minor independent label to fall in love with the project. The minor independent label turned out to be Reprise Records. And its enlightened artistic director was Duke Ellington.

Founded by Frank Sinatra in the late fifties, Reprise Records initially produced albums featuring The Voice's friends, from the members of the Rat Pack (Sammy Davis Jr. and Dean Martin) to Bing Crosby. Before Warner incorporated it in 1963, it succeeded in signing on Ellington as well. Sinatra, whose present to himself for his fifty-second birthday was an LP with the Duke Ellington Orchestra, entrusted the Duke with the AR department (Artists and Repertoire), meaning he became a talent scout. Ellington gave contracts to a number of artists (from Alice Babs to Bud Powell and Dollar Brand), but most of all, looked out for himself, and after *Afro-Bossa*, the first record released by the label, devoted his efforts to *The Symphonic Ellington*, the album that ultimately documented his big band's encounter with some of Europe's most renowned symphony orchestras. The Duke's creatures of the night were immortalized on this recording.³⁵

Night Creature, when all is said and done, did not meet with such an adverse fate; it didn't have to wait thirteen years for an official recording, like *Harlem* (symphonic version), or two decades, like *New World A-Comin'*. Nevertheless, recording this score was not as easy as it might seem. On the contrary, so many obstacles appeared along the way that "Blind Bug" and "Stalking Monster" didn't make it to the finish line.

THE CREATURE IN PARIS

Norman Granz organized a European tour packed with dates in the winter of 1963. Between January 9 and early March, the Duke not only performed almost every day in a myriad of cities in the Old Continent, but between one live show and the next, he also got together in recording studios with a number of classical orchestras to work on his first symphonic album.[36] So, with this twofold goal, on Monday, January 28, his orchestra flew from London to Paris. Here, in two days (on Friday and Saturday, February 1 and 2, at the Olympia), he gave three concerts that brought to a close a tour de force that began with two recording sessions scheduled for Wednesday, January 30, and Thursday, January 31, when his big band joined forces with the Orchestre de Paris.

On Thursday, January 31, in the morning and early afternoon, not without some difficulties, as discussed in chapter 3, *Harlem* was recorded. The day before was dedicated to *Night Creature*, which turned out to be an even bigger headache.[37] Various factors turned the session into an ordeal, not least the fact that the French orchestral musicians, not unlike their Italian counterparts at the Teatro della Scala, took the whole thing a bit too lightly. Critic Charles Delaunay, who, like Giuseppe Giannini a few days later in Milan for CGD, organized the session on behalf of the French franchisee of Reprise Records, the French label Vogue, and this is how he recalls the encounter:[38]

> In 1963, the Duke signed an exclusive contract with Reprise, Frank Sinatra's record label, and Vogue was responsible for its distribution in France. This was a fantastic experience for me. . . . For the session with the orchestra, he gave me the task of hiring an orchestra with about seventy members. He also insisted that it include the horn player [Georges] Barboteu, whom he had probably heard and liked on a previous occasion. Neither Albert Ferreri nor I had any experience in this field, so we turned to Gérard Calvi to choose the musicians first and then the conductor. The Duke needed an assistant, because he didn't speak French.
>
> We didn't know of any recording studio in Paris that could accommodate, at the same time and in proper working conditions, seventy classical musicians and a jazz orchestra like Duke Ellington's. In the end we chose the Salle Wagram, which was used for a variety of events, including sports (catch wrestling and boxing), dancing (with groups such as the Catherinettes) and recording sessions. It dated back to the late nineteenth century, and wasn't in excellent shape. The walls were partially covered in mirrors, which was no good for the acoustics. But since nothing else was available, it was generally used to record very large orchestras.
>
> In the end, it wasn't such a good choice. No matter how many screens or mobile room dividers were used to block off the noisier

instruments, like the drums or the brass section, and no matter how far away you placed the microphones, they still kept recording them.

Above and beyond the issues involved in recording, those among the ranks of the orchestra Delaunay also spotted a number of musicians who certainly didn't help things, i.e., a worrying group of "sharks." Delaunay explains the metaphor as follows: these "sharks" were no other than "recording professionals who, at our expense, played a game all of their own, a sort of musical chairs. While a piece was being repeated, they would at times be replaced by others, who had never played it. These working methods, far from being an exception, were even provided for in their union contracts!"[39]

But then things got even more complicated, as we discover listening to some of the unreleased tapes containing the rehearsals and the recording sessions themselves. That day, the work began with "Blind Bug," which, for the occasion, had been slightly modified. A *rubato* introduction was added in which the trombone played the first phrase of the theme and the double bassoon the second, followed by the drums keeping time for four bars, which led to the theme in the reeds (while in the master take, the theme first appears played by the piano alone). This movement was recorded repeatedly, but none of the takes was convincing enough; the contrapuntal passage mentioned above was performed rather shoddily each time.[40]

Then Ellington skipped directly to the third movement, of which various takes were made. "Dazzling Creature," too, was adjusted here and there in the studio; for example, the brass accompaniment of the repetition of the first theme after the exposition of the second was eliminated (probably because it covered the oboe melody).[41] A few blunders were made by the symphony orchestra in this movement as well: the final break, which put every ensemble that performed this score to the test, once again proved a tough nut to crack. Ellington had to sing it repeatedly, spelling out its swing phrasing and articulation; the passage was only performed clearly after quite a few takes. Even the Duke himself didn't seem at ease; he repeated his piano solo at length and, after a few takes, didn't seem overly inspired.

Not much time was left, but Ellington thought he would take advantage of the remainder and try to get "Stalking Monster" down on tape. One thing is clear from those takes, above and beyond the mistakes made in some passages: the Duke had changed his mind. *Night Creature* was originally conceived as an almost entirely notated score, but here in Paris, Ellington decided to embellish the central movement with improvisations played by the members of his big band.

As we have already pointed out, "Stalking Monster" was the part of this score that saw the most revision over the years; in the Salle Wagram, the boogie-woogie-loving monster underwent a considerable restyling. First, the Duke asked Ray Nance to improvise on the violin over a vaguely defined structure based on minor blues chords; then, in the 12/8 section, Johnny Hodges played a clearer passage during two twelve-bar choruses. In the following take, Ellington himself tried out a piano solo.

The session ended. The Duke knew that none of those takes of "Stalking Monster" could be released on an album. All things considered, the first movement, with all its blemishes, could not have been included in a Reprise recording either. So the bandleader left the hall vexed by the thought of having to find another orchestra willing to come back to his creatures of the night. He was eventually saved by the Stockholm orchestra. But before we move on to another European capital city, once again hoping to eavesdrop on the studio recordings of *Night Creature*, let us pause to discuss some features of "Dazzling Creature," the only movement that reached its definitive recorded version in the Paris studio.

Bongos and a hi-hat hint at a Latin atmosphere by way of a 3–2 clave, evoking a bolero (with little thought to historical accuracy). Over this backdrop but without further accompaniment, the first theme rises in the oboe. In E minor, it is one of Ellington's most fascinating melodies, with its leap of a descending major sixth that, after a triple *acciaccatura* on a repeated note, falls by a diminished fifth; the harmonic color given by the leading note and the expressive major sixth at the end of the melody are further brilliant touches.

This first theme, repeated by the baritone sax and the trumpet with a plunger mute, now sustained by a dark background of horns and trombones, gives way, after a brief transition, to a second theme. This latter sixteen-measure phrase develops the beginning of the opening theme and similarly gives prominence to the major sixth of a minor chord; the Phrygian color that emerges halfway through also helps create a parallelism with the minor hues of the first theme. The two themes are furthermore united by tonal affinities; the minor setting is not abandoned, with the chords continuously shifting between G major and minor.[42]

The reappearance of the first theme acts as a bridge toward that which, in the initial version of *Night Creature*, was to be the only improvised moment within the score: Ellington's solo, which unfolds over the harmonies of the second theme. A sudden increase in tempo and a swell in the dynamics, which reaches fortissimo, then gives the music fresh impetus, and the two

Ex. 4.1. "Dazzling Creature," improvisation by Ellington, mm. 1–8.

themes are presented once again a semitone higher before the convulsive finale is closed by a chromatic break played by both orchestras.

Among all these passages, summarily described hereto, let us focus for a moment on Ellington's solo (ex. 4.1). The Duke approaches this improvisation like a Latin pianist, insisting on the percussive repeated thirds and tracing out a simple melody; the first eight bars come to a close with a phrase repeated in diminution, in which an expressive tritone appears.

This same leap of an augmented fourth, played by both hands two octaves apart, reappears at the end of the solo (ex. 4.2).[43]

Ellington, in the various takes, kept quite close to these ideas. Only one of them opens up into an improvisation that distances itself from this outline, and, truth be told, it is among the most inspired.

The beginning is remarkably simple. The three notes of the G major triad are enough to sketch out a lyrical theme. The following measure, too, is

Ex. 4.2. "Dazzling Creature," improvisation by Ellington, m. 16.

Ex. 4.3. "Dazzling Creature," improvisation by Ellington, alternate take, beginning.

extraordinarily cantabile, with the Duke insisting on only using notes that are part of the underlying harmony; in fact, what unfolds here is a diminished G chord with extra tension coming from a major seventh, the same chord played at that point by the saxophones (ex. 4.3). And yet Ellington discarded this improvisation. Most likely, for this Latin piece, the Duke had decided to exclusively use stylistic features coming from that musical culture, which are somewhat absent in this take, even though this led him to sacrifice originality.

Moreover, there seem to be subtle ties between the solo released on *The Symphonic Ellington* and the most well-known Caribbean piece in Ellington's repertoire. The final measure, in which both hands play an augmented fourth, calls to mind a similar ploy the Duke had adopted in all versions of his "Caravan" as of the midfifties. When he arrived at the bridge, he developed the habit of playing a melodic pattern in both hands, rhythmically and in unison, based solely on a diminished triad in its second inversion, a position that brings out the tritone.[44]

In that workshop, only a few steps away from the Arc de Triomphe, a "Dazzling Creature" came to life in its definitive form. But a "Stalking Monster" and a "Blind Bug" were still knocking on the door. And so, our demiurge the Duke proceeded to the capital city of Sweden with this idea on his mind.

DEAR OLD STOCKHOLM

On February 3, 1963, Ellington and his men landed in Malmö, at the southern tip of Sweden, and after heading to Lund, they immediately got back to their tight schedule: four concerts in three days spread out over three different cities, zigzagging between Sweden and Finland.[45]

Between Wednesday, February 6, and the afternoon of Friday, February 8, the band stayed put in Stockholm, but the Duke didn't even consider taking advantage of this pause to catch his breath. On the contrary, he took on even more engagements. Thursday, February 7, proved to be a particularly long day: rehearsals in the morning, a television appearance in the afternoon (in a program titled *Indigo* produced by Sveriges Television, Sweden's national broadcasting corporation), and studio recordings at night. The next day, he and his big band left for Denmark, where an audience was waiting at the Falkoner Theater in Copenhagen.[46]

And so, during the night between Thursday and Friday, at the Europa Film Studio in Stockholm, the Duke Ellington Orchestra, along with the Stockholm Symphony Orchestra, completed the work on *Night Creature* that had begun in Paris. The unreleased tapes of the rehearsals inform us that the two ensembles immediately connected: the very first take of "Blind Bug," played through without interruption, shows that the orchestra knew perfectly well how to approach this score. Two more takes to polish off a few details, and the fourth recording wound up directly in the Reprise album.

Then the sound technician announced, "*Night Creature*, second movement"; Ellington was extremely careful about the dynamics in his piano

Ex. 4.4. "Stalking Monster," improvisation by Ray Nance, accompaniment by Billy Strayhorn.

theme, but the orchestra's shaky entrance ruined the take. The next one didn't turn out well either. Then, the Duke had an idea: he would stand up and watch over both ensembles. Who could take his place at the piano? The only musician present who was able to play that piece on the fly: Billy Strayhorn. The simple riff that accompanies the violin solo is indicative of his style. Typically, a triad in root position and a fleeting bluesy flourish (later transposed to various other degrees of the scale) were enough to create an effective background; above this, a diabolical Ray Nance began improvising with an A minor harmonic arpeggio, particularly expressive thanks to the *acciaccaturas* (ex. 4.4).

The tape, after four violin choruses and the beginning of Johnny Hodges's solo, suddenly breaks off. The following take is dedicated to the twenty-four measures of the alto sax improvisation. It's truly a shame that such an outstanding solo didn't wind up on the album! Hodges, who, since the Paris session, had been coming up with different melodic ideas for each take, all of which are splendid, outdid himself here. His entire improvisation remains within a fragment of the blues scale; in the first phrase, he is able to cast a spell on the listener with only four notes (tonic, minor third, blue fifth, and perfect fifth); in the second and the third, only three of these four pitches are sufficient. Then, unexpectedly, departing from this uniform context, in the second chorus, he makes room for a single minor sixth underlined by a crescendo: the pathos contained in this isolated F natural is overwhelming. All of this is sprinkled with strategic ghost notes, expressive *acciaccaturas*, glissandos, vibrato, and changes in dynamics; in other words, embellished with extremely good taste.[47]

The next take was Ellington's last chance to ponder over the team of soloists to be used in this movement. After having decided on Williams, Nance, and Hodges, he thought he would also try out trombonist Lawrence Brown, who (as could have been expected) fully convinced him. Meanwhile, the symphony orchestra had another opportunity to rehearse the more challenging passages (which were still somewhat imprecise). The following take became the master take that made its way onto the album.

All three movements were fit to be included in the final recording. But the session ended a bit early. It was late at night during a northern winter. The band members, many of whom were over fifty, had gone through a hellish day and only a few hours later would find themselves in a different country for yet another concert along their tour. Any normal bandleader would have let them go back to their hotel and get some sleep, at least for a few hours. But Ellington was Ellington. Probably not entirely convinced of the quality of the Paris recording of "Dazzling Creature," he decided to record a Swedish version as well. The exhausted musicians obeyed their exacting Duke, who decided to experiment with a few new ideas. Almost as though he was picking the scarf that would best match the dress worn by his "Dazzling Creature," he tried out various introductions for the opening theme.

Right from the first take, the Swedish orchestra seemed more concentrated than the Parisian one, for example, performing the virtuoso final break rather well. In the following takes, Ellington considered giving some room to improvise to Paul Gonsalves (whose solo appeared during the B theme and the following A theme) but then went back to the original layout. Furthermore, in take 4, he left the piano to Billy Strayhorn once again, who played a magnificent solo.

In the opening measures, Strayhorn kept close to Ellington's idea, but his own personal features emerged all the same. One notices that the melodic movement in measure 6 is harmonically motivated: the pitches E, F♯, and G are supported by three chords (A7, D, and G major), which are part of a II7-V-I progression. In the second half of the improvisation, Strayhorn's typical harmonic daring is even more evident: in measure 12, he uses a Lydian scale on the D flat dominant over a G7 chord as a sort of tritone substitution and surprisingly continues in the following measure with the

Ex. 4.5.1 "Dazzling Creature," improvisation by Strayhorn (take 4, Stockholm).

same scale, even over the E7 chord played by the saxophones. As is the case with Hodges's solo mentioned above, it is a bit of a disappointment that this solo excursion was not chosen for the album. As we know, the "Dazzling Creature" ultimately released was the one recorded at the Salle Wagram, while the Stockholm orchestra saved the first two movements, which we shall now discuss.

"Blind Bug" begins with a blue note as an upbeat; as mentioned earlier, this piece appears on the album without its orchestral introduction, starting directly with an eight-measure piano episode inspired by the theme. This theme, while being the only structural element of this part of *Night Creature*, seems like it has been pared down to the bone. Only eight bars long, it is actually made up of a more succinct four-measure idea, repeated twice, and upon further inspection, those four measures result from an assembly of two almost identical two-measure motives. But that's not all. Even the smallest of these Russian dolls can be opened up; here, we realize that the basic cell

Ex. 4.5.2. "Dazzling Creature," improvisation by Strayhorn (take 4, Stockholm).

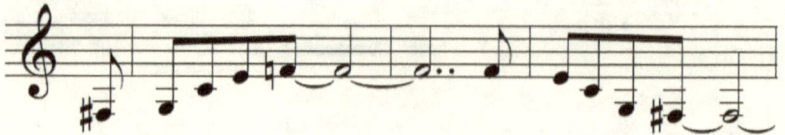

Ex. 4.6. "Blind Bug," theme, mm. 1–3.

is only one measure long and that the second measure is no other than a retrograde version of the theme's opening riff (ex. 4.6).[48]

Put simply, "Blind Bug" is a meditation on this single measure, a meditation that lasts four minutes. Only Ellington's boundless imagination and Henderson's technical mastery could have based an entire movement on such a Lilliputian, albeit rich, musical idea.

His use of modulating transitions to transpose the theme into distant keys is one important device: the melody reappears along a cycle of thirds, in C major, E-flat major, and then G major, finally returning to the basic tonality. Rhythmic and melodic elaborations of the theme also contribute, and the two transformations given to the trombones are particularly ingenious.[49] The backgrounds to the ever-changing riffs are equally effective, as are a few virtuoso passages in Henderson's orchestration; the flamboyant *tutti* before the repetition of the theme is an explosion of joy, detonated by someone who truly knew how to write for a pop orchestra.[50]

Then comes "Stalking Monster," the shiniest pearl in the score, in which the Duke's irony reaches its peak. Music history has a long-standing tradition of "scherzos" that goes well beyond the third movement of symphonies. Verdi's crafty *hoquetus*, Mozart's musical jokes, or Prokofiev's parodies of Haydn are only a few examples from an endless encyclopedia of musical humor.[51] Jazz, with Mingus's grotesque inventions, Ornette Coleman's wacky marches, Sonny Rollins's desecrating quotations, or Count Basie's bizarre and hilarious chords, is simply the most (auto)ironic genre of the twentieth century. And Ellington leads the way in this procession. Humor is clearly at the heart of many of his compositions, but then again, from the comedian who maintained on the *Dick Cavett Show* that the plunger mute was created first for the trumpet and was only later used to unclog sink drains or the joker who refused to take collect calls, informing the operator that it wasn't Ellington on the phone but his cat, we couldn't have expected anything else.[52]

The Duke sometimes used melodies to bring a smile to his listeners' lips, such as when, in "Take the 'A' Train," he had fun playing the theme on the piano without finishing the second phrase that was thus left hanging on a

Ex. 4.7. "Stalking Monster," theme, mm. 1–4.

harsh dissonance.[53] Other times, instrumentation was responsible for the jest: the "pep section," a trio made up of two trumpets and a trombone, all muted and busy making gurgling sounds, provided many enjoyable moments.[54] But even form was a means for the Duke to have fun. "Blues in Blueprint" (1959) has a sort of retrograde structure, ABCDBA; after the second to last theme, the listener guesses that the simple opening melody in the bass clarinet and the double bass at the lower octave may well follow (with finger-snapping as a rhythmic accompaniment), and this is what happens. What is created is a sense of gratification, and a relieved smile may well appear. Then, as a coda, the only instrument that has not yet played, the piano, chips in with the last word, a single disjointed chord. Our smile grows wider.

In "Stalking Monster," Ellington's irony comes out in the huge gap between the pitches used. The theme is first stated by the piano, accompanied only by the hi-hat: these thirty bars allude to blues both in the presence of blue notes and the path followed by the melody, which, in measure 9, moves upward by a fourth. This is, in the words of the program, "a monster we all fear we should have to meet some midnight." But this was never truly intended to be a scary beast. Not by chance, the tonality is A minor and will remain so until the end (this being the only movement of the suite without modulations). This tonal setting allows Ellington to begin the theme with the lowest and the highest note of the entire keyboard: A_1 and C_7. The rest of the music insists on this exaggerated gesture: the left hand spells out a very weighty theme, and the right plays a riff made up of three rapid, chromatically descending notes that are continuously repeated (ex. 4.7).

And so, his arms spread wide across the keyboard, the Duke manages to put us at ease as to the monster's intentions. The apparently gloomy theme turns out to be hilarious, like the polka in Šostakovič's ballet *The Bolt*, whose melody is played in the low register by the bassoon and doubled many octaves higher by a shrill piccolo. Ellington, in cahoots with Henderson, plays this joke on us repeatedly. For example, immediately after the piano theme, in only three measures, the descending riff passes from the flute to the double bassoon. The ending of the movement is once again based on this idea: an arpeggio slips from the flute (doubled by the violin) to the double bassoon (in unison with the double bass).[55]

Roughly a third of the way through the score, after a few elaborations of the first four measures of the theme and a few sparkling *tutti* passages, the twelve-bar blues form takes shape and acts as a trampoline for the soloists' bravura: first Ray Nance, who, like in some of the solos played during the rehearsals, doesn't move away from the color of A minor, then Cootie Williams with a plunger mute, and lastly Johnny Hodges followed by Lawrence Brown.[56]

The last two musicians improvise in 12/8 time: clearly, a reference to the boogie-woogie in the Duke's grotesque program. In the end, the opening theme reappears, lowering the curtain over this superb farce.

In 1962, the National Academy of Recording Arts and Sciences (the organization responsible for the Grammy Awards) chose *Night Creature* as the "Best Original Jazz Composition" while Ralph Gleason had words of praise for the entire album: according to this critic, the Reprise album was definitive proof of "Ellington's virtuosity and depth as a composer."[57]

Meanwhile, only a few months after the album was released, another symphonic suite was being prepared for its debut. This score was perhaps less refined than *Night Creature*, but it still had its interesting points and quite a few features in common, in addition to its visionary program, with the composition we have just discussed.

A GOLDEN BROOM, A GREEN APPLE, AND A GURU

On the first of April 1966, no jokes were in store for the Italian jazz buffs tuned in to the country's national television broadcaster. That evening, the RAI transmitted a curious documentary titled *Duke Ellington: Jazz e simpatia*. The first part of this short piece features a party held by the family of Dr. Arthur Logan (the Duke's most trusted doctor); the guest of honor is Ellington, surrounded by his closest friends. In the second sequence, the setting shifts to 333–34 Riverside Drive, almost at the corner of West 106th Street, right inside the Duke's apartment, where Ruggero Orlando is being received by a rather eccentric host who is first seen in bed, tucked under the sheets. But he isn't resting; on the contrary, he is absorbed in reading his latest score: *The Golden Broom and the Green Apple*. Ellington makes sure that the spectators are aware of both the imaginary narrative program underlying this work and that the piece had been performed in July by a classical orchestra.[58] And so he was proud of his symphonic output and personally took part in promoting it, even though, in order to do so, he had to set up this little prank.

That suite had kept Ellington on his toes until the end. The main cause for concern was that only two weeks before the premiere, the score was still far from being complete, as he confessed to the African American weekly *Jet*.[59] What's more, two factors made things even more complicated: the Duke had conceived a suite that was entirely notated (like the first version of *Night Creature*); in other words, it wouldn't have been possible to stretch things out by including an improvisation here and there. Furthermore, the orchestrator wasn't the veteran Luther Henderson, whom the bandleader could trust with anything, but Joe Benjamin.

Benjamin had worked with Ellington for the first time in 1950, acting as a copyist for *Harlem*. In spite of this, the services he later offered to the Duke's court essentially saw him working as a double bassist; that was how he contributed to the premiere of *Harlem*, and he would play the same role in the orchestra off and on for over three decades.[60] Even outside of Ellingtonia, this jazzman made a name for himself as a bassist, not an orchestrator. But this was what the bandleader had decided, and no one, not even Billy Strayhorn, could make him change his mind.

In any case, whether he was an expert or not, Benjamin handed in the score on time. Only one part was missing: the drums. And this didn't go over very well with Louie Bellson at all. According to what we know from Don George, this drummer was literally terrified at the rehearsal held on July 29. Only forty-eight hours were left until the debut, and the poor man didn't even have a written trace to follow. Ellington, as usual, played things down and, halfway between reassuring him and making fun of him, commented, "Hey Lou, don't worry about a thing, the first part's in 3/4."[61] But Bellson did worry and, by transcribing a guideline from the score, he made himself a safety net for the big concert at Lincoln Center. Naturally, the drummer, bassist John Lamb, and Ellington were about to present the work not in a modest music club but at the Philharmonic Hall, where no other than the New York Philharmonic Orchestra was waiting for them. The context, moreover, was the distinguished French American Festival, with its ten days of concerts held between July 14 and 31, given by classical musicians from both countries.[62]

Ellington's schedule, as usual, was packed. On July 28, he had played at Tanglewood as a special guest of the Boston Pops, with Arthur Fiedler conducting works by the Duke, arranged by Richard Hayman, in front of 18,000 people; the day after, he took on a grueling round of rehearsals.[63] July 30 was the big day. He appeared on the stage of the Philharmonic Hall playing three different roles: "Not only did I conduct *The Golden Broom and the Green Apple* and play the piano part in *New World A-Comin'*, but I was also honored by being asked to act as narrator in Aaron Copland's *Preamble for a Solemn Occasion* which was performed in memory of Adlai Stevenson."[64] We have an unreleased recording of the performance.[65]

The next afternoon, candidate for mayor of New York City, Paul Screvane, awarded him the city's highest honor: the Bronze Medallion. Outside City Hall, he was recognized for his extraordinary contribution to cultural life of the Big Apple. On that occasion, before taking his leave, the mayoral candidate felt he would comfort the Duke for not winning the Pulitzer Prize, emphasizing the fact that he was a die-hard classic: "Duke Ellington has survived the Charleston and he will outlast the Watusi!" Screvane blurted out.[66] Ellington probably appreciated the mayoral candidate's words but didn't add any fuel to the fire: the Duke had no time to mull over the past; he had other things to worry about. That evening, he was to appear once again on the podium at Philharmonic Hall for a repeat performance of his new suite and to improvise at the piano on "Take the 'A' Train" and "Satin Doll."[67]

The outstanding string section of the New York Philharmonic was particularly sharp and, except for a few blunders (the horn solo in the second movement, which ended on a wobbly low C, and the imprecise entry of the double bassoon in the following measure), the only problem was Louie Bellson's drumming, perhaps too insistent and heavy for this score. So, with a few critics expressing their approval, including Carter Harman, who described the work in *Life* as being full of charm and vitality, Ellington began taking his creation on tour across the United States.[68]

Between 1965 and 1969, the golden broom flew first to Los Angeles (Los Angeles Symphony Orchestra, August 23, 1966) and then to the Lyric Baltimore (Baltimore Symphony Orchestra, December 17, 1966), then headed back to the West Coast, touching on Hollywood (Hollywood Bowl Symphony Orchestra, August 3, 1968) and Stanford University in Palo Alto (California Youth Symphony Orchestra, March 9, 1969), before one last side trip to Ohio (Cleveland Symphony Orchestra, June 21, 1969). Finally, on February 19, 1967, it also took an intercontinental flight, landing at the Royal Albert Hall in London, where the London Philharmonic Orchestra was waiting for it.

Not all of these performances were particularly brilliant. For example, the London Philharmonic (the percussionists in particular) seemed at a loss at certain moments, as did a few soloists of the renowned Los Angeles Symphony (the trumpet solo had more than one glitch). The Cleveland Orchestra's performance, however, was very good, excellent even in its attention to dynamics.[69]

Unlike *Night Creature*, this score did not undergo substantial changes from one concert to the next, with one exception: the first fifteen measures of the second movement were erased, disappearing from the recordings of the concerts with both the Los Angeles Symphony and the London Philharmonic. It seems difficult to find a musical reason for this amputation; the lyrical solo played by the horn at the beginning of the movement, a melody that has its twists and turns but is highly cantabile, is one of the high points of the suite. No doubt, it is a difficult passage: the instrumentalist is required to leap across the entire range of his instrument, playing extremely wide intervals.

In 1970, conductor Maurice Peress asked the Duke himself for an explanation: "Did you give such a high solo to the French horn? It's in nosebleed territory and might more easily be given to a saxophone." Ellington not only reassured him as to the quality of the instrumentation but, more importantly, taught him how a conductor should deal with those measures during rehearsal: by beginning right after the horn theme. In this case, the soloist, if and when they were truly convinced of their own technique (and, in the end, of the value of this passage), would raise their hand and complain about the cut. Upon hearing this, Peress immediately saw the Duke as (in his own words) "a new guru." What we find is a plausible reason for the revisions of the second movement, as well as an illuminating example of how Ellington based his creations, including the symphonic ones, on instrumentalists instead of instruments.[70]

A few months after the debut of *The Golden Broom and the Green Apple*, in the previously mentioned documentary *Duke Ellington: jazz e simpatia*, he stated, "When I write music, I imagine the person who will perform it. When I write a part, I already have in mind the guy who will play it on the sax, the trumpet, or the trombone." From another point of view, this might be paraphrased as follows: "If the horn player of the London Symphony, whom I have no way of knowing musically, does not appreciate a certain passage, well, in that case, I might consider eliminating it."[71]

READING THROUGH THE STANZAS

Within five years, the piece was deemed worthy of a recording contract: Decca opened its Cincinnati studios and the city's symphony orchestra, conducted by Erich Kunzel, recorded it on May 28, 1970. The same orchestra, again conducted by Kunzel, had already played this suite some years earlier. From April 13 to 16, 1966, Ellington was in Cincinnati. Wedged in between conferences at the university, piano recitals, masterclasses, and a concert for the employees of General Electric, he found the time to rehearse the suite on April 14 and perform it two days later. On Saturday, April 16, indeed, after an afternoon ceremony in which Ellington was handed the keys to the city,

| Cm x4 | Fm x4 | Cm x4 | Fm x4 | Cm x4 | Fm x4 | Cm x4 | G7 x4 |

| Cm x4 | Fm x4 | D9 x2 | D♭9 x2 | Cm x4 |

Ex. 4.8. "The Golden Broom," second theme.

he proceeded to the Wilson Auditorium to present a solid program that alternated piano solos with two symphonic works: *New World A-Comin'* and *The Golden Broom and the Green Apple*.

That evening, Joe Benjamin replaced the regular double bassist, John Lamb, no doubt due to Benjamin's deep knowledge of the score, having orchestrated it a few months earlier. According to Stanley Dance, Ellington was highly satisfied with this performance. And surely enough, four years later, when it was time to record the work, he called on the same roster.[72] For this occasion, the orchestration was thinned down, above all, in the second movement, to the benefit of the suite as a whole. Furthermore, the Duke didn't miss the chance to record a narration of the program of the "three stanzas" that made their way onto the album, going back to the studios for this very purpose on May 28 that same year.[73]

The first stanza is rather full of events, with three different themes running through the movement and setting out a kaleidoscopic mixture of tonalities, which incessantly shift in "The Golden Broom," often based on parallel key modulation. The first theme is a cheerful little waltz that, as of its first appearance in the clarinet, reveals its roots in blues. In only a few measures, it goes from F major to E major, then back to the original key before switching to F minor. Constantly reworked, it later touches on many other tonal centers. One of its transformations has a specific sense: in measure 102, measures 6–7 of the theme are reshaped as a four-bar blues riff; the entire fragment is repeated over the following four measures.[74]

This is a sort of premonition of what comes across more clearly in the second theme, beginning in measure 192; as of this point, three distinct melodies are heard along a forty-eight-bar harmonic progression: first, the violas in unison (in C minor), then the glockenspiel (in C♯ minor), and lastly the violins harmonized in sixths (in F minor). These melodic profiles are a sort of chorus over a spartan blues harmony (ex. 4.8).

Indeed, these forty-eight measures are the result of an eight-bar blues grafted onto a sixteen-bar blues; in both cases, the harmony remains on each chord for twice as many bars as in the traditional blues form.[75]

Then the atmosphere suddenly changes. A bolero in F minor appears in the middle of the first stanza. Ellington, as far back as March 1930, had recorded "Admiration," a composition by W. H. Tyers, the mixed-race ragtime master who was crazy about the habanera. This was the first time he encountered the world of Latin music in a recording studio if we exclude the second theme of "Swampy River," a sign of his interest in this music dating to 1928. From the times of the Great Depression until his death, the Duke put together a sizeable catalog of pieces that evoked rumbas, cha-chas, mambos, habaneras, tangos, calypsos, bossa novas, and sambas. Entire LPs were dedicated to this world, from *Afro-Bossa* (Reprise 1963) to *Latin American Suite* (Fantasy, 1970). Sometimes, he was simply following the trends of the moment (the rumba craze in the thirties or the mambo fever in the fifties); elsewhere, even without getting hung up on philological issues, he showed greater awareness in his way of approaching this tradition. His boleros fall within the second category. The Duke grasped the typical dark color and ardently erotic mood of this Latin genre, which, since the nineteenth century, had changed shape more than once.[76] In his later years, he came back to the bolero with "Afro-Bossa" (1963), "Oclupaca" (1968), "Tina" (1970), and "Bourbon Street Jingling Jollies," without forgetting the third theme of "The Golden Broom": the music heard as of measure 336 of this suite (along with "Tina") comes the closest to its authentic Latin American model. What's more, Ellington had given a name to this melody...

On March 17, 1970, Ted O'Reilly, a promoter active in the Canadian jazz scene, met up with Ellington in a hotel in Toronto. Their brief conversation was mainly concentrated on the bandleader's astounding number of recordings. The Duke revealed that, not satisfied with official recordings, he had been privately recording on tape for a few years. When O'Reilly asked if any unreleased compositions were found among those tapes, Ellington answered: "Oh yeah! I've got... I don't know how deep that thing is."[77]

What he had in mind was the mountain of tapes that collectors refer to as "stockpile recordings." After his death, quite a few record labels (including Reprise, Atlantic, Fantasy, and Pablo) acquired some of those recordings and officially released them. The amount of unreleased material circulating increased sharply in the eighties, partially due to a donation made by Mercer Ellington to the Danish public radio company: the Duke's son gave this broadcaster a treasure trove consisting of 781 tapes. A true monument, the International Association of Jazz Record Collectors (IAJRC) has estimated that it contains at least 120 studio recording sessions (without counting interviews and innumerable live concerts).[78]

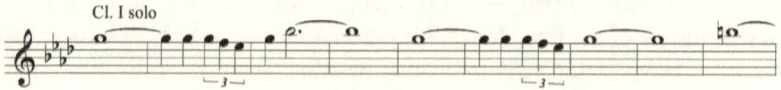

Ex. 4.9. "The Golden Broom," third theme / "P.S. 170."

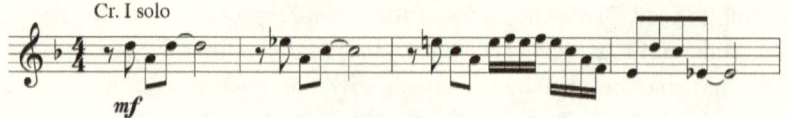

Ex. 4.10. "The Green Apple," opening theme, horn.

Among all these recordings, which span a quarter of a century, let us dwell on a single take recorded on tape on May 20, 1965, in a Chicago studio. That day, Ellington conducted his big band in an enchanting bolero that he called "P.S. 170."[79] Two months later, this piece found its way into the first stanza of *The Golden Broom and the Green Apple*, acting as its third theme (ex. 4.9).[80] All that Ellington took from "P.S. 170," which contained two similar harmonic progressions, was the first episode. Just like in the unreleased tape, in the suite as well, he gave the melody to the clarinet; Benjamin added the oboe and the bassoon in the background. These sixteen bars in F minor are highly inspired: the music is sinister and provocative, with unexpected twists appearing in the harmony.[81]

In the stanza titled "The Green Apple," something that had only been alluded to previously is now stated loud and clear: a blues, in the canonic twelve-bar form, appears as of the first measure. But it does not burst onto the scene; on the contrary, it begins quite elegantly. Ellington gives the horn (or rather, as noted above, the horn player) a graceful melody supported by appropriate chords: for example, as of the first bar, he avoids the typical blues chord, the dominant seventh, substituting it with a more delicate F6; the characteristic move to the IV in the second bar is also replaced with a leap of a major third (A7Bb13 instead of Bb7) that gives the passage a melancholic gospel atmosphere. Still anchored to its basic tonality, the blues, after an inspired contrapuntal section featuring different chords, is played by the vibraphone and then reappears in the main theme (ex. 4.10).

The third stanza reiterates all that was previously heard, but it does so less convincingly. "The Handsome Traffic Policeman" is a conventional blues that, accompanied by a shuffle that hints at the style of rock heard during those years, passes through various tonalities. And yet, since we are, in any case, dealing with a composition by Duke Ellington, a few passages worthy of note do emerge; one of them in particular is quite powerful. For the first bar of the second phrase of the blues in A flat major, instead of the habitual Ab7, Ellington opts for the following vertical combination: Ab7 (strings), F minor (trumpets) and, dramatically, G, C, and B in the trombones. The result is a chromatic blues chord that contains both the minor and the major seventh![82]

Eddie Lambert noticed a resemblance between this third movement and the boogie-woogie strings in "Stalking Monster." He was right. And this is not the only thing in common with *Night Creature*.[83] The two works, which we compared at the beginning of this chapter owing to their highly visionary programs, share other features. For example, the Latin element is crucial in both: while *Night Creature* makes room for an exquisitely Cuban improvisation on the piano keyboard, in *The Golden Broom*, we find one of the most authentic and intriguing boleros in all of Ellingtonia. But above all, and the reader will certainly have noticed this, the factor that definitively binds the two scores together is the predominant presence of the blues. The two suites begin with a theme that makes a veiled allusion to that world, leaving the task of fully revealing it to the second movement.

The blues, even in the restricted field of the Duke's symphonic works, is not in the least confined to these two compositions; it also underpins the compositions discussed at length in the previous chapters. A blues vein runs through *Harlem* (to be precise, at 132nd Street) and *New World A-Comin'*, even without turning to the twelve-bar structure, permeated by the atmosphere of the blues (a fresh glance at the second theme is enlightening in this sense); *La Scala*, needless to say, is completely given over to this form of music.

Ellington, to succeed in gleaning from this folk material a blues that was sophisticated but not contrived, a tribute to tradition even while overcoming it, turned yet again to his idols of the Black Renaissance. We have already shown how convinced the founders of the Harlem Renaissance were that, except for classical music, only spirituals had a right to exist in the world of the "new Negro." This was what the founding fathers of the movement believed. But sons, it goes without saying, only rarely agree with their fathers.

5

LA SCALA, PART II
FATHERS, SONS, AND THE BLUES

THE BLUES AIN'T...

On November 28, 1974, American television audiences, seated comfortably in their living room on the evening of Thanksgiving Day, were treated to a series of choreographies by Alvin Ailey with music by the Duke. The show was titled *Ailey Celebrates Ellington*, and in one memorable moment, a close-up highlights the Venusian squint detectable in the eyes of a decidedly seductive Gladys Knight. Her words are no less alluring: while snapping her fingers to keep time, she recites a definition of the blues coined by the Duke. "The blues is the accompaniment to the world's greatest duet, a man and a woman going steady. And if neither one of them feels like singing 'em, the blues just vamps 'till ready!"[1]

Understood this way, the blues is something that lurks inside the music. To be more precise, it lies dormant in the "vamp 'till ready" section (the ad lib ostinato that, in popular music, often prepared the entrance of the voice) and is prepared to leap to the forefront of a sentimental relation if and when one of the two lovers feels the need to sing. In this sense, the blues is a trickster, a Legba from the Vodou tradition, a Puck always ready to stir up trouble for the two lovers.

On another occasion, when speaking of Othello, Ellington told a journalist from the *Miami Herald*: "What a melodrama! What a subject for the blues. Blues in the night!" While this ironic reference to a song by Harold Arlen ("Blues in the Night") may not do justice to Shakespeare's drama, the Duke's statement still suggests that the twelve-bar blues form could indeed render the dark atmosphere of this tragedy. Surely enough, "Such Sweet Thunder" (1957), a roaring blues balanced between major and minor underpinned by a severe habanera rhythm, is dedicated to the figure of Othello.

At Carnegie Hall in 1943, Ellington's presentation of "The Blues," part of the second movement of the suite *Black, Brown and Beige*, was decidedly lugubrious. Singer Betty Roché delivered the Duke's message, accompanied by a desolate landscape consisting in a harmonic minor key with a good dose of chromaticism: "The blues ain't nothing but a cold gray day. . . . The blues ain't nothing but a black crepe veil ready to wear . . . sighin', cryin', feel most like dyin' . . ." Ellington expresses this lament within a structure that is similar to a twelve-bar blues without truly being one. After this phantasmal allusion to the blues, the trombones fleetingly sketch out a real one during a twelve-bar intermezzo where, for the first and only time in the entire suite, the blues appears in flesh and blood.

What we have here is a definition, a fragment of an interview, and a text: three different visions of the blues. The Duke made no secret of the fact that this musical tradition had many different connotations. In his memoirs, he describes the blues as conveying both misfortune and optimism, a symbol of both hard times and perfect bliss. It may cast you into poverty and dejection, or it may spur you on to fight.[2]

When described in words, however, this range of expression sounds almost monotonous compared to the complex variety of his works: in over half a century of composition, Ellington indeed perfected the most versatile conception of the blues found in the entire history of American music.

"TRANSBLUCENCY"

Some of Ellington's blues pieces revolve around a single element, the riff.[3] "C-Jam Blues" (1941) and "Main Steam" (1942) are two well-known works that fall into this category and mix swing and bebop. The Duke kept adding new pieces to this series until the end of his life, such as "Ocht O'Clock Rock" (1967), with its funk cadence, or the rock-influenced "Didjeridoo" (1971). The Duke also brought a bit more variety into this series with rhythm and blues numbers, including "Happy Go Lucky Local" (1946) and "Ray Charles' Place" (1962). These are all compositions full of vitality, vigor, and vivacity, but their inebriating rhythmic drive, ensured by the straightforward repetition of a single riff, often covers up formal structures that are anything but ordinary.

"Diminuendo in Blue" (1937), which might be classified as a simple blues based on a series of rhythmic-melodic fragments, is actually a rather complex creature that, in three minutes, passes through no fewer than five tonalities. Its main section is made up of one fourteen-bar chorus, a second one lasting twelve bars (that closes with a four-bar modulating transition), and a third with fourteen; none of the three harmonic patterns respects the canonic blues progression.[4]

The Duke's sparkling "Crescendo in Blue" (1937) as well, even while it does not change keys, presents two anomalous fourteen-bar choruses, reaffirming its individual profile with a ten-bar blues the seventh time around.

Various deviations from the established form are also found in "Battle of Swing" (1938). Basically, the Duke lengthened or shortened the blues form whenever he saw fit to do so. Some pieces with parts trimmed away include "Merry-Go-Round" (1935), whose third-last and second-last choruses are both ten bars long; "Sonnet to Hank Cinq" (1957), whose first theme lacks the last two bars; and "Flirtibird" (1959), whose first four bars seem to have been clipped off. Ultimately, Ellington had been reshaping this material since the early thirties, coming up with original forms. The various themes heard in "Creole Rhapsody—Part I" (1931) include a sixteen-bar blues whose harmonic rhythm is a bit crooked: five bars on I, two on IV, three on I, and then four bars of resolution that lead to the last two on I. In "Transblucency" (1946), he maintains the classic frame of twelve bars but inserts an asymmetrical phrase structure within it, 4+3+5 bars.

Even when he left the overall outline and harmonic pillars of this form intact, Ellington often gave it a prominent role within the overall structure of larger forms having more than one theme. In "Birmingham Breakdown" (1926), a blues appears as the last of the three themes; in "Black and Tan Fantasy" (1927), it is the main theme out of two; and in "Echoes of the Jungle" (1931), it is the second of a three-part form with two themes. The formal plan of these early works is at least partially due to general compositional practice at the time, which tended toward rather large forms. Pieces such as "Sepia Panorama" (1940), however, the first and last of whose four harmonic patterns are in blues form; the mature work "Sonnet to Hank Cinq" (1957), a three-part form with two themes; or the late pieces "Oclupaca" (1968) and "Portrait of Mahalia Jackson" (1970), which both have a blues as one of their two themes, suggest that over his entire career, the Duke used this traditional form as part of broader narrations. The last two works, furthermore, reveal even more refined intentions given that they both have two themes, one of which is an actual blues and the other that resembles one.

"Portrait of Mahalia Jackson" and "Oclupaca" have, indeed, one blues theme and another that falls within twelve bars. The second theme of "The Swingers Get the Blues, Too" (1959) lasts twenty-four bars and also takes up the blues phrase structure A8A8B8. This is the same strategy used by the Duke decades earlier in "The Mooche" (1928), whose first chorus (twenty-four bars long, subdivided AAB) is like a curtain being raised whose color matches the clothes worn by the leading actor, which is a blues alternating between E flat major and E flat minor. In his symphonic works, the Duke took up this idea of narration, where every event leads into the next like a cross-fade. The first theme of the "Stalking Monster" movement in *Night Creature*, played by the piano, with its blue fifths, its phrasing, and a few peculiar harmonic passages, introduces the second episode, which is a genuine blues that soon acts as a trampoline for the improvisers. Similarly, the first theme of "The Golden Broom" (the first movement of *The Golden Broom and the Green Apple*) has much in common with the second chorus, which is a progression constructed out of a sixteen-bar blues (stretched over thirty-two bars) and an eight-bar blues (stretched over sixteen); this slow unveiling continues in the second and the third movement, where the blues finally emerges in its standard structure.[5]

As we have seen, for half a century, Ellington continually strove to renew this long-standing tradition. He did it not so much to demonstrate what a wide range of music a composer (or at least an extremely talented one) could glean from those simple twelve bars but because, for him, the blues was like a theater mask. That is, it was capable of conveying the innermost inclinations of the human soul, speaking to us of solemnity and lightheartedness, religion and worldliness, expressionist turmoil and sublime serenity.

On the wittier side of things, we find, in addition to the previously mentioned "Blues in Blueprint" and "Stalking Monster," a "C-Jam Blues" whose playfulness lies in the extremely limited resources of its theme: the melody is built around two notes, the dominant and the tonic, and that's all.[6] One of the tracks on the album *Money Jungle* (1962) plays another "private joke" on us. A twelve-bar structure with a gospel feel, complete with a plagal cadence at the end of the chorus, this piece somehow or other also manages to express the essence of the blues. The Duke seems to have had fun turning things around, switching places between the IV and the V chords, and giving us the solution to this musical riddle in the title itself: "Backward Country Blues."

There is certainly no room for such pranks in "Portrait of Mahalia Jackson." Ellington paid tribute to this great African American sacred music singer by reproducing the timbre of an organ without, however, calling on Wild Bill Davis, his orchestra's organist, who, in fact, does not appear in this piece. He and his pipes are replaced by a few of the musicians in the Duke's band (three trombones, three trumpets, three clarinets—one of which is a bass clarinet—and one flute) who sketch out a blues in E minor, one of the most painful and solemn ever written. The harmony is monochromatic, like the sky in a nineteenth-century photo, shuffling slowly back and forth between the only two chords that appear (both minor, I and VIb).

At times, Ellington is even more scathing, reaching forms of acute expressionism in a few blues movements of the *Sacred Concerts*, such as "The Biggest and Busiest Intersection" (1968) or in works like "The Clothed Woman" (1947). The latter composition opens with a piano solo: all the instrument's registers are brought violently into play, and in the ensuing whirlwind of harmonics, the vertical combinations of sounds appear to be atonal. Only upon listening more closely can one make out a highly chromatic dominant seventh chord with a flat fifth, pointing toward a delirious blues in F with an overwhelming sonic power.

The harmonies in a few passages of "Oclupaca" and "Ko-Ko" (1940) are also extremely somber. In both works, we find major sevenths within minor keys instead of the more familiar and bluesy minor seventh, giving them an original but also very bitter touch. In the first piece, the theme in the winds slowly advances on an E natural within a blues in F minor. In "Ko-Ko," Ellington, in his piano solo, produces a similarly lacerating effect with a whole-tone scale on C played over a blues in E flat minor (thus emphasizing the major seventh, as well as a harsh minor ninth).[7]

At times, in his more dissonant blues pieces, both sevenths (minor and major) are blended together in a destabilizing cluster. Two such cases appear in his symphonic works. In the blues section of *Harlem* in A flat major, the brass instruments explode simultaneously with a diminished F chord in the trombones and a C7 chord in the trumpets. G natural and G flat come together, suspending the concept of tonality for twelve bars.[8]

A similar style of writing reemerges in the more modest third movement of *The Golden Broom and the Green Apple*, to be precise in bar 84, where a blues in A flat begins. Here, in the first four bars, while the strings play a bluesy A flat 7 chord (reinforced by an A flat 6 in the trumpets), the trombones intervene with B-C-G. The Duke then embellishes the harmony in the low register with a blue third (B) and a major seventh (G), giving the strident clusters heard in this episode a ferocious elegance.[9]

Worlds apart from this expressionist mood, we find other blues pieces with different stories to tell. More delicate and subtle, these works convey an idea of enchantment or unblemished beauty and have no equals in the African American repertoire. Not even the Modern Jazz Quartet, which produced extremely refined blues pieces, was able to take this down-to-earth tradition to the heights of sublimation reached by Ellington. Often, he achieved this metamorphosis through his choice of chords. In "Saddest Tale"

| B♭ B⌀ Cm F$^{add♯11}_{add♭9}$ | B♭6 D7 | Fm G7 E♭m F7 | A♭ Gm A♭△ B♭7 |

Ex. 5.1. "Saddest Tale," third blues chorus, reed chords.

| D F7 | E7 E♭7 | D6 F♯7$^{♭9}$ | B♭m |

Ex. 5.2. "Carnegie Blues," second chorus, harmonization.

(1934), during the first four bars of the third blues chorus, the woodwinds, instead of the two or three chords that would customarily be found here, play no fewer than sixteen, none of which has the typical blue seventh. This is an extremely sophisticated progression in the context of a blues (ex. 5.1).

The harmonization of the second chorus of "Carnegie Blues" is equally elaborate, in particular the first four bars, which contain a move to the spiritual atmosphere of the III and an incisive modulation to the relative minor (ex. 5.2).

In "Blue Light" (1938), the blues is given a velvety feel mainly through timbre, making it almost unrecognizable. Here, Ellington uses the voicing he had perfected in 1930 for the ballad "Mood Indigo": muted trumpet and trombone play in thirds in the treble clef (that is, with the second instrument projected into its upper register), with the clarinet quite some distance away, playing in the bass clef, confined to the dark chalumeau register.[10] He would later elaborate this voicing, adapting it for four woodwinds in the enigmatic blues piece "Subtle Lament" (1939) and then revised to a further degree a few years later in the masterpiece "Transblucency" (1946).

For this latter work, perhaps to make the basic principle underlying this twelve-bar form even more evident, he coined the neologism that gives the piece its title. It's as though the Duke was saying to us: "Ladies and gentlemen, here is a transfiguration of the blues!" "And one of its highest moments," we might add.[11] For this important occasion, he modified the voicing used for "Mood Indigo," substituting the trumpet with a singer's voice: soprano Kay Davis appears here as an instrument in a homophonic-chordal combination with the trombone and chalumeau clarinet, bringing to life to one of the noblest timbres composed in the twentieth century (ex. 5.3).[12]

This metamorphosis of the blues is not limited to the opening bars of "Transblucency." Later, Ellington takes up the trombone solo written by Lawrence Brown for "Blue Light" and uses it as a sort of *cantus firmus* for Davis's voice, coupling it with a clarinet. This is one of the contrapuntal pinnacles of Ellingtonia, and, at the same time, one of his most sophisticated treatments of the blues (ex. 5.4).

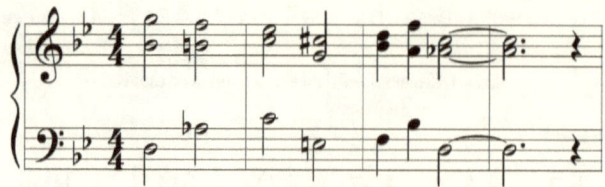

Ex. 5.3. "Transblucency," theme, mm. 1–4.

Ex. 5.4. "Transblucency," counterpoint, Kay Davis (1st voice), Jimmy Hamilton, clarinet (2nd voice).

In "Fugi," the first movement of the suite titled *Ad Lib on Nippon* (1964–66), the Duke also came up with a range of tactics to camouflage the blues tradition.[13] This highly charming piece includes a Latin bass that supports a Dorian melody with a lowered second (the theme is based on the II of G harmonic minor) that leads to a hexatonic ending. This blues in A minor, with its atmosphere reminiscent of pointillism, ends on an original resolution (ex. 5.5).

Other times, all the Duke needed was the melody to camouflage the blues. The theme of "Angu" (1963) is shaped to emphasize the major seventh through an ascending leap that would seem to be the negation of the

| G7$^{\#11}$ E7$^{\#11}$ | D7$^{\#11}$ C7$^{\#11}$ | Am6$^{\flat 9}$ | Am6$^{\flat 9}$ |

Ex. 5.5. "Fugi," harmonic resolution.

Ex. 5.6. "Angu," theme.

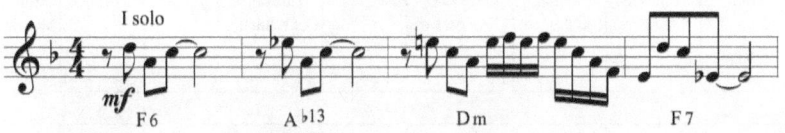

Ex. 5.7. "The Green Apple," horn theme.

melodies from the Mississippi Delta, which gradually descend toward the tonic, clinging to the blue notes along the way. And yet this lyrical sequence of notes unfolds over a standard twelve-bar blues in D (ex. 5.6).

In much the same way, the horn melody that opens the second movement of *The Golden Broom and the Green Apple* sounds like an elegiac and sentimental *andante* from a symphony, even though it is set within the same harmonic frame as the one heard in "Angu." This background is partially disguised, however, once again by a delicate major seventh, which appears repeatedly in the third bar (ex. 5.7).[14]

Over his entire lifetime, therefore, Ellington pursued this peculiar ideal of refining the blues. Using the same ingredients from the Mississippi Delta, from which everyone had concocted the same sort of gut-wrenching expression, he demonstrated that it was possible to distill a vintage brandy. And so, in 1963, he produced one of his most precious bottles ever: *La Scala*. What's more, Ellington succeeded in getting one of the world's most famous symphony orchestras involved in this process of sublimation; too appealing to refuse, this occasion would give him the last word in a discussion (or perhaps a monologue) revolving around tradition and innovation. All of this probably helped convince him to endure more than one setback in order to reach what was, for him, such a lofty goal.

Ex. 5.8. *La Scala*, Introduction, piano.

Intro	A	B	C	D	E	F	B'	A'	Coda
12	12	12	12	12	12	12	12	12	12
Rhythmic section	Theme orchestra	background *a*	background *b*	background *c*	Special orchestra	background *d*	background *e*	Theme orchestra	
C major		G major	C major		F major	D minor	F major		
Soloists		trombone L. Brown	clarinet R. Procpe	tenor sax P. Gonsalves		trumpet C. Williams			trombone/clar/trumpet/tenor sax
Timing CD									
0:00	0:40	1:16	1:52	2:29	3:06	3:43	4:19	4:55	5:32

Ex. 5.9. *La Scala*, formal outline.

"LA SCALA": DISTILLING THE BLUES

Right from the opening bars of the introduction, Ellington puts things clearly. The parallel triads in stepwise ascending motion do not have a swing phrasing: nothing could be further from the blues, meaning that this might be a piece by Ravel but certainly not the music sung by Bessie Smith. Only as of bar 5 do we begin to realize, to our surprise, that we are dealing with a twelve-bar form and its respective theme; moreover, at this point, the tonality is also revealed. The ingenious dominant pedal in the opening bars immerses us in what is apparently a Mixolydian mode on G, disguising a sophisticated blues that is actually in C major. Later, these same bars become all the more elegant when they contain a major seventh instead of the blue seventh, with a gesture that is repeated after the modulation to the IV (ex. 5.8).

The theme sketched out in the introduction becomes more well-defined when played by the symphony orchestra in the following chorus. Here, an evocative timbre in the woodwinds confirms this tendency toward purification; as it continues, passing through five tonalities, the entire suite will remain faithful to this credo (ex. 5.9).

The diatonic background *a*, with its light stepwise motion in the strings in the section in G major, and the similar background *b* that unfolds in section C, in which the first motif of the theme begins to appear, are two examples

Ex. 5.10. *La Scala*, trombone solo, mm. 1–5.

Ex. 5.11. *La Scala*, trumpet solo, mm. 2–4.

Ex. 5.12. *La Scala*, horn harmonization, mm. 1–4, solo by Paul Gonsalves.

of this tendency. Not only in Ellington's score, moreover, does *La Scala* show this inclination. The trombone solo feels like an improvisation on a sentimental ballad, and it may not be by chance that Lawrence Brown began with the first six notes of the heartrending "In a Sentimental Mood" (ex. 5.10).

This solo excursion, with its calibrated alternation of calls and responses, climaxes and anticlimaxes, rapid outbursts and meditative rests, has a unique grace. In a similar vein, the trumpet chorus in the section in F major seems to set aside the stylistic features of blues in favor of gentle major-seventh arpeggios and delicate sixths (ex. 5.11).

Within this composition's measured pace, like a sonnet or rather an ode to the transfiguration of an age-old tradition, the Duke also found a way to include a few experimental verses. Underneath the ethereal solo played by Paul Gonsalves, in only four bars, the horns summarize all possible variations on the blues (ex. 5.12).

The atmosphere we breathe in the first bar resembles a minor blues: the four brass instruments, in fact, play a Cm7 chord. The E flat probably has a twofold function here, acting as an augmented ninth and a peculiar blue note. The minor key is nevertheless palpable, not merely suggested: the double bass plays an arpeggio on the C minor triad, and furthermore, when the Fm6 arrives in the following bar, it seems to confirm this suspicion. The key actually is major (with the double bass and horns presenting misleading blue notes), but the visionary sonorities created by Ellington show little regard for a rigid application of music theory.

Bar 3 shifts into a luminous C major 7. This is an unexpected gleam of light that, however, almost seems out of place in this ashen-colored landscape, and rather than providing illumination, it confuses us. The following bar is filled by a more appropriate C9. Thus, what we find here is a minor blues, a tonal one on major seventh chords, and a traditional one: the entire history of jazz condensed into four bars![15]

For his Italian suite, the Duke used some of the most refined words in his vocabulary: never had the blues been put forward with such elegance. And yet it was not only his wish to reach the highest peaks, assisted in his climb by a prestigious orchestra, that led Ellington to record this work in spite of the myriad of difficulties that barred his way on that day in February 1963. Perhaps, on that occasion, the African American Ellington felt like he was charged with a task whose importance went far beyond music, a task he had to fulfill at all costs.

FATHERS AND SONS

"Music should sound, not screech; music should cry, not howl; music should sweep, not bawl; music should implore, not whine."[16] The preacher speaking here is mixed-race pianist Maud Cuney-Hare. Her pulpit is the volume *Negro Musicians and Their Music*. The evil against which her sermon is directed and that screeches, howls, bawls and whines is jazz. Miss Cuney-Hare, editor of the music section of the *Chicago Defender*, had nothing kind to say about syncopated music in the book she published in 1936; Ellington was given a few lines in this 438-page text, but even he was written off as a composer of "light music."[17] Nor did critic Lucien White mince his words when writing from Harlem for the *New York Age*, where he railed against that "conglomerate mixture of dissonances" that could only arouse "sensuous and debasing emotions."[18] Moving back toward the Windy City, a music lover looking for suggestions would have heard the voice of African American pianist Dave Peyton loud and clear. Peyton, even while being part of Chicago's jazz scene, warned everyone, young musicians in particular, to keep clear of it: "Put two or three hours a day on your scale work and stay away from jazz."[19]

The blues was given much the same treatment, in particular, the urban—and corrupted—blues played in the Roaring Twenties. The fathers of the Harlem Renaissance had much the same opinion: in their world, permeated by the sounds of the classical European tradition and the symphonic spiritual, blues had no citizenship. These were two separate planets and no one should dare try to bring them into contact, even though this is precisely what a few impudent musicians were attempting to do.[20] That vulgar tradition, which was born in the Deep South where ignorance was rampant and flourished in the indecent cabarets of Harlem, left them indifferent at best or simply embarrassed, and since their sense of diplomacy prevented them from taking a more radical position, on the whole, they just ignored it.

The most reticent of these intellectuals was Du Bois, who, as editor of *The Crisis*, carefully avoided writing about the blues. At the time, he was busy encouraging Black artists to break the color barrier and thus could not abide the thought of African American musicians becoming overly comfortable in the ghetto of jazz.[21] As scholar Arnold Rampersad has observed, the only musical events worthy of being reviewed in his journal were those in which a Black interpreter played classical European music.[22] James Weldon Johnson described the blues in *Black Manhattan* (1930) simply as a "repository of folk poetry," showing that he didn't have much respect for its musical side; along similar lines, in the preface to his *The Book of American Negro Poetry*, he had earlier praised spirituals as "the greatest body of song."[23]

A more nuanced vision was expressed by Alain Locke, the Renaissance's ideological leader. Having taken it upon himself to write about African American music, publishing various essays and an entire volume in the process, he was forced to say something about the blues. He did become more interested over time but, on the whole, remained rather timid.[24] Not by chance, indeed; the bibliography that accompanies the chapter titled "Secular Folk Songs, The Blues and Work-Songs" of his *The Negro and His Music* (1936) was not prepared by Locke himself. This professor had to rely on the knowledge of a younger colleague at Howard University, Sterling Brown. The latter, with his first collection of poems titled *Southern Road* (1932), had already won over the literary figures of the Black Renaissance. His verses were inspired by Southern folklore, including its dialect (which did, in fact, worry James Weldon Johnson, who felt that the use of Black slang risked slipping into caricature, along the lines of a minstrel show), and above all, the blues, of which he had deep knowledge.

Ma Rainey, a portrait of the singer whom Brown had met personally in a theater on Cedar Street, Nashville, in 1928, is a moving tribute to this music, whose folkloric verses, taken from "Backwater Blues," to be precise, appear in its last strophe. Brown believed that the blues and jazz were as dignified as the spiritual, and he took off his hat to the artists who had created those traditions, men and women who certainly "cannot be dismissed as clowns."[25] For his sociological, anthropological, and musicological projects dedicated to Black folklore, Professor Brown repeatedly collaborated with another indomitable daughter of the Harlem Renaissance: Zora Neale Hurston.

Even though she was warmly admired by the fathers of the Renaissance (her story "Spunk" was included in the fundamental anthology *The New Negro*), Zora Hurston did not obey all the dictates of the movement. For example, she did not subscribe to the idea that all Black musical culture should be modeled on the concert spiritual. An anthropologist, folklorist, and intellectual, she strongly preferred the songs sung by farmers in Florida to the educated voices of Roland Hayes or Paul Robeson. For her, what came first was folklore, expressed in the blues and elaborated in jazz, and then all the rest. According to Pulitzer Prize–winner Alice Walker, who worked hard to promote her works in the seventies, Zora Hurston was part of a secular trinity alongside Billie Holiday and Bessie Smith. Ethnomusicologist Alan Lomax considered her "the best informed person on Western Negro Folklore" and gave her most of the credit for the success of their trip to Florida in 1935, where they made 227 field recordings.

After all, Zora Hurston had been wandering around the Deep South for about a decade, discovering unknown melodies, doing research on religious rites that were falling into neglect, and collecting information on obscure beliefs. During one of her tours, which took place in 1927 (the year she married a jazz musician), she brought a poet friend along with her. The two had met in Harlem, and in 1926, along with Wallace Thurman, they created the journal *Fire!!* In 1930, they collaborated on a theatrical work. Her traveling companion, who couldn't wait to see that fascinating world of folk artists firsthand, was called Langston Hughes.[26]

Brown and Hurston's attraction to the blues worried the fathers of the Renaissance, but Hughes's boundless enthusiasm for this tradition, which even extended to vulgar jazz, was a source of even greater pain for the movement's founders. He loved them (he once said that the Bible and Du Bois were his main influences) and they loved him (they, in particular Alain Locke and Weldon Johnson, admired and endorsed his earliest writings), but their strong dislike of that music enraged him. So much so that he showed a lack of respect toward them on more than one occasion. In 1926, writing for *The Nation*, he blurted out the following irreverent statement: "Let the blare of Negro jazz bands and the bellowing voice of Bessie Smith singing the Blues penetrate the closed ears of the colored near-intellectuals until they listen and perhaps understand." That same year, he came into contact with the affected milieu of Washington's Black aristocracy, which, from a musical point of view, he found conventional and pretentious compared to the scene at Seventh Avenue, which was teeming with blues and jazz.[27]

During those same months, Hughes's first collection of poetry was published under the title *The Weary Blues*. The culture of the blues, which had cast its spell on him since 1918, underpinned a large portion of his output by the late twenties. Not only do his poems, some of which were published by periodicals including *Opportunity* and *Vanity Fair*, employ the three-part structure of the blues and frequently quote the singers of the Delta, but various short stories of his also have to do with that world (the most well-known of which is perhaps "The Blues I'm Playing" from *The Way of White Folk*, 1934), as do many of his essays.[28] Even his last publication, a photographic history of the African American arts that was published posthumously in 1967, contains a chapter dedicated to the blues and one about the birth of jazz.[29]

And that's not all. As of the fifties, Hughes began participating in concerts and making recordings with a number of prominent jazz artists. In 1957, he wrote and recited, along with Lonne Elder, the text for "Scenes in the City," the first track on the album by Charles Mingus's *A Modern Jazz Symposium of Music and Poetry*. The following year, he worked with Mingus again for the album *Weary Blues*; to promote this work, Hughes gave various jazz readings in New York (at the Village Vanguard), Hollywood, a music festival at Fisk University, and the Ontario Shakespeare Festival, accompanied by Mingus, Phineas Newborn, Ben Webster, and Earl Hines. He recited on TV with Doug Parker's white band and Red Allen's Black ensemble, wrote a text for Randy Weston's fundamental album *Uhuru Afrika* (1960), and contributed to the 1960 Newport Jazz Festival with "Goodbye Newport Blues," a number performed at that venue by John Lee Hooker, Muddy Waters, and Jimmy Rushing, along with the Sonny Price Trio.[30]

In his later years, as part of a piece written for *African Forum*, Hughes sketched out his memories of Harlem when he was a young man. "I was nineteen when I first came up off the Lenox Avenue subway one bright September afternoon and looked around in the happy sunlight to see if I saw Duke Ellington on the corner of 135th Street."[31] Straight out of a movie, this magical scene is full of suspense. Unfortunately, however, at this point, we have to stop the reel and turn on the lights: our poet has gotten things mixed up. In 1921, the young Ellington was still in Washington. He hadn't yet set foot in New York, and above all, was completely unknown, meaning that Hughes couldn't have wished to meet him on a street corner. Nevertheless, while this reminiscence may be somewhat blurry, it eloquently conveys his burning desire to meet this man. And from this point of view, the scene portrayed by Hughes is completely reliable.

4.
WE, TOO, SING AMERICA (AND THE BLUES)

Ellington and Hughes kept trying to get together for over thirty years without ever actually meeting. Not even once did their collaborations lead to anything concrete or meaningful. In 1936, they were both busy working on the musical *Cock of the World*, which should have involved Paul Robeson as well. In spite of coauthor Kaj Gynt's efforts to find a producer, however, it never saw the light of day.[32] In 1940, they flopped twice. The theater piece *Jubilee: A Cavalcade of the Negro Theatre*, for which Ellington wrote "Diamond Jubilee" to a text by Hughes, fell through due to a lack of funding. Hughes then abandoned the show *Negro Revue* after a drawn-out conflict between the various scriptwriters who were working on it. He did, however, succeed in selling the rights to his texts before the production definitively collapsed.[33]

Jump for Joy was born out of the ashes of that show. Ellington wrote all the music and also included a song with lyrics by his friend Hughes that had been part of *Negro Revue*: "Mad Scene from Woolworth's." Hughes, who bought a new suit with the check he got for the royalties, probably felt that this song would have set off fireworks and led to a long artistic collaboration. But it fizzled out quite soon. At the premiere, this song, in particular, didn't go over well and was eliminated in the (few) repeat performances. Speaking with his friend Carl Van Vechten, all Hughes could do was grumble that he'd wasted his money on a suit he could no longer afford.[34]

A few years later, in 1945, they sketched out a song titled "The Heart of Harlem," dedicating the copyright money to a white liberal group called the City-Wide Citizens' Committee on Harlem. But it didn't come to much: the song never became part of the Duke's immense discography.[35]

After a couple of decades with no shared projects, in the midsixties, Hughes got Ellington involved in the TV show *The Strolling Twenties*. This tribute to the Harlem Renaissance was conceived by Harry Belafonte, who had just read Hughes's autobiography, *The Big Sea*. Notwithstanding its star-studded cast (Sammy Davis Jr., Sidney Poitier, Harry Belafonte, and Diahann Carroll were only a few of the celebrities who appeared in it), the show, which went on the air on February 21, 1966, wasn't all that successful. Ellington didn't write any new pieces for it, simply playing "Mood Indigo" and "Rockin' in Rhythm" with his orchestra.[36] One year later, Hughes died.

And yet, despite the bad luck that continually afflicted their plans, both benefited from their reciprocal influence. Things couldn't have gone otherwise: the two were bound by a deep mutual esteem. Hughes attended the Duke's most important concerts (including his first performance at Carnegie Hall on January 23, 1943), praised some of his most unusual works (such as

A Drum Is a Woman, of which he wrote: "It was wonderful that the towering talent of so fine a composer and musician was made available to the nation via television"), rejoiced for the orchestra's rebirth at the 1956 Newport Festival ("Duke made the cool night hot"), was delighted to be at the Duke's side in Dakar in spring 1966 for the first World Festival of Negro Arts, promoted by the president of Senegal Léopold Senghor, and repeatedly wrote about him as a friend in his memoirs and short stories (such as *A Toast to Harlem*).[37] As for Ellington, in his autobiography, he referred to Hughes as a hero of Harlem, enthusiastically agreed to participate in all of his projects, and repeatedly provided evidence that Hughes's ideas had a considerable influence on his own aesthetics and ideology.[38]

In 1926, Hughes wrote the manifesto *The Negro Artist and the Racial Mountain*, an essay in which he continually affirms the concept of Black beauty, coining the phrase "We know we are beautiful." Two years later, Ellington composed "Black Beauty."[39] At a time when many African Americans used bleaching cream to whiten their skin, Hughes and Ellington were on the same wavelength. This piece, one of the Duke's early masterpieces, is not the only one of his works that seems to have been inspired by Hughes. His first suite, *Black, Brown and Beige* (1943)—intended to narrate Black history from Africa to the United States using an authentically African American musical idiom—also has a precedent in the play *Don't You Want to Be Free?* (1937), which Hughes wanted to be accompanied by spirituals and blues pieces performed live.[40]

In 1941, in its *Speech of the Week* column, the *California Eagle* published the words offered by Ellington at the Scott Methodist Church in Los Angeles for the Annual Lincoln Day Services. The title he chose for the speech, "We, Too, Sing America," paraphrases the poem "I, Too, Sing America," found at the end of the volume *The Weary Blues* (1926). The Duke clarified the source of this quotation, explicitly referring to the title of "a very significant poem" written by the "distinguished poet and author, Langston Hughes."[41]

What the two truly sang together, however, was the blues. As of the late twenties, both demonstrated that it was possible to find continual inspiration in that tradition. They taught us that this extremely concise form contained plenty of room for bold experiments. Between the lines of this rustic folklore, they found sublime examples of Black beauty: not a savage splendor (following an idea that goes back to Rousseau) but an authentically noble grace. According to this vision, the jungle made of tinsel at the Cotton Club turns out to be a true "black mother." The same spellbinding Africa is seen in the poem "Nude Young Dancer" by Hughes (published in *The New Negro*) and is the one where the "Fleurette Africaine" sprang to life. This delicate piece, composed by Ellington, along with Max Roach and Charles Mingus, in 1962, is a metaphysical minor blues whose underlying story—an uncontaminated creature, protected from the eyes of men and safeguarded in (and by) the jungle—was told by the Duke to the musicians in the recording studio. This piece, when all is said and done, is a soaring expression of all creation, like the blues in *The Golden Broom and the Green Apple*, in whose program Ellington speaks of purity, virtue, and virginity.[42]

But while the Duke paid tribute to the blues through a symphonic sublimation, Hughes appears to have appreciated its innermost authentic beauty without feeling any desire to elevate its status.[43] The poem "Note on a Commercial Theatre" (published in *The Crisis* in 1940) is quite clear on this point, unequivocally stating about the blues that "you sing 'em on Broadway / and you sing 'em in Hollywood Bowl / and you mixed 'em up with symphonies / and you fixed 'em / so they don't sound like me."[44] Nevertheless, in an article dedicated to W. C. Handy, published in the *Chicago Defender* on November 28, 1942, under the title "Maker of the Blues," Hughes heralded the works presented by this bluesman on no other than Broadway. He furthermore praised his sophisticated reharmonizations of folk music and declared that he fully agreed with Handy (the Father of the Blues), who believed that the potential of this great music had no limits and was certain that "someday the blues will be the basis for great ballets, great sonatas, and great new forms still unevolved."[45]

In a nutshell, Hughes had little patience for businessmen who disrespectfully exploited that folk repertoire, nor could he abide narrow-minded and conservative composers who altered its stylistic features, having no knowledge of the culture in which it was originally produced. Someone like Handy was welcome to rework this music, but it was another can of worms altogether if an Ellington took the pains to bring that sincere rural tradition to the world's concert halls. The Duke's experimental blues pieces, with their sophisticated chords, may have aroused John Hammond's disapproval; all the same, they are not only evidence of a compositional research that lasted over half a century; they were also signs of a true faith this white producer had no way of understanding.

EPILOGUE: A BLUES TRIUMPH

With *La Scala*, Duke Ellington brought an entire movement to fulfillment. His traveling companions included classical composer William Grant Still, who had attempted to elevate the blues "into the highest of musical forms" and who, after collaborating with the leading literary figures in the movement (including Hughes) and arranging jazz and blues numbers for a record label established by Handy, used the twelve-bar form in his famous *Symphony n. 1 "Afro-American"* in A flat major (1930).[46]

His companions also included, in addition to his friend Langston Hughes, the younger and more daring members of the Renaissance, such as Zora Hurston and Sterling Brown. He found other companions among the painters associated with the Renaissance whom, as we saw in chapter three, the bandleader knew very well. In the same years in which Ellington was elaborating on the blues, indeed, it also appeared in the highly modern style of Aaron Douglas with works such as *On De No'thern Road* and *Play De Blues* (both dating to 1926). It was colorfully portrayed in works by Archibald J. Motley Jr., such as *Blues* (1929); it was given deeper substance in the series of oil paintings titled *Blues Singer #1* by Charles Alston (1954); and it was transfigured in a large number of outstanding works by Romare Bearden, among which was the early abstract work *The Blues Has Got Me* (1944).

In 1966, journalist Ruggero Orlando asked Ellington about his thoughts on Italy. He replied with words of praise and continued by expressing his satisfaction for having recorded *La Scala*.[47] A tactful man, this was all the Duke could have said. We, however, with the knowledge we now have of the mortifying events that took place behind the scenes, cannot help but feel slightly embarrassed; more than slightly, if we took a peek at what local experts had to say about the work. The influential critic Arrigo Polillo, for example, belittled *La Scala*, calling it a "dull, weak" piece.[48]

In Ellington's own country, not many people noticed the true quality of this score (even though Woody Herman called it "the epitome of the blues"), and probably no one fully realized its cultural importance.[49] Those who could have appreciated what was truly at stake were either too old (like Du Bois, who turned ninety-seven only a few hours after *La Scala* was recorded) or had already passed away. But the Duke had not forgotten them, nor could he fail to recall the *mos maiorum* of the Harlem Renaissance. It was probably his memory of those elders, their customs and social norms, and their teachings that, alongside his constant desire to experiment with the blues, drove him to complete this recording. From this point of view, *La Scala* was, in spite of everything, a triumph. Better yet, the celebration of a victory, to take up the definition of "art" formulated by Romare Bearden. In a description of the blues idiom and the phrasing of a trumpet player in Ellington's orchestra, this painter, masterfully combining three different points of view, wrote the following: "A blues singer up at the old Lafayette, she sings about waking up one morning, there's a letter from my man, he done left me, I'm going down to the river and God knows what I'll do—but then here comes

Freddy Jenkins on the trumpet, playing with the mute in, and he does a funny kind of riff that turns what might have been tragic into something else, into farce, so you don't feel like going out and committing suicide after all. Life is going to triumph somehow."[50]

Ellington meeting with the director of the General Record Company (Compagnia Generale del Disco), Giuseppe Giannini (left), who organized the session, and with the musician Piero Rizza (center), who served as a copyist. Photo: Archivio Giancolombo.

Ellington arm in arm with bassoonist Oreste Canfora, who took care to gather the "professors" of the Teatro alla Scala for the recording of the suite *La Scala*. Photo: Archivio Giancolombo.

Ellington and the orchestral parts of *La Scala*. On the right side, near the double bass player Ernie Shepard, who is tuning his instrument, almost entirely out of the field of the photograph, we can glimpse Billy Strayhorn. Photo: Archivio Giancolombo.

Ellington and the rhythm section. Drummer Sam Woodyard and bassist Ernie Shepard, the Ellingtonian rhythm section that took part in the recording of "La Scala." Photo: Archivio Giancolombo.

Ellington rehearsing a passage on the piano while in the background trumpeter Ray Nance (hired for the session and later replaced by Cootie Williams, who recorded the part in the US) talks to the critic Daniele Ionio. Photo: Archivio Giancolombo.

Ellington, during the recording sessions for "La Scala," providing instructions to the Theater's percussionists, for whom he had not written parts. Photo: Archivio Giancolombo.

A shot during the recording of "La Scala" portraying the bandleader while he conducts the "professors" of the La Scala Orchestra in the work dedicated to them. Photo: Archivio Giancolombo.

6

THREE BLACK KINGS
A TRIBUTE TO BLACK HISTORY

"NO FOUR KISSES PLEASE"

In spring 1974, anyone passing through Columbia Presbyterian Hospital's Harkness Pavilion would probably have come across a strange sign. Next to the door of one room, a notice read: "No four kisses please."[1] The only patient who could have gone to the pains of prohibiting this gesture was Duke Ellington. As a greeting, he was indeed in the habit of exchanging four kisses. He did so with everyone, his closest friends and heads of state, jazz fans and reverends, lovers and university deans. When questioned about this eccentric ritual of his, his reply appears to have been provocative, even impudent: "I give a kiss to each of your cheeks."[2]

It is heartening to know that not even a tumor could ruin Ellington's sense of humor. Admittedly, he decided to suspend this rigid protocol, exhausted as he was. On the other hand, the need he felt to excuse himself and communicate this change in his code of behavior, even when he was at death's door, was his way of mocking fate. His illness dictated that he would give no more concerts (his last was held in Indiana on March 22, 1974) and eventually took him away (on May 24 of that same year). But it could not unnerve the Duke during his last two months spent in the hospital. As always, he had plenty of work to do and no time to give any thought to death.

Indeed, even though the support shown by his family and the visits made by his friends lifted his spirits (as did the flowers sent by Frank Sinatra and the caviar delivered by Norman Granz), truth be told, he had only one thought: putting the final touches on two scores. And while the entire country celebrated his birthday on April 29, 1974, with a host of initiatives, the Duke was busy giving instructions to the musicians charged with completing these works. They got together at his bedside, sheet music in their hands, with an electric piano placed next to his bed, which kept him company as though it was a fellow patient in his hospital room.[3]

One of the two scores gave him less to worry about. The comic opera *Queenie Pie* had been virtually completed in the summer of 1973, even though it may be significant that his main collaborator for this project, Betty McGettigan, often visited the Duke at the Harkness Pavilion (and was apparently the last person to see him alive).[4] But the other score still needed a lot of work. It was a ballet that Ellington wanted to present in symphonic form in addition to its big band version; the score was to be completed by his loyal orchestrator, Luther Henderson. Indulging his penchant for playing with words, especially in French, he titled it *Les trois rois noirs* (*The Three Black Kings*): a tribute to three great figures in Black history. Ellington made every effort to communicate his ideas to his son Mercer and also tried to get the eminent musicologist and composer Gunther Schuller involved, but the latter had previous commitments and left for a tour.[5] At 3:10 a.m. on May 24, when the Duke was forced to meet the only deadline he could not avoid, the Black Kings were not entirely ready. But the Duke Ellington Orchestra, led by Mercer, decided to perform it all the same for audiences in Europe, which took place in winter and spring 1975, during this ensemble's first European tour.[6]

THE JOURNEY OF THE KINGS

The day after the funeral, Mercer left with the orchestra for Bermuda to honor a commitment his father had accepted, fully confirming the saying "like father, like son." After a few gigs with Lloyd Mayers at the piano, Mercer quickly took the big band to the recording studio for two sessions, held on July 16 and 17, 1974, which led to good results. Then, between the January 6 and 7, 1975, sessions and the ones held on May 12, the band left for its first European tour, which gave it the chance to present the previously unheard suite titled *Three Black Kings*.[7]

In Paris, on February 6, the audience wholeheartedly applauded the work even though the performance seems to have shown a few loose ends, mostly in the first movement. The performances given on February 20 at the Hammersmith Odeon in London and on March 14 in Barcelona were similarly marred, and the version heard on March 21 in Reading also proved to be unsatisfactory since the trumpets were not in good shape. The poor acoustics at the Stokesay Castle restaurant (a rather kitschy imitation of a medieval English castle) were even more ill-suited for a jazz orchestra.[8] Be this as it may, the three kings, a bit the worse for wear, came back to the United States from a tour that, in any case, got the ball rolling. In the end, the true premiere, where the *Three Black Kings* would have been treated with all due respect for their station, had yet to come. And it came.

The *New York Times* announced on April 20, 1976, that with an initiative promoted by New York Governor Hugh Carey and Mayor Abraham Beame, April 29 would be "Duke Ellington Day." For the composer's birthday, the Cathedral of St. John the Divine was to host the orchestra conducted by Mercer: *Three Black Kings* was on the program, now to be unveiled in the United States.[9] The newspaper omitted that the occasion, to which celebrities coming from well outside jazz circles (including Muhammad Ali) had been invited, was to be graced with an exceptional female presence: the First Lady herself. Mrs. Betty Ford, even though she could only stay for fifteen minutes before rushing to another event (at the Mark Hellinger Theatre at 8:00 p.m.), had words of praise for the initiative, adding that she herself was "one of the many, many fans of his music."[10]

At that evening concert, titled "Ellington Is Forever," *Three Black Kings* was played with a precision unequaled by the European performances (for example, the trumpet theme in the second movement finally sounded like it was supposed to). Mercer had also gotten over a few doubts as to the tempo of the first movement, speeding things up this time by at least thirty notches on the metronome.[11] Furthermore, while the orchestra was taking the kings back and forth between Europe and America, another man was at work, a key figure in this work's transformation into what the Duke had desired.

African American choreographer Alvin Ailey had told the *New York Times* on April 13, 1975, that the New York State Theater, during the month of August, would celebrate the Duke's music for two weeks with a myriad of choreographies. For this sumptuous million-dollar project, in addition to presenting his own works, Ailey wanted to invite leading artists of the world of dance, such as George Balanchine and Jerome Robbins.[12] In the end, these two masters did not participate, but for two weeks in mid-August 1976, no fewer than seventeen choreographies created by ten different dancers came to life at Lincoln Center Theater.

Ailey's dream only partially came true, not just because instead of famous choreographers, he had to settle for the less-renowned ones (some of whom were, in any case, extremely talented, such as Louis Falco) but also because everything came together too late. His idea of paying tribute to "our black

Stravinsky" with a huge event to "celebrate this man while he's alive" went up in smoke, given that the first edition of *Ailey Celebrates Ellington* was created for TV in November 1974, a few months after the Duke's death.[13] In 1975, no funds were available, so Ailey only worked on a theater adaptation of "The Mooche" and *Night Creature*, two numbers he had worked on for the TV celebration one year earlier, which were included in his ballet season. 1976, instead, turned out to be the right year for the second official edition. This is because the bicentennial of American independence gave the event an even more prestigious backdrop; the poster, indeed, featured a photo of a blue-colored Ellington against a background of red and white stripes.

Between August 10 and 22, the festival presented choreographies by Lester Horton (*Liberian Suite*), Talley Beatty (*The Road of the Phoebe Snow*), Milton Myers (*Echoes in Blue*), Louis Falco (*Caravan*), Cristyne Lawson (*Still Life*), Raymond Sawyer (*Afro-Eurasian Eclipse*), Dianne McIntyre (*Deep South Suite*), Gus Solomons Jr. (*Forty*), Alvin McDuffie (*New Orleans Junction*) and—obviously—Ailey. The latter proposed a few of his previous works such as *The River* (danced for the occasion by the prestigious company American Dance Theater), Night Creature, "The Mooche," *Reflections in D* and *Blues Suite* (only the latter was not set to music by Ellington). He also included specifically created works such as the sumptuous *Black, Brown and Beige*, a pas de deux, or rather a *Pas de Duke* as he ironically titled it, that featured ballet star Mikhail Baryshnikov, and a ballet in three parts to a posthumous work intended for dance by Ellington himself: *Three Black Kings*.

The choreography with the "three kings" was the most recent sign of the great esteem Ailey had felt for Ellington since the early fifties. As a young man, he heard the Duke live on various occasions and had the chance to meet him personally in 1952, when he was called by choreographer Lester Horton to dance in his latest work, *Liberian Suite*. Ellington was present at the rehearsals. Ailey began creating ballets to music by Ellington in 1963, the year in which he completed the sublime solo *Reflections in D*. During the summer of that same year, the two were in direct contact for the project *My People*, an opera for jazz orchestra, choir, solo voices, narrator, and two dance companies. One was led by Talley Beatty, with whom Ellington had previously collaborated in *A Drum Is a Woman*, and the other was the Alvin Ailey American Dance Theater. In 1970, Ailey commissioned a score that the famous American Ballet Theatre soon staged: *The River*, one of the most outstanding pieces in Ellington's late production and one of Ailey's most successful ballets.[14]

In the summer of 1976, when *Three Black Kings* saw the light, Ailey had choreographed a dozen or so works by Ellington. In order to make sure he got everything just right, since the dance had been rehearsed according to a rather tight schedule, he tried it out one month before the premiere, giving the public a preview of it at the Artpark in Lewiston (New York) on July 7. The official debut took place on August 13 at Lincoln Center's State Theater. And while on August 10, the speech for the celebration's opening night was given by the First Lady, Mrs. Betty Ford, three days later, for *Three Black Kings*, the same task went to Coretta Scott King, the widow of Martin Luther King Jr., to whom the third movement is dedicated.

On that occasion, the Duke Ellington Orchestra, conducted by Mercer in front of a particularly attentive audience, which included the Duke's sister Ruth, played this posthumous score and a medley of famous melodies by Ellington. Arnold Jay Smith, writing for *DownBeat*, found that the big band was in great shape and the dance was captivating.[15] Even though Ailey's work on *Three Black Kings* didn't convince everyone (the November 1976 issue of *Dance Magazine* had harsh words for this ballet, calling it "vulgar"), his choreography represented a crucial step that brought the work closer to Ellington's original idea.[16] And yet the three Black kings, as the Duke had decreed, deserved to appear in a symphonic guise. And this was the very form in which they went to Yale University to receive their due.

The *Yale Daily News* announced on September 23, 1977, that on October 14 at 8:30 p.m. in the University's Woolsey Hall, a number of jazz giants would come together for a very special concert.[17] This live event, planned by horn player and bassist Willie Ruff, was intended to raise the funds required to create a "Duke Ellington Scholarship Program." The musicians that paid homage to the Duke that evening included Dave Brubeck, Louie Bellson, Count Basie, Billy Eckstine, Lionel Hampton, Benny Carter, Slam Stewart, Milt Hinton, and Jaki Byard.

This important event did not receive much attention (only the *New York Times* dedicated a short article to it on October 9), but it did feature two highlights. The first was a surprise performance by Bellson's wife, who was invited onstage to sing "The Way We Were." Since the woman in question was the great Pearl Bailey, this unexpected moment turned out to be magical. The second was the world premiere of the concerto grosso version of *Three Black Kings*.[18] This work, whose score had been finished by Luther Henderson, saw the Duke Ellington Orchestra (with Bellson on the drums) performing together with Yale's Philharmonia Orchestra. Mercer, even while complaining that some orchestral musicians had abandoned their posts and were replaced by younger colleagues, stated that the audience's response was absolutely extraordinary.[19]

Only one thing was missing for the three kings to be enthroned: a recording. Even if only indirectly, it turned out to be the State Department that took care of this. While preparing his second European tour planned for autumn/winter 1977, Mercer called the State Department, which put together a series of concerts in Poland, one of which would also involve the Polish National Philharmonic Orchestra.[20] Notified in late August, the organizers of the famous Jazz Jamboree Festival programmed two concerts by the Duke Ellington Orchestra for the event's opening and closing dates. On October 19, it performed at the Palace of Culture and Science Congress Hall for an audience of two thousand, and on October 24, it appeared at the Philharmonic Concert Hall alongside the Polish National Philharmonic Orchestra.[21] That evening, the jazz orchestra played some famous pieces by the Duke; together with the symphony orchestra, in addition to an enjoyable version of Stevie Wonder's "Sir Duke," it also performed *New World A-Comin'* (with Adam Makowicz at the piano) and *The River* conducted by Wojciech Rajski while Mercer took the baton for *Three Black Kings*. The concert, which was broadcast on national television, was partially released on the album *Remembering Duke's World* (Polijazz) and partially on *Three Black Kings* (Frog Box). The latter contains the first official recording of the work currently under discussion.[22] The three kings, after a long journey, had reached their destination. But who were these three dignitaries to whom a dying Duke of jazz had dedicated his last thoughts?

"KING OF THE NATIVITY": THE BLACK AND BEAUTIFUL KING

From the stage of the Palau de la Música Catalana in Barcelona, during a concert held on March 14, 1975, Mercer Ellington introduced the first king with the following words: "The first [of the three kings] I'm sure was inspired by our visit to Santa Maria del Mar, where you'll find a glass window with the three Kings of the Nativity, one of which is black."[23]

The Duke had given a triumphal sacred concert in Barcelona's Gothic cathedral on November 24, 1969, and returned on November 10, 1973, only a few months before his death. In all likelihood, he admired the eight stained-glass windows and the central rose window. He did not, however, conceive the "King of the Nativity" here for one simple reason: among the religious themes portrayed in this church's glass mosaics, there is no reference whatsoever to the adoration of the Magi. The Duke must have come across this Black king somewhere else. Mercer had gotten things mixed up.[24] In itself, this is unsurprising because the story of the Magi, as seen over the history of art, is rather confusing in itself. Incredible as it may seem, a brief glance at the history of these representations, starting from the earliest centuries of Christianity, will lead us back to Harlem and the Black Renaissance, thus giving us a better understanding of the deepest meaning of the Duke's score.

As we were saying, the whole thing is rather perplexing; how else to define a story whose protagonists are three kings when the Bible does not state that they were kings nor that there were three of them? Even their famous names, Caspar, Melchior, and Balthazar, are a problem. They do not appear in the only canonical text that refers to the Magi who came from the East to visit the newborn King of the Jews. Over the centuries, new details were invented and added to the story: first, the magi priests became kings, and then, around the tenth century, were considered symbols of the three ages of man (a white-haired old man, a middle-aged man with a dark beard, and a clean-shaven youth). Around one hundred years later, they acquired the names by which we know them today, after which the idea took hold that the Magi represented the three continents known at the time: Europe, Asia, and Africa. This is where, slowly but surely, the Black king comes into the picture.[25]

Indeed, even though the *magio fuscus* became part of Western iconography as of 1300, this troublesome figure had some difficulty in establishing a place for himself; sometimes, he didn't succeed in the least. If we were to go for a stroll among the paintings found in Turin's Galleria Sabauda, we would discover that Renaissance artist Defendente Ferrari did not include a Black king in his Adoration of the Magi (nor does one appear in the many other works with the same subject found in that gallery). Or, if we chose to visit London's National Gallery, we would come across a delicate Adoration painted by Filippino Lippi in 1480, whose magi are all patently white. Art history, therefore, offers us, as though under an intermittent or stroboscopic light, examples in which the young king is Black and cases in which he is white.[26]

Seen this way, naming one movement after the African king of nativity was not in the least an innocuous gesture. It's as though the Duke had respectfully agreed to disagree with the many painters (including almost all of Italy's great masters, such as Botticelli, Raffaello, Ghirlandaio, and Leonardo) who opted for a Caucasian Balthazar, denying that this biblical figure was Black.[27] Put briefly, what Ellington did in his score is similar to what the German artist Hans Memling did on canvas in 1464 when he made an almost identical copy of Rogier van der Weyden's 1460 Adoration of the Magi, introducing, however, a Black king instead of the white one.

But the Duke's tribute didn't only consist in underlining the presence of the Black king. His "king of nativity" was to be, first and foremost, noble, gracious, and dignified; in the words of the "new Negro," beautiful. Art history had almost constantly denied this "black beauty." The king in the Adoration by Mantegna (1500), with full red lips and his markedly flat nose, falls into the stereotype of the grotesque Black that stretches from the thirteenth century to the minstrel show. The king depicted by Bosch, in some interpretations, has even been taken to incarnate the Antichrist. We must only add that Balthazar was often represented as the least important of the three (the farthest from the Virgin and her Child), sometimes even cut out of the picture, as in one illumination found in an early fourteenth-century Austrian missal. Here, inside a capital "A," there is room for the Virgin, Jesus, and two Magi, but not for Balthazar. Covered by the initial letter of the word, only a glimpse of his face remains. Seeing him look onto the scene from behind that letter, as though he was outside a window peeking at a party to which he hadn't been invited, is truly touching![28]

The Duke's "King of the Nativity" is, on the contrary, the only protagonist present. He is Black. And he is beautiful. Locke would have been proud of this first movement. This Harlem Renaissance ideologist was strongly interested in visual art and, beginning in the twenties, dedicated essays, articles, and two volumes to it. In the latter, *Negro Art: Past and Present* (1936) and *The Negro in Art: A Pictorial Record of the Negro Artist and of the Negro Theme in Art* (1940), he chastised all European and American artists who used racist clichés when portraying Blacks and praised those who showed them in their natural beauty. In the second volume, he reflected on the theme of the adoration of the Magi, and in so doing, didn't mince his words. When speaking of how the Black king was depicted, he states without reserve that it was "the most artificial of all the Negro art stereotypes" in art history. Lamenting the complete lack of realism, he concludes that "it added little to true Negro portrayal." As though trying to set the record straight on centuries of iconography, he then mentions a carefully selected list of works by masters including Van Leyden, Massys, Grunewald, and Dürer, all artists who had shown respect for the African king and brought out his true grace.[29] Langston Hughes probably recalled this lesson when conceiving *Black Nativity* (1961), a sort of gospel musical with an all-Black cast in which Alvin Ailey also participated. The Three Wise Men were interpreted by prominent members of the local Black community.

While we have no way of knowing whether the Duke was acquainted with Locke's writings, the chances are he was not. Nevertheless, the fact that both of them felt the same need to bring the king who had been relegated to the margins back to center stage and restore the beauty of one who had lost it tells us that the precepts of the Harlem Renaissance (regardless of whether he learned them directly or indirectly) were still part of the Duke's poetics in the seventies.

The second theme of "King of the Nativity," in particular, has much to tell us about Ellington's desire to change the history books. Beauty permeates this minute portion of music; only ten bars long, this theme is strong enough to sustain the musical narration covering the entire thirty-six-page score. Here, what the Duke offers us is the painting that was missing in the entire history of art: the Black king is alone in front of Baby Jesus. And, during this fleeting yet eternal moment, he is joyfully overwhelmed by the force of this encounter. For this ecstatic vision, Ellington composed a sober theme in long notes whose cantabile expression mainly revolves around the leading notes of the chords. The melody is given to the trumpets in the big band version and doubled by the violins in the symphonic orchestration. It is sustained by an interesting harmonic progression with direct modulations by thirds: the last measures, which pass from F major to D flat major and ultimately come to rest on the basic tonality, B flat major, perfectly render Balthazar's sense of disorientation.[30]

The passage dedicated to this encounter with the Savior is preceded by a marvelously descriptive first theme: this fragmentary melody, only four notes with a pentatonic profile, suggests the three wise men's long pilgrimage across the desert. It is accompanied by intricate rhythms in the drums, representing the various tribes that live here.[31] The motif G-C-Bb-F, obsessively repeated à la Steve Reich, comes together with other rhythmic figures and goes through a few changes in meter. Scattered here and there in the middle of the relentless forward motion, Ellington included small spaces that express a relative peace, mostly rendered with the octatonic scale, thus using a sequence of notes that, in music history, has often been associated with the supernatural.[32]

"KING SOLOMON": REFLECTED SHADES OF BLACK

Whatever the case may be with Balthazar, there is no lack of Moors in the Bible. We find two Ethiopian eunuchs: Ebed-Melech, who saved the prophet Jeremiah's life, and an anonymous one, often represented in illuminated bibles in the act of converting to Christianity. Then there is the Egyptian Agar who, as narrated in Genesis, gave birth to Abraham's son, Ishmael; the uncompromising Ethiopian pharaoh, Tirhakah; the Egyptian Asenath, who became Joseph's wife after giving up her false idols; and Moses's wife, Zipporah, mentioned in the book of Exodus, who is portrayed in all her beauty in a painting by Jacob Jordaens (1650).

The list might go on even if we were to exclude Church Fathers (such as the North African Augustine of Hippo) and saints (such as the Roman commander St. Maurice). But it would certainly not include Solomon. Mercer Ellington may well have maintained that this biblical character was Black because he was an ancestor of the last Ethiopian emperor, Haile Selassie, but virtually no Biblical exegesis has come to the same conclusion. Surely enough, in Western iconography, he is only represented as being white.[33]

What the Duke had in mind when including this character in his score was probably not the color of his skin but his relationship with Africans. Solomon's attraction toward beautiful dark-skinned women is well-known, such as the one who introduces herself in the Song of Songs with the words "I am black but beautiful" (Song of Songs, 1:5); this declaration, even with the adversative conjunction, is somewhat like a precursor of the expression "Black is beautiful" long before it was coined. In the end, he married her; the illuminated Bible of Evert Zoudenbalch (1465) shows the two of them (portraying her very Black and very beautiful) a second before their lips meet in a kiss, like in a snapshot.[34] But the most famous Black wife of Solomon (who seems to have had wives aplenty) is no doubt the Queen of Sheba, whom the Duke knew quite well. In 1959, he dedicated the "Apes and Peacocks" movement of the *Queen's Suite* to her, referring to the gifts she brought to Solomon. Ellington, as his son later recalled, scrupulously annotated the respective passage in the First Book of Kings before writing the music, and when biographer Stanley Dance confessed that he did not grasp the link with the scriptures, the Duke chastised him, telling him to read the Bible as soon as he could, all of it, the Old and the New Testament![35] So it may well have been the black projected onto the figure of Solomon by the Queen of Sheba or by his "black but beautiful" wife that gave him the honor of becoming the second of Ellington's three Black kings.[36]

In the score, the entrance of the wise ruler is announced by augmented-triad arpeggios that lead to the key of C major. At this point, a carefully devised sixteen-bar melody begins, once again based on arpeggiated figures, which then leads to a second section, having the same length but with an even more lyrical melodic line.

In the big band orchestration, the melody of the first episode, which we will indicate as A, was written for the piano with only the winds in the background; in the symphonic version, the theme went to the harp and the strings were added to the saxophones. The second thematic moment of this

| C^6_9 | $E7^{\sharp 9}$ | $A7^{\sharp 9}$ | D^{13} | G^{sus} | $G^{sus\flat 9}$ | C^6_9 | C^6_9 |

Ex. 6.1. "Melancholia," chords.

| C^6_9 | $E7^{\sharp 9}$ | $A9^{\sharp 11}$ | $A9^{\sharp 11}$ | D^9 | G^{13} | $C7^{\sharp 9}$ | $C7^{\sharp 9}$ | $(F^\triangle)$ |

Ex. 6.2. "King Solomon," harmony, episode A'.

episode, which we will call A', was instead given to a solo trumpet in both scores. It doesn't seem possible for such an inspired and delicate moment to be based on the simplest, most threadbare harmonic progression imaginable: a series of descending fifths. Nor should we forget that the Duke had demonstrated, years before, how enchanting this Baroque formula can be if used with refined voicing and associated with the right sort of melody. This was the case with the chords in "Melancholia," a masterful ballad composed in 1953, which we have transposed from D flat to C major to make the comparison easier (ex. 6.1).

The first eight bars of A' in "King Solomon" initially follow the same path. The longer theme associated with Solomon then deviates toward the subdominant, touches on other intermediate chords, and winds up where it started, on a C6/9 chord (ex. 6.2).

Then episode B arrives: the tempo goes from andante to allegro, and a fairly raw sixteen-bar bossa nova gradually leads from F minor back to the basic tonality. Once this Latin moment has come to a close, the peaceful A theme comes back to the center of our attention.

At this point, King Solomon—interpreted on the tenor sax by Ricky Ford in the live concerts held during the first European tour and by David Young in a symphonic concert in Poland in 1977—is given a sixty-four-bar AA'BA chorus that consists only in the harmonic outline of the various episodes previously heard, over which he improvises, now turning to wild pleasure. The King reaches 240 beats per minute to the quarter note in the third and last solo choruses. Mercer maintained that this section portrayed our biblical character's huge sexual appetite (it is said that Solomon had seven hundred wives without counting his concubines, who apparently numbered about three hundred). The reappearance of A', with the enchanting *andante* theme played on the trumpet by Willie Singleton, brings us back to decency in a dignified finale.

"MARTIN LUTHER KING JR." IN BIRMINGHAM AND THE FAR WEST

Martin Luther King Jr. asks his driver to stop the car. He's just seen a man whose hand he wants to shake. That man is Duke Ellington. This story, told by an immensely proud Duke in his memoirs and relayed in greater detail by their common friend Marian Logan, took place in Chicago in August 1963. On the sixteenth of that same month, as part of the "Century of Negro Progress Exposition," a celebration of the centennial of Lincoln's Emancipation Proclamation, five thousand people flocked to the debut of Ellington's stage show *My People*. One of them was Martin Luther King Jr., who, at the end of the concert, gave him a plaque in recognition of "his contribution to American society through music." The Duke reciprocated by giving the Reverend the manuscript of a composition inspired by him.[37] This piece was "King Fit the Battle of Alabam,'" an arrangement of the spiritual "Joshua Fit the Battle of Jericho." The Duke had written a new, sardonic text for this piece, transferring the combat from the ancient city in Canaan to today's Birmingham, the capital of Jefferson County (Alabama), continually in the news due to the turmoil between the racist police and the pacific African American demonstrators led by King. The champion of the Civil Rights Movement, who listened to the rehearsals in the afternoon, was moved by this dedication.[38]

After King's death, a host of twentieth-century musicians paid tribute to him. In 1968, the year of his assassination, Rostropovič commissioned Oskar Morawetz to write the cello concerto *A Memorial to Martin Luther King*, Luciano Berio wrote *O King*, African American composer Olly Wilson conceived the work for chorus and electronic sounds of *In Memoriam Martin Luther King, Jr.*, Mary Lou Williams had her say with "I Have a Dream," and George Russell contributed with his *Electronic Sonata for Souls Loved by Nature*. These were only the first voices in a chorus that eventually comprised hundreds of musicians active in any and all genres (a list of works could range from Petrassi's chamber oratorio *Beatitudines: Testimonianza per Martin Luther King* [1969] to the lullaby "MLK" [1984] by U2).[39] And yet the world of music offered very few tributes to the Reverend while he was still alive: the list would be rather short but would include the piece by Ellington mentioned above, which proves the admiration he felt for King. This was a man whom, in Mercer's words, he considered "his main man" and he literally "adored."[40]

As of the summer of 1963, Ellington remained close to King, partially owing to their mutual friends, the Logan family. Marian, the wife of Dr.

a4	a4	a4	b8	a4	Transition 2	a4	b'9	a4	b'9	a4	Transition 4	a4	Coda (=Tr.2)
C maj.							mod. from C maj. to Eb maj.	Eb maj.	mod. from Eb maj. to C maj.		C maj.		

Ex. 6.3. "Martin Luther King," formal outline.

Arthur Logan, the Duke's private physician, met King on various occasions and sided with him in many battles, for which she also recruited prominent musicians such as Lena Horne and Billy Strayhorn.

When, on April 4, 1968, King was killed by a rifle shot at a Memphis motel, Ellington was extremely grieved. To alleviate the pain felt by King's widow and ease her worries, left alone with four children, he gave a few fundraising concerts. Six years later, from his hospital room, he expressed his most sincere feelings in the final movement of the ballet discussed in this chapter. And yet, as we know, death came a bit too early, and the Duke was unable to put the finishing touches on this same third movement, which was so important to him.

"Martin Luther King," it must unfortunately be said, has one clear compositional weakness. The first to realize this was Mercer, who, almost as though apologizing, said, "One of Pop's superstitions was not to write the finale or ending of a piece until the last day before a performance . . . unfortunately [in this case] he had taken this finale with him."

A 12/8 meter and a straightforward harmonic progression, both inspired by gospel music, underpin a concise theme, the only one heard in this third movement, whose formal outline is shown in example 6.3.

The very fact that only a single theme appears might point toward an unfinished work, considering that "King of the Nativity" and "King Solomon" both feature two main themes inserted in the broader narration of a three-part form. What's more, upon closer inspection, the theme of "Martin Luther King" is only found in the *a* section, which is four bars long; the *b* section, which lasts eight bars, does not have a true melodic line. It is as though we were dealing with a work in progress, a song form interrupted before the harmonic frame of the bridge was provided with a melody.

One must add that the orchestrations, both for symphony orchestra and, above all, for big band, instead of patching things up, only made the situation worse. The prosaic, monotonous riff inserted in almost all the *a* sections may be well suited for an album by the Platters, but not a ballet by Ellington (ex. 6.4).

Ex. 6.4. "Martin Luther King," riff.

In the jazz orchestra version, where this figure is given the full sonority of the brass, it seems even more clearly in bad taste. A few trite harmonic cadences, inserted along the lines of a transition after the exposition of melody A, ruin one of the most inspired passages in the score, the four-bar theme itself (whose outline is Tr.2; Tr.'4; Coda). The decision to include a two-voice improvisation in the part of the score in E flat major (a4-b'9) seems equally unoriginal. In the jazz orchestra adaptation, Mercer and Henderson opted for a counterpoint between the trombone with plunger mute and the trumpet. Joint improvisation, given to two or three instruments, appears throughout Ellington's music from the twenties to the works of his late period, but something doesn't seem to work in this passage of "Martin Luther King." It may not be by chance that this tactic was not repeated in the symphonic version.

Each new orchestration of the third movement of *Three Black Kings* that appeared after the big band arrangement, which was finished sometime between the date of Ellington's death and January 1975, conveys the difficulty of trying to refine a piece often weighed down by a sense of awkwardness. Each recording made, indeed, makes a further effort in this direction. In the one that appeared in 1977, the riff mentioned above, now played by the strings, sounds a bit less crude; furthermore, the inappropriate collective improvisation was eliminated from this version. The 1988 recording conducted by Maurice Peress, who prepared a new orchestration, shows great attention to detail and tends toward a more elegant expression, most notably with Jimmy Heath's contribution on the soprano sax, which makes up for the lack of melodic themes by providing highly tasteful improvised melodic ideas.[41]

The recording made by the Buffalo Philharmonic Orchestra in 2012 returns to Luther Henderson's score, making, however, a number of changes to it: for example, a concertante clarinet is introduced that gives a delicate color to the various sections.[42] Other musicians have adopted a more radical approach: Enrico Intra, conducting the Civica Jazz Band and the Giuseppe Verdi Symphony Orchestra of Milan, decided to eliminate the third movement of *Three Black Kings* entirely, recording only the first two movements, arranged in a novel order: here, "King of the Nativity" not only opens but, after "King Solomon," also closes the work.[43]

Walter Rutledge, in an interview with his fellow dancer Dudley Williams, who, in Ailey's version, danced the role of Martin Luther King Jr., also expressed some skepticism about this music, which, in his opinion, sounds "uncharacteristically gospel for Ellington."[44] Actually, the Duke wrote plenty of gospel pieces, a few of which, such as the ones found in *My People* and the three *Sacred Concerts*, are extremely well crafted, and "Portrait of Mahalia Jackson," part of the *New Orleans Suite*, is a masterpiece. As a young African American man, Rutledge worked with Ailey's company and certainly knew Ellington; with these words, he clearly meant that he felt uncomfortable with a piece of music that was much too ordinary to have been written by the Duke.

"We searched for a piano tape or an illustration record, anything that might provide a clue to the way he wanted the work to end."[45] Once again, this is a desperate Mercer begging our forgiveness. And yet the Duke's son, before giving up, should perhaps have looked a bit harder for that tape.

In 1961, photographer Sam Shaw, who for many years had immortalized celebrities in the world of cinema, decided to play a new role in that same environment. Now working as a producer, he created *Paris Blues*.[46] The soundtrack was composed by Duke Ellington. While the two men had briefly encountered one another in a professional context around twenty years earlier, this was their only project that was successfully completed.

Shaw initially wanted to become an artist, which led him to rent a studio together with the young Romare Bearden. As of the forties, he chose photography and began collaborating with *Collier*, often collaborating with journalist Harry Henderson for this magazine.[47] Among the stories they published jointly, whose subjects ranged from miners in West Virginia to jazzmen in New Orleans, the one that appeared in the January 30, 1943, issue under the title "This Strange Bright Land" caught the Duke's attention. He wished to transform its narrative, based on a group of English sailors captivated by Broadway, into a musical. Unfortunately, the show, to be titled *H.M.S. Times Square*, never saw the light of day.[48]

Two decades later, as mentioned above, Shaw and the Duke were in France for *Paris Blues*, interpreted by Paul Newman and Sidney Poitier. On this occasion, the two went from being simple acquaintances to friends. When, in 1968, Shaw wished to try his hand at yet another profession, now working behind the camera as a director, he asked Ellington to look after the music. The idea was to make documentaries dedicated to great painters; Shaw and Ellington, indeed, shared a passion for art history. None of the films were ever completed. Work on the one dedicated to Matisse never even began. The only film that almost reached its finished form was the one on Degas.

Ellington had already recorded the music, and yet things came to a halt when the film was just about to be completed.[49] Moreover, between one session and the next of his work on *Racing World* (which was to be the film's title), Shaw frenetically took on even more work, proposing a third project that was also to involve Ellington: an obscure documentary about the Far West. Nothing whatsoever was known about this film until quite recently. In this sense, the information provided by Edie Shaw, the director's son, who, in 1968, had just graduated from Pratt Institute in Brooklyn and was involved in working on these documentaries, turned out to be very precious.[50]

The film was not intended to deal with the Far West in a general way but to specifically focus on paintings by two of the great American artists who, in the late nineteenth and early twentieth centuries, created the iconography of the Old Wild West: Frederic Remington and Charles Marion Russell.[51] For this film, featuring paintings of landscapes, cowboys, and Indigenous Americans, Edie Shaw was entrusted with the graphics, preparing the slides and designing the cover for the soundtrack. In addition to compositions by the Duke, the latter was also to include other music, more in sync with the subject, such as the *Concert for 5-String Banjo* by Earl Robinson, which virtuoso Eric Weissberg premiered in 1967, accompanied by the Boston Symphony conducted by Arthur Fiedler. The film, titled *Remington & Russell West*, was never released in theaters due to a lack of funding.

The only sound document that survived from this project is a tape recorded by Ellington on December 3, 1968. It is a musical portrayal of the Duke's impressions while observing a painting of a family of Indigenous Americans crossing a barren landscape on horseback. With this painting in his mind's eye, during the third session for the *Degas Suite*, Ellington recorded a score initially titled "Elous" (a sort of anagram of "soul," with an "E" added at the beginning to fool the overly curious) and eventually copyrighted as "Elos."[52] I was able to examine various contact sheets of the photos of the paintings but could not, however, obtain a complete list of the works to be included in *Remington & Russell West*. Nonetheless, the oil painting that fascinated Ellington may have been Charles Russell's *Piegans* (1918).

While the painting cannot be definitively identified, the music can most certainly be recognized: "Elos" is identical to the third movement of *Three Black Kings*, "Elos" is "Martin Luther King"! While examining the masterpieces by Remington and Russell, the Duke most likely drew a parallel between the dignity of the Native American communities, in spite of their slow decline, and the great pride felt by African Americans, even at that difficult point in history. After the project for the film fell through, Ellington perhaps thought it would be natural to return to that music, transforming

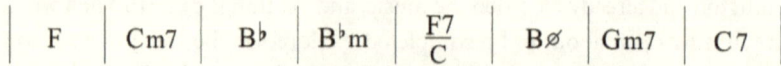

Ex. 6.5. "Elos," bridge (*b* section).

it into a portrait of his friend Martin, the man who instilled an unshakable self-respect in his people. The recording of "Elos" is, therefore, the track that Mercer and Henderson spent so much effort looking for and that could have radically changed the fate of the third Black king.

"Elos" is little more than a recorded rehearsal containing a sort of song form with the bridge unexpectedly inserted between the *a* sections (ex. 6.5). The piece's structure, indeed, diverges from the typical *aaba*.[53] As a sketch, however, it is extremely pure and always inspired. "Elos" does not suffer from heavy riffs and is not compromised by inelegant harmonic cadences; its chords, simple as those in gospel music, have no need of being transposed to other keys, coming across naturally in F major from the beginning to the end. Little does it matter if the *b* section does not have a theme of its own: both times it appears, Johnny Hodges would have improvised an appropriate melody. The appearance of the alto sax during the bridge, furthermore, creates an evocative contrast with the *a* section which, on the contrary, insists each time on the melodic line written by Ellington, with improvisation only providing brief comments on it.

To avoid monotony, the Duke decided that each time this section appeared, it would have a different timbre. He thus chose five shades of color: the entire orchestra, with fills by trombonist Buster Cooper; Paul Gonsalves, with comments by the other tenor saxophonist Harold Ashby; trombones and then winds, with fragments added by Buster Cooper; and, in the last *a* section, the orchestra with the lead given to the clarinet, along with free interpolations by Cooper and the winds. This is a hymn to simplicity, as is also clear in the harmonic foundation, consisting in only a few—yet uniquely fascinating—chords.

The bridge, too, is admirable: the *b* section begins in the same key as *a*, but in its second bar starts to move toward IV, passing through a moving minor dominant.[54] An interesting effect also comes from the F7 with a C in the bass and a gospel feel that leads chromatically to an expressive semi-diminished chord. While the *a* section, based on the simple progression I-vi-IV-ii-V in F major, does not require any analysis, a note on the number of bars might be helpful. These eight bars unfold in 12/8 time, with the dotted quarter note proceeding at 55 bpm, meaning that the harmonic rhythm is extremely slow. This adagio, with its distended chords, takes a very different shape in "Martin Luther King," whose *a* section was condensed into only four bars. The idea of boundless landscapes, infinite prairies, and noble souls animated by an immense feeling of pride completely disappears. Four bars, whose harmonic rhythm is twice as fast, do not express any of this; they are simply a turnaround.

In the belief that musicology, once it has completed its examination of scores and historical documents, must bring its results to the attention of musicians, artistic directors, and institutions and thus transform its conclusions into real projects, I decided to contact composer and arranger Bruno Tommaso, who has vast experience in both classical and jazz music and an excellent knowledge of Ellington, requesting that he rewrite the last movement of *Three Black Kings* based on "Elos" and its meaning.

This piece, freed from the less-inspired elements of "Martin Luther King" and modeled on the transparency of the music written for the documentary, was conceived for concertante clarinet, an instrument to which Ellington turned on more than one occasion for solo passages in his symphonic works. As in the Duke's own practice, the score was written to highlight the specific technical and expressive skills of a particular musician, virtuoso Bepi D'Amato (esteemed by Tony Scott and Buddy DeFranco, with whom he collaborated on various occasions). Tommaso wrote a sixteen-bar introduction, divided symmetrically in half. In the first part, he gave a pentatonic motif to the winds (similar to the one that appears repeatedly within the first theme of "King of the Nativity"). Here, the imitative writing creates a dense counterpoint supported by long notes in the strings, which only use harmonics (once again suggesting the idea of wide-open spaces). In the second part, he decided to introduce a chordal figure in the trombones while at the same time letting the strings take part in the contrapuntal writing.

The theme was then divided among various solo instruments and orchestral combinations, following the example of "Elos" yet opting for different solutions. The solo clarinet was inserted in an eight-bar modulating section, which, passing through B flat major and E flat major, then leads to the basic key of F major for the last appearance of the *a* section, still embellished by D'Amato's solo. This virtuoso then plays a free cadenza that eventually leads to one bar of written music full of perilous high notes (one of this Italian clarinetist's specialties). The second eight-bar phrase of the introduction then rounds off the work.

A chance to perform this score in front of an audience soon arose. With the support of the Società Italiana di Musicologia Afroamericana, Bruno Tommaso conducted the Orchestra del Teatro Marrucino di Chieti and the SIdMA Jazz Orchestra, presenting his own arrangement as part of a concert featuring other rare works by Ellington (conceived by the author of this book). A recording was made of the concert held in Chieti on March 6, 2007, in order to be publicly released. The recording of that performance, made accessible on the ICAMus channels, thus represents the final step along the voyage, strewn with obstacles, made by a king envisioned by a Duke of jazz half a century ago. Today, the protagonist of that vision no longer needs us to tell his tale. He can speak with his own voice.

Scan the QR code to access the music files that complement this book.

CELEBRATION

THE SCORE FORGOTTEN ON THE BOTTOM OF THE RIVER

A WELL-MANNERED GUEST

The Imperial Room, a five-hundred-seat hall located on the lobby level of Toronto's luxurious Royal York Hotel, has welcomed some of the brightest stars in showbiz, with names ranging from Marlene Dietrich to Tina Turner, Liberace, and Jim Carrey. For over forty years, the Imperial Room's maître d' was Italian American Louis Jannetta, famed for his strict insistence on etiquette. Jannetta once showed Bob Dylan the door because he refused to put on a tie. On another occasion, he agreed to let in a group of bikers, who had come to see Raquel Welch, as long as they behaved like true gentlemen, which they did. One can only assume that our unbending head waiter found no reason to object to the Duke, with his refined attire and conduct, given that Ellington performed at this hotel for thirty-five years. He first played at this venue in 1938, and his last concert here took place in spring 1973.

On the evening of March 17, 1970, the bandleader, pleased to see that the Imperial Room was packed with four hundred fans, gave an interview to Ted O'Reilly from CJRT Radio between the first and second sets of the concert.[1] In addition to letting his Canadian listeners in on his favorite cocktails (a topic on which he had some expertise), Ellington praised Charlie Barnet's interpretations of his music. Barnet's scores were often signed by Billy May. And since May had looked after the arrangements for an album the Duke Ellington Orchestra recorded with Frank Sinatra, the radio host naturally continued with a direct question: "Can other people write for your orchestra?" The bandleader nodded but, as an example, only mentioned one name: Ron Collier.

Actually, quite a large number of people arranged or composed pieces for the Duke above and beyond Strayhorn and Mercer. In his memoirs, Ellington declared his gratitude for the work done by Jimmy Jones, Wild Bill Davis, Dick Vance, Ron Collier, Luther Henderson, Calvin Jackson, Hilly Edelstein, Raymond Fol, Ernie Burkhardt, and Gerald Wilson.[2] This list is nevertheless incomplete and should include the names of other accomplished musicians such as Kay Parker, Buck Clayton, Jimmy Hamilton, Louie Bellson, Mary Lou Williams, Chappie Willett, Ben Webster, and Joe Benjamin.[3]

So it is rather curious that Ellington, while speaking of arrangers that Tuesday evening at the Royal York Hotel, only mentioned Collier. Perhaps it was a way of winning his Canadian listeners' goodwill, something the Duke was quite good at. A respectful guest at this Toronto hotel, while speaking over an Ontario radio station, he praised the only Canadian orchestrator on his payroll. Or perhaps there is more to the story. Perhaps that musician truly was important to Ellington. And as we shall see, Collier unquestionably was a key figure in the very last years of the Duke's career.

A CANADIAN AT THE DUKE'S PALACE

The two had met for the first time in 1956. That summer, they both appeared onstage at the Stratford Shakespeare Festival, which, for its fourth edition, opened its doors to jazz. And so, while classical music lovers had the chance to listen to Benjamin Britten's *The Rape of Lucretia* and Shakespeare buffs got to see stagings of a number of tragedies and comedies, including a magnificent *Henry V*, jazz fans could enjoy Dave Brubeck, Wilbur de Paris, Oscar Peterson (who shared his two evenings with the Modern Jazz Quartet), Phil Nimmons, Calvin Jackson, Paul Draper, Duke Ellington, and Norman Symonds's octet, whose trombonist was no other than Ron Collier. The man who invited all these musicians was composer and artistic director Louis Applebaum, the same person who one year later commissioned the Duke to write his famous suite *Such Sweet Thunder* for this very festival.[4]

Ellington, who went on to play many other times in Stratford (even only performing unrecorded pieces during his last appearance here in 1966), felt a certain affinity with Canada. "I'm always partial to Canada and Canadians," the Duke once confessed.[5] In a radio interview given in 1968, he was able to recall the exact year in which he first performed north of the 49th Parallel and the name of the theater, even though the event took place almost four decades earlier. The first time the Duke set foot in Canada was indeed on May 29, 1931, for a concert in Toronto.[6] As of that moment, he went on tour north of the border almost every year. So when his old friend Lou Applebaum asked him to take part as a pianist in a recording of pieces by Canadian jazz composers, he accepted without reservation.[7]

At the Hallmark Studios in Toronto on July 24 and 25, 1967, Ellington joined forces with three different groups (a big band, a string ensemble, and a large pops orchestra), improvising on compositions by three Canadian composers. He seemed to have some difficulty with the pieces by Norman Symonds, *Nameless Hour* and *Fair Wind*, as he did with *Song and Dance* and *Collage #3*, the two scores by Gordon Delamont, which, in any case, are very well written. Furthermore, regardless of the enthusiasm shown by the critic working for *DownBeat*, Canadian John Norris, who listened to the recording in the studio, Ellington's contribution at the piano was not overly significant for the two works titled *Aurora Borealis* and *Silent Night, Lonely Night* for large orchestra. They were composed by Ron Collier, who also conducted the ensemble.[8]

Decca soon released the album under the title *North of the Border in Canada: The Ron Collier Orchestra with Duke Ellington Soloist*. The Duke did his utmost to promote the work of these musicians, going as far as drawing a sketch for the back cover of the LP, portraying the three composers along with himself at the piano. On at least one occasion, he performed some of these works live. For example, on July 2, 1969, he played twice (at 5:30 p.m. and 8:30 p.m.) at the Ford Auditorium in Detroit with the Ron Collier Orchestra, performing a few of the pieces that appeared on *North of the Border*, including the challenging ballet *Aurora Borealis*.[9] Above and beyond the musical result, however, the album produced by Applebaum gave Ellington the chance to see how Collier dealt with scores written for large ensembles and also to hear the improvisations of a flugelhorn soloist whom he would soon call in his own right, Fred Stone.[10]

The first step the Duke took was to give Collier work as a big band arranger. On September 2, 1969, and during the two following days, his orchestra was in the recording studio for an album not intended to be distributed in music stores. The LP, titled *The Big Bands Are Back! Swinging Today's Hits*, was sold as an attachment to *Reader's Digest*, which, in those years, had millions of subscribers. The arrangements were done by Luther Henderson, Wild Bill Davis, and Collier. The latter was responsible for "Manhã de Carnaval," written by Luiz Bonfá for the film *Orfeu negro*, and "A Taste of Honey," a song by Bobby Scott taken from the Broadway musical with the same name, whose melody was loved by many jazzmen (including Paul Desmond, who made a splendid version of it) and even the Beatles. Collier gave the Brazilian piece a rich array of countermelodies and brilliant passages, which must have put the trumpet section to the test. For "A Taste of Honey," instead, he opted for a more sober but no less detailed arrangement. The modulation that comes before the closing theme, played by Cootie Williams, is very well devised.[11]

The Duke had spotted the right man and promptly welcomed Collier to Ellingtonia. At any rate, this Canadian musician was no novice. Born in 1930, he first studied with Gordon Delamont, whose composition and arrangement texts have been translated into various languages and are still today a reference point in music education. Later, he took lessons in New York from George Russell and Hall Overton, two of the most important jazz masters and theoreticians in the second half of the twentieth century. A versatile trombonist (he played jazz in the ensembles led by Norman Symonds, classical music with the Toronto Symphony, and pop for the radio and television), as of the midfifties, he led groups of his own that performed his compositions, including a *Sonata* for piano and jazz quintet. Collier eventually became, along with Symonds and Delamont, one of the leading figures in the Canadian third stream, as theorized by Gunther Schuller in 1957, which brought together elements of classical and jazz music in the midfifties and the sixties. In this vein, he composed works such as *Waterfront Night Thoughts* (1965), written for classical flutist Robert Aitken; scores for music theater (*The Mechanic*, 1965) and ballet (*Aurora Borealis*, conceived for CBC-TV in 1966 and adapted for the album with Ellington one year later); and various pieces that included a narrator, such as *The City* (1960), *Hear Me Talkin' to Ya* (1964), whose libretto consists of quotes from early jazz musicians taken from the book with the same name edited by Nat Hentoff in 1955, and *Carneval* (1969).[12]

Ellington, in Collier, therefore found a musician who had worked his way up the ladder. Since he was perfectly at home with a wide range of ensembles and musical genres, the first task he gave him involved a sort of musical that brought together gospel and jazz and called for a small choir. On May 29, 1970, a new library at the Mount Angel Abbey in St. Benedict, Oregon, was inaugurated in grand style. Ellington's big band played a few of his most successful works, including the *Harlem* suite, and a new composition written for the occasion by composer-in-residence Ann Henry. Singer, actress, dancer and choreographer, she was first endorsed by the Duke, who asked her to take part in the debut of *Harlem* (January 21, 1951) at the Metropolitan Opera House. The same show also included *Threesome*, a piece written for three dancers, one of whom was Henry. An entertainer widely known as "the female Sammy Davis Jr.," in 1952, she began a successful career that, however, came to a rapid halt in the midsixties when she was operated on for spinal meningitis. After years of therapy, which allowed her to walk but only with crutches, she retired to the Mount Angel Abbey and dedicated herself to composition. The Duke did not forget her and, in 1970, asked Collier to arrange her musical titled *Pockets: It's Amazing When Love Goes on Parade*. This is a sort of short gospel musical, with both music and text written by Henry.[13] Collier took care of the arrangements, which also called for a small choir of seminarians. At the inauguration of the library, Ellington first performed *Harlem*, then left the podium to the man he presented as an "incomparable conductor."[14] The care given by Collier to this rather modest composition convinced Ellington even more of his worth as a musician. And surely enough, not long after, he gave him a chance to appear as a composer as well.

On June 22, 1972, Ellington, on his way back from Honolulu, where the American Federation of Musicians honored him for his longstanding activity in this union, joined his musicians at the Thunder Sound Studio in Toronto to record a couple of compositions by his new arranger. "Vancouver Lights" is a classical blues influenced by the Duke's "Jeep's Blues," embellished with solos by Cootie Williams and Norris Turney on the alto sax. "Relaxing" has a swaying theme inserted within an AABA song form in which the amber color of the clarinets prevails (with the B flat clarinet played by Russell Procope and the bass clarinet by Harry Carney). The instruments are asked to improvise but also play sections of the theme, sometimes in a chordal texture (such as in the second exposition of A).[15] These are perfectly respectable pieces but perhaps not good enough to deserve being included in an album. Or at least this must have been the Duke's opinion since he never released them.[16]

So the aurora borealis seen "north of the border" didn't seem to bring much luck, and things went even worse with the blue nights in Vancouver. In other words, no shooting stars appeared in the sky over Canada. But in the water flowing through a geographically unspecified and perhaps even metaphysical river, Ellington and Collier found their element.

"THE RIVER"

On the morning of Saturday, May 3, 1970, the Duke arrived in Canadian homes just in time for lunch: Toronto's CBLT-TV broadcast its weekly show *The Morning After*, featuring Ellington as its guest. Introduced by the first eight bars of "Take the 'A' Train" played by the Don Thompson Quartet, the Duke sat down to answer Danny Finkleman's questions. He mentioned the Canadian musicians now working for him (Collier and Stone) and, after expressing his esteem for the Beatles, informed Finkleman of one of his new projects: "I'm working on a ballet for the American Ballet Theatre," he remarked in a relaxed tone of voice.[17] We have no way of knowing whether or not Ron Collier, Alvin Ailey, and Lucia Chase saw this television interview, but one thing is certain: if they did, they would have been outraged by the serene Duke's unflustered attitude.

America's most prestigious ballet company was preparing to dance to a score that, only a few weeks before the debut, was still in its composer's head. And he wasn't worried about it in the least. Ellington was holding everyone up. Collier, who was entrusted with orchestrating it, was left idle. So was Ailey, in charge of choreographing the entire work. The dance company was left waiting at the barre for instructions. But the company's director, Lucia Chase, who had included the ballet in its 1970 season, had no intention of waiting any longer. She sent Ailey on a mission to Vancouver, where the Duke Ellington Orchestra had recently been playing at a club, telling him to find out how much progress had been made on the score. Ailey arrived at the Cave Supper on April 11, 1970, at one in the morning. The bandleader was still on the stage. Early the next day, the band had to fly to Los Angeles. So there was only one thing poor Ailey could do: follow the Duke to his hotel and try to make the most of the few hours that were left to gather as much information as possible. He found out that Ellington had started working on a few movements, some of which he played for him on an electric piano, to show him that things were moving along. Back from his mission, Ailey could only report that the ballet was still very much up in the air. Only one thing had been defined, its name: *The River*.[18]

One month later, slightly concerned (to say the least) since he still hadn't received any music his dancers could start rehearsing to, Ailey took another plane to Canada. This time, he landed in Toronto, where he found Ellington busy writing at the Imperial Room (where he performed from May 1 to 9). He was completely surrounded by aquatic scores, from Debussy's *La Mer* to Britten's *Peter Grimes*, without forgetting Händel's *Water Music*, but still hadn't recorded a single note. Ailey begged him.[19] The Duke understood his point of view and, since he still hadn't written anything for big band, reassured him that he would record a few movements at the piano as soon as he got back to New York. It was the only promise he maintained.

On May 11, a dreadful day marked by the death of Johnny Hodges, he recorded six movements of *The River*.[20] The tape was first given to Martha Johnson, the American Ballet Theatre's piano accompanist charged with transcribing the music, and then wound up in Alvin Ailey's hands. In the meantime, Ellington, who had started studio rehearsals for the work on March 9, recorded the eleven movements of the suite, partially in Chicago (on May 25) and partially in New York (on June 3, 8, and 15).[21] But by now, it was too late. For the premiere on June 25 at Lincoln Center, Ailey only managed to stage six of them. The ballet was presented to the audience as a work in progress in six sections: "The Spring," "The Lake," "Vortex" (a new title for "The Whirlpool"), "Falls," "Riba," and "Two Cities" (which actually brought together two compositions, "The Neo-Hip-Hot Cool-Kiddies Community" and "The Village of the Virgins"). For the following season, he had time to add "The Meander," "The Giggling Rapids," and "The Sea," even though one year later, in 1972, he decided to eliminate the latter, meaning that the definitive version of the suite *The River* has eight sections.[22]

In his memoirs, Ellington provided a comment for each of the suite's eleven movements. Taken as a whole, they make up a program in which the course of a river, from its source to the sea, passing through rapids and lakes, is a metaphor for human existence. Through water, the Duke speaks to us about life from the newborn's cradle in "The Spring" and is eventually embraced by "The Mother, Her Majesty the Sea," which, in Ellington's spiritual vision, corresponds to a rebirth.[23] Actually, this narrative framework is less closely reflected by the score than is the case in other works by the Duke and sometimes seems to be a mere pretext. For example, a few of the movements had already been written before *The River* became a project in its own right. The Duke could well describe the second movement, "The Run," as the gurgling of the river, still a stream when it meets up with a puddle, but we now know that this composition was originally called "Marcia Regina" and written for the 1968 documentary on Degas (discussed in the previous chapter).[24] Bearing this in mind, this suite (which in any case is strongly linked to its program and occasionally descriptive) is one of Ellington's most inspired late works. Movements such as "The Spring," with its Middle Eastern feel (which reappears in various other parts of the suite), and "The Lake," with its melodic eloquence, are outstanding compositions, as are "The Village of the Virgins," that contains a fragile blues, and "The Meander," whose languid development gives us a sense of malaise tinged with bitterness.

Ron Collier played a crucial role in *The River*'s difficult advancement. Ellington was not asked to conduct the music for this ballet, not even at its debut. Instead, he was to prepare a symphonic score, of which the American Ballet Theatre Orchestra would then make a recording and to which the dancers would perform. Collier was in charge of the orchestration. This was a rather laborious task, which became more demanding every day that Ellington procrastinated with his own recordings.[25] Indeed, since he didn't have the time to write a complete score for big band, he simply notated the most important passages and got the rest down on tapes that were recorded, as mentioned above, in the form of piano solos or with his big band. Basically,

Ex. 7.1. "The Spring," horn introduction.

Ex. 7.2. "The Giggling Rapids," piano introduction.

these were recorded rehearsals. While for the Duke, they were like entries in a writer's journal, for Collier, they were the source from which he was to assemble a symphonic score.

The eleven movements of *The River* recorded by Ellington were released posthumously as part of the CD *Duke Ellington, The Private Collection, Volume Five: The Suites, New York 1968 & 1970* (WEA), but the takes selected by Mercer for the recorded edition are not necessarily the same as the ones chosen by Collier as the starting point for his orchestration.[26] For example, as a basis for his work on "The Spring," he did not turn to the orchestral version recorded in Chicago on May 25, 1970, later included in the CD, but opted instead for the superb piano solo recording made in New York on May 11. Collier gave the first four bars, in which Ellington on the ivories had traced out a generically Spanish modal color, to the horn (ex. 7.1).

He then assigned the luxuriant theme to the oboe in unison with the horn, leaving the strings to define the movement's center of gravity, i.e., the tonic D. The resulting sound is polymodal, halfway between Phrygian and Phrygian with a major third.[27]

For the sparkling piece titled "Giggling Rapids," Collier also chose a different take than the one released on CD, which, once again, comes from the session held on May 25, 1970. His choice went to a recording made in New York on June 3, 1970.[28] The piano introduction, which perfectly renders the impression made by the piece's title, probably caught Collier's attention, given that he left it for the same instrument and also included it as a coda (where it does not appear in Ellington's take) for his arrangement (ex. 7.2).

He began his work on "The Meander" with the take mentioned above from the posthumous CD recorded on May 25, 1970.[29] Collier condensed the structure with respect to the more drawn-out performance by Ellington (who, on the whole, didn't pay too much attention to formal aspects, given that it was a rehearsal), and for the doleful theme, he searched for more refined timbral solutions. In particular, the mixture of strings (violas and violins), horns, and clarinet is splendid. Put briefly, Collier did an excellent job, perhaps most notably with the orchestration of "The Village of the Virgins," where the first exposition of the theme is given to the clarinet, cornet and trombone, vaguely reproducing the color of "Mood Indigo."

According to his indications on the manuscript score, Collier finished working on the six movements necessary for the premiere of *The River* in June 1970. For the 1971 version, he also arranged "The Giggling Rapids" and "The Falls," finishing that June, as is once again visible on the score. Ellington was not present at the ballet's debut on June 25, 1970, nor at any of the repeat performances. Collier's work was heard by others, not only those who flocked to the theater (including President Lyndon Johnson, who expressed his wholehearted approval) but also television viewers who tuned in to a program broadcast on October 8, 1973, by WNET titled *American Ballet Theatre: A Close-Up in Time*. In this documentary, which features Alvin Ailey, among others, Lucia Chase discusses a few ballets staged by her company. One of them is *The River*, and the video includes a clip with Cynthia Gregory and Marcos Paredes dancing to "The Lake."[30]

Later, an even broader audience had the chance to hear Collier's orchestration. A fragment of it was included in the film *The Turning Point*, shot in 1977 by Herbert Ross, formerly a choreographer for the American Ballet Theatre, and interpreted by Shirley MacLaine and Anne Bancroft. A film focused on the world of dance, and the ABT in particular, it contains a sequence in which aspiring prima ballerina Emilia Rodgers (Leslie Browne, who, a few years after the film was released, became the star of the American Ballet Theatre) shows her mastery of both classical and modern ballet styles; for the latter, the director chose "Vortex" ("The Whirlpool") from *The River*.[31]

Meanwhile, on October 24, 1977, just when Ross's film was about to appear in movie theaters, Ellington's big band performed the score by Ellington–Collier along with the Polish National Philharmonic Orchestra during the Jazz Jamboree Festival. Here, Mercer, after leaving the baton in the hands of Polish conductor Wojciech Rajski, announced to the audience that what they were about to hear was the world premiere of the orchestral form of a composition by Duke Ellington titled *The River*. For the occasion, Collier's score was revised to make room for the big band. And yet all the solo passages were still played by the classical musicians, and in a few movements, such as "The Falls" and "The Whirlpool," the jazz ensemble remained completely silent. Even the improvisations the jazzmen could have offered were reduced to a bare minimum. Without changing the structure of the compositions, first trombonist Booty Wood and then trumpet player James Bolden presented their solos for "The Village of the Virgins," while Michael Bolivar's bebop alto sax followed the meanders of "The River," which closed the concert in a blues vein.[32]

Actually, even though Mercer (more or less deliberately) neglected to mention it in his presentation, *The River* had already been performed in concert form three years earlier. On April 29, 1974, Collier, to wish the Duke well on his seventy-fifth birthday, conducted Toronto's CJRT Orchestra for the premiere of *The River*. The movements heard on this occasion included "The Spring," "The Meander," "The Giggling Rapids" (in which the pianist bungled the introduction), "The Lake," "The Whirlpool," and "The River," rounded off by an impressive performance of "The Village of the Virgins."

Collier made sure that Ellington received a recording of the performance, but since the Duke was in the hospital, nearing death, he most likely didn't listen to it.[33] In any case, as mentioned above, he wasn't present at the prestigious debut held on June 25, 1970, at Lincoln Center, either (since he had a gig in Chicago), nor did he follow the work when it came back to New York, and all the less so when it traveled to Caracas or Budapest. Precisely due to the Duke's unexplainable lack of interest and his refusal to supervise progress on the symphonic version, *The River*, while discussed at length in this chapter, plays a marginal role in this book as a whole. This is not the case for another work conducted by Collier that very same evening in Toronto, a work that remained submerged for many years and that we will attempt to bring to the surface in the following pages.

THE "CELEBRATION" AT THE BOTTOM OF THE PAGE

The name of CJRT Radio, founded by Toronto's Ryerson Institute of Technology, comes from the three main programs offered here, journalism, radio, and technology, along with a letter indicating the nation. Ted O'Reilly graduated from the Institute in 1963, and two years later, was hired by its radio station. He shortly succeeded in producing and presenting a show called *The Jazz Scene*, which, for the following thirty-seven years, kept Canadians up-to-date about the music he loved most, six times a week. One of his favorites was the Duke, who, on April 29, 1974, turned seventy-five. As a birthday present, O'Reilly organized a nineteen-hour Ellingtonia marathon, whose last miles included a concert with two symphonic debuts. That Monday evening, while in New York, minister John Gensel was paying tribute to the dying Duke at St. Peter's Church with a selection of pieces from his sacred concerts, Ron

Collier, at the new Ontario Science Center in Toronto, conducted the CJRT Orchestra in the world premiere of *The River* and another score that, while having been performed previously, was equally unknown to Canadian listeners or just about any other audience for that matter. Its title was *Celebration*.

The concert, for which entrance was free, had been promoted by The Music Performance Trust Fund and CJRT Radio, as Collier informed those present in his introduction. And yet, it did not obtain the recognition it deserved.[34] Ted O'Reilly, desolate, informed me that the press took virtually no interest in the event whatsoever. The arts and entertainment section of the *Toronto Star* only made room for a brief article with a few scraps of information, with more space going to Robert Altman's latest film, some new works commissioned by Yehudi Menuhin, and a piece decrying cuts in arts funding. So the Duke wound up at the bottom of the page.[35]

The "celebration" referred to in the title of the work performed by Collier and a sixty-six-member orchestra had nothing to do with Ellington's birthday. The Duke was an ambitious man and did not suffer from low self-esteem, but he never would have celebrated himself. Instead, he wanted to pay tribute to Jacksonville's Jackson's Jax, an attractive woman named Jacqueline who married violinist Jackson, in turn from Jacksonville (Florida). Her husband affectionately called her Jax, even though Jax is also clearly short for Jacksonville... So we are dealing with a program by the Duke, a narrative that, doing our best not to gloss over its ambiguities, we will now try to explain.

IN THE HANDS OF THE ORCHESTRA

Speaking over the microphone at Ted O'Reilly's radio show, Ron Collier expressed his curiosity about something to Ellington. In a calm tone of voice, this Canadian musician put together a question that, truth be told, was not overly diplomatic: "I can understand that, for economic reasons, the band has to keep working and you have to keep fresh material in the book, etc. Do you ever have an interest in writing for a different type of organization, a different type of orchestra, different musicians?" The Duke felt no need to make any clarifications about the first part nor to justify himself in any way and went straight to the point: "Oh, sure! I wrote something for the New York Philharmonic: *The Golden Broom and the Green Apple*."[36] As of the thirties, Ellington had certainly written for other ensembles: for example, "Blue Bells of Harlem" (commissioned by Paul Whiteman in 1938 for his own orchestra), *Turcaret* (1960) for theater, and again, in a certain sense, *My People* (1963), a fair amount of film music and yet more scores scattered over decades of composition. This interest, while somewhat restrained, was to bear further fruit less than four years after this radio interview. And Collier, almost as though he himself had sparked things off, was involved in the project.

Ellington may have intended to mention this project in his memoirs given that, in a notepad with the Palmer House (Chicago) hotel's letterhead, right beside the note "River ballet," he jotted down the word "Celebration." In the end, however, all he wrote down here was the title. The only reference to this score in *Music Is My Mistress* is the same title, which is listed in his catalog of works.[37] Not much more appeared in the biographical-musicological literature in the years to come; some information can be gleaned from Klaus Stratemann's precious *Duke Ellington, Day by Day and Film by Film* but only in the space of four lines (which contain some slightly imprecise information).[38] This *Celebration*, nevertheless, definitely doesn't deserve to be forgotten. Nor does the Jacksonville Symphony Orchestra, which, after a deep crisis that may have led to its demise, found the strength to raise its head, or even, in the words of the June 10, 1972, issue of the *National Observer*, to "rise from the grave."[39] In this resurrection, the Duke and his *Celebration* played a significant role.

Before giving our full attention to Ellington's symphonic work, a brief overview of this Jacksonville ensemble's history would be in order.[40] Jacksonville, Florida, which in the 1880s introduced Frederick Delius to African American music, saw musical activities flourish during the following decade thanks to the effort made by Claudia L'Engle Adams, a patron of the arts who, before dying prematurely at the age of thirty, succeeded in bringing a few musicians together in a sort of cultural association that, twenty-five years later, was still alive and well under the name of The Friday Musicale. That small group of refined amateurs gave birth to the community's first symphony orchestra, led by violinist George Orner. Over the next twenty years, with funding coming from the state during the years of the Great Depression, the ensemble progressed rapidly, and by the fifties, now conducted by Van Lier Lanning first and James Christian Pfohl later, held its first acclaimed concert seasons. It still brought together professionals and amateurs (for example, flutist Margaret Garrison made a living as an accountant, and horn player Henry Cornely was a banker) but was accomplished enough to play in the television show *The Magic of Music*. The sixties started out well: John Canarina, who was one of Leonard Bernstein's assistants (along with Maurice Peress) at the New York Philharmonic, accepted to conduct this orchestra, which in the meantime had been given a new five-million-dollar facility: the Civic Auditorium, a concert hall with 3,200 seats. Unexpectedly, however, the ensemble's good luck ran out. At the end of the decade, the Jacksonville

Symphony Orchestra was threatened by serious economic problems and probably would have reached its end if its new president, Ira Koger, hadn't stepped in. First of all, he found an experienced conductor and entrusted him with both a contract and a mission: to give the orchestra new life at any cost. Somehow or other, they would come up with the money. The conductor was Willis Page, who held the baton for the next twelve years. First bassist at Arthur Fiedler's Boston Pops and the Boston Symphony Orchestra, Page immediately got on the phone, calling some of his fellow musicians from these ensembles and inviting them to join the Jacksonville Orchestra. They were nearing the end of their careers but were nevertheless solid professionals who provided valuable reinforcement.[41] Page's second step consisted in contacting Arthur Fiedler himself, who gave one successful concert in the 1970–71 season. And yet he kept the biggest occasion in store for the following year: a program with two world premieres for the city's 150th anniversary. Composer Carlisle Floyd was invited; he had already gained esteem for his opera *Susannah* and got to work on a monodrama whose vocal part, enriched by *Sprechstimme*, was to be sung by the famous soprano Phyllis Curtin, the only character to appear on stage during the work's forty-five minutes. For the second score, the conductor called his "good friend Duke Ellington."[42] Page had shared the stage with the Duke on July 23, 1957, when he led the Buffalo Philharmonic Orchestra in *New World A-Comin'* and the second movement of *Night Creature*. Impressed with these symphonic scores, fifteen years later, he requested a new one, freshly written.[43]

The media began giving attention to the project as early as January 1972. The January 28 issue of the *Florida Times-Union* featured the title *Symphony to Perform Ellington Composition*, announcing that Floyd and the Duke were to write new pieces for a concert commemorating Jacksonville's 150th anniversary. The event was given a precise date and venue: May 16, 1972, Civic Auditorium. But this article goes even further. It also informs us that the same program would be performed at the John F. Kennedy Center in Washington on May 18 and the following day at Carnegie Hall. As an impresario, Ira Koger was not bad![44] On April 25, the same newspaper went into more detail and, without publishing the titles of the pieces, revealed: "Ellington's work is a musical remembrance of a concert date he had here [in Jacksonville] many years ago."[45] On the day of the debut, a lengthy article gave most of its emphasis to the work by Floyd, mentioning its title and the names of the performers, while—only a few hours before the performance—Ellington's score was still not referred to by name. The review that appeared the day after, instead, gave much more weight to the composition by the Duke, who was praised alongside Phyllis Curtin as one of the "two stars [who] add to [the] city's cultural crown."[46]

Celebration was the special guest during the evening at the Civic Auditorium, and as such, appeared on stage last. The entire program began with a work by Howard Hanson titled *Dies Natalis*, in which a soft figure in the timpani introduces a delicate chorale, and continued with Floyd's dark composition, which concluded the first part of the concert. After the intermission, virtuoso Mary Lou Wesley Krosnick performed Carl Maria von Weber's *Konzertstück* in F minor for piano and orchestra op. 79, after which the last word was given to Ellington.

It was a huge success. The Duke was given the key to the city and drank champagne, toasting with the mayor and other local authorities.[47] At dawn, the elderly maestro left for Texas. He didn't have time to follow the Washington and New York performances. The day after the Jacksonville debut, the Duke Ellington Orchestra had a concert with Sarah Vaughan and a gig in Houston in the next few days; his men needed their bandleader. Even though he did not attend the repeat performances, Ellington was able to hear the piece again. He had asked for the concert to be recorded, and while waiting for a connecting flight at the Atlanta airport, he found a few minutes to listen to those tapes. The Duke, as Stanley Dance later recalled, was satisfied.[48]

Celebration is a unique piece in Ellington's entire output. It is the only score that does not give a single note to the members of his big band; none of them took part in the performance, and even the Duke himself, who for his similar works was always present as a pianist or conductor, listened to it from the first row of the audience. Ellington, therefore, entrusted his last symphonic work to a large, generic orchestra. And he did so with the help of Ron Collier.

JACKSONVILLE'S JACKSON'S JAX

Ron Collier should have been considered an "almost associate composer" for his contribution to *Celebration*. Or at least this is the opinion expressed by Ted O'Reilly, to whom Collier showed Ellington's manuscripts, which essentially contain the themes and a few indications as to the arrangement and nothing more.[49] Surely enough, the Canadian orchestrator, as we will shortly prove, played a considerable role. And yet the Duke did more than was asked of him. Conductor Maurice Peress, while working in the Ellington archives on *Queenie Pie*, found one page from a symphonic score entirely in the Duke's handwriting. This is a fragment of the piece currently under discussion, which Ellington fully orchestrated upon request by Collier who, worried he might not be able to finish his work in time, asked for the Duke's help.[50]

Ex. 7.3. *Celebration*, mm. 1–3

Put briefly, for this work, unlike *The River*, the two worked in close collaboration. The result is the longest composition ever written by Ellington. It lasts roughly half an hour, compared to the fifteen or twenty minutes of his other symphonic pieces. The size of *Celebration* can be gauged by the number of pages in the manuscript: 192. Thanks to the generosity of Cathy Collier, the orchestrator's widow, it was possible for me to study this hefty score.[51] A quick glance is enough to be impressed by the incredible variety of this piece, which alternates between blues moments and Latin sections, intimate nocturnal passages and blaring fanfares, and thundering rock episodes and sorrowful spirituals. This kaleidoscope is made all the more astonishing by quick changes in meter and key, which appear more frequently than anywhere else in Ellington's works.

Let us examine the first few minutes of *Celebration* to get an idea of the various threads that are woven together. A fanfare, that at times sounds like a march but never loses its poise, opens the score. Two clarinets and a bass clarinet in triads, playing *mezzo forte*, are sustained only by the snare drum as they set out a theme that, in only a few bars, touches on three different keys (ex. 7.3).

The first two times this march appears, it is delicate and reserved, having nothing of the solemnity of "Timon of Athens March" nor the boundless joy of "Klop," and not even the shambling wryness of "Marcia Regina" ("The Run"). Then, the dynamics increase, leading to the second theme. This episode opens once again in a subdued tone. A calm spiritual with a blues undercurrent, it continues for nine bars, played by the bass clarinet, initially sustained by a pedal of open fifths in the double bass and cello. The melody is a variation on the first theme, but now the key, the fourth to appear in only a few bars, is D minor.

The third section remains in D minor but changes time signature: from 4/4, we pass to a waltz. Here, a flute plays softly in the upper range over a

Ex. 7.4. *Celebration,* bass clarinet ostinato.

delicate orchestration, leading to two secondary themes. The second of them gives us reason to believe that Ted O'Reilly was right. In G♯ minor, a bass clarinet ostinato that uses only two notes (the tonic and the perfect fifth) accompanies a theme in the English horn; eight bars later, the piece suddenly swerves to B minor (ex. 7.4).

This is an idea that Collier used in various compositions. The clarinet ostinato found in "Relaxing" is in some senses similar; in *Silent Night, Lonely Night*, this device, which accompanies the modal theme, shows a clearer resemblance with the bars discussed here; and *Aurora Borealis* contains the main precedent: in 3/4 time and in a minor key, we encounter the same bass clarinet obbligato that, like in *Celebration*, is then transposed to another key.

The piece continues with the blues. There are three of them in a row. One is in B flat major and lasts twelve bars, followed by a sort of blaring rock 'n' roll, sixteen-bar-long piece (in the same tonality) that leads back to the first theme (ex. 7.5). For this third appearance, Collier's orchestration is highly refined, with the theme in a counterpoint played in the low register of the first and second violins. The dark color of this episode, however, is not only a question of timbre. Here, Ellington newly proposes the first blues, in B flat major, now in the parallel minor key (ex. 7.6). This device, which has the effect of a *coup de théâtre*, comes up periodically over his entire career, beginning with early masterpieces such as "Black and Tan Fantasy" (1927) and "The Mooche." Somehow, inexplicably, it is surprising every time.[52]

No room is given to improvisation in these episodes, nor for that matter in the rest of the work. In the closing passages, two solo moments are entrusted to the alto sax, the work's only instrument, along with the drums, not traditionally found in a symphony orchestra. First over the harmonies of a blues in F minor and then over the chords of a broader section in C minor, the saxophonist is not asked to improvise but to read the notes (ex. 7.7). This is exactly what medical doctor Bernard L. Kaye, president of the American Society of Aesthetic Plastic Surgeons, did in the three concerts held in 1972. The Duke had been informed that the orchestra's flutist was also an excellent saxophonist, even though, by day, he practiced an entirely different profession. So he called him at home and asked him to play a few phrases over the

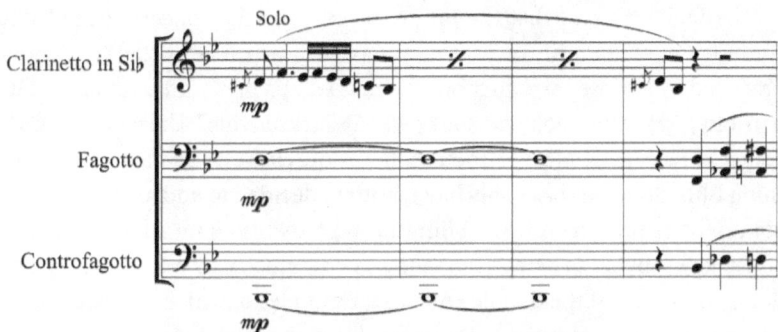

Ex. 7.5. *Celebration*, blues in B-flat major.

Ex. 7.6. *Celebration*, blues in B-flat minor.

Ex. 7.7. *Celebration*, alto sax solo.

phone. After half a century, Ellington was still firmly convinced that music should be written for instrumentalists, not instruments. It also seems that, while listening to the tapes at the airport, he was highly satisfied with that saxophonist, who "played like Rabbit."[53]

These initial themes, the first of many found in *Celebration*, give a good idea of the wide range of colors in the Duke's last symphonic piece. The considerable assortment of musical events, often simply juxtaposed, leads to a sense of fragmentation that arises on more than one occasion. Nevertheless, this variety is partially explained by what Ellington wrote, not on the staves but in words, on a sheet of paper.

The Duke insisted that the program notes for the concert at the Civic Auditorium contain his own program as well, which consisted in a poem preceded by a prose introduction: "Here is what a pretty little century-and-half-old girl should look and sound like in Jacksonville." The program note editors, unaware that this introduction was the clearest and most intelligible thing Ellington could possibly have written, decided to add an explanatory comment of their own: "Mr. Ellington regards his composition as a love affair. Jacksonville is being romanced by the musicians and music." In so doing, they ruined the double entendre, examples of which had been present in the Duke's elusive narrations for decades, which informs us that this piece is a musical allegory.[54]

The story of Jax, which is the name of both the city in Florida and the attractive girl in Ellington's introduction, is narrated through a series of portraits arranged in chronological order, each of which corresponds to one section of the piece. While Ellington may have turned to T. S. Eliot's *Ash Wednesday* as a model for his text "The Blues," here he seems to have been inspired by Yeats's *Brown Penny* (an adaptation of which he set to music for a theater show). Its refrain, "Ah penny, brown penny, brown penny," indeed, sounds much like "Jacksonville's Jackson's Jax."[55] Seen in the light of Ellington's program, the series of musical tableaux heard in *Celebration*—from the folk dances heard when Jax is a young girl to the sounds of her first ball (perhaps a waltz), all the way to the swing she dances as an adult woman, without forgetting the blues sung by her suitors—gains a certain coherence.

> She was a dancer
> She was a beaut
> Old enough to vote
> But still cute.

Then, beginning from the third verse, Jax begins to attract attention.

> Cowboys and Indians
> Cops and Robbers
> Brought her all the bouquets they could bring her.

She is now center stage:

> Newsmen and Bluesmen
> And party goers and party givers
> And hangers on
> All acclaimed her as a swinger.

But among all of them, the one who steals her heart is "a boy with a fiddle." In the last verse, he will take her, whom he calls "*Sweet as a peach / And so out of reach*," to Jacksonville, to the sound of the tongue twister Jacksonville's Jackson's Jax.

Celebration saved the Jacksonville Symphony Orchestra. The fanfare that opens this piece seems to have inspired its musicians to raise their heads and move toward a rebirth. But it did not bring a similar amount of luck to its composer. Ellington died without being able to record it. By now, we well know that a desire to record his symphonic works tormented him during the last years of his life. So, even though the Duke had no interest whatsoever in posterity (perhaps his way of fending off the thought of death), it seemed appropriate to make amends by presenting his last symphonic work during the same concert in which a new version of the movement titled "Martin Luther King" was presented.

On Tuesday, March 6, 2007, the Orchestra of the Teatro Marrucino (Chieti, Italy) and a few members of the SIdMA Jazz Orchestra, conducted by Bruno Tommaso as part of an event titled *Ellington Celebration*, recorded the score for the first time.[56] Musicology had already played its part before the curtain rose; now it was time for music to speak. The music performed that night also included a comment, which appeared immediately after *Celebration*. The comment was by John Lewis. An exact transcription of the opening bars of "For Ellington," written by the leader of the Modern Jazz Quartet in his old age, provided an additional tribute. The words of that gentle gospel would have been appreciated by the composer of *Celebration*. Appreciated and understood. Because they came from a fellow musician who shared the same conviction as the Duke: the idea that jazz can live in a musical world that is far more vast than the one to which critics, recording executives, and sometimes even fans themselves would rather it be confined.

Ellington initially formulated this principle in *New World A-Comin'* and later developed it with *Harlem*, *Night Creature*, *La Scala*, and *The Golden Broom and the Green Apple*. Even on his deathbed, he insisted on this same idea with *Three Black Kings*. Today, those who listen to the music related to this book, made accessible on the ICAMus channels, will hear further evidence of his belief and will perhaps be won over by this patient Duke.

Scan the QR code to access the music files that complement this book.

NOTES

INTRODUCTION

1. In his volume *Paul Whiteman: Pioneer in American Music. Vol. 1, 1890–1930* (Oxford: Scarecrow Press, 2003), Don Rayno provides detailed information on the 1924 concert "An Experiment in Modern Music" and on Whiteman's role as a promoter of symphonic jazz. The CDs *Paul Whiteman: Music for Moderns* (Naxos 8.120505), *Jazz Nocturne—American Concertos of the Jazz Age* (Naxos 8.559647) and *Skyscrapers: Symphonic Jazz* (Naxos 8.120644), with their accurate liner notes written respectively by Peter Dempsey, Peter Mintun, and David Lewis, provide an excellent introduction. Ellington's *Creole Rhapsody* (1931) was conducted by Whiteman as part of his "Fifth Experiment in Modern Music" at Carnegie Hall in 1933.

2. David Ross Baskerville's dissertation *Jazz Influence on Art Music to Mid-Century* (University of California, Music Department, 1965), while dating to some decades ago, remains the most complete discussion of this topic.

3. In 1953, during a radio interview broadcast by Boston's WLAW, Ellington revealed to critic Nat Hentoff that ever since he was a young man, he had made an effort to imitate the powerful sound of a symphony orchestra with the modest ensemble of six men he could count on in the twenties. He repeated this same idea in front of the cameras of the Italian national broadcaster in 1965 (*Duke Ellington: Jazz e simpatia*, RAI documentary by Alfredo Di Laura and Ruggero Orlando).

4. The Duke, unlike many jazzmen, was never interested in the European avant-garde that in the postwar years fascinated many of his colleagues. On the relations between jazz and dodecaphony, see Luca Bragalini, *Organizzare il suono: Dalla dodecafonia alle aree intervallari*, preface to the text by Franco D'Andrea and Luigi Ranghino, *Aree Intervallari*, Milan: Volonté & Co., 2011.

5. John Howland, *Ellington Uptown: Duke Ellington, James P. Johnson, and the Birth of Concert Jazz*, Ann Arbor, MI: University of Michigan Press, 2009. The second chapter of the book by Lawrence Levine, *Highbrow/Lowbrow: The Emergence of Cultural Hierarchy in America* (Cambridge, MA: Harvard University Press, 1988), dedicated to nineteenth-century American classical music, is particularly stimulating. Even more interesting, from our present point of view, is the article by the same scholar, "Jazz and the American Culture," *Journal of American Folklore* CII, 403 (January–March 1989), 6–22.

6. Samuel A. Floyd Jr., *The Power of Black Music: Interpreting Its History from Africa to the United States*, New York: Oxford University Press, 1995. Henry Louis Gates Jr., *The Signifying Monkey: A Theory of African-American Literary Criticism*, New York: Oxford University Press, 1988.

7. Paul Allen Anderson, *Deep River: Music and Memory in Harlem Renaissance Thought*, Durham, NC: Duke University Press, 2001. Houston A. Baker Jr., *Modernism and the Harlem Renaissance*, Chicago, IL: University of Chicago Press, 1987.

8. W. E. B. Du Bois, *The Souls of Black Folk*, Chicago 1903, is available in an excellent critical edition: Henry Louis Gates Jr. and Terri Hume Oliver (eds.), W. E. B. Du Bois, *The Souls of Black Folk*, New York: W. W. Norton & Company, 1999. Catherine Parsons Smith, *William Grant Still: A Study in Contradictions*, Los Angeles, CA: University of California Press, 2000.

9. Christopher Coady, *John Lewis and the Challenge of "Real" Black Music*, Ann Arbor, MI: University of Michigan Press, 2016.

10. Information as to the large number of publications on this topic will be provided in the bibliography of chapters 3, 4, and 5.

11. Ellington expressed this dislike in an interview with Leonard Feather published in the January 26, 1951, issue of *DownBeat*; an extract from this article is found in Eddie Lambert, *Duke Ellington: A Listener's Guide*, Lanham, MD/London: Scarecrow Press, 1999, 246.

12. There are multiple definitions of symphonic jazz, as David Schiff points out in his article "Symphonic Ellington? Rehearing *New World A-Comin'*," *Musical Quarterly*, XCVI, 3–4 (Autumn-Winter 2013). My monograph addresses Ellington's works expressly written for symphony orchestra (such as *La Scala* and *Celebration*) and Ellington's works written for big band that included a symphonic arrangement at Ellington's request and with his supervision (e.g., *Harlem* and *New World A-Comin'*) or partial supervision (such as *Three Black Kings*). Symphonic works by other composers recorded by Ellington, works arranged for symphony orchestra after Ellington's death or without his supervision, and Ellington's compositions that have a symphonic feel but do not feature a symphony orchestra (such as *Creole Rhapsody* or *Reminiscing in Tempo*, and a number of other scores starting from the early *Rhapsody Jr.* of 1926) did not fall within the scope of investigation of my book.

1. LA SCALA, PART I

1. Video interviews with Bruno Schiozzi (November 4, 2005) and Gian Mario Maletto (December 13, 2005). My research at the Hotel Duomo and the Hotel Palace did not provide any additional evidence. Upon Ellington's arrival, waiting for him on the platform at Milano Centrale stood photographer Riccardo Schwamenthal, who took a few shots, along with a welcoming committee organized by Arrigo Polillo, who was then working as a journalist for the magazine *Musica Jazz*. A cultural animator and future author of an important book on the history of jazz, Polillo had invited his colleagues Gian Mario Maletto and Bruno Schiozzi; the latter personally drove Ellington to the hotel.

2. The only dissenting voice came from prominent critic Giampiero Cane in the March–April edition of the magazine *Jazzland*. The concerts were released posthumously in two

albums, *In the Uncommon Market* (Pablo 2308) and *The Great Duke Ellington* (MJCD 1091). According to producer Luciano Massagli, who attended both concerts, a video recording was made by Italy's RAI that has yet to be released (interview held on December 5, 2005).

3. Licia Sirch, in a personal email, January 13, 2006.

4. As early as the second half of the twenties, the Mediolana Jazz Band recorded in a hall at the Verdi Conservatory. In this case as well, the physical contact between the two worlds did not imply any kind of cultural closeness. Details on these recordings are found in Adriano Mazzoletti, *Il jazz in Italia dalle origini alle grandi orchestre*, Turin: EDT, 2004, 551. Not even the music suspended between baroque and jazz played by the Modern Jazz Quartet succeeded in gaining the theater's sponsorship; this group played in the Verdi Hall in May 1960, and the concert was a huge success.

5. Livio Cerri, "I concerti di Ellington a Milano," *Musica e dischi*, March 1963.

6. Telephone interview with Tano Ponzoni, October 1, 2005.

7. Franchini wrote "Duke Ellington and La Scala: The World's Most Famous Jazz Musician Conducts the World's Most Famous Orchestra"; Daniele Ionio published "The Duke and the La Scala Orchestra: The Italian Suite" in the March–April 1963 issue of *Jazzland*, as well as "Ellington Conducts La Scala" in *L'Unità* (February 23, 1963). Video interviews with Vittorio Franchini, Ennio Miori (November 28, 2005) and Gianni Tollara (November 3, 2005). The periodical *Jazzland* was basically a fanzine whose first number came out in January 1963; written mainly by Daniele Ionio, Arrigo Arrigoni, and Gianni Tollara, it was in some ways a reply to *Musica Jazz*, which, in 1963, had already been releasing issues for twenty years. *Jazzland* had a short life: the last issue appeared in January 1966. The name of the newspaper that published the article by Vittorio Franchini cannot be determined.

8. The supervisors of the Music Archive, Franco Tabarelli, and the Microfilm Service, Giuseppe Busetta.

9. Virtually nothing has been published on the composition *La Scala*, which is one of the reasons I presented "La Scala, She Too Pretty to Be Neglected: History and Analysis of an Ellington Composition" at the International Conference on Black Music Research. Society for American Music, 32nd Annual Conference, Chicago, March 15–19, 2006.

10. The binders were labeled "Reading office," "Recording company correspondence 1962, 1963, 1964," "Orchestra," "Ensembles," and "General secretary correspondence 1962."

11. Labeled "Artistic direction," "Copies of letters 1962, 1963," "Artist Contracts," and "Scala Recordings [1960–1969]."

12. Labeled "Newsletters, service orders," "Memos for Management," "Press Review 1962/1964," and "Orchestra Payrolls."

13. Letter by Busetta, dated December 30, 2005.

14. Luciano Massagli, Liborio Pusateri, Giovanni M. Volonté, *Duke Ellington's Story on Records 1963–1965*, self-published, 1979. The list mentioned was obtained by Liborio Pusateri through Bruno Cavallo, the *La Scala* flutist present at the session. Interview with Liborio Pusateri, October 2005.

15. Video interview with Ennio Miori, November 28, 2005.

16. The photographer was Erio Piccagliani. Personal email from Elena Fumagalli, La Scala Photographic Archive, November 22, 2005.

17. Tabarelli also recalled that the orchestra's bassoonist, Oreste Canfora, had been suspended during his apprenticeship at the conservatory on account of his flirtation with popular music. Tabarelli himself confessed that one year prior to graduating from the conservatory, in 1963, he accepted a gig with a pop orchestra. For this lighthearted decision, he risked being "expelled from the conservatory." Video interview with Franco Tabarelli, November 22, 2005.

18. Livio Cerri's volume, *Mezzo secolo di jazz* (Pisa: Nistri-Lischi, 1981) offers an interesting portrait of jazz in Italy during the period in question, including the relations between this tradition and the world of classical music.

19. Luciano Chailly, *Buzzati in musica*, Turin: Ada Martello Editore, 1987, 211. The extraordinary quality of *Ghosts at the Grand Hotel*—which unfolds in three movements, "The Meal," "Ballet of the Bottles," and "Dance of the Sorceress"—expresses the interest shown elsewhere by Chailly toward aspects of jazz composition such as Gerry Mulligan's themes and Stan Kenton's voice leading. The three pieces, which I rediscovered in 2007 while working alongside Chailly's first daughter, Floriana, received their world debut on February 20, 2007, performed by the big band of the Parco della Musica Auditorium in Rome.

20. Video interview with Bruno Cavallo, October 27, 2005.

21. Video interview with Franco Fantini, January 23, 2006. In 1961, Fantini took part in a recording in Milan featuring jazz musician Buddy Collette, titled *The Soft Touch of Buddy Collette* (Music LPM 2095). In 1975, he became the first violin of the La Scala String Quartet, the group with which he recorded Livio Cerri's *Third Quartet in D Minor*, a work mingling classical music and jazz (Durium MS AL 80009). The name "Il Quartetto della Scala," which appears on the Cerri LP, while not literally representing the prestigious institution's trademark, is in any case indicative of a change in the cultural climate. In 1971, Fantini participated in recording the LP *La Scala Pops interpreta Frank Sinatra*, made possible by the winds of change seen since the conservative early sixties.

22. Video interview with Armando Burattin, January 25, 2006.

23. Video interview with Michelangelo Mojoli, January 16, 2006.

24. *Musica Jazz*, May 1984: this issue, dedicated to the ten-year anniversary of Ellington's death, contains an unreleased LP titled *Le Suites sinfoniche*, and *Musica Jazz*, December 1991: also dedicated to Ellington, this issue contains the CD *The Great Duke Ellington* with the live performances at the Verdi Conservatory on February 20 and 21, 1963. Research done by Ines Mosconi in her late husband's archives definitively confirmed that any further material had been lost. Telephone interview with Ines Mosconi, January 13, 2006.

25. The other three photographers were Tullio Farabola, for Farabola; Fedele Toscani, Oliviero's father, for Rotofoto; and Vincenzo Carrese, for Publifoto. The foremost collaborator of Luigi Tonali's agency also photographed the concerts held at the Verdi Hall in the evening. Over his career, Gian Battista Colombo took photos of heads of state, Nobel Prize winners, movie stars and intellectuals; in the world of music, to mention only a few names, he portrayed Maria Callas, Arturo Toscanini, Arthur Rubinstein, and Igor Stravinsky, along with jazz musicians including Miles Davis, Bud Powell, Lester Young, and Frank Sinatra. Colombo passed away on February 24, 2005, only a few months before the photos were found.

26. Oreste's younger brother was Bruno Canfora, a songwriter and highly respected popular music arranger, and the two occasionally collaborated. In 1977, Bruno Canfora recorded a piece significantly titled *Tribute to Ellington*, Via Asiago 10 TWI CD AS.

27. The following musicians from La Scala have confirmed Canfora's "unofficial" role, and above all, his involvement in organizing the session with Ellington: Bruno Cavallo, Franco Fantini, Ennio Miori, Armando Burattin, Michelangelo Mojoli, Battistino Bacchetta, and Franco Tabarelli. Video interviews were carried out between October 2005 and February 2006.

28. Identifying Giannini was quite arduous: I contacted a considerable number of people who worked at CGD in the sixties, hoping that they would recognize their colleague; the one who did so was Johnny Porta, who closely collaborated with Giannini. Video interview, Milan, January 21, 2006.

29. Video interviews with Bruno Cavallo, Franco Fantini, Ennio Miori, Armando Burattin, and Michelangelo Mojoli were carried out between January and March 2006.

30. That day, Glauco Cambursano (1st flute), Paolo Budini (1st clarinet), Mario Cazzola (1st horn), Enrico Minetti (1st violin), Alfredo Valdinoci (1st viola), and Giuseppe Russotto (1st double bass) did not show up at 57 Via Ludovico il Moro, the address of Regson Recording Studios, better known to the Milanese as Studio Zanibelli. The data concerning the official first chairs of the orchestra in 1963 was provided by the La Scala Microfilm Archive. Those who acted as first chair were identified by way of their colleagues' recollections and an inquiry based on the photos.

31. In my research on the technical equipment, an important contribution came from sound engineer Fabio Marchesi. I visited the former Studio Zanibelli on December 28, 2005 (video recording).

32. The equipment it hosted, sold to the Zanibelli brothers by the company Oberto Giannuzzi Savelli, in fact included very prestigious microphones and recording devices. Roberto Beppato, general manager of Audio International and engineer Savelli's assistant at the time, was able to find a note with a list of the devices sold to Studio Zanibelli: an Ampex 440 stereofonico; a Telefunken mono M5 recorder; Georg Neuman M48 and M49 microphones; and SM2 stereo microphones. The mixer was assembled ad hoc by the technicians at the RAI (telephone interview with Roberto Beppato, January 16, 2006). This fact gives further credit to the hypothesis that the problems that arose that day in the studio, on which we dwell further on in this paragraph, were not due to the recording studio, which was provided with high-quality equipment, but to other factors.

33. In 1967, the Duke visited the establishment no fewer than twice. On January 14, Ellington mainly rehearsed music for the film *Assault on a Queen*; on February 25, he tested a few new arrangements and played some older compositions for piano solo. In both sessions (which currently have not been released), producer Luciano Massagli was present. Telephone interview, January 23, 2006.

34. Grieder worked in Italy during the early sixties, and for one year was involved in prestigious contexts such as Philips. His efficiency (and his identity as the technician responsible for recording *La Scala*) was recalled by sound engineers Gualtiero Berlinghini and Tonino Paolillo, Joker manager Vanni Moretto, and jazzman Paolo Tomelleri; the

latter emphasized Grieder's excellent ear. Interviews were carried out in November 2005 and February 2006.

35. Daniele Ionio, "La suite italiana," *Jazzland*, March–April 1963, 27.

36. Video interview with Gianni Tollara, November 3, 2005.

37. At this writing, the record producers have yet to identify the date of the session during which the solos were recorded, which in any case must have been held between March and the latter part of 1963.

38. Ellington nevertheless rehired the trumpeter (as well as violinist, singer, and refined entertainer) in 1965. Nance continued to work with Ellington periodically after 1965. He died an alcoholic in 1976.

39. Video interview with Bruno Schiozzi, November 4, 2005.

40. Piero Rizza was identified in the photo by Italian jazz historian Adriano Mazzoletti, to whom I sent a copy of the shot.

41. On Piero Rizza's career until the fifties, see Adriano Mazzoletti, *Il jazz in Italia dalle origini alle grandi orchestre* (Turin: EDT, 2004), which contains an account of his meeting with Ellington in 1932 (407) and the quotation (351). On his later life, crucial information came from interviews with Mazzoletti (November 20, 2012) and Luciano Massagli, who visited Rizza at the Giuseppe Verdi Foundation retirement home for musicians toward the end of his life (interview on January 23, 2006). To have an idea of how little interest Rizza received, the date of his death has never previously been published, and I was forced to search for it in the SIAE archives. I owe my knowledge of his role in copying the piece currently being examined to Bruno Schiozzi (video interview November 4, 2005), backed up by the recently found photos.

42. The three takes have not been released, and the scores seen in this chapter were transcribed by myself and Marco Marzi.

43. Eugenio Montale, "Butterfly," *Corriere d'Informazione*, February 22, 1963.

44. W. E. Timner, *Ellingtonia: The Recorded Music of Duke Ellington and His Sidemen*, Lanham, MD: Scarecrow Press, 2007, 255. This volume provides two alternative subtitles, *She Too Pretty to Be Blues* and *She Too Pretty to Be Blue*, of which only the second is correct. In all likelihood, Timner took the subtitle *She Too Pretty to Be True* from the catalog of works included in Duke Ellington's autobiography; still, it is a misprint. Duke Ellington, *Autobiografia*, Italian trans. by E. Mancini, Trento: Emme Edizioni, 1981, 516; orig. ed. *Music Is My Mistress*, New York: Da Capo Press, 1973.

45. A copy of these notes has been provided by Luciano Massagli.

46. Additional confirmation of this has come from Gloria Cruz Sanchez at the music publishing company G. Schirmer (email dated January 25, 2006).

47. Archivist Annie Kubler supplied a rich documentation on *Boogie Bop Blue* between December 2005 and February 2006. Ellington's handwriting, also found in the parts for symphony orchestra, has been recognized by archivist Marcia Rodwin; from this perspective, *Boogie Bop Blue*, while remaining a rough sketch, is the first experiment in symphonic writing conceived and orchestrated by Ellington.

48. Concerning this "little thing," see the liner notes written by Stanley Dance for *The Symphonic Ellington* (Discovery 71003).

49. The author drew attention to various points of contact between the score of *Boogie Bop Blue* and *Non-Violent Integration* in his contribution "La Scala: She Too Pretty to Be Neglected: History and Analysis of an Ellington Composition" at the Conference on Black Music Research—Society for American Music, Chicago, March 15–19, 2006. More recently, musicologist John Howland once again emphasized the close relation between the two works: John Howland, *Ellington Uptown: Duke Ellington, J. P. Johnson and the Birth of the Symphonic Jazz*, Ann Arbor: University of Michigan Press, 2009, 256–61.

50. There is no trace of this first theme in *Boogie Bop Blue* even though, according to John Howland, it is "vaguely derived from a sax blues riff heard in the background of the second chorus of the big band arrangement of *Boogie Bop Blues*." Howland, *Ellington Uptown*, 258.

51. *La Scala* is also the only one of Ellington's orchestral works that was actually released on LP immediately upon being conceived; as will be clarified below, his other similar works had to wait years, sometimes decades, before appearing on an official recording.

2. NEW WORLD A-COMIN'

1. Within the perspective of "Signifyin(g)," this is at the same time an instance of subversive black humor; Samuel A. Floyd Jr., *The Power of Black Music: Interpreting Its History from Africa to the United States*, New York: Oxford University Press, 1995. Henry Louis Gates Jr., *The Signifying Monkey: A Theory of African-American Literary Criticism*, New York: Oxford University Press, 1988.

2. This unreleased documentary, broadcast by ORTS on August 7, 1970, does not have a definitive title. It recently appeared on YouTube, referred to as *Duke Ellington Piano Solo Concert*. The order of the pieces is not the same as in Ellington's recording, where "Black Beauty" appears as the fourth piece and *New World A-Comin'* is the eighth. Luciano Massagli and Giovanni M. Volonté, *The New DESOR: An Updated Edition of Duke Ellington's Story on Records 1924–1974*, 2 vols., Milan: Private edition published by Massagli, 1999, I, 577–8.

3. A fundamental text for the three sacred concerts is Wilbert Weldon Hill's dissertation, *The Sacred Concerts of Edward Kennedy "Duke" Ellington*, Washington, DC: The Catholic University of America, 1994. The premiere of the *First Sacred Concert*, broadcast on June 16, 1967, on NET Public Television, is available on the DVD titled *Duke Ellington: A Concert of Sacred Music/Love You Madly*, Jazz Casual Productions, 2005.

4. The live performance is dated April 10, 1972.

5. Eddie Lambert, *Duke Ellington: A Listener's Guide*, Lanham, MD: Scarecrow Press, 1999, 266. The concert was released on *Duke a Goutelas* (JBP 91); Ellington's reflections are found in *Music Is My Mistress*, New York: Da Capo Press, 1973; the *Goutelas Suite* was recorded on April 27, 1971, and is contained in the CD *The Ellington Suites* (Pablo OJCCD-446-2).

6. The live performance at New York's Museum of Modern Art has recently appeared on a CD released by the French cultural association La Maison du Duke, titled *The 1962 MOMA Recital* (MDD001).

7. On other unreleased tapes dating prior to the *First Sacred Concert* (1965), Ellington plays piano solo versions of the work in question; one of the most outstanding is the recital held at Columbia University on May 20, 1964.

8. The four-minute length of the *First Sacred Concert*'s premiere is likely due to the time available during television broadcasts; only the first theme was played in the concert dedicated to Roosevelt, bringing it to last for three minutes.

9. The program for the premiere of the *First Sacred Concert* is reproduced in Klaus Stratemann, *Duke Ellington, Day by Day and Film by Film*, Copenhagen: JazzMedia, 1992, 516; the liner notes, written by Stanley Dance, music critic and close friend of Ellington, are included in the CD *Concert of Sacred Music* (BMG-RCA 74321192542).

10. "Words of the Week," *Jet*, xxxi, 13, January 5, 1967, 30; Ellington, *Music Is My Mistress*, 342.

11. One must also note that jazz had previously been programmed at the Robin Hood Dell, beginning in 1935, with Paul Whiteman, Benny Goodman, and Hazel Scott playing here.

12. On this occasion, *Grand Slam Jam* was also performed; see chapter 1.

13. Ellington, *Music Is My Mistress*, 475.

14. The extraordinary turnout for this concert has been described by Stratemann, *Duke Ellington, Day by Day and Film by Film*, 304. A positive review and brief history of the summer concerts at the Robin Hood Dell can be found in the August 6 edition of the African American newspaper *Pittsburgh Courier*; this article also draws attention to the Black musicians who had been invited to the Philadelphia Orchestra's previous festivals.

15. The performance of *New World A-Comin'* was rather bland; even though Ellington congratulated the classical musicians repeatedly for their ability to play without a conductor, they may have done better to use one, as can be read in Ken Vail, *Duke's Diary: The Life of Duke Ellington, 1950–1974*, 2 vols., Oxford, MA: Scarecrow Press, 2002, II, 19. Further information is included in Stratemann, *Duke Ellington, Day by Day and Film by Film*, 327. This concert also saw the debut of *Harlem*, but this piece will be discussed in the next chapter.

16. This concert, titled *Excursions in Jazz*, will also be discussed in greater detail in chapter 4, given that *Night Creature* saw its premiere on that occasion.

17. Along with Shirley, drummer Gil Cuppini's big band performed in this ballet (choreographed by Mario Pistoni). One cannot say, however, that La Scala opened its doors to jazz, as is suggested by the title of the article written by Pino Candini and published by *La Notte* on November 19, 1965, "Il jazz entra alla Scala"; if anything, the Theatre hesitantly opened its doors just a crack to Gershwin, whose music, in Italy in the sixties, was beginning to be considered part of the twentieth-century classical tradition.

18. The liner notes written by disc jockey Al Jazzbo Collins are found in *Don Shirley, Tonal Expressions/Piano Perspective*, 2CD set, Collectables (COL CD 2755).

19. As late as a few interviews carried out in 2007 with musicologist John Howland, Shirley still maintained that Ellington should not be considered along the same lines as a classical composer: "It's an insult to Johann Sebastian Bach if you're going to call [my friend Duke Ellington] a composer." John Howland, *Ellington Uptown: Duke Ellington, James P. Johnson, and the Birth of Concert Jazz*, Ann Arbor, MI: University of Michigan Press, 2009, 177–8, 275. The quotation is on page 178.

20. Even in the morning rehearsal, his cadenzas were admired and enthusiastically applauded by the orchestral musicians. The unreleased tapes of the rehearsals also prove that they were improvised and that Ellington left Shirley a certain degree of interpretative freedom as well as the liberty to add brief passages. The evening's live recording was not released for decades until the magazine *Musica Jazz* decided to attach it to its May 1984 issue as an LP titled *Duke Ellington, Le Suites sinfoniche* (2MJP—1021).

21. Ellington, *Music Is My Mistress*, 183.

22. Shirley can be pardoned to some extent, considering that he was not given a transcription of the piano part (which Ellington generally played by heart) but a simple lead sheet to which he had to add many missing parts, some of which were included just before the rehearsals for the concert.

23. On this live performance and the possibility of releasing an LP, see Stratemann, *Duke Ellington, Day by Day and Film by Film*, 364. From the host's spoken introduction, we can presume that this fourth recording was made on the occasion of what actually was the fourth symphonic performance of the work.

24. Labels such as Columbia and Capitol rejected Ellington's symphonic works, considering them "not jazz enough."

25. The performance with the Buffalo Philharmonic Orchestra conducted by Willis Page, whom we shall encounter again as a leading figure in chapter 6, is excellent, above all, in the solo part: Ellington played with great conviction (unreleased recording).

26. Critic Daniele Ionio, in the March–April 1963 issue of the Italian fanzine *Jazzland*, tells us that the Reprise album was also intended to contain a version of *New World A-Comin'* with the Stuttgart Radio Symphony Orchestra. Trombonist Chuck Connors has also mentioned a recording of this work made during the 1963 European tour in Kurt Dietrich, *Duke's Bones: Ellington's Great Trombonists*, Rottenburg: Advance Music, 1996, 165. No other evidence exists, however, and still today, the world of collectors (consulted by record label executive Luciano Massagli upon my request) is not aware of any tapes. The accounts given by Ionio and Connors are, in any case, enough to surmise that Ellington truly did wish to record the work even though he probably did not resolve to proceed.

27. In the unreleased tapes featuring these three orchestras, the composition is performed by three different types of ensembles: New York Philharmonic (Ellington's rhythmic section and classical orchestra), Los Angeles Symphony Orchestra (concerto grosso with both orchestras), and London Philharmonic (classical orchestra with Ellington as a soloist). This shows how open Ellington was to presenting the work in concert with modifications to his original symphonic conception.

28. In 1977, a new live recording was made with the Polish National Philharmonic Orchestra: *The Duke Ellington Orchestra Conducted by Mercer Ellington with the Orkiestra Filharmonii Narodowej* (Polijazz ZSX675). The big band's pianist, a young Mulgrew Miller, was replaced by Adam Makowicz, who at times does not seem to be in his element, above all, in the ragtime passages. *New World A-Comin'*, ably conducted here by Wojciech Rajski, was the only one of Ellington's symphonic works included in this recording that required a classical conductor.

29. Precious biographical information on Luther Henderson can be found in: Peter Lavezzoli, *The King of All, Sir Duke: Ellington and the Artistic Revolution*, New York:

Continuum, 2001, 189–203; liner notes of the CD *Luther Henderson, Clap Hands!/The Greatest Sound Around*, Collectables Jazz Classics (COL-CD-6895); *Luther Henderson Papers*, Schomburg Center for Research in Black Culture, 515 Malcolm X Boulevard, New York, NY 10037; Ben Sisario, "Luther Henderson, 84: Arranged Broadway Music," *New York Times*, August 1, 2003.

30. Ruth Ellington, who became the chairman of Tempo Music in 1941, directly mentioned the works by Henderson that were published: "Mostly we published Duke's music, but we pulled in around thirty composers in the end—some of the musicians in the band, and people like Harry James, Luther Henderson, Randy Weston." In Derek Jewell, *Duke: A Portrait of Duke Ellington*, London: Elm Tree Books, 1977, 73. "A Slip of the Lip," recorded for RCA on July 28, 1942, out of the four pieces composed by Henderson and recorded by Ellington, is the one that met with the most success, being recorded fourteen times. Another work by Henderson was published six years later, "She Wouldn't Be Moved," once again cosigned by Mercer, but only three recordings were made (one of which, however, was at Carnegie Hall on November 13, 1948). Two more pieces written by him alone eventually appeared: "Oh! Well," which was recorded in 1953 for Capitol but never made its way into the repertoire, and "Hey, Cherie," which was occasionally played live between 1955 and 1956 (seven recordings). This discographic information is available in Luciano Massagli and Giovanni M. Volonté, *The New DESOR*, I.

31. On the relations between Strayhorn and Henderson, see David Hajdu, *Lush Life: A Biography of Billy Strayhorn*, New York: North Point Press, 1997. In 1956, Henderson wrote the music for a Broadway show titled *The Crystal Tree*, a score that was meant to have been composed by Ellington who, however, overworked, ultimately decided to pass the commission on to Luther. John Franceschina, *Duke Ellington's Music for the Theatre*, Jefferson, NC: McFarland Company, 2001, 86–7.

32. For a musical dating to late in his life, *Jelly's Last Jam*, based on the life of Jelly Roll Morton, Henderson received the Drama Desk Award for outstanding orchestration, while the Tony Award was given to the show's two main actors (Gregory Hines and Tonya Pinkins). The arrangements prove that Henderson was also capable of writing superbly for smaller ensembles. *Jelly's Last Jam: Original Broadway Cast Recording* (Mercury 314 510 846-2, 1992).

33. Ellington, *Music Is My Mistress*, 43.

34. Four scores by Henderson were used in the session for *Reader's Digest*: "La Dolce Vita," "Spanish Flea," "One Note Samba," and "Misty"; the latter is perhaps the most refined. Interestingly, Henderson's career came to a distinguished close once again surrounded by the Duke's aura, with two recording projects to which he contributed with excellent arrangements: the well-received *Classic Ellington* (1999), recorded by the City of Birmingham Symphony Orchestra conducted by Simon Rattle, and *Take The "A" Train* (2000) by the Canadian Brass, a work that was nominated for the Grammy Award for Best Classical Crossover Album. Henderson died in 2003.

35. On the relations between Mercer Ellington and Calvin Jackson, see Mercer Ellington, *Duke Ellington in Person: An Intimate Memoir*, Boston, MA: Houghton Mifflin Company, 1978, 74–5, 79.

36. Howland, *Ellington Uptown*, 265.

37. The two quotations come from an audio interview given in 1956 to journalist Carter Harman; Howland, *Ellington Uptown*, 265.

38. Ulanov's observations are found in Vail, *Duke's Diary*, I, 247; the other reviews are brought together in Kenneth Steiner's excellent liner notes for the CD *Duke Ellington, Live at Carnegie Hall Dec. 11, 1943* (Storyville 103 8341).

39. Ellington, *Music Is My Mistress*, 183; the beginning and end dates of his engagement at the Capitol appear on the site *The Duke—Where and When, A Chronicle of Duke Ellington's Working Life and Travels*, a meticulous work reconstruction by David Palmquist, www.tdwaw.ca/.

40. Richard O. Boyer, "The Hot Bach," *The New Yorker*, June 24, 1944, quoted in Mark Tucker (ed.), *The Duke Ellington Reader*, New York: Oxford University Press, 1993, 219. The voyage Boyer refers to could plausibly have taken place on November 29 or 30, 1943.

41. Howland, *Ellington Uptown*, 269.

42. Inquiries on the work's formal outline have led to differing results, above all concerning the number of main themes, which varies from three to six. The most coherent analyses have been done by John Howland, who, based on the manuscript, considers the ragtime theme (see ex. 2.2) alongside the three main themes described in this paragraph; David Schiff, who identifies six themes grouped into pairs owing to their motivic ties; and Wilbert Hill, with whom I agree, who in his dissertation reduces the number of main themes to three. Howland, *Ellington Uptown*, 270–2 (which also includes a detailed formal description of the entire work); David Schiff, "Symphonic Ellington? Rehearing New World A-Comin'," *Musical Quarterly*, XCVI, 3–4 (Autumn–Winter 2013), 471–6; Wilbert Hill, *The Sacred Concerts of "Duke" Ellington*, dissertation, Washington, DC: The Catholic University of America, 1995, 123–41 (with a formal outline of the piano solo version that, according to Hill, is a sort of rondo-sonata).

43. Schiff, *Symphonic Ellington?*, 469.

44. The recording contains an impeccable performance from the orchestra, while to some extent, the soloist seems less focused: Ellington seems to have had some formal uncertainties. For example, he hints at a repetition of the second theme in a section intended for the orchestra, and again, some of his hesitations involve technique, such as the unclear exposition of the third theme. *Duke Ellington, V-Disc: A Musical Contribution by America's Best for Our Armed Forces Overseas* (Collectors' Choice Music 617742359428).

45. The instruments available to Henderson for his concerto grosso are the following: two flutes, two oboes, an English horn, three clarinets and a bass clarinet, two bassoons, four French horns, four trumpets in B flat, three trombones, one tuba, timpani, percussions, double bass (played pizzicato as part of the big band), drums, violins, violas, cellos, and double basses. The present analytical observations are based on the score published in 1949 by G. Schirmer under the title Duke Ellington, *New World A-Comin' Arranged by Luther Henderson, Edited by Jeff Tyzik. Ellington Piano Transcription by John Nyerges*; the discographic point of reference is the official 1970 recording: *Duke Ellington, Orchestral Works* (MCAD-42318).

46. Liner notes for the CD *Duke Ellington, Live at Carnegie Hall Dec. 11, 1943* (Storyville 103 8341).

47. Ellington dedicated a single line of his autobiography to the relationship between the book and his composition: "The title was suggested by Roi Ottley's best-selling book of the same name." Ellington, *Music Is My Mistress*, 183.

48. William Pease and Jane Pease, *Black Utopia: Negro Communal Experiments in America*, The State Historical Society of Wisconsin, 1963. Robert Owen, the founder of New Harmony, while against slavery, excluded African Americans from his colony; in Ahmed Shawki, *Black Liberation and Socialism*, Chicago, IL: Haymarket Books, 2006, 111.

49. Both quotations come from Giorgio Rimondi's interesting essay, "Il jazz venuto da Saturno: Sun Ra e la science fiction afroamericana," *Jazzit*, 59 (July–August 2010), 154–63.

50. Brent Hayes Edwards, "The Literary Ellington" in Robert G. O'Meally, Brent H. Edwards, and Farah J. Griffin (eds.), *Uptown Conversation: The New Jazz Studies*, New York: Columbia University Press, 2004, 326–56.

51. Ellington, *Duke Ellington in Person*, 95.

52. Unless otherwise indicated, the biographical information about Roi Ottley has been taken from Mark A. Huddle's excellent introduction to the volume he edited, *Roi Ottley's World War II: The Lost Diary of an African American Journalist*, Lawrence, KS: University Press of Kansas, 2011.

53. The *Roi Ottley Collection* website, edited by St. Bonaventure University, contains a great deal of precious information: web.sbu.edu/friedsam/archives/ottley/.

54. The impact of the Popular Front on American and African American culture, music included, has been well documented by Michael Denning's lengthy study, *The Cultural Front: The Laboring of American Culture in the Twentieth Century*, New York: Verso, 1997.

55. See Elliott Parker, *African-American Correspondents during World War II*, presented at the conference of the Association for Education in Journalism and Mass Communication in Toronto, August 2004. Parker notes that the names of the African American reporters, including Ottley, never appear in studies on World War II correspondents. The previously mentioned *Roi Ottley's World War II* is a good anthology of Ottley's writings on the war.

56. Roi Ottley, *New World A-Coming: Inside Black America*, Boston, MA: Houghton Mifflin Company, 1943, 243.

57. This conversation is found in the paragraph "Politics" from George's monograph on Ellington: Don George, *Sweet Man: The Real Duke Ellington*, New York: G. P. Putnam's Sons, 1981, 112–3.

58. George, *Sweet Man: The Real Duke Ellington*, 113, for both citations.

59. Ellington, *Music Is My Mistress*, 175–80; in his memoirs, Ellington dedicated an entire paragraph to this musical, *Jump for Joy Extension*. The show's political implications have been brought out by Graham Lock, *Blutopia: Visions of the Future and Revisions of the Past in the Work of Sun Ra, Duke Ellington, and Anthony Braxton*, Durham, NC, London: Duke University Press, 1999, 93–9; and even more so by Denning, *The Cultural Front*, that dedicates to *Jump for Joy* the paragraph "Fare Thee Well, Land of Cotton: Duke Ellington," 309.

60. The quotations are from Boyer, *The Hot Bach*, in M. Tucker (ed.), *The Duke Ellington Reader*, 238.

61. Duke Ellington, "The Duke Steps Out," *Rhythm*, March 1931, in M. Tucker (ed.), *The Duke Ellington Reader*, 49; Ellington, *Music Is My Mistress*, 180.

62. Lock, *Blutopia*, 95.

63. Near a small train station in Scottsboro (Alabama), nine young African Americans were accused of raping two white women. After a trial that only lasted four days, an Alabama courthouse sentenced them to death. Lawyers from the American Communist Party then stepped in and, after two more trials, succeeded in having the five men definitively found guilty receive sentences ranging from twenty-three years to life in prison.

64. The information on Ellington's political and civil engagement in the early thirties is found in Lock, *Blutopia*, 121.

65. Ingrid Monson, *Freedom Sounds: Civil Rights Call out to Jazz and Africa*, New York: Oxford University Press, 2007, 61, 202, 209.

66. While Ellington's involvement with the cultural agenda of the Popular Front is sprinkled throughout the aforementioned volume by M. Denning, *The Cultural Front*, the paragraph entirely dedicated to the ties between the world of jazz and that movement is titled "Cabaret Blues," 323–61. Ellington's links with the left are part of a tendency toward communism that, from the midtwenties to the Second World War, concerned a significant portion of the African American community, Harlemites in particular. On the relations between the left and the African American community, see Ahmed Shawki, *Black Liberation and Socialism*, Chicago, IL: Haymarket Books, 2006; Cedric J. Robinson, *Black Marxism: The Making of the Black Radical Tradition*, Chapel Hill, NC: University of North Carolina Press, 1983; Michael C. Dawson, *Black Visions: The Roots of Contemporary African-American Political Ideologies*, Chicago, IL: University of Chicago Press, 2001 (that does not overlook Ellington's contribution, 190); Michael C. Dawson, *Blacks In and Out of the Left*, Cambridge, MA: Harvard University Press, 2013; Winston James, *Holding Aloft the Banner of Ethiopia: Caribbean Radicalism in Early Twentieth-Century America*, New York: Verso, 1998. The latter volume is interesting, given that Ottley's parents were Caribbean; nevertheless, he only makes two fleeting appearances.

67. John Hammond, "The Tragedy of Duke Ellington," *Brooklyn Eagle*, November 3, 1935, in Tucker (ed.), *The Duke Ellington Reader*, 118–20.

68. FBI dossier, "Edward (Duke) Kennedy Ellington 100-HQ-434443," 4–5.

69. Judith E. Smith, *Visions of Belonging: Family Stories, Popular Culture, and Postwar Democracy, 1940–1960*, New York: Columbia University Press, 2004. The entire first chapter, "Ordinary Families, Popular Culture, and Popular Democracy, 1935–1945 is richly documented regarding this period of time, 1–37. Aaron J. Johnson, "A Date with the Duke: Ellington on Radio," *Musical Quarterly*, Winter 2013, 394.

70. Barbara Dianne Savage, *Broadcasting Freedom: Radio War and the Politics of Race, 1938–1948*, Chapel Hill, NC: University of North Carolina Press, 1999, 251.

71. *New World A-Coming* concentrated on the problems faced by African Americans and thus relied on Ottley for its first two seasons. From 1946 until 1957, the last year it was on the air, it broadened its civic engagement to include other minorities (Italian immigrants, Puerto Ricans, victims of Apartheid in South Africa, etc.).

72. The excerpts from reviews are in Savage, *Broadcasting Freedom*, 254–5. In its first year alone, *New World A-Coming* won seven prizes, and Ottley received the Peabody Award for the radio adaptation of his bestseller.

73. The conductor and the arranger changed over the various episodes; sometimes John Guard filled both roles. The chromaticism in the transition episode seen in ex. 2.8 has some

features in common with "Mood Indigo," as noted by David Schiff in his aforementioned analysis, *Symphonic Ellington?*, so it is not by chance that the transformation of the end credit theme resembles this ballad by Ellington. "Mood Indigo" is furthermore present in the episode "The Negro in the Entertainment" (March 26, 1944), more precisely in the narration of a musician playing jazz in the racist South.

74. Biographer John Hasse makes no mistake when he writes that the only composition in Ellingtonia directly tied to the war is "A Slip of the Lip," written by Mercer Ellington and Luther Henderson. Nevertheless, here we have shown that *New World A-Comin'*, above all in its radio version, also falls within this category of composition. John Edward Hasse, *Beyond Category: The Life and Genius of Duke Ellington*, New York: Omnibus Press, 1993, 277.

75. The points of contact between Ellington and Canada Lee have been brought to light in the biography by Mona Z. Smith, *Becoming Something: The Story of Canada Lee, The Untold Tragedy of the Great Black Actor, Activist, and Athlete*, New York: Faber and Faber, 2004.

3. HARLEM

1. Ellington's memories of his encounters at the White House are found in *Music Is My Mistress*, New York: Da Capo Press, 1973, 424–33; an accurate account of the galas with Nixon, of which partial audio and video recordings also exist, is provided in Edward Allan Faine's volume, *Ellington at the White House 1969*, Takoma Park, MD: IM Press, 2013.

2. The details of Truman and Ellington's meeting are available online on the website for the Harry S. Truman Library & Museum, www.trumanlibrary.org. The quotation is in Ellington, *Music Is My Mistress*, 361.

3. The photo has been reproduced in various texts and on the internet, but the publication with the best resolution is Scott Yanow, *Duke Ellington*, New York: Friedman/Fairfax Publishers, 1999, 15. Making hypotheses on this score based on the photo is the only option currently available, given that the manuscript score given to Truman has never been found; Stanley Slome, *Harlem: Duke and the Classical Connection*, *Blue Light*, iv, 1 (March 1997), 1–14; *Blue Light*, iv, 2 (June 1997), 9–10.

4. The White House's stance on any possible involvement in a concert tied to the civil rights movement was made clear by the president's absence and his eloquent silence. Furthermore, a private note written at the White House at the end of Ellington's letter of invitation by an unknown person dispels any ambiguity with one single syllable: "No!" underlined twice. John Edward Hasse, *Beyond Category: The Life and Genius of Duke Ellington*, New York, Omnibus Press, 1993, 297.

5. In July 1952, Ellington invited Truman to a date of his own choice among the many concerts held during his three-week engagement at the Blue Note in Chicago; Ellington offered the tapes of the live performance to the president as a gift. A PDF version of the correspondence is available at the website: www.trumanlibrary.org.

6. Truman Record Collection, www.nps.gov/hstr/learn/historyculture/truman-record-collection.htm.

7. "Six Composers to Collaborate on NYC Portrait," *DownBeat*, October 20, 1950, 3.

8. According to the article "Six Composers to Collaborate on a NYC Portrait," "each composer conducting his section"; according to the August 30, 1950, issue of *Variety*, "The NBC [Symphony Orchestra] was to be conducted by Toscanini, or by each composer batoning his own movement of the suite"; quoted in Klaus Stratemann, *Duke Ellington, Day by Day and Film by Film*, Copenhagen: JazzMedia, 1992, 480.

9. Ellington remained closely tied to NBC throughout the fifties; in 1952, his big band was on the air no fewer than seventeen times, setting a record for the African American ensemble most frequently broadcast by NBC. Michele Hilmes, *NBC: America's Network*, Los Angeles, CA: University of California Press, 2007, 134.

10. Ellington, *Music Is My Mistress*, 188–89. The interview with Ruth Ellington is found in Harvey G. Cohen, *Duke Ellington's America*, Chicago, IL: University of Chicago Press, 2010, 292.

11. Ellington, *Music Is My Mistress*, 188.

12. David Palmquist, *The Duke—Where and When, A Chronicle of Duke Ellington's Workings Life and Travels*: www.tdwaw.ca/.

13. Ellington dedicated his *Uwis Suite* to this week-long celebration.

14. Duke Ellington Week has been analyzed in detail by Stratemann, *Duke Ellington, Day by Day and Film by Film*, 633–9. In addition to Baker, stride piano specialist Brooks Kerr and Ellington also took turns at the piano.

15. In his memoirs, the Duke included a highly affectionate recollection of hefty Two Ton amusing children while dressed up as Santa Claus: "In size and personality, he was the perfect Santa Claus. He would sit and play piano, and give presents to the kids, and everybody came and brought their children. They loved Two Ton Baker." (Ellington, *Music Is My Mistress*, 246). Two photos, one of Two Ton Baker dressed as Santa Claus and the other of the comedian next to Ellington and two kids, both taken at the Blue Note sometime around 1952, are available online at the site The Dick Two Ton Baker Home Page, www.twotonbaker.com.

16. An unreleased video contains the performance given by the two.

17. The tape of the party has not been released.

18. This demonstrates that studying manuscript scores, in jazz studies in particular, is not always able to reconstruct the coordinates of the compositional act.

19. The reference score of *Harlem* is the one published by Schirmer with Luther Henderson's symphony orchestration (and Maurice Peress's editing). To locate the sections of the work discussed here, one can use the following timings from the CD *The Symphonic Ellington* (Reprise) Discovery 71003: from measure 9 of A until D1 = 1:42–4:36.

20. The clarinet's sextuplets are heard at 2:01.

21. Section B2 = 3:17; sections B and B1 = 3:04–3:17. A slighter deviation from the score appears in the melody of the C section: in the piano version, it takes up the first theme in an almost identical form, while in the score, it is split apart by brief concertante interventions by the clarinet.

22. Most likely, Steiner was stimulated by Selznick to write such important scores, both in terms of their duration and as regards their extradiegetic comments. The producer decided to give the soundtrack a leading role in all his films; Selznick often collaborated with his composers in conceiving the soundtracks even without any formal training in music. On

this matter, see the interesting dissertation by Nathan R. Platte, *Musical Collaboration in the Films of David O. Selznick, 1932–1957*, Ann Arbor, MI: University of Michigan Press, 2010.

23. It was director (and producer) Merian C. Cooper who rejected Harling's music on the grounds that it was not suited to the sinister atmosphere of the jungle. On the origin of the score for *The Most Dangerous Game*, interesting information is contained in John Morgan's liner notes for Max Steiner's CD, *The Son of Kong—The Most Dangerous Game*, Naxos 8.570183.

24. The opening has been analyzed by Michael Slowik, *After the Silents: Hollywood Film Music in the Early Sound Era 1926–1934*, New York: Columbia University Press, 2014, 199–205.

25. In some senses, the score can be read as a modern adaptation of the traditional genre of the *chasse*.

26. The reader may judge these affinities by comparing the outset of *Harlem* with the beginning of the film, which is currently available on YouTube. The motif returns clearly at 48:51 and is echoed six further times during the hunting scene.

27. My private conversation with Lasker took place in Portland during the international conference *Ellington and Strayhorn: A Celebration*, Reed College Greenberg Distinguished Scholar Program, Portland, OR, November 6–8, 2015.

28. The theater referred to in the piece is the Howard Theatre in Washington, DC, known for its Black clientele since its opening in 1910. The engagement lasted from December 3 to 9, 1932. Ken Vail has reproduced two posters in which it is clear that the week's shows saw Duke Ellington and His Cotton Club Band followed by the screen feature *The Most Dangerous Game*; Ken Vail, *Duke's Diary: The Life of Duke Ellington, 1950–1974*, 2 vols., Lanham, MD: Scarecrow Press, 2002, i, 70. Many thanks to Steven Lasker for providing a copy of the article that appeared in the *Pittsburgh Courier*.

29. Not by chance, the same interval, a minor third, also appears at the beginning of the theme indicated in the score as "Russian Waltz," i.e., the minor key composition played at the piano by Count Zaroff, evoking his fatherland. This melody is all that survived of Harling's score.

30. Section Y = 13:38 to the end.

31. Strayhorn's presence on the transatlantic is confirmed by his boarding card ("William Strayhorn, age 35, single, 1619 Broadway, New York") in Palmquist, *The Duke—Where and When*.

32. "The larger things like *Harlem* or *Black, Brown and Beige* I had very little to do with other than maybe discussing them with him. That's because the larger works are such a personal expression of him," Bill Coss, "Ellington & Strayhorn, Inc.," *DownBeat*, June 7, 1962, quoted in Mark Tucker (ed.), *The Duke Ellington Reader*, New York: Oxford University Press, 1993, 501.

33. On Strayhorn's unrecognized contribution, see Walter van de Leur, *Something to Live For: The Music of Billy Strayhorn*, New York: Oxford University Press, 2002, 115.

34. Mark Tucker, "The Genesis of Black, Brown and Beige," *Black Music Research Journal*, xiii, 2 (Fall 1993), 67–86.

35. Duke Ellington, *Beige*, in *Black, Brown and Beige*, ms n.d., Duke Ellington Collection, Series 4: Scripts, Box 3, Archives Center, Smithsonian Institution, 1, 3. Ellington

himself believed that this narration would help the listener understand the work. He had, in fact, revealed to *Variety* that he intended to explain the story behind his much-discussed composition *Black, Brown and Beige*, elaborating the typewritten copy and publishing the result in a book; the layout was to contain narration and music transcribed like a sort of parallel text translation. This project was never brought to completion. "Duke's Book Will Explain His Carnegie Hall Symph," *Variety*, June 9, 1943, 2.

36. Acute observations on the manuscript, in particular the section that refers to Harlem, can be found in John Howland, *Ellington Uptown: Duke Ellington, James P. Johnson, and the Birth of Concert Jazz*, Ann Arbor, MI: University of Michigan Press, 2009, 290–2; Graham Lock, *Blutopia: Visions of the Future and Revisions of the Past in the Work of Sun Ra, Duke Ellington, and Anthony Braxton*, Durham, NC: Duke University Press, 1999, 110–2; Brent Hayes Edwards, "The Literary Ellington," in Robert G. O'Meally, Brent H. Edwards, and Farah J. Griffin (eds.), *Uptown Conversation: The New Jazz Studies*, New York: Columbia University Press, 2004, 343–5.

37. The notes printed for the premiere of *Black, Brown and Beige*, edited by Irving Kolodin, are reproduced in *The Duke Ellington Reader*, 160–5 [163]. Ellington's presentation is recorded in *The Duke Ellington Carnegie Hall Concerts: January 1943*, Prestige (2PCD 34004-2). The narration underlying *Black, Brown and Beige*—which would pass, as mentioned, from the manuscript to the typewritten copy and then into the program notes—was summarized in Ellington's presentation at Carnegie Hall and eventually preserved in Ellington, *Music Is My Mistress*, 143–5.

38. A narrative outline not unlike *Black, Brown and Beige* and *Harlem* also appears in a short film dating to 1934 titled *Symphony in Black*; the film is subdivided into four episodes: "The Laborers," "A Triangle" (in turn divided into "Dance," "Jealousy," and "Blues"), "A Hymn of Sorrow," and "Harlem Rhythm." The concept of "more churches than cabarets," not by chance included at the heart of the score with "Hymn of Sorrow," took shape for the first time in an extended work by Ellington.

39. The symphony is examined in chapter 5, "Harlem Love Song: The Symphonic Aspirations of James P. Johnson, 1930–1945," of John Howland's monograph, *Ellington Uptown: Duke Ellington, James P. Johnson, and the Birth of Concert Jazz*, Ann Arbor, MI: University of Michigan Press, 2009, 200–45.

40. Ellington played in Fort Lauderdale on November 20 and in Tampa on November 22: Palmquist, *The Duke—Where and When*. The passage by James Weldon Johnson is in Howland, *Ellington Uptown*, 212.

41. *Harlem Symphony* was Johnson's classical composition most performed during his life; in spite of this, it was only recorded many years after his death, in 1992, conducted by Marin Alsop. J.P. Johnson, *Victory Stride: The Symphonic Music of James P. Johnson*, MusicMasters Classics (01612-7140-2).

42. Actually, Johnson's music, which, according to the program notes, intended to evoke a "rhumba of the Spanish section" of *Harlem*, sounds more like a Brazilian tango; a maxixe, to be specific (comparable, for example, to "Corta Jaca" by Chiquinha Gonzaga); Ellington, instead, at the point of his score indicated as a "Rhumba," wrote a Cuban danzón.

43. An analysis of the "Baptist Mission" movement is found in Howland, *Ellington Uptown*, 237–9.

44. Ellington, *Music Is My Mistress*, 36.

45. The exact dates of this first visit to New York have not been identified; the concerts at the Lafayette Theatre were held, according to various sources, sometime between March 1 and 11. Mark Tucker, *Ellington: The Early Years*, Chicago, IL: University of Illinois Press, 1995, 80–2.

46. Leonard Harper got Ellington involved, as a piano accompanist, in a show he was staging at the Hollywood Café, an off-Broadway club located at 203 West 49th Street; Steven Lasker's liner notes for the three-CD compilation *Early Ellington: The Complete Brunswick and Vocalion Recordings of Duke Ellington, 1926–1931* (MCA—GRP 36402), page 32. Ellington's son conserved a vivid recollection of that block and that house, his father's first residence in Harlem: Mercer Ellington, *Duke Ellington in Person: An Intimate Memoir*, Boston, MA: Houghton Mifflin Company, 1978, 16–7.

47. More precise information on immigration to Harlem in the fundamental text by Gilbert Osofsky, *Harlem: The Making of a Ghetto: Negro New York, 1890–1930*, Chicago, IL: Ivan R. Dee, 1996. Osofsky notes that there was a strong rivalry between Blacks who were originally from New York and those who immigrated from the South; the latter caused the former some embarrassment, as is sarcastically rendered in a poem by Langston Hughes, *High to Low*: "God knows / We have our troubles, too / One trouble is you: / You talk too loud, / Look too black." Ellington's "Immigration Blues" seems to, instead, suggest a possible "Harmony in Harlem."

48. The invitation is reproduced on page 152 of the chapter dedicated to the rent party, titled "The Saturday Night Function," of the volume by Jervis Anderson, *This Was Harlem: A Cultural Portrait, 1900–1950*, New York: The Noonday Press, 1981. Further details on the topic are found in Jonathan Gill, *Harlem: The Four Hundred Year History from Dutch Village to Capital of Black America*, New York: Grove Press, 2011, 232–5; David Levering Lewis, *When Harlem Was in Vogue*, New York: Penguin Books, 1977, 107–8; Osofsky, *Harlem*, 138–40.

49. While Carl Van Vechten mentions these parties in his famous *Nigger Heaven* (1926), Wallace Thurman titled Part Four of his novel *The Blacker the Berry* (1929) "Rent Party," which contains one of the most evocative descriptions of these events; Carl Van Vechten, *Nigger Heaven*, New York: Alfred A. Knopf, 1926, 56–7; the quotation of Willie "the Lion" Smith is in Lewis, *When Harlem Was in Vogue*, 107. Ellington considered Smith to be one of the great masters of stride piano, a perfectly Harlemite piano style that was often heard at rent parties. Not by chance, he dedicated two compositions to this virtuoso, "Portrait of a Lion" and "The Second Portrait of the Lion."

50. "Gimme a Pigfoot (And a Bottle of Beer)," written by Wesley Wilson and recorded by Bessie Smith in 1933 for Okeh Records.

51. Andrew S. Berish, *Lonesome Roads and Streets of Dreams: Place, Mobility, and Race in Jazz of the 1930s and '40s*, Chicago, IL: University of Chicago Press, 2012. This musicologist, who dedicated to Ellington a chapter titled "A Locomotive Laboratory of Place: Duke Ellington and His Orchestra," adopts a concept developed by historian Josh Kun, *Audiotopia: Music, Race, and America*, Los Angeles, CA: University of California Press, 2005.

52. Meyer formulated the theory of connotation. Put briefly, he maintains that music can stimulate certain associations with images, places, and cultures by emphasizing certain

parameters (instrumentation, harmonic or rhythmic context, etc.). Leonard B. Meyer, *Emotion and Meaning in Music*, Chicago, IL: The University of Chicago Press, 1961.

53. Duke Ellington, "Ellington: My Hunt for Song Titles," *Rhythm*, August 1933, 22–3, reproduced in Tucker (ed.), *The Duke Ellington Reader*, 87–9.

54. The colorful description of café aromas, flirting couples, and boisterous dancers all wafting through the air shafts was published by Richard O. Boyer in the second of three pieces dedicated to Ellington with the title "The Hot Bach," *The New Yorker*, July 1, 1944, later included in Tucker (ed.), *The Duke Ellington Reader*, 235. A deeper exploration of the work's descriptive elements is found in Edward Green, "Harlem Air Shaft: A True Programmatic Composition?" *Journal of Jazz Studies*, vii, 1 (Spring 2011), 28–46.

55. This catalog could be enlarged by including the Duke's compositions dedicated to the cultural heroes most closely tied to the history of the ghetto, such as "Black Beauty: A Portrait of Florence Mills," "Bojangles: A Portrait of Bill Robinson," "Portrait of a Lion" and "The Second Portrait of the Lion," and "A Portrait of Bert Williams." Furthermore, pieces linked more generically to New York, excluding those with references to neighborhoods other than Harlem, may have a right to be included in the list; among the latter, we would find "New York City Blues (An Urban Fantasy)" and "Asphalt Jungle." Nonetheless, adjusting our focus slightly, only those works that explicitly deal with Harlem have been included here.

56. Floyd Henderson, "The Image of New York City in American Popular Music: 1880–1970," *New York Folklore Quarterly*, xxx, 4 (December 1974), 267–78.

57. Similar results were reached by Nancy Groce in the chapter "Harlem on My Mind" of her *New York: Songs of the City*, New York: Watson-Guptill Publications, 1999, 82–9.

58. The list includes a "Harlem Mania" (1932) with words and music by Donald Heywood, a "Harlemania" (1930) by the famous team Rodgers & Hart, and a third "Harlemania" (1929) by the duo that wrote for the Cotton Club in collaboration with Ellington, Dorothy Fields, and Jimmy McHugh; the Duke recorded this latter song in 1929. The short by Vitaphone, *Harlem-Mania* (1929), features Norman Thomas's white ensemble.

59. Cinema, both white and Black, had a severe case of Harlemania. Midway between gangster movies and musicals, dozens of Harlemite films appeared from the late twenties through the following decade. On this topic, see the fundamental volume by Paula J. Massood, *Making a Promised Land: Harlem in 20th Century Photography and Film*, New Brunswick, NJ: Rutgers University Press, 2013.

60. I have analyzed a selection of fifty songs (excluding compositions by Ellington), chronologically situated between "The Harlem Strut" by J. P. Johnson (1921) and "I Remember Harlem" by Roy Eldridge (1950).

61. While a discussion of "exotic Africa" in Western music would certainly take us well beyond the limits of the current volume, we must still note that the ingredients of "jungle style" were not personally devised by Ellington; the bandleader inherited them from a long-standing tradition. Not by chance, the "Air pour les esclaves africains" in Rameau's 1735 *Les Indes galantes* is an unsettling tribal dance in a minor key marked by obsessive repeated notes to be played, according to the composer's indications, *lourdement* (heavily). The same clichés echoed in America beginning in the 1870s and reached their peak between 1900 and 1909: ragtime, indeed, overflowed with an Americanized

"Africa." From here, Hottentots, Senegalese, Zulu, and Congolese figures (all obviously made of paper mâché) made their way into jazz during the Roaring Twenties with titles such as "Senegalese Stomp" (Clarence Williams, 1926), "African Jungle" (Jungle Town Stompers, 1929), and "Congo Love Song" (Dixie Rhythm Kings, 1929). I presented my study of exoticism in "400 Years of Jungle Style" during the convention promoted by the Società Italiana di Musicologia Afroamericana, *Black Atlantic, From Africa to Jazz and Back*, Piacenza, March 19, 2005.

62. Widening our field of observation beyond Ellington, one notices that other pieces in the *Harlemania* craze also tell us, in their words and music, that in the end, the Black jungle and Black Manhattan are one and the same thing. While "Harlem Congo" (1937) by Chick Webb merely alludes to exoticism in its title, "Harlem Serenade" (1929) by George Gershwin, Ira Gershwin, and Gus Kahn makes this allusion explicit with a text that invites us to go on a safari in the ghetto ("Listen to that uptown jungle wail / Book your passage to that Harlem Congo trail"), while "Tarzan of Harlem," a 1939 hit by Cab Calloway, underlines this even more with jungle devices including ostinatos played by "African tom-toms" set in a minor key. The quotation is from Barry Ulanov, "The Ellington Programme," in Robert G. O'Meally (ed.), *The Jazz Cadence of American Culture*, New York: Columbia University Press, 1998, 169.

63. Here, I am referring to the typewritten manuscript containing the program for *Black, Brown and Beige* discussed above. One exception could be the impressionistic "Blue Bells of Harlem" that, not by chance, Ellington never officially recorded and that he wrote for Paul Whiteman. The term "stereotype" does not refer to the artistic quality of these Harlem compositions but the image of the ghetto conveyed by them. From a purely aesthetic point of view, this repertoire contains minor works (such as "Savoy Strut"), highly interesting compositions (including "Immigration Blues"), and true masterpieces (for example, "Echoes of Harlem").

64. Konrad Bercovici, "The Black Block of Manhattan," *Harper's*, October 1924, in Anderson, *This Was Harlem*, 172; Winthrop D. Lane, "Ambushed in the City: The Grim Side of Harlem," *Survey Graphic—Harlem Mecca of the New Negro*, March 1925, 692–4, 713–5; Beverly Smith, "Population Rises Steadily: Illness Takes Heavy Toll; Employment and Low Wages Result from Race Prejudice," *New York Herald Tribune*, February 10, 1930, in Allon Schoener (ed.), *Harlem on My Mind: Cultural Capital of Black America, 1900–1968*, New York: The New Press, 1995, 125.

65. This data is found in Osofsky, *Harlem: The Making of a Ghetto*, 140.

66. For the situation of Harlem during the Great Depression, the reference text, with abundant statistical information and precise details concerning the events that triggered the racial revolts, is the volume by Cheryl Lynn Greenberg, *Or Does It Explode? Black Harlem in the Great Depression*, New York: Oxford University Press, 1991; the engrossing chapter "Self-Help in Hard Times" is in the text by radical historian Howard Zinn, *A People's History of the United States*, New York: Harper & Row 1980; an equally stimulating chapter, "Moon Over Harlem, The Great Depression Uptown, 1929–1943," is found in Gill, *Harlem*, 282–333.

67. Fannie Hurst, "The Other and Unknown Harlem," *New York Times Sunday Magazine*, August 4, 1946, quoted in Anderson, *This Was Harlem*, 186.

68. This is where he lived with his son Mercer and his new sweetheart Mildred Dixon, a dancer at the Cotton Club. In 1931, Ellington's parents also moved into this apartment. Lasker, liner notes for *Early Ellington*, 49–50; M. Ellington, *Duke Ellington in Person*, 17–8.

69. Claude McKay, *Harlem: Negro Metropolis*, New York: A Harvest Book, 1960, 25–8.

70. "Sugar Hill," *Ebony*, November 1946, quoted in Anderson, *This Was Harlem*, 341.

71. Adam Clayton Powell Jr., "Harlem Declares Its Rent Too High," *Washington Post*, March 28, 1935, in Anderson, *This Was Harlem*, 340.

72. In 1976, Ellington's apartment became a National Historic Landmark. Photos of and information concerning the apartment on St. Nicholas Avenue can be downloaded from the Library of Congress website, www.loc.gov/pictures/item/ny1647/.

73. In the fifties and sixties, Ellington also had two apartments at 333 and 334 Riverside Drive, almost on the corner of West 106th Street (Central Park West). One of them acted as his office, while the other was used by his family and Tempo Music, whose president was his sister Ruth. In 1977, West 106th Street, to which he dedicated "Park at 106th Street," was renamed "Duke Ellington Boulevard." In the early sixties, he moved to 400 Central Park West and spent the last decade of his life with his partner Beatrice "Evie" Ellis on the twenty-second floor of 140 West End Avenue on the Upper West Side.

74. Van de Leur, *Something to Live For*, 88.

75. The vexed reaction shown by Manhattan's white inhabitants to the real estate investment concerning St. Philip's Church is discussed in the article "Loans to White Renegades Who Back Negroes Cut Off," *Harlem Home News*, April 7, 1911, in Schoener (ed.), *Harlem on My Mind*, 24–5.

76. Osofsky, *Harlem: The Making of a Ghetto*, 113–7, 143–6.

77. James Weldon Johnson, *Black Manhattan*, New York: Alfred A. Knopf, 1930, 163–8.

78. George E. Haynes, "The Church and the Negro Spirit," *Survey Graphic: Harlem Mecca of the New Negro*, March 1925, 695–7, 708–9; Johnson, *Black Manhattan*, 165–6.

79. Greenberg, *Or Does It Explode?*, 103–5.

80. Mark Tucker believes that the first theme of "Immigration Blues" most likely has a spiritual character; Tucker, *Ellington: The Early Years*, 232–3.

81. Musicologist Marcello Piras is inclined to see a religious element in the saxophones' four-measure introduction to "Harlem Air Shaft"; see his stimulating essay "Duke and Descriptive Music," in Edward Green (ed.), *The Cambridge Companion to Duke Ellington*, Cambridge, MA: Cambridge University Press, 2014, 221.

82. Another brief allusion consists in the reappearance of the spiritual "Come Sunday" in the *Beige* movement (set in North Manhattan and Harlem) of the suite *Black, Brown and Beige*; the theme, however, is developed by Ellington in *Black* (which refers to the rural nineteenth century), while in *Beige*, it only fleetingly appears for a few measures, as though reminding us that the values of the "old South" were transplanted into the modern urban setting. It may be useful to point out here that the spiritual "Hymn of Sorrow," the third part of the previously discussed short film *Symphony in Black* (1934), does not necessarily refer to the New York ghetto. In the entire film, the only explicit reference to "black Manhattan" is (not by chance) the final "Harlem Rhythm," where dancer "Snakehips" Tucker, who had worked with Ellington at the Cotton Club, shows his talent; Stratemann, *Duke Ellington, Day by Day and Film by Film*, 118–28.

83. Sara Blair, *Harlem Crossroads: Black Writers and the Photograph in the Twentieth Century*, Princeton, NJ: Princeton University Press, 2007, 5–6.

84. Melissa Rachleff, "Photojournalism in Harlem: Morgan and Marvin Smith and the Construction of Power, 1934–1943" in Deborah Willis et al. (eds.), *Harlem: A Century in Images*, New York: Skira Rizzoli, 2010, 5.

85. The American tradition of photojournalism has deep roots, from the photographers who documented the Civil War, such as Mathew B. Brady and Timothy O'Sullivan, to the ones who chronicled the Great Depression, including Walker Evans and Dorothea Lange, without forgetting figures like Jacob Riis and Lewis Hines who, in the late nineteenth and early twentieth centuries, focused their work respectively on the extreme poverty in New York's slums and child labor. The following texts are dedicated to American photojournalism in the thirties and forties: Alan Trachtenberg, *Reading American Photographs: Images as History: Mathew Brady to Walker Evans*, New York: Hill & Wang, 1989; Peter Walther, *New Deal Photography: USA 1935–1943*, Köln: Taschen, 2016; Oliver Lugon, *Le style documentaire: D'August Sander à Walker Evans 1920–1945*, Paris: Editions Macula, 2001. The series *Fields of Vision*, published by the Library of Congress and mainly based on the work of photographers from the Farm Security Administration and the Office of War Information, is remarkable, above all, for the quality of its images; at present, the volumes printed include monographs by Ben Shahn, Jack Delano, Arthur Rothstein, Esther Bubley, Russell Lee, John Vachon, Marion Post Wolcott, and Gordon Parks. Black issues interested some of these photographers, in particular Delano, Lee, Shahn, and the African American Parks; in 1941, Lee published a book of photography with text by Richard Wright titled *12 Million Black Voices*, New York: Basic Books, 2002.

86. Blair, *Harlem Crossroads*, 7.

87. A rich iconography of these racial revolts is found in Blair, *Harlem Crossroads*; Golden et al. (eds.), *Harlem: A Century in Images*; and above all, Shoener (ed.), *Harlem on My Mind*. See also the extraordinary monumental collection with texts by Manning Marable and Leith Mullings, edited by Sophie Spencer-Wood, *Freedom: A Photographic History of the African American Struggle*, London: Phaidon, 2002.

88. Aaron Siskind, *Harlem Document: Photographs 1932–1940*, Providence, RI: Matrix Publications, 1981.

89. The photos of Parks's scoop, published in the November 1, 1948, issue of *Life*, have been marvelously reproduced in a series dedicated to this photographer: *Gordon Parks, Collected Works*, 6 vols., Göttingen: Steidl/Gordon Parks Foundation, 2012, II, 24–73, and V, 24–34; the volume with the photo report "Harlem 1943, 1944," 62–73, is also pertinent to the present context. Roy DeCarava, with texts by Langston Hughes, *The Sweet Flypaper of Life*, New York: Hill & Wang, 1967.

90. The portraits made by Van Der Zee and others of the middle-class members of their community represented a reaction against decades of images that forced African Americans into grotesque stereotypes. This form of liberation had begun in the early twentieth century with the photographs taken by Du Bois of the Black elite in Georgia and by the photography studio belonging to the African American Scurlock family in Ellington's Washington. Deborah Willis, *Reflections in Black: A History of Black Photographers, 1840 to the Present*, New York: W. W. Norton & Company, 2002, 36; Deborah Willis-Braithwaite,

VanDerZee, Photographer 1886-1983, New York: Harry N. Abrams, 1993; Shawn Michelle Smith, *Photography on the Color Line: W. E. B. Du Bois, Race and Visual Culture*, Durham, NC: Duke University Press, 2004; Paul Gardullo et al. (eds.), *The Scurlock Studio and Black Washington: Picturing the Promise*, Washington, DC: National Museum of African American History and Culture, Smithsonian Institution, 2009. The enormous distance between Van Der Zee and DeCarava's generations can be measured by comparing two photos of the same subject: a young Black woman portrayed on the day of her graduation. Van Der Zee's "Graduation Portrait" (1939) is a studio photo of a girl dressed in white and surrounded by flowers and a few books; the female protagonist of DeCarava's "Graduation" (1949) is still wearing a ceremonial white dress, but the backdrop is now walking across a dirty alley in Harlem, tellingly passing from a well-lit area to a shadowy zone. These two worlds are bridged by the production dating to the thirties and the forties by Black photographers Morgan and Marvin Smith who, concentrating on Harlem, on the one hand still portrayed the Black bourgeoisie but on the other also documented strikes, breadlines, and demonstrations against lynching; M&M (Morgan and Marvin) Smith, *Harlem: The Vision of Morgan and Marvin Smith*, Lexington, KY: University Press of Kentucky, 1998.

91. Patricia Hills, *Painting Harlem Modern: The Art of Jacob Lawrence*, Berkeley, CA: University of California Press, 2009; for the present discussion, see in particular the chapter "Home in Harlem: Tenements and Streets," 168-203, focused on the works he dedicated to the ghetto beginning in the thirties in relation to a few photos dating to the same period. Lawrence's most important paintings dedicated to Black Manhattan are the thirty works in the *Harlem Series* (1943), interpreted by Hills as a comment in images on Ottley's essay *New World A-Coming*. Many thanks to the Portland Art Museum for providing PDFs of a few paintings from the *Harlem Series* that are not displayed for those visiting the permanent collection.

92. In Ann Petry, *The Street*, New York: Houghton Mifflin Company, 1974, 141.

93. In the area of music, the last echoes of the fascination for exotic Harlem were heard in 1942-43.

94. Actually, there is another composition dating to the same years that portrays a Black Manhattan free from stereotypes: "I Remember Harlem," written by trumpet player Roy Eldridge in 1950 while living in France, is a fascinating work that does not, however, have the same density as Ellington's imposing and eloquent suite.

95. The passage by Parks—who, in addition to being a photographer, was also a composer, film director, and writer—is found in his autobiography, *A Choice of Weapons* (1965), and has been reprinted in Herb Boyd (ed.), *The Harlem Reader*, New York: Three Rivers Press, 2003, 108-13; the stream of consciousness also mentions the Duke and his "The Mooche." Introduction by Peter Galassi to the catalog of the exhibition *Roy DeCarava: A Retrospective*, New York: Museum of Modern Art, 1996, 19, quoted in Blair, *Harlem Crossroads*, 51.

96. Vail, *Duke's Diary: The Life of Duke Ellington, 1950-1974*, II, 12; Stratemann, *Duke Ellington*, 324.

97. Duke Ellington, "Ellington on Career Highlights," *DownBeat*, November 5, 1952, quoted in *The Duke Ellington Reader*, 267.

98. This concert was recorded by the Voice of America (and broadcast in Italy by the RAI in June 1951) and released on the LP *Duke Ellington, 1951 at the Metropolitan Opera House*, Vee Jay RJL-2638(M). The passages with blemishes, the beginning of the Latin and blues sections, appear at 1:02 and 4:46.

99. This recording was later included in Columbia's prestigious Masterworks series on the LP *Duke Ellington, Uptown*, Columbia (ML 4639).

100. Stratemann, *Duke Ellington*, 327; Vail, *Duke's Diary: The Life of Duke Ellington, 1950–1974*, ii, 19. No recordings have survived of this concert, organized to raise funds for cancer research.

101. Ellington, *The Symphonic Ellington*, 2:04–2:12.

102. The passage in question is found at 7:53–7:56.

103. The spiritual theme mentioned here corresponds to section Q, 8:57–9:21; in this passage, trombonist John Sanders, famous for his perfect intonation and harmonious sound, plays out of tune.

104. Nevertheless, upon carefully listening to this recording, a few weak spots appear, including the tricky Latin groove and imprecise exposition of the spiritual theme in section U.

105. The passage for the reeds and woodwinds is in section A1, 2:23–2:30.

106. *Duke Ellington, Orchestral Works*, Decca (MCAD 42318).

107. This can be heard in a comparison between the passage on *The Symphonic Ellington* (Reprise, 5:58–6:12) and the Decca album (5:48–6:02).

108. This revision has other interesting points, such as section R1, which maintains two of the original three voices (i.e., the spiritual theme in the clarinet and the other two melodies), eliminating the spiritual melody (already repeatedly presented in the previous sections); these measures thus maintain the countermelodies but not the main theme, which, in any case, is suggested by the harmonic rhythm. On the CD, the passage appears at 9:53–10:18.

109. An unequivocally negative sentence was only passed by critic Ron Collier, who wrote off the work as one of Ellington's most disappointing. James Lincoln Collier, *Duke Ellington*, New York: Oxford University Press, 1987, 283.

110. Many thanks to Steven Lasker for providing me with a photostatic copy of the original program notes.

111. I have reconstructed a macro program, on which the observations found in these pages are based, which combines information on *Harlem* found in the following sources: program notes by Leonard Feather (January 21, 1951); spoken introduction by Ellington, live concert, March 25, 1952, *Duke Ellington, 1952 Seattle Concert*, Victor (ljm1002); spoken introduction by Ellington, live concert, October 7, 1956, unreleased tape; spoken introduction by Ellington, live concert, February 20, 1964, *Duke Ellington, The Great London Concerts*, Musicmasters (65106-2); spoken introduction by Ellington, live concerts April 28–29, 1964, *Duke Ellington in Concerto, New York 1964*, "I Maestri del Jazz," LP attached to part 4, vol. ii, Novara: Istituto Geografico De Agostini, 1990; poetic commentary, May 28, 1970, CD Decca, *Duke Ellington, Orchestral Works*; spoken introduction by Ellington, live concert, April 28, 1972, unreleased tape; Ellington, *Music Is My Mistress*, 155–6.

112. In-depth analyses of the elaborations of the "Har-lem" motto have been carried out by Andy Jaffe, "An Overview of Duke Ellington Composition Techniques," *Jazz Research Papers*, 1996, XVI, 71–90; and more recently by David Berger, "The Land of Suites:

Ellington and the Extended Form," in Green (ed.), *The Cambridge Companion to Duke Ellington*, pages 253-4.

113. The reference work on the impact of Caribbean radicals on American culture and politics in the first decades of the twentieth century is the text, accompanied by statistics on flows of migration, by Winston James, *Holding Aloft the Banner of Ethiopia: Caribbean Radicals in the Early Twentieth-Century America*, London: Verso, 1999. See also the chapter "The West Indians" in the volume by Anderson, *This Was Harlem*, 299. The quotation is from Anderson, *This Was Harlem*, 299.

114. A history of Latin music in the Big Apple is found in Max Salazar, *Mambo Kingdom: Latin Music in New York*, New York: Schirmer Trade Books, 2002. A brief but precise discussion is also contained in the chapter by Juan Flores, "Before Mambo Time: New York Latin Music in the Early Decades 1925-1945," in Edward J. Sullivan (ed.), *Nueva York 1613-1945*, New York: Scala Publishers, 2010, 256.

115. Ned Sublette based an entire chapter of a sizable volume on "The Peanut Vendor": *Cuba and Its Music: From the First Drums to the Mambo*, Chicago, IL: Chicago Review Press, 2004, 392-402; for more general information on the rumba era, see John Storm Roberts, *The Latin Tinge: The Impact of Latin American Music on the United States*, New York: Oxford University Press, 1999, 76-99.

116. Concerning Latin music's impact on jazz, see Basilio Serrano, *Puerto Rican Pioneers in Jazz 1900-1939: Bomba Beat to Latin Jazz*, Bloomington, IN: iUniverse, 2015; the same scholar has written a biography of Ellington's trombonist, titled *Juan Tizol, His Caravan Through American Life and Culture*, Bloomington, IN: Xlibris, 2012. Both texts, however, lack in-depth analyses, unlike the excellent unpublished study by Edu Hebling, *Juan Tizol, Una rumba per l'uomo comune*, master's thesis, Adria Conservatory, 2013.

117. Ellington, who later composed pieces that truly belong to the genres of the habanera, cha-cha, mambo, bossa nova, tango, and bolero, shows here that the form he was less acquainted with was precisely the rumba. In any case, the rumba craze was not initially concerned with authenticity: "The Peanut Vendor," which launched the fashion and that Ellington recorded in 1931, is a son-pregón, not a rumba; a conspicuous number of compositions called rumbas, in particular the ones that filled up Broadway and Hollywood, did not actually match this genre. Many thanks to Edu Hebling for a series of stimulating discussions on the classification of Latin genres, an area in which musicological-analytical publications are few and far between.

118. A snapshot of Harlem's nightlife taken by an insider is found in the book *The Night Club Era* that *New York Herald Tribune* journalist Stanley Walker published in 1933 (New York: Frederick A. Stokes Company). The study by Shane Vogel, *The Scene of Harlem Cabaret: Race, Sexuality, Performance*, Chicago, IL: University of Chicago Press, 2009, reconstructs the cultural context. The text by James Haskins, *The Cotton Club*, London: Robson Books, 1977, while not being particularly accurate, still contains useful information on the music club that had such a large influence on Ellington's career. A highly detailed list of the most important cabarets in Black Manhattan is found in Anderson, *This Was Harlem*, 168-80; much information is also found in Gill, *Harlem*, 267-72. It is sufficient to flip through Ellington's discography (or consult online the meticulous *The Duke—Where and When*; www.tdwaw.ca/) to realize that those music clubs, as of 1923, were a home away

from home for the bandleader; not by chance, his autobiography contains various memories of those places.

119. The passage can be heard at 6:41.

120. The scene with the funeral concerns sections O1 and, above all, P (7:36–8:44); the chromatic motif appears for the first time in the last measure before A (1:15).

121. The bass clarinet ostinato appears at 8:44.

122. Section Q, 8:57.

123. Section R, 9:23.

124. Section R1, 9:49.

125. Section S, 10:13. In the Decca recording *Orchestral Works* with the Cincinnati Symphony alone, the brass section does not perform the shake, and the descending riff is only played by the strings (without the saxophones). The passage thus becomes more dramatic than sexy, and the reference to the prostitute ("hip chick") is completely lost. This demonstrates that an awareness of the narrative aspects of Ellington's music is crucial in order to correctly perform his repertoire.

126. Section T, 10:42.

127. Section U, 11:15.

128. The grandiose spiritual fanfare, which is followed by the ten-measure coda written by Strayhorn (section Y), corresponds to section X, 12:52.

129. Ellington's religious side has not as yet been studied at length, leaving a gap that neither the book by Janna Tull Steed (*Duke Ellington: A Spiritual Biography*, New York: The Crossroad Publishing Company, 1999) nor the article by Frank A. Salomone ("It's All Sacred Music—Duke Ellington from the Cotton Club to the Cathedral," in Jeffrey O. G. Ogbar (ed.), *The Harlem Renaissance Revisited: Politics, Arts, and Letters*, Baltimore, MD: The Johns Hopkins University Press, 2010, 31–41) have been able to fill; the dissertation by Wilbert Weldon Hill, *The Sacred Concerts of Edward Kennedy "Duke" Ellington*, Washington, DC: Catholic University of America, 1994, while prevalently analytical, is currently the reference work.

130. Ellington's typical touch, which consists in adopting a "quasi-religious" attitude toward Tin Pan Alley numbers, has been described by Mark Tucker in the liner notes for *Duke Ellington, The Blanton–Webster Band*, Bluebird (74321-13181-2).

131. The ties between Ellington and O'Connor and Garcia Gensel, along with Ellington's involvement in New York's Jazz Vespers, has been discussed by Mark Sumner Harvey, "Jazz Ministry in Manhattan: The Shepherd, the Night Flock, and the First Church of Jazz," in Aaron Rosen (ed.), *Religion and Art in the Heart of Modern Manhattan: St. Peter's Church and the Louise Nevelson Chapel*, Farnham: Ashgate, 2016, 157–82; the relation between the Duke and Rev. Garcia Gensel also surfaces in the 1975 documentary *The Shepherd of the Night Flock*, by George C. Stoney, Documentary Educational Resources, 2009.

132. This quotation is from the famous essay by Alain Locke, "Enter the New Negro," published first in the March 1925 issue of the periodical *Survey Graphic* and later included in the anthology published the same year titled *The New Negro. Survey Graphic—Harlem Mecca of the New Negro*, Baltimore, MD: Black Classic Press, 1980; Alain Locke (ed.), *The New Negro*, New York: Simon & Schuster, 1997, 5.

133. Both quotations are from Lewis, *When Harlem Was in Vogue*, 24.

134. An enormous number of texts have been dedicated to the Harlem Renaissance; for an overview of the phenomenon, see Houston A. Baker Jr., *Modernism and the Harlem Renaissance*, Chicago, IL: University of Chicago Press, 1987; Ogbar (ed.), *The Harlem Renaissance Revisited*; Vogel, *The Scene of the Harlem Cabaret*; Lewis, *When Harlem Was in Vogue*; Harold Bloom (ed.), *The Harlem Renaissance*, Philadelphia, PA: Chelsea House Publishers, 2004; George Hutchinson (ed.), *The Cambridge Companion to the Harlem Renaissance*, Cambridge, MA: Cambridge University Press, 2007.

135. The observation by Weldon Johnson, taken from correspondence with Carl Van Vechten dated March 1926, appears in Osofsky, *Harlem: The Making of a Ghetto*, 182.

136. The motto is in Lewis, *When Harlem Was in Vogue*, xxviii. Du Bois had various afterthoughts about the concept of Black art as propaganda, but as of the midtwenties, he maintained this position.

137. Mark Tucker, "The Renaissance Education of Duke Ellington," in Samuel A. Floyd Jr. (ed.), *Black Music in the Harlem Renaissance*, New York: Greenwood Press, 1990, 111–28 (quotation on 112).

138. The reference work is the catalog of the exhibition *Rhapsody in Black: Art of the Harlem Renaissance*, ed. R. Powell, Berkeley, CA: University of California Press, 1997. Richard Powell has written a lengthy essay titled "New Negroes, Harlem, and Jazz (1900–1950)" for the fifth volume of the colossal work *The Image of the Black in Western Art*, 5 vols., ed. D. Bindman and H. L. Gates, Cambridge, MA: Howard University Press, 2014 (V: *The Twentieth Century*, part 2: *The Rise of Black Artists*, 53–104). Also pertinent, even though only a small number of works belong to the Harlem movement, is the luxurious catalog of the exhibition *African American Art: Harlem Renaissance Civil Rights Era and Beyond*, ed. R. Powell and V. M. Mecklenburg, New York: Skira Rizzoli, 2012. Among the monographs dedicated to single artists, we will only mention the ones on Douglas, Motley, and Alston, the three painters most directly involved in the Harlem Renaissance: Susan Earle (ed.), *Aaron Douglas: African American Modernist*, New Haven, CT: Yale University Press, 2007; Amy Helene Kirschke, *Aaron Douglas: Art, Race, and the Harlem Renaissance*, Jackson, MS: University of Mississippi Press, 1995; Amy M. Mooney, *Archibald J. Motley Jr.*, *The David C. Driskell Series of African American Art*, IV, San Francisco, CA: Pomegranate, 2004; and Alvia J. Wardlaw, *Charles Alston, The David C. Driskell Series of African American Art*, VI, San Francisco, CA: Pomegranate, 2007. The recent catalog of the exhibition *Archibald Motley: Jazz Age Modernist*, ed. R. Powell, Durham, NC: Duke University Press, 2014, contains many of the paintings reproduced in Mooney's monograph but is also interesting for the text by Powell himself.

139. The relations between Alston and Ellington are discussed in Wardlaw, *Charles Alston*, and, above all, in the article by Lemoine D. Pierce, "Charles Alston: An Appreciation," *The International Review of African American Art*, XIX, 4, 2004, 28–42, which in the iconography contains the cover of *Black, Brown and Beige*, created by Alston. Two crucial interviews with Alston date to September 28, 1965, and October 19, 1968: in the first, he reveals that Ellington completed "Sophisticated Lady" during one of their encounters. The audio and the transcriptions are available on the website of the Smithsonian Institution, Archives of American Art, *Oral History Interview with Charles Henry Alston*, www.aaa.si.edu/collections/interviews/oral-history-interview-charles-henry-alston. Stephen James, Ruth Ellington's son, in a personal email, confirmed the close relationship between his uncle and the artist in question.

140. This knot of relations is complicated by a few sources claiming that Ellington was also Romare Bearden's cousin. My research has not led to any evidence supporting this claim. Stephen James, in a personal email, categorically excluded this relation.

141. Bearden's relationship with jazz, and with Ellington in particular, has been examined in Robert G. O'Meally, "We Used to Say 'Stashed': Romare Bearden Paints the Blues" and "Blues and the Abstract Truth or Did Romare Bearden Really Paint Jazz?" both in G. Lock and D. Murray (eds.), *The Hearing Eye: Jazz & Blues Influences in African American Visual Art*, New York: Oxford University Press, 2009, 173–93, 194–218; and in Calvin Tomkins, "Profiles: Putting Something Over Something Else," in O'Meally (ed.), *The Jazz Cadence of American Culture*, 224–42. Bearden speaks about Ellington in a July 31, 1980, interview, Smithsonian Institution, Archives of American Art, *Oral History Interview with Romare Bearden*, www. aaa.si.edu/collections/interviews/oral-history-interview-romare -bearden. For our current analysis, particular note must go to the polyptych *The Block* (1971), an enormous collage dedicated to Harlem with a church; in the center, there is a clear reference to the suite *Harlem*.

142. The famous painting portraying Strayhorn and the sketch on the back of the Decca LP *North of the Border* (DL 75069) are only two examples of a significant artistic production, of which Ellington's heirs possess various pieces. On this topic, two curious photos published in *Look* in 1949 that immortalize the composer with a paintbrush in his hands are available online on the website of the Museum of the City of New York, www. org/collections; some sources credit Stanley Kubrick with taking these photos, but expert Filippo Ulivieri (who, along with Emilio D'Alessandro, published *Stanley Kubrick e me*, Milan: Il Saggiatore, 2012) did some research, on my request, whose results exclude that the director was involved. Some of the colorful titles alluded to are "Magenta Haze," "Mood Indigo," "Lady of the Lavender Mist," and "Sepia Panorama," which indicate a certain intimacy with the painter's palette; one might add "Azure," "Light Blue," "On a Turquoise Cloud," "Lady in Blue," "Purple Gazelle," "Purple People," and the synesthetic "Crescendo in Blue," "Diminuendo in Blue," and "Piano Pastel." For the synesthetic translation of the musical notes into colors, see Don George, *Sweet Man: The Real Duke Ellington*, New York: G. P. Putnam's Son, 1981, 226.

143. The first quotation has been taken from Lewis, *When Harlem Was in Vogue*, 96; the following are instead found in Alwyn Williams, "Jazz and the New Negro: Harlem's Intellectuals Wrestle with Art of the Age," *Australasian Journal of American Studies*, XXI, 1 (July 2002), 1–18, quotations on page 14, an essay that deeply examines the African American press's aversion toward jazz in the twenties. One must point out that the anthology *The New Negro* also contains an article on jazz that is not in the least disparaging; in the same vein, in Locke's volume, *The Negro and His Music* (Salem, MA: Ayer Company Publishers, 1991, first edition 1936), does not show hostility toward syncopated music. And yet one clearly perceives the low opinion these intellectuals had of this music; not by chance, in Locke's text, the bibliography on blues was not compiled by the author (who likely did not know enough about it) but by young writer Sterling Brown.

144. Alain Locke, *The Negro and His Music & Negro Art: Past and Present*, Salem, MA: Ayer Company Publishers, 1991. This publication brought together in a single volume two monographs, both dating to 1936. This scholar had already written about spirituals

both in his anthology *The New Negro* (*The Negro Spiritual*, 199–213) and in an article titled "Toward a Critique of Negro Music," published in 1934 in the periodical *Opportunity*, in *The Works of Alain Locke*, ed. C. Molesworth, New York: Oxford University Press, 2012, 136–45. An extremely well-documented work is the volume by white pianist Maud Cuney-Hare, who was also a musicologist and an activist: *Negro Musicians and Their Music*, New York: G. K. Hall & Co., 1996 (original edition 1936). Important recent studies include Jon Michael Spencer, *The New Negroes and Their Music: The Success of the Harlem Renaissance*, Knoxville, TN: University of Tennessee Press, 1997, the collection edited by S. Floyd, *Black Music in the Harlem Renaissance*, and above all, Paul Allen Anderson, *Deep River: Music and Memory in Harlem Renaissance Thought*, Durham, NC: Duke University Press, 2001.

145. Spirituals were so central to the Harlem Renaissance that they concerned not only music but also literary works by various authors, including Jean Toomer, who, in his 1923 masterpiece *Cane*, cites various titles of sorrow songs; James Weldon Johnson, who, along with his musician brother Rosamond, edited the anthologies *The Book of American Negro Spirituals* (1925) and *The Second Book of Negro Spirituals* (1926), now republished in a single volume as *The Books of American Negro Spirituals*, Boston, MA: Da Capo Press, 2010, and Johnson also wrote a collection of poetry inspired by Black religion, *God's Trombones: Seven Negro Sermons in Verse*, London: Penguin Books, 2008 (orig. ed. 1927); Du Bois, who set the transcription of a spiritual at the beginning of each chapter of his masterpiece *The Souls of Black Folks* and who dedicated to this genre the seminal essay "The Sorrow Songs." Art was no less involved: the painting *Swing Low Sweet Chariot* by Malvin Gray Johnson, the famous sculpture by Augusta Savage, *Lift Every Voice and Sing*, and the sublime religious illustrations and murals by Aaron Douglas are only a few examples.

146. Spencer, *The New Negroes and Their Music*.

147. Ellington, in spite of the fact that Cuney-Hare, in her aforementioned volume *Negro Musicians and Their Music*, reserved no more than a couple of sentences for him, never received the jibes given by the Harlem Renaissance to jazzmen; Locke, in his *The Negro and His Music*, ranks him just one notch below classical music.

148. *Nigger Heaven* split African American critics into two categories: while a very small portion (Hughes, Weldon Johnson, and a few others) held it to be a good novel, the majority felt that it was an insult to the Black community. In any case, it was reprinted fourteen times in a single year (1926). On the way in which Black critics described Van Vechten's book, see Anderson, *This Was Harlem*, 217–20; Vogel, *The Scene of the Harlem Cabaret*, 32–3, 75–6; Anderson, *Deep River*, 50; and Lewis, *When Harlem Was in Vogue*, which dedicates the entire chapter "Nigger Heaven," 156–97, to this novel. The quotation of Du Bois is in Anderson, *Deep River*, 50.

149. Ellington and Du Bois never visited one another, nor does the composer's name appear in the latter's correspondence (or rather, it appears one single time, to take his distance from him). There is no trace of Ellington in the lengthy volume by David Levering Lewis, *W.E.B. Du Bois: A Biography*, New York: Henry Holt & Company, 2009; and yet it is clear that Ellington was aware of the thought of the man who wrote *The Souls of Black Folk*. They both fundamentally agreed with the majority of the African American press, irritated by the fact that Harlem was considered no more than an enormous cabaret: "Is This Really Harlem?" (*New York Amsterdam News*, October 23, 1929), "Harlem Breakfast

Caps Gotham Night" (*Daily News*, October 31, 1929), and "Socialites Mix in Harlem Club" (*Daily News*, November 1, 1929); these articles are found in Schoener (ed.), *Harlem on My Mind*, 79–84.

150. Johnson, *Black Manhattan*, 161.

151. The passage from the interview with Carter Harman is reproduced in Howland, *Ellington Uptown*, 292.

152. These two quotations have been taken respectively from Locke (ed.), *The Image of the Black in Western Art*, 24, and *The New Negro*, 199; with the second expression, Locke describes the enchantment of African American religious melodies in his essay *The Negro Spirituals*.

153. On the life and work of Coleridge-Taylor and his relationship with Black culture, see Jeffrey Green, *Samuel Coleridge-Taylor: A Musical Life*, London: Routledge, 2016, which is the most detailed biography; the text by W. C. Berwick Sayers, *Samuel Coleridge-Taylor, Musician: His Life and Letters*, dating to 1915 and republished by Kessinger Publishing in 2008, is the first study dedicated to this composer and contains a rich correspondence; the essay by William Tortolano, *Samuel Coleridge-Taylor: Anglo-Black Composer, 1875–1912*, Lanham, MD: Scarecrow Press, 2002, is the only study with analytical elements.

154. The Englishman's dry response is found in Tortolano, *Samuel Coleridge-Taylor*, 41.

155. The two quotations have been taken from Sayers, *Samuel Coleridge-Taylor*, 149, which reproduces a letter dated January 3, 1904, and Tortolano, *Samuel Coleridge-Taylor*, 55.

156. On Coleridge-Taylor's crucial contribution to the success of "Deep River" in the American musical scene, see the highly detailed essay by Wayne D. Shirley, "The Coming of Deep River," *American Music*, XV, 4 (Winter 1997), 493–534.

157. In this recital, the piano was played by Maud Cuney-Hare, the author of the aforementioned *Negro Musicians and Their Music*.

158. See the essay by Jeffrey J. Green, "The Negro Renaissance in England," in the collection edited by S. A. Floyd, *Black Music in the Harlem Renaissance*, 151–71. On Burleigh, in the present context, one relevant study is the dissertation written by Brian Alan Moon, *The Old Songs Hymnal: Harry Burleigh and His Spirituals During the Harlem Renaissance*, Boulder, CO: University of Colorado, 2006. Rebaptizing Harry Burleigh as "the American Coleridge-Taylor" marks a clear reversal compared to the habit of labeling Black personalities as copies of whites; singer Sissieretta Jones, who became "the black Patti" (with reference to Adelina Patti), and abolitionist Samuel Ringgold Ward, nicknamed "the black Daniel Webster" (after the white politician), are only two cases.

159. On the relationship between Garvey, the Black Renaissance and African British composer, see Tony Martin, *Literary Garveyism: Garvey, Black Arts, and the Harlem Renaissance*, Dover, DE: The Majority Press, 1983 (the articles on Coleridge-Taylor that appeared in *Negro World* are discussed on 110–2); John W. Work, "Negro Folk Song," *Opportunity*, I, 10 (October 1923), in Anderson, *Deep River*, 79; the cover of the August 1925 issue of *The Crisis*, reproduced in *The Image of the Black in Western Art*, 21; and the poem "To Samuel Coleridge-Taylor, Upon Hearing His" is in Locke (ed.), *The New Negro*, 146.

160. The concert given on June 15, 1933, whose program was dedicated to Black composers (Florence Price, Margaret Bonds, and Coleridge-Taylor) is discussed by Samuel A. Floyd Jr., *The Power of Black Music: Interpreting Its History from Africa to the United States*, New York: Oxford University Press, 1995, 120.

161. This play, written by Du Bois, debuted in New York in 1913 and was staged in Washington in 1915 at the American League Ball Park, where young Ellington earned change selling beverages; it is thus possible that the Duke saw it. This opinion is maintained by Tucker, *The Genesis of Black, Brown and Beige*, 69; *The Star of Ethiopia*, in addition to two arias from *Aida*, contained music written by Black composers Bob Cole, Rosamond Johnson, Charles Young, and Coleridge-Taylor.

162. See note 54.

4. NIGHT CREATURE

1. This anecdote appeared in *Swing Magazine* in 1940, and Ellington's words were reprinted in Nat Shapiro and Nat Hentoff, *Hear Me Talkin' to Ya: The Story of Jazz as Told by the Men Who Made It*, London: Peter Davies, 1966, 211.

2. Things were probably made worse by the fact that the Palace regularly featured leading vaudeville stars, seasoned entertainers such as the ones who appeared on the same billboard as Ellington in April 1929: The Marx Brothers. Information on that engagement is found in David Palmquist, *The Duke—Where and When, A Chronicle of Duke Ellington's Working Life and Travels*, www.tdwaw.ca; Klaus Stratemann, *Duke Ellington, Day by Day and Film by Film*, Copenhagen: JazzMedia, 1992, 2.

3. In a series of broadcasts at the Cotton Club from March to May 1938, it is clear that Ellington preferred to leave almost all presentations to the disc jockeys; in the famous concert held in Fargo in 1940, the bandleader simply announced the title of the piece and the names of the soloists; at his first live appearance at Carnegie Hall in January 1943, he only had a few words for "Cotton Tail" and "Jumpin' Pumpkins" and to outline the program of his first suite, *Black, Brown and Beige*, without, however, indulging in an imaginative presentation.

4. On November 24, 1962, the *Kansas City Times* wrote, "The audience awaits the lengthy tone-poems and gets a show"; the article, written by James W. Scott, was discovered by David Palmquist and shared with the members of the Duke-LYM mailing list on August 20, 2016.

5. A sense of humor and a penchant for the absurd emerge in more than one of the Duke's narratives for his religious production. The text Ellington wrote to be recited before "In the Beginning God" (1965), the opening movement of his *First Sacred Concert*, may as well have been conceived by a new-world Dadaist and consists in an endless catalog of things that would not have existed without the Lord. The list, alternating between the prosaic and the sublime, includes aspirin and glory, bills to be paid and mountains, heroes and TV ads. In "My People/The Blues Ain't" (1963), from *My People*, the Duke plays the part of a Baptist preacher and, using emphatic tones worthy of Martin Luther King Jr. and a touch of irony, delivers a caustic sermon.

6. *Duke Ellington, Carnegie Hall, November 13, 1948*, VJC 1024/25–5.

7. Barry Ulanov, "The Ellington Programme," in Ken Williamson (ed.), *This Is Jazz*, London: George Newnes Ltd., 1960, 145.

8. Stanley Dance, *The World of Duke Ellington*, Boston, MA: Da Capo Press, 1970, 43.

9. Ellington, *Music Is My Mistress*, New York: Da Capo Press, 1973, 200.

10. In July 1966, Ellington and Miró met at the Maeght Foundation, and their encounter was filmed for a documentary on improvisation produced by Norman Granz. On that occasion, the Duke played the piano part of the trio "Blues for Miró" (which, two years later, he included in his *Second Sacred Concert*, renaming it "The Shepherd"). No sources inform us whether Ellington saw any of Miró's many paintings titled *Personnages dans la nuit*.

11. Critic Leonard Feather, who wrote an article on the concert for the April 1955 issue of the magazine *Melody Maker*, included a few excerpts from the eccentric program notes; Leonard Feather, *The Night Creature at Carnegie, Melody Maker*, April 2, 1955, 3.

12. This is the case of the July 10, 1956, concert with the New Haven Symphony Orchestra and the May 31, 1962, event with the National Symphony Orchestra, when he told the story twice, first during a radio show and then, that evening, on stage. Both concerts, and the interview by Patti Cavern for NBC, are on unreleased tapes.

13. Only in Ellington's imagination; however, D major, A flat major, and A minor do not appear in the movement titled "Dazzling Creature." This nocturnal diva could be a cross between an insect and a transvestite. Only once did Ellington mention transvestism, speaking about *Night Creature* with journalist Carter Harman in 1956. Stuart Nicholson, *Reminiscing in Tempo: A Portrait of Duke Ellington*, Boston, MA: Northern University Press, 1999, 342. The quotations are in Ellington, *Music Is My Mistress*, 191.

14. For the interview, see note 12.

15. The program for "Fantazm," at least in the version narrated by Ellington at Cornell University in 1948, expressly involves a dream.

16. Not by chance, in 1974, choreographer Alvin Ailey created a ballet inspired by the three dances suggested in the program. He turned to modern dance for the first movement, boogie-woogie for the second, and classical arabesque for the third.

17. Here, we are not referring to Ellington's pieces intended for dance but to compositions whose programs allude to that milieu.

18. Feather, *The Night Creature at Carnegie*, 3.

19. Gillis's program included the world premiere of *Boogie in Brass* and the New York debut of *Bobby Sox*, along with *Bing, Bang, Bong*; *Lullaby Tango*; and *A Dance Symphony*. This music, while written with some degree of skill (such as the theme and variations *Bing, Bang, Bong*) is fairly unremarkable. Gillis most likely performed in this prestigious venue thanks to the roles he had previously covered as a producer for the NBC Symphony and president (after Toscanini's death) of the Symphony Foundation of America.

20. Feather, *The Night Creature at Carnegie*, 3.

21. Charles Mingus, "Duke Ellington, Carnegie Hall," *Metronome*, LXXI, 5 (May 1955), 41–2.

22. The *New York Times* article written by Howard Taubman is mentioned by David Schiff in his essay "Symphonic Ellington? Rehearing New World A-Comin'," *Musical Quarterly*, XCVI, 3–4 (Autumn–Winter 2013), 459. Feather expressed the same opinion as Taubman, writing that "[Ellington] successfully joined two art forms that had often been called irreconcilable"; Feather, *The Night Creature at Carnegie*, 3.

23. Only a few passages are not perfectly polished, such as the entry of the trumpets at measure 106 of the first movement. The tapes of this live performance remained unreleased

for three decades until they were published on an LP included with the May 1984 issue of *Musica Jazz*, titled *Duke Ellington, Le Suites Sinfoniche* (2MJP-1021).

24. On Henderson's discouragement upon not being recognized for his orchestration, see chapter 2, note 35.

25. Peter Lavezzoli, *The King of All, Sir Duke: Ellington and the Artistic Revolution*, New York: Continuum, 2001, 196–202.

26. With reference to the Reprise LP and the Schirmer score (critical edition by Gunther Schuller, published in 1992), in m. 78 (after the orchestral climax in mm. 74-7), the two-blues chorus played by Ray Nance on the violin does not appear. Instead, the piano theme returns, reduced to sixteen measures, after which the Carnegie Hall performance continues by proceeding directly to m. 102, where Cootie Williams's trumpet fills are heard. At m. 126, when the time signature changes to 12/8, Johnny Hodges's two alto sax blues choruses are not heard, nor is Lawrence Brown's trombone improvisation; we find ourselves at m. 162 with brief one- or two-bar phrases in the woodwinds that, in *The Symphonic Ellington*, provide the background for Brown's solo, but here, since this improvisation is not present, take on the function of a theme.

27. Even though the tapes have not been released, chronometric indications from the CD *The Symphonic Ellington* and references to the Schirmer score will be provided here. In this case: first movement, m. 90–6, CD 1:57; third movement, m. 152–5, CD 3:57.

28. Ellington, *Music Is My Mistress*, 390.

29. This tape has not been released. "Stalking Monster" was shortened at the passage corresponding to mm. 78–149, between 2:36 and 5:00 on the LP. The break appears at mm. 152–5 of the third movement, CD 3:57.

30. This tape has not been released. The added chorus corresponds to mm. 102-13 of the Schirmer score, at which point the album contains the first twelve measures of the trombone improvisation (CD 3:25–3:48).

31. Duke Ellington, "The Jazz Fakers Can't Make It Now," *Negro Digest*, XII, 1 (November 1961), 77–8.

32. The passage in question appears in the score at mm. 31–4, CD 1:02. On the album, it appears only once in the woodwinds and reeds; in the Washington live concert, it is repeated twice more, the last acting as a coda for the movement. The percussive introduction to the third movement is also quite long here, lasting 1 minute 43 seconds (compared to a handful of measures in the previous versions).

33. Feather, *The Night Creature at Carnegie*, 3.

34. On Capitol and Columbia's reluctance to make an LP, see John Edward Hasse, *Beyond Category: The Life and Genius of Duke Ellington*, New York: Simon & Schuster Press, 1993, 316, 352.

35. Ellington's relationship with Reprise Records is perfectly described, with particular attention to details concerning the studio recording sessions, in Mark Tucker's liner notes for the box set *Duke Ellington, The Complete Reprise Studio Recordings*, Mosaic (MD5-193).

36. This tight schedule also included other studio recording sessions for albums (such as the violin session, the one with singer Bea Benjamin, and the one with Alice Babs, which also featured a few French jazz musicians and four classical horn players) and appearances for various radio and television broadcasts. Extremely tired, on March 5, Ellington wound

up in the hospital with a bad case of pneumonia that forced him to spend a week in bed. He flew back from Paris to New York on March 15.

37. Scholars have not reached an agreement as to the exact dates on which these two symphonic works were recorded; actually, consulting a few sources, including a 1963 article published in the magazine *Epoca*, reveals that (only) *Night Creature* was recorded on January 30, while the following day was dedicated to *Harlem*. On the problems that arose while recording *Harlem*, see chapter 3 on page 77, note 105. Jean Durieux, "Violini, consolate il vecchio negro," *Epoca*, XIV, 646 (February 10, 1963), 58.

38. Disques Vogue, a label that specialized in jazz, was founded by Delaunay in 1947.

39. Charles Delaunay, *Delaunay's Dilemma: De la peinture au jazz*, Mâcon: Editions W., 1985, 179–81. Many thanks to Nicola Baudo for his translation. The horn player referred to by Delaunay in this excerpt from his autobiography is Georges Barboteu, who wrote important books on instrumental technique and was a great classical interpreter who also knew how to approach jazz. One month after the session for *The Symphonic Ellington*, Barboteu returned to the studio with Ellington to record the album *Serenade to Sweden*.

40. This is the same passage discussed in note 27.

41. The theme in question appears at mm. 47–54, CD 1:16.

42. "Dazzling Creature," second theme, mm. 31–46, CD 0:49.

43. Ellington's chorus begins at m. 55, CD 1:29.

44. The phrase, based on a diminished triad, can be heard in the November 20, 1958, February 20, 1964, and May 9, 1966, performances of "Caravan," to mention only a few. Ellington also played this pattern in the famous version of "Caravan" included in *Money Jungle* (1962), which Matthew J. Cooper has transcribed and discussed in his excellent *Duke Ellington as Pianist: A Study of Styles*, Missoula, MT: The College Music Society, 2013, 90–2.

45. On Sunday morning, February 3, 1963, the Duke was in Lund speaking at a TV station, and in the afternoon, he led his orchestra in a double concert; on Monday, February 4, they performed in Göteborg, flying to Finland the next day to play in Helsinki and returning to Sweden on February 6 for a concert at Stockholm's Konserthuset.

46. The entire program is available on YouTube under the title *Ellington in Sweden 1963 (feat. Alice Babs)*.

47. The unreleased tape referred to here is the fourth take of "Stalking Monster."

48. Musicologist Marcello Piras has studied Ellington's use of retrograde forms in detail; according to Piras, this compositional strategy may indicate a will to translate palindrome-like dance steps into music. One of the examples he mentions is the theme of "Blind Bug." Thus, the program narrated by the Duke, with its constant reference to dance, seems to be precisely reflected in the music from this point of view as well. Marcello Piras, "Duke and Descriptive Music," in Edward Green (ed.), *The Cambridge Companion to Duke Ellington*, Cambridge, MA: Cambridge University Press, 2014, 219–21.

49. The two highly convincing variations of the theme in the trombones are found at m. 56 and m. 129, CD 1:06, 2:49.

50. The orchestral *tutti* referred to begins at m. 137, CD 3:00.

51. An insightful overview by Leonard Bernstein is found in "Humor in Music," in *Leonard Bernstein's Young People's Concerts*, Jack Gottlieb (ed.), Pompton Plains, NJ: Amadeus Press, 2005, 133–50. This text is a revision of the script written for the episode

with the same title as the TV series *Young People's Concerts*. The complete original script is available at www.leonardbernstein.com, in the section "Television Scripts."

52. These are only two of Ellington's many pranks related by his friend and collaborator Don George in *Sweet Man: The Real Duke Ellington*, New York: G. P. Putnam's Sons, 1981, 103, 73.

53. Bill Dobbins had noted that the suspended D flat (in the key of C major) is often erroneously sung as a D natural. Most likely, Ellington took evil pleasure in pointing out this mistake. Bill Dobbins, "Duke Ellington and the World of Jazz Piano," Green (ed.), *The Cambridge Companion to Duke Ellington*, 209.

54. In 1966, Strayhorn used similar techniques, typically Ellingtonian, in his delightful arrangement of the Beatles' "I Want to Hold Your Hand" heard on *Ellington '66*, Reprise (8122-79684-4).

55. The first time occurs at m. 31, CD 1:02, and the second at m. 196, CD 6:28. Jelly Roll Morton was a master in using wide gaps in pitch (and register) to create playful effects; for example, in the coda of "The Pearls" (1926), a tuba ostinato is answered by a strident clarinet trill, and in only three bars of the introduction to "Kansas City Stomp" (1928), a clarinet motif is answered by the trumpet, the trombone, and lastly the tuba.

56. The canonic blues form appears as of m. 78, CD 2:26. Quite commonly, in modern performances of "Stalking Monster," the soloists more or less freely imitate the improvisations heard on *The Symphonic Ellington*. In any case, as early as 1972, Ellington tells us, the violinist of the National Symphony Orchestra, Redentor Romero, transcribed the solo played by Ray Nance in order to perform it identically in a live concert; Ellington, *Music Is My Mistress*, 382.

57. Gleason's comment is included in the liner notes for the Mosaic box set dedicated to the Reprise collected works, 17. Not all critics had words of praise for the suite: Collier wrote that *Night Creature* is "alternatively insipid and pompous." James Lincoln Collier, *Duke Ellington*, New York: Oxford University Press, 1987, 284.

58. The score seen in the documentary is a photographic print. Therefore, when the documentary was shot in November 1965, Ellington had not yet published the suite.

59. "Duke Captivates Audience; Gets N.Y. City's Highest Award," *Jet*, XXVIII, 16 (August 19, 1965), 60–1.

60. Joe Benjamin only played stably with the Duke Ellington Orchestra in his later years; he was an official double bassist from 1970 until early 1974.

61. George, *Sweet Man: The Real Duke Ellington*, 171. However, it is worth pointing out that Don George has not always proved to be a reliable source. Conductor Maurice Peress was also present at the rehearsal and, feeling that Benjamin's orchestration was rather clumsy, resolved to revise it in the late sixties; Maurice Peress, *Dvořák to Duke Ellington: A Conductor Explores America's Music and Its African American Roots*, New York: Oxford University Press, 2004, 155–7.

62. The complete program of the entire 1965 edition of the French-American Festival is available on the New York Philharmonic's official website, www.nyphil.org.

63. Some radio interviews tied to Ellington's collaboration with the Boston Pops, along with the rehearsals for the concert and the entire live event, have been published on the CD *Duke Ellington, Live and Rare*, Bluebird. In the liner notes for the Victor LP

released in 1965, *The Duke at Tanglewood*, Ellington praised Richard Hayman's arrangements of his compositions.

64. Ellington, *Music Is My Mistress*, 200. Adlai Stevenson II, the American ambassador to the United Nations, had died a few days earlier.

65. The date of the unreleased tape is mistakenly reported as July 31, 1965, in Luciano Massagli and Giovanni M. Volontè, *The New DESOR: An Updated Edition of Duke Ellington's Story on Records 1924–1974*, 2 vols., Milan: private edition published by Massagli, 1999.

66. "Duke Captivates Audience; Gets N.Y. City's Highest Award," *Jet*, August 19, 1965, 61. The Watusi was a very fashionable dance in America in the early sixties, almost as popular as The Twist.

67. Given that discrepancies are found in the sources as to the works performed at the French-American Festival on the evenings of July 30 and 31, 1965, at Lincoln Center's Philharmonic Hall with the New York Philharmonic Orchestra, the complete program played over those two days is as follows:

Friday, July 30 (8:30 p.m.): conductor Lukas Foss: Ch. Ives, *From the Steeples and the Mountains*, Ch. Wuorinen, *Orchestral and Electronic Exchanges*, W. Schuman, *Fantasy for Cello and Orchestra*, with Leonard Rose; conductor and soloist Duke Ellington: *New World A-Comin'*, *The Golden Broom and the Green Apple*; conductor Lukas Foss, narrator Duke Ellington: A. Copland, *Preamble for a Solemn Occasion*.

Two changes were introduced into the program played on Saturday, July 31: instead of the composition by William Schuman, Edward MacDowell's *Concerto for Piano and Orchestra in D minor opus 23* was performed, with Van Cliburn as the soloist (substituting André Watts at the last minute), and two pieces by Strayhorn, "Take the 'A' Train" and "Satin Doll," in piano solo interpretations by Ellington, took the place of *New World A-Comin'*.

68. Carter Harman, "The Duke Clicks in Squaresville: Ellington at the Philharmonic," *Life*, August 27, 1965, 15.

69. These remarks are based on unreleased tapes with recordings of all the concerts listed in this paragraph.

70. Peress and Ellington's encounter is related in Peress, *Dvořák to Duke Ellington*, 157.

71. In this sense, Ellington's working methods are similar to the ones used by Mozart, who tailored his *Concerto for Horn and Orchestra* No. 1 in D Major to the skills of soloist Joseph Ignaz Leutgeb. The bandleader knew much more about his musicians than their mere technical ability. Decades spent onstage with them all over the world, playing over three hundred concerts a year, taught him much about their subtlest musical inclinations; Ellington knew who among them loved the blues and who preferred Latin melodies, who would be at their best in a ballad and who would have given a scintillating performance in a fast tempo. The Duke, in short, did not write for alto sax, he wrote for "the Rabbit" (John Cornelius Hodges); he never composed a trumpet concerto; he composed a "Concerto for Cootie" (Charles "Cootie" Williams).

72. Details as to the grueling schedule for those four days in Cincinnati in April 1966 are found in Stratemann, *Duke Ellington, Day by Day and Film by Film*, 536; and in Ken Vail, *Duke's Diary: The Life of Duke Ellington, 1950–1974*, 2 vols., Lanham, MD: Scarecrow Press, 2002, I, 287–8. Vail's volume contains (with no bibliographical indications) an article by Stanley Dance titled "April in Cincinnati."

73. The suite and Ellington's "poetic commentaries," published in two different albums in 1970, later appeared together in the CD *Duke Ellington, Orchestral Works*, Decca (MCAD 42318).

74. The measures refer to the score published by G. Schirmer; chronometric indications from the Decca CD *Duke Ellington, Orchestral Works* are also provided here for easier reference to the passages discussed. In this first case: Stanza 1 "The Golden Broom," mm. 102–9, CD 2:50.

75. Stanza 1 "The Golden Broom," second theme, m. 192, CD 4:38.

76. The bolero that a twentieth-century American musician would have known belonged to another tradition compared to the boleros that fascinated Chopin and Verdi, and in some senses, even Ravel. On the internationalization of this genre, see John Storm Roberts, *The Latin Tinge: The Impact of Latin American Music on the United States*, New York: Oxford University Press, 1999, 23.

77. Many thanks to Louis Tavecchio and Geoff Smith for sharing the unreleased tape recording of the interview.

78. The Duke Ellington Music Society (DEMS) dedicated a special number of their bulletin to the stockpile; *DEMS Bulletin* 86, II, 3–10. A partial list of the albums released posthumously containing materials from this collection can be consulted online in Matthew Asprey Gear, *Duke Ellington: A Guide to the Stockpile*, www.matthewasprey2.wordpress.com/2015/04/18/duke-ellington-a-guide-to-the-stockpile/.

79. This piece was officially released in 1992 by the small label LaserLight: *Duke Ellington, Cool Rock* (15782).

80. The clock was most likely ticking, so instead of writing a new one, the Duke opened his giant closet and found the most suitable melody.

81. Stanza 1 "The Golden Broom," third theme, m. 336, CD 7:46.

82. Stanza 3 "The Handsome Traffic Policeman," m. 84, CD 2:39.

83. Eddie Lambert, *Duke Ellington: A Listener's Guide*, Lanham, MD/London: Scarecrow Press 1999, 297. This critic admired the work but not as much as Dan Morgenstern, who, in the September 9, 1965, issue of *DownBeat*, expressed his enthusiasm by describing it as "Ellington's most valid and finished symphonic work." Quoted in Antonio Berini and Giovanni M. Volonté, *Duke Ellington: Un genio, un mito*, Florence: Ponte alle Grazie, 1994, 605.

5. LA SCALA, PART II

1. Ellington is referring to both musical terms (the duet, which would translate into a sort of *pas de deux*, and the vamp) and elements of African American folklore. The blues is singular when it acts like a living being, a Kuntu in African philosophy (the blues just vamps), and is plural at the same time as a contraction of "blue devils" (singing them).

2. Duke Ellington, *Music Is My Mistress*, New York: Da Capo Press, 1973, 417.

3. Some of the observations in this chapter are indebted to Ben Givan's excellent essay "Ellington and the Blues" in Edward Green (ed.), *The Cambridge Companion to Duke Ellington*, Cambridge, MA: Cambridge University Press, 2014, 173–85.

4. Richard Crawford has dedicated a detailed analysis to this composition, defining it as "a commentary on the nature of the twelve-bar blues"; Richard Crawford, "Duke Ellington (1899–1974) and His Orchestra," *The American Musical Landscape: The Business of Musicianship from Billings to Gershwin*, Berkeley, CA: University of California Press, 1993, 199–210; the quote appears on page 207. Important remarks have also been made by Schuller, who, nevertheless, erroneously counts fourteen bars in the second chorus; Gunther Schuller, *The Swing Era: The Development of Jazz 1930–1945*, New York: Oxford University Press, 1989, 91.

5. These two passages are discussed in chapter 4 on pages 103–4 and 118.

6. On the irony found in "Stalking Monster" and "Blues in Blueprint," see chapter 4 on page 113.

7. While "Ko-Ko" has been the subject of various analyses and a scrupulous transcription by David Berger for Classic Editions (SST-107–002), the neglected masterpiece "Oclupaca" has only been discussed by the present author, in an article titled "'Mexicanticipation' e 'Latin American Suite,' Metamorfosi nella fucina del Duca," *Musica Jazz*, March 2000, 56–9, and chapter 4 of Eric S. Strother's master's thesis, *The Development of Duke Ellington's Compositional Style: A Comparative Analysis of Three Selected Works*, University of Kentucky, 2001, 48–60.

8. In the symphonic score published by Schirmer and the recording contained in *The Symphonic Ellington*, this passage is found at letter M and heard at 6:41. In this type of writing, Ellington tends to create bluesy effects by placing clusters around the fifth and the seventh.

9. These bars can be heard on *Orchestral Works*, "The Handsome Traffic Policeman," at 2:39. In Ellington's music, the clash between the two sevenths in a bluesy context does not always create an expressionistic effect. The same procedure in "Flirtibird" and "Blues for New Orleans," as arranger Michele Corcella has noted, produces an effect that is not as harsh.

10. The harmonies produced by the three voices might sound rather strident (as of the first chord, F-Bb-E, which seems to allude to a G7) if they were not softened by the delicacy of the timbre.

11. "Transblucency" is an utterly polysemic creative neologism that moves from "translucency" as dialectically opposed to "transparency" (to the extent that clarity of direct light and opacity of diffused light can be regarded as opposed). By means of grafting the "B" of the (color) blue into the word, Ellington causes a consequent modification of the meaning that is refracted in a spectrum of multiple directions. This is also inherently suggested by the alternate title *A Blue Fog That You Can Almost See Through*, which intertwines the color blue with the blues and evokes precisely those effects of musical translucency so masterfully displayed in the musical score.

12. Here as well, the harmony is admirably delicate: the progression I-VI-II-V-I (Bb / G7b9 / Cm / C7b9 / Bb) that ends in bar 3 on a Bb major triad (transformed into Bb major 7 in the second movement, later stabilizing on a Bb7) involves various blue notes, and yet it gives one a very faint perception of the blues.

13. *Ad Lib on Nippon* was born as a piano piece during the Duke's Japan tour in 1964 and arranged for big band the following year. This suite, made up of the four movements—"Fugi,"

"Igoo," "Nagoya," and "Tokyo"—was recorded for RCA on December 20, 1966, and included in the LP *Far East Suite*. Musicologist Riccardo Scivales painstakingly transcribed the seven choruses of the movement titled "Fugi" for the periodical *Piano Today*, Winter 2000, 42–5.

14. The harmony sustains the idea proposed by the melody: the chord on I is a F6 (and therefore does not contain the blue seventh), and the passages in 2 and 3 are not in the least orthodox, with a leap of a gospel third leading to the relative minor. All things considered, the F7 in the following bar is not bluesy either but a simple dominant seventh that resolves in bar 5 on IV.

15. In the third chorus of "Across the Track Blues" (1940), Ellington had alternated the blues chord on I of D7 with the graceful DMaj7, but for *La Scala*, as has been explained, he was even more daring.

16. Maud Cuney-Hare, *Negro Musicians and Their Music*, New York: G. K. Hall & Co., 1996 (original edition 1936), 156.

17. Cuney-Hare, *Negro Musicians and Their Music*, 153.

18. Lawrence W. Levine, "Jazz and American Culture," *Journal of American Folklore*, xii, 403 (January–March 1989), 12.

19. Levine, "Jazz and American Culture." Regarding Peyton as a critic, an interesting thesis has been written by Sarah Waits, "'Listen to the Wild Discord': Jazz in the Chicago Defender and the Louisiana Weekly, 1925–1929," University of New Orleans, 2013.

20. Lucien White, "Decrying the Use of Spirituals as Companion Pieces to Blues and Jazz," *The New York Age*, November 29, 1924, 6. Other serious recriminations of jazz and blues music written by African American critics and leading figures in the Harlem Renaissance can be seen in chapter 3 on pages 87–88.

21. On this aspect of Du Bois's ideology, particularly interesting reflections are found in Paul Allen Anderson's volume *Deep River: Music and Memory in Harlem Renaissance Thought*, Durham, NC: Duke University Press, 2001, 13–57.

22. Arnold Rampersad, *The Art and Imagination of W.E.B. Du Bois*, New York: Schocken, 1990, 188.

23. James W. Johnson, *Black Manhattan*, New York: Alfred A. Knopf, 1930, 228; James W. Johnson, *The Book of American Negro Poetry*, Champaign, IL: Book Jungle, 2008, 10 (original edition New York: Harcourt, Brace and Company, 1922).

24. For the anthology *The New Negro*, which he edited, in addition to an essay on African American sacred music, Alain Locke put together a sizeable bibliography on Black music. It does not, however, contain any discographic references, which led him to exclude both jazz and blues, to which significant recordings had been dedicated by 1925 but very few articles and no books. In his list, therefore, recognized artists such as Bessie Smith or excellent musicians close to the aesthetics of the "new Negro" such as Fletcher Henderson were not included. In his following publications—the article "Toward a Critique of Negro Music" for *Opportunity* (1934), the volume *The Negro and His Music* (1936), and the article "Negro Music Goes to Par" for *Opportunity* (1939)—he acknowledged that blues and jazz, and Duke Ellington in particular, had a certain dignity. Alain Locke (ed.), *The New Negro*, New York: Simon & Schuster, 1997; Alain Locke, *The Negro and His Music, Negro Art: Past and Present*, Salem, MA: Ayer Company Publishers, 1991; the two articles that appeared in *Opportunity* have been republished in Charles Molesworth (ed.), *The Works of Alain Locke*, New York: Oxford University Press, 2012.

25. For a brief discussion of Sterling Brown's relationship with the blues tradition, see Steven C. Tracy, *Langston Hughes and the Blues*, Chicago, IL: University of Illinois Press, 2001, 28–33; the quote is on page 31. Interesting observations have also been made by Houston A. Baker Jr. as to the poem *Ma Rainey* in his volume *Modernism and the Harlem Renaissance*, Chicago, IL: University of Chicago Press, 1987, 91–8.

26. From this point of view, many interesting points are made in the chapter "Zora Neale Hurston and Billie Holiday, Improvisation through Interpretation," found in the volume by Alfonso W. Hawkins Jr., *The Jazz Trope: A Theory of African American Literary and Vernacular Culture*, Lanham, MD: Scarecrow Press, 2008, 79–118. Steven C. Tracy has described Lomax's praise for Hurston in *Langston Hughes and the Blues*, 33.

27. Hughes's polemical statements were published by *The Nation* (in the June 23, 1926, issue) as part of his famous *The Negro Artist and the Racial Mountain*, a manifesto that, insisting on the concept of Black beauty six times in only a few lines, encouraged African American artists to proudly express their individuality. This poet, who collaborated with historian Carter G. Woodson in Washington, wrote about the time he spent with the Black elite in his autobiography *The Big Sea*, which was published in 1940; Langston Hughes, *The Big Sea*, New York: Hill & Wang, 1993, 207–9.

28. Steven C. Tracy's volume *Langston Hughes and the Blues* contains a detailed bibliography of Hughes's writings linked to jazz and the blues, 266–8. A significant analysis has been published by Jane Olmstead, "Black Moves, White Ways, Every Body's Blues: Orphic Power in Langston Hughes's *The Ways of White Folks*," chapter 3 of Saadi Simawe, *Black Orpheus: Music in African American Fiction from the Harlem Renaissance to Toni Morrison*, New York: Garland Publishing, 2000, 65–90.

29. Langston Hughes—Milton Meltzer, *Black Magic: A Pictorial History of the African-American in the Performing Arts*, New York: Da Capo Press, 1967. This work is a history of African American culture in dance, music, theater, film, and television, and references to jazz and blues artists are found throughout it, not only in the chapters "Birth of Jazz" (73) and "The Blues" (80).

30. A detailed description of the relationship between Hughes and jazz in the fifties and sixties can be found in "I, Too, Sing America," chapter 5 of Josh Kun's volume *Audiotopia: Music, Race, and America*, Los Angeles, CA: University of California Press, 2005. In a certain sense, the beginning of this collaboration between Hughes and jazz musicians could be seen in his joint work with J. P. Johnson, which, in 1940, led to the socialist opera *De Organizer* (1940), for which Hughes wrote the libretto.

31. Langston Hughes, "The Twenties: Harlem and Its Negritude," *African Forum*, I, 4, 1966, 12.

32. This musical is discussed by Arnold Rampersad in the first volume of his weighty monograph dedicated to this poet, *The Life of Langston Hughes*, 2 vols., 1: *1902–1941: I, Too, Sing America*, New York: Oxford University Press, 2002, 328–9. As regards the Duke's contribution, see also John Franceschina, *Duke Ellington's Music for the Theatre*, Jefferson, NC: McFarland & Company Inc., 2001, 29–30, 41.

33. Important information on the two shows can be found in Franceschina, *Duke Ellington's Music for the Theatre*, 30, and in Rampersad, *The Life of Langston Hughes*, vol. I. The music for "Diamond Jubilee" has been lost.

34. The collaboration between Hughes and Ellington for the musical *Jump for Joy* is discussed in Rampersad, *The Life of Langston Hughes*, vol. I: *I Dream a World*, 26–8; the text by Franceschina, *Duke Ellington's Music for the Theatre*, is once again helpful, 30–45. Hughes wrote about his discouragement following the elimination of his song (and, consequentially, his loss of copyrights) in a letter dated October 8, 1941, published in Emily Bernard (ed.), *Remember Me to Harlem: The Letters of Langston Hughes and Carl Van Vechten*, New York: Vintage Books, 2002, 189–91.

35. The text of this song, which showcases the great cultural heroes of Black Manhattan (including boxer Joe Louis, intellectual Du Bois, classical singer Marian Anderson, and Adam Clayton Powell Jr., reverend and politician), has been published in *The Collected Works of Langston Hughes*, edited by Leslie C. Sanders, 16 vols., vi: *Gospel Plays, Operas, and Later Dramatic Works*, Columbia, MO: University of Missouri Press, 2004, 635–7.

36. In December 1965, Ellington's orchestra recorded these two numbers for the show but did not appear in it; only the bandleader was seen on TV, with a small band of CBS musicians serving as a "stand-in" for his ensemble. Accurate information on the broadcast is included in Klaus Stratemann, *Duke Ellington, Day by Day and Film by Film*, Copenhagen: JazzMedia, 1992, 518–22. Hughes's biographer Rampersad also discusses it in the second volume of *The Life of Langston Hughes*, 392.

37. The two quotations appear respectively in Rampersad, *The Life of Langston Hughes*, vol. II, 254, and in Harvey G. Cohen, *Duke Ellington's America*, Chicago, IL: University of Chicago Press, 2010, 333. *A Toast to Harlem* is included in Herb Boyd (ed.), *The Harlem Reader*, New York: Three Rivers Press, 2003, 172–9; it is one of the stories featuring Jesse B. Simple, Hughes's alter ego. In the choreography of *Night Creature*, Jennifer Dunning sees a link with Simple's "double nature" (alternately naïve and savvy), "so cherished by Hughes, Ellington and Ailey"; Jennifer Dunning, *Alvin Ailey: A Life in Dance*, Cambridge, MA: Da Capo Press, 1998, 300.

38. Ellington, *Music Is My Mistress*, 198.

39. The piece written for *The Nation* can be consulted online, www.english.illinois.edu/maps/poets/g_l/hughes/mountain.htm.

40. A probable relationship between the two works has been hypothesized by Cohen in *Duke Ellington's America*, 233.

41. The article "We, Too, Sing America" appears in Mark Tucker (ed.), *The Duke Ellington Reader*, New York: Oxford University Press, 1993, 146–8; the passage quoted is on page 147.

42. From this point of view, the story underlying "Fleurette Africaine" (or "African Flower") has a great deal in common with the program of "The Little Purple Flower."

43. Truth be told, not even all the intellectuals who contributed to the Black Renaissance were in favor of symphonic transformations of the spiritual; Claude McKay expressed his skepticism in the wonderful verses that close his poem *Negro Spiritual*: "To fashion thee for virtuoso wonders, / Drowning thy beauty in orchestral thunders"; Claude McKay, *Selected Poems*, New York: Dover Publications, 1999, 29.

44. This poem was republished in Romare Bearden's volume *The Block*, New York: Viking, 1971.

45. Reprinted in the January 1943 issue of *Negro Digest* (37–8), this article is included in *The Collected Works of Langston Hughes*, vol. IX: *Essays on Art, Race, Politics, and World Affairs*, ed. C. De Santis, Columbia, MO: University of Missouri Press, 2004, 224–6. Handy and Hughes's relationship and collaborations, which included writing a few blues pieces together, are examined in Tracy, *Langston Hughes and the Blues*, 171–2.

46. This musician's relationship with blues (which he incorporated in various works, in addition to his first symphony, such as the ballet *Lenox Avenue*) is explored in Catherine Parsons Smith's monograph *William Grant Still: A Study in Contradictions*, Berkeley, CA: University of California Press, 2000. The quotation appears on page 52.

47. This conversation is included in the Italian national television broadcaster's documentary, *Duke Ellington: Jazz e simpatia* (1966).

48. Review by Arrigo Polillo of the album *The Symphonic Ellington* in *Musica Jazz*, February 1964, 35–6 (quotation on page 36). This periodical had insistently expressed its biased view of that sector of the Duke's work for years; for example, Romano del Forno's comments in the article *Sul sinfonismo di Ellington* were on the verge of insulting, defining the works in question as an "unrestrained hodgepodge . . . that knocks on the door of art without getting any answer," *Musica Jazz*, July–August 1953, 25–9.

49. Critic Leonard Feather asked Woody Herman to listen to *La Scala* in one of his famous blindfold tests and published his answers in the April 23, 1964, issue of *DownBeat*, 34. Herman, while admitting he didn't know the piece, guessed that it was by Ellington and, after identifying three of the four soloists, praised the composition. Four years later, saxophonist James Moody was given the same test (*DownBeat*, February 22, 1968, 32). He was not able to identify the album either but recognized the Duke's skillful hand.

50. Calvin Tomkins, "Profiles: Putting Something over Something Else," in Robert G. O'Meally (ed.), *The Jazz Cadence of American Culture*, New York: Columbia University Press, 1998, 242.

6. THREE BLACK KINGS

1. This amusing request is described in Derek Jewell, *Duke: A Portrait of Duke Ellington*, London: Elm Tree Books, 1977, 172.

2. Although it is highly unlikely that Ellington revealed this secret to President Nixon in 1969, as has at times been claimed, a few of his acquaintances have confirmed that the entire ceremonious gesture was at least partially a prank. The Duke said it was a prank to Willie Ruff, and so did Ruff to those involved in the convention titled *Ellington & Strayhorn: A Celebration*, held in Portland, OR, at Reed College on November 7, 2015.

3. A large amount of information as to who visited the Duke in his hospital room and the national celebrations for his seventy-fifth birthday is found in Harvey G. Cohen, *Duke Ellington's America*, Chicago, IL: University of Chicago Press, 2010, 574–6.

4. The project for *Queenie Pie* began to take shape in the fifties. It was first conceived for television and reworked for theater after negotiations with broadcaster WNET fell through. This comic opera, set in Harlem during the Black Renaissance, was only staged in 1986 thanks to a collaboration between McGettigan and Maurice Peress and was released as a

recording, after further revision, in 2010. The music is not entirely new, with fragments of old melodies by Ellington reappearing in a different guise in addition to out-and-out transplants of pieces such as "Creole Love Call," "Such Sweet Thunder," and "Second Line" under new titles. An entire chapter dedicated to a musicological reconstruction of the genesis of this work, titled "Gilbert and Sullivan on Hallucinogens," is available in the volume by John Franceschina, *Duke Ellington's Music for the Theatre*, Jefferson, NC: McFarland Company, 2001, 170–82. Further precious information has been provided by Maurice Peress, who was part of the project as of 1972, in the chapter "Ellington's Queenie Pie" of his volume *Dvořák to Duke Ellington: A Conductor Explores America's Music and Its African American Roots*, New York: Oxford University Press, 2004, 161–70. The recording features Count Basie's former singer, Carmen Bradford: *Queenie Pie*, LHM2010003.

5. Schuller's initial involvement, and his reluctant abandonment of the idea, is recounted by Mercer Ellington in *Duke Ellington in Person: An Intimate Memoir*, Boston, MA: Houghton Mifflin Company, 1978, 206.

6. Very little bibliographical information on Mercer Ellington and the orchestra is available for the period following the Duke's death. Almost all texts, including the book by M. Ellington, *Duke Ellington in Person*, only cover up to May 1974. Two exceptions include the September/November 1996 issue of the *International DEMS Bulletin*, in which Bjarne Busk, to commemorate the recent death of the Duke's son, prepared a discography updated to 1995, and the bulletin of the Duke Ellington Society of Sweden published in May 2014 and dedicated to Mercer. In the latter case as well, however, very little information is provided about any events that took place after spring 1974.

7. The three sessions came together in the album *Continuum*, released by Fantasy in 1975 (the CD edition is Fantasy 00025218246521).

8. These concerts can be heard on unreleased tapes. The audience in London on February 20 included biographer Derek Jewell, who briefly mentions this concert in his *Duke: A Portrait of Ellington*, 179.

9. The concert was intended to raise funds for a college in Liberia; "Concert to Celebrate Duke Ellington Day on April 29," *New York Times*, April 20, 1976, 37. The benefit concert is discussed in the April 1977 issue of *National Chairmen's Report* in the article "Duke Ellington Orchestra Concert to Benefit Cuttington College."

10. This speech was prepared by Frances K. Pullen, who began writing for the president in 1974 and focused on speeches for the First Lady as of 1976. Five versions were prepared, all slightly different, but all explicitly expressing Madam First Lady's admiration for the Duke's music. Typewritten copies are conserved at the Gerald R. Ford Presidential Library, Box 1, Folder "1976/04/29—Duke Ellington Concert, New York City," Frances K. Pullen Papers.

11. These observations are based on unreleased tapes of the radio broadcast *Ellington Is Forever*.

12. Joseph H. Mazo, "Alvin Ailey's Dance Tribute to the Duke," *New York Times*, April 13, 1975.

13. In the interview given to Harriett Milnes on April 7, 1983, Ailey was probably referring to the fact that the New York City Ballet only created a Stravinsky Festival after the Russian composer's death (one year later, to be precise). Many thanks to Yale University for providing a transcription of the tape: *Alvin Ailey Talking with Harriett Milnes*, Ailey Alvin OHIII 577 A-C.

14. On the relation between Ailey and Ellington, see the two monographs dedicated to Ailey: Jennifer Dunning, *Alvin Ailey: A Life in Dance*, Boston, MA: Da Capo Press 1998, and Thomas F. DeFrantz, *Dancing Revelations: Alvin Ailey's Embodiment of African American Culture*, New York: Oxford University Press, 2004. The text by Dunning reports that Ailey cultivated relations with a few members of the Harlem Renaissance, including Carl Van Vechten and Langston Hughes; with the latter, he worked on two projects, *Black Nativity* and *Jerico-Jim Crow*.

15. Arnold Jay Smith, "Alvin Ailey Dance Company/Duke Ellington Orchestra," *DownBeat*, January 1977, 35–6.

16. John Franceschina, in his *Duke Ellington's Music for the Theatre*, quotes reviews of some of the choreographies to music by Ellington in the 1976 edition of *Ailey Celebrates Ellington*, 167–8.

17. This announcement appeared in the *Yale Daily News* on September 23, 1977, 3, and was reprinted in the October 6 (17), October 7 (4), October 10 (10), October 11 (3), and October 13 (3) issues. Many thanks to Suzanne Eggleston Lovejoy, music librarian for Reference and Instruction—Yale University Library, for providing this information from the *Yale Daily News*.

18. Jim Gardner, "Jazz Musicians Assemble to Benefit Ellington Scholarship," *Yale Daily News*, October 17, 1977, 6.

19. This is what the bandleader told Manheim Fox, a producer at the record label The Frog Box Inc., during an interview given on January 24, 1981, later included in the liner notes for the LP *Three Black Kings* (Frog Box TFB 100/2).

20. The tour took place from October 17 to mid-December. Files coming from the American State Department, which can currently be consulted at wikileaks.org under "Mercer Ellington," were used to reconstruct the big band's participation in the Jazz Jamboree Festival and their journey in Poland.

21. Between the two performances at the jazz festival, Mercer led the big band in Łódź on October 20, in Katowice on October 22, and the following day in Wrocław. The program of the 1977 Jazz Jamboree is online as a PDF on the Polish site www.polishjazzarch.com/jazz-jamboree.html.

22. The works played during the October 24, 1977, concert are now found in three different sources: the unreleased video seen on Polish television that contains "Sir Duke"; the LP *Remembering Duke's World* (Polijazz- SX0675) that includes "Take the 'A' Train," "Do Nothin' Till You Hear from Me," "Satin Doll," "Caravan," "In a Sentimental Mood," and *New World A-Comin'*; and the LP *Three Black Kings* (Frog Box TFB 100/2), which in addition to the title piece, includes *New World A-Comin'* and *The River*.

23. This introduction appears on an unreleased tape of the concert, which was organized by the Barcelona Hot Club in collaboration with Ayuntamiento de Barcelona (the city's public administration).

24. Mercer reaffirmed this link between the first movement and the stained-glass windows at Santa Maria del Mar in the 1981 interview mentioned above. It then made its way into the liner notes for the LP *Three Black Kings* and, from there, into the musicological literature.

25. A particularly detailed historical account of the Magi is found in the text by Franco Cardini, *I re magi: Storia e leggenda*, Venice: Marsilio, 2000. The volume by Madeleine Félix, *I re magi*, Milan: Jaca Book, 2000, mainly focuses on their presence in art history.

26. On the figure of the Black Magus in art history, see the scrupulously researched and magnificently illustrated volumes edited by David Bindman and Henry Louis Gates Jr.: *The Image of the Black in Western Art, II: From the Early Christian Era to the Age of Discovery, Part 1: From the Demonic Threat to the Incarnation of Sainthood* and *Part 2: Africans in the Christian Ordinance of the World*, Washington, DC: Howard University Press, 2010.

27. Even the late fourteenth-century *Adoration of the Magi*, painted for the church that, according to legend, hosts the mortal remains of the three kings, the Basilica of Sant'Eustorgio in Milan only contains white Magi.

28. The *Missale secundum usum ecclesiae s. Floriani*, which dates to 1400–1405, is reproduced in Bindman and Gates (eds.), *The Image of the Black in Western Art, II, Part 2*, 62.

29. Alain Locke, *The Negro in Art: A Pictorial Record of the Negro Artist and of the Negro Theme in Art*, Washington, DC: Associates in Negro Folk Education, 1940; in particular, the chapter *The Negro in Art*, 138–40; the quotation appears on page 138. The catalog of the exhibition *Black Is Beautiful: Rubens to Dumas*, Amsterdam: Waanders Publishers, Zwolle, 2008, carries on along the same lines as Locke's volume; in our context, see the chapter *The Black Magus in the Netherlands from Memling to Rubens*, 32.

30. Ellington always had a penchant for modulations by thirds, and in January 1956, recorded "Blue Rose." This piece is almost exclusively based on this sort of modulation and anticipates the harmonies used by John Coltrane in 1959 and 1960 in works such as "Like Sonny," "Giant Steps," and "Central Park West."

31. Mercer Ellington's discussion of the narrative aspects of the three movements is included in the liner notes for the Frog Box LP *Three Black Kings*.

32. Listening to the unreleased tapes and the LP *Three Black Kings*, it becomes clear that both the big band and the musicians of the Polish National Philharmonic Orchestra came across more than one stumbling block while playing "King of the Nativity." The first theme, in particular, seems rhythmically confused in the recordings from the European tour. The tempo itself, which is quite different from one performance to the next, shows that Mercer wasn't entirely certain about how to conduct this piece.

33. Mercer justifies Solomon's place as the work's second Black king in the liner notes for *Three Black Kings*. In his live presentations, based on the recordings that can currently be consulted, he never explained the reasons for which Solomon was included.

34. The work in the Bible of Zoudenbalch is reproduced in Bindman and Gates (eds.), *The Image of the Black in Western Art, II, Part 2*, 158; the phrase from Song of Songs is discussed in *Part 1*, 202–5.

35. Ellington's annotations are described in M. Ellington, *Duke Ellington in Person*, 120; the remark he made to Stanley Dance is found in Cohen, *Duke Ellington's America*, 449.

36. In art history, even in ancient times, the Queen of Sheba was often portrayed as a Black woman; nevertheless, much like Balthazar, a parallel iconography exists in which she is white. According to some exegeses, the queen and Solomon's Black wife mentioned in Song of Songs are the same person.

37. Duke Ellington, *Music Is My Mistress*, New York: Da Capo Press, 1973, 309; Marian Logan recalled the event in Robert Levi's documentary, *Duke Ellington: Reminiscing in Tempo* (1992); the quotation appears in Cohen, *Duke Ellington's America*, 395.

38. In the literature dedicated to King, no significant information is found on his presence at the performance of *My People* nor his relations with Ellington, not even in the 800-page monograph written by Pulitzer Prize–winner David J. Garrow, *Bearing the Cross: Martin Luther King, Jr. and the Southern Christian Leadership Conference*, New York: William Morrow Paperbacks, 2004. Given that during those very hours King was planning the March on Washington, scholars have understandably chosen to concentrate on this historical event, which took place in August 1963.

39. For an overview of these musical tributes, see Anthony McDonald (ed.), *A Catalog of Music Written in Honor of Martin Luther King, Jr.*, Lanham, MD: Scarecrow Press, 2012. Inevitably, this catalog is incomplete; from our point of view, one work that should be added, and that is similar to *Three Black Kings*, is the ballet *Martin*, written in 1990 by the great African American photographer Gordon Parks, who had portrayed both Ellington and King.

40. Ellington's son made these remarks during a series of interviews given in 1990–91, and they appear in Cohen, *Duke Ellington's America*, 398. Among the few works dedicated to Martin Luther King Jr. before his death (which include pieces by Black composers such as Mark Fax and Margaret Bonds), in addition to the piece composed by Ellington for *My People*, mention must go to John Coltrane's masterpiece "Alabama." In 1963, Coltrane wrote this musical prayer based on the funeral oration given by King for the four young Black girls killed in the dynamite attack that destroyed a Baptist church in Birmingham on September 15 of that same year. Neither of these works appears in the catalog edited by McDonald.

41. American Composers Orchestra, *Four Symphonic Works by Duke Ellington*, Musical Heritage Society (512335T). The United States Air Force Band used Peress's orchestration for a 2011 recording released on the CD *The Symphonic Portrait* (ALT70942), which demonstrates the quality of this orchestration and is worth listening to even without Jimmy Heath's solos.

42. Duke Ellington, *Black, Brown and Beige*, Naxos (8.559737), Buffalo Philharmonic Orchestra conducted by JoAnn Falletta. The solo clarinetist is Sal Andolina, perfectly at home with both classical and jazz music.

43. *The Symphonic Ellington: Night Creature*, Civica Jazz Band and the Giuseppe Verdi Symphony Orchestra of Milan, conducted by Enrico Intra, Soul Note (121319-2). This is a live recording of the concert held at the Teatro Lirico in Milan on February 17, 1999.

44. The video interview, *Three Black Kings*, can be viewed on Walter Rutledge's YouTube channel.

45. Liner notes for the LP *Three Black Kings*.

46. A splendid selection of works by this photographer, including a few shots from the set for *Paris Blues*, is found in the volume by Lorie Karnath, *Sam Shaw*, Ostfildern: Hatje Cantz, 2010; as regards the film with Ellington, see pages 170–3.

47. The three men's careers overlapped repeatedly during the following decades. Bearden used photos by Shaw in his magnificent collages, which often portrayed jazz musicians (and, most prominently, Ellington). Along with Henderson, whom he met through Shaw,

he also wrote a fundamental text, Romare Bearden and Harry Henderson, *A History of African-American Artists: From 1792 to the Present*, New York: Pantheon, 1993.

48. Information on this show, whose text was to be written by Bob Russell, the author of the lyrics for "Don't Get Around Much Anymore," is found in John Franceschina, *Duke Ellington's Music for the Theatre*, 46–8.

49. *Racing World* still required editing and a narrator. For the latter, in addition to Ellington himself, prestigious actors such as Anthony Quinn and Simone Signoret were to be involved; Klaus Stratemann, *Duke Ellington, Day by Day and Film by Film*, Copenhagen: JazzMedia, 1992, 579–82. The music for this documentary was recorded by Ellington for his stockpile collection under the title *Degas Suite* and was released posthumously by various labels. The American edition is the only one that indicates the single movements of this suite: Duke Ellington, *The Private Collection, Volume Five: The Suites, New York 1968 & 1970*, Saja (7 91045-2).

50. Many thanks to Edie Shaw who, in October and November 2016, answered many of my questions with detailed emails.

51. For a general overview of the masters who portrayed the Far West, see the book by Kate J. Jennings, *Remington & Russell and the Art of the American West*, Greenwich: Brompton, 1999; the reference monographs for the two artists featured in the documentary are Carpenter Troccoli (ed.), *The Masterworks of Charles M. Russell: A Retrospective of Paintings and Sculpture*, Norman, OK: University of Oklahoma Press, 2009; and Brian W. Dippie, *Frederic Remington: The Frederic Remington Art Museum Collection*, New York: Harry N. Abrams, 2001. Since these bibliographical indications are intended to allow the reader to have an idea of the works that were under Ellington's eyes while he was working on the film, they are all richly illustrated with color reproductions.

52. Stanley Dance, who wrote the liner notes for the various editions of the recordings that make up the *Duke Ellington Private Collection*, is the only source who has given us brief indications on "Elos." The most detailed liner notes regarding the composition in question are the ones for the CD *Duke Ellington, The Private Collection, Volume Nine: Studio Sessions, New York 1968*, WEA (255 925-2).

53. The structure of "Elos" is intro/aaabaabaa/.

54. The C minor chord is obviously a ii, part of the progression ii-V-I in B flat major with the F7 not explicitly present, and thus not a true minor dominant, such as, for example, the one found in bar 3 of the theme of "Mood Indigo" (1930). Nevertheless, the effect of this chord, perhaps precisely because the F7 is missing, is extraordinarily similar.

7. CELEBRATION

1. The tape of this interview, which lasts almost thirty minutes, has not been released.
2. Duke Ellington, *Music Is My Mistress*, New York: Da Capo Press, 1973.
3. This incomplete list includes the names of the arrangers whose work for Ellington appeared on an album. Others were not so fortunate: Tadd Dameron and Fred Stone's arrangements never made it to the recording studio.

4. Information on Ellington's pieces written for the Stratford Shakespeare Festival is provided by Jack Chambers in his essay "Bardland: Shakespeare in Ellington's World," published in the *International DEMS Bulletin*, April–July 2005.

5. The limited-edition album *Live Performances by Duke Ellington and His Orchestra: 1956 Stratford, 1973 Winnipeg*, distributed to those who participated in the Duke Ellington Society convention held in Toronto in 1987, contains accurate liner notes by musicologist Andrew Homzy on Ellington's relation with Canada. The quote appears in Stanley Dance's liner notes for the LP *Duke Ellington, North of the Border* (ACDM 1425).

6. The radio interview was carried out by Ted O'Reilly and the founder of the Canadian jazz magazine *Coda*, John Norris, on CJRT Radio on November 25, 1968, and is contained in the CD version of *North of the Border*, released by Attic Records (ACDM 1425).

7. On the friendship between Ellington and this Canadian film music composer and artistic director, see the biography by Walter Pitman, *Louis Applebaum: A Passion for Culture*, Toronto: Dundurn, 2002, 112.

8. Norris's article for *DownBeat* is reproduced in Ken Vail, *Duke's Diary: The Life of Duke Ellington, 1950–1974*, 2 vols., Lanham, MD: Scarecrow Press, 2002, II, 319.

9. One day earlier, on July 1, Ellington rehearsed with this ensemble. The unreleased tapes of the concert, which was broadcast over the radio, are indicated in the fifth edition of the discography by W. E. Timner, *Ellingtonia: The Recorded Music of Duke Ellington and His Sidemen*, Lanham, MD: Scarecrow Press, 2007, 400, but not in Luciano Massagli and Giovanni M. Volontè, *The New DESOR: An Updated Edition of Duke Ellington's Story on Records 1924–1974*, Milan: Private edition, 1999. In Detroit, during the part of the concert in which Ellington participated, the pieces performed included *Song and Dance*, "Satin Doll," *Nameless Hour*, "Take the 'A' Train," and *Aurora Borealis*.

10. Fred Stone, who, in the fifties, was part of the ensembles led by Norman Symonds in which Collier appeared as a trombonist, joined Ellington's Orchestra in March 1970. He did not, however, remain for very long. Stone left the big band after the European tour held in the summer of that same year. Nevertheless, he was able to participate in one of the most significant recordings in late Ellington: *The New Orleans Suite*. Stone gave Ellington a score of his titled "Maiera," a modal composition that the bandleader recorded privately in Milan on July 23, 1970, and that he played a few times live without, however, releasing a recording of it. The complete tapes of the Milan session, along with a few photos, were discovered by myself during interviews with sound technician Luigi Pessani.

11. The recordings that involved Collier took place on September 2. All the takes for the *Reader's Digest* project were released in 2002 on the CD *Duke Ellington, Live and Rare*, Bluebird (09026 63953 2).

12. Mark Miller, *The Miller Companion to Jazz in Canada*, Toronto: The Mercury Press, 2001, 46–7.

13. The ninety-two-page score and the twenty-two-page libretto were registered under that title on May 11, 1970.

14. Many thanks to David Palmquist, who, on May 29, 2016, reported to the Duke-LYM mailing list that a number of clips of the concert held on May 29 are now online. These recently restored videos cover most of the live concert and a few moments backstage and can be seen on YouTube under the title "Duke Ellington with Ann Henry at the Mount Angel

Abbey Library, 1970." The February 1971 issue of *Ebony* dedicated a touching article to Ann Henry, written by Louie Robinson and titled "Ann of Mount Angel Abbey: Stricken Dancer Finds Success at Monastery," which includes some information concerning the event with Ellington, of whom a photo appears, 29–36.

15. "Relaxing," which Collier recorded as bandleader in 1965 for the LP *Ron Collier Tentet* (CTLS-5059), was released posthumously by Laserdisc on the CD *Duke Ellington, Cool Rock* (La15782), under the erroneous title "Vancouver Lights." The latter composition has yet to be released.

16. Collier, five days later, took Ellington to a jazz club. The Duke was asked to evaluate a singer who performed that evening as a candidate for an upcoming engagement at the Playboy Club Hotel in Great Gorge (New Jersey). Romanian Canadian Aura Rulli passed the test; not only did she sing with the orchestra for a week, but on July 8, the Duke took her to Carnegie Hall. Some sources maintain that Ellington commissioned Collier to write specific arrangements for this singer; this, however, is not plausible because listening to the unreleased tapes of Aura Rulli's virtuoso scat in "Blem" and "Mood Indigo" at Carnegie Hall confirms that this was indeed a jam session.

17. Klaus Stratemann, *Duke Ellington, Day by Day and Film by Film*, Copenhagen: JazzMedia, 1992, 598. The audio tapes of the interview have not been released.

18. Information on the ballet can be found in the following volumes: *Jennifer Dunning, Alvin Ailey: A Life in Dance*, Boston, MA: Da Capo Press, 1998, 255–8; and Thomas F. De Frantz, *Dancing Revelations: Alvin Ailey's Embodiment of African American Culture*, New York: Oxford University Press, 2004, 148–59. Many details also appear in John Franceschina, *Duke Ellington's Music for the Theatre*, Jefferson, NC: McFarland Company, 2001, whose chapter "Water Music" is dedicated to *The River*, 161–9.

19. All the choreographer's memories concerning *The River* understandably convey a sense of growing concern for the tapes, which never seemed to arrive. Particularly detailed oral recollections appear in the interview given to Harriett Milnes on September 7, 1983 (many thanks to Yale University for the transcription), and on the CD (track 23) attached to the book by Vivian Perlis and Libby Van Cleve, *Composers' Voices from Ives to Ellington: An Oral History of American Music*, New Haven, CT: Yale University Press, 2005.

20. The music recorded by Ellington at the National Recording Studio in New York on May 11, 1970, consists in the following sections: "The Spring," "The Run," The Meander," "The Giggling Rapids," "The Lake," and "The Neo-Hip-Hot Cool-Kiddies Community," and it was partially released on the cassettes Azure 3 and 25, tapes for collectors with ties to the DEMS (Duke Ellington Music Society) and more recently in the CD *Duke Ellington, The Piano Player*, Storyville (101 8399), which, however, contains an erroneous recording date for the session held in New York.

21. On March 9, Ellington rehearsed "The Giggling Rapids" (dedicating many takes to it), "The Meander," and "The River." On May 25, he recorded "The Run," "The Meander," "The Lake," "The Giggling Rapids," and "The Spring"; on June 3, "The Village of the Virgins," "The Whirlpool," "The Neo-Hip-Hot Cool-Kiddies Community," and "The River"; on June 8, "The Falls"; on June 15, "The Mother, Her Majesty the Sea."

22. The author of this book attended a magnificent performance given by the ballet company of the Teatro alla Scala, which, in the 1999–2000 opera and ballet season, danced

The River, following the structure defined by Ailey in 1972. A video document of the 1972 edition in eight movements (I. "Spring," II. "Meander," III. "Giggling Rapids," IV. "Lake," V. "Vortex," VI. "Falls," VII. "Riba," VIII. "Two Cities") is held in the Dance Collection of the New York Public Library. It is a film shot by Gardner Compton and Emilie Ardolino in August 1972. The score is for only two pianos (Martha Johnson and Howard Barr).

23. Ellington, *Music Is My Mistress*, 201–2.

24. "The Giggling Rapids" had also been recorded on tape with the title "Gigl" in a private session on November 29, 1968, released posthumously on the CD *Duke Ellington, The Private Collection, Volume Six: Studio Sessions, New York 1968*, Caz CD (506). "The Lake" was included in a few concerts in 1969, such as the second live concert held in Rotterdam on November 7, 1969, where it was played in a Latin tempo by a quartet; this take was recently included in the CD *Duke Ellington, An Intimate Piano Session*, Storyville (1018445).

25. The orchestrator, in an article by Roger Burford Mason, "Ron Collier: Memories of Duke," *The Canadian Composer*, Spring 1991, 8, confessed that working with the Duke was quite difficult since he didn't respect any of the deadlines.

26. At the Duke Ellington Society convention held in Toronto in 1996, Collier expressed his (partially justifiable) dissatisfaction that these recordings were released: "I'm sure if Duke were alive, he would never have released this . . . . The River numbers were really very rough and their function was not to be a commercial record." Stanley Slome has written about the orchestrator's involvement and more in general about the birth of this ballet in his article "The River," *Duke Ellington Society, Southern California Chapter Newsletter*, available online at www.ellingtonweb.ca/Slome-River.htm.

27. Collier carefully wrote down indications for stage lighting and the entrance of the dancers. In "The Spring," for example, he noted that the lights were to be turned on after the entrance of the horn, which would thus take place in the dark ("curtain up in darkness"). The score in question is the one published by G. Schirmer and registered in 1970 by Tempo Music Inc.

28. The take chosen by Collier as a starting point for his orchestration is New DESOR catalog number DE7042X. This recording is largely unreleased, given that it only circulated as cassette Azure 25, a collectors' tape solely intended for members of the Duke Ellington Society.

29. Four days after the session, Ellington still had that theme in mind. During the breaks from rehearsals for the concert at Mount Angel Abbey on May 29, 1970, the Duke played "The Meander" at the piano.

30. This documentary was released on VHS and has been described by Brian Geoffrey Rose, *Television and the Performing Arts: A Handbook and Reference Guide to American Cultural Programming*, Westport, CT, Greenwood Press, 1986, 46–8.

31. The scene begins with a superimposed title: "Ellingtonia. Choreography: Arnold Berger. Music: Duke Ellington." Actually, the piece is "Vortex," and the fictional choreographer Berger was interpreted in the film by Daniel Levins, who in real life was an esteemed dancer and choreographer. Levins was white. The Black Alvin Ailey thus disappeared from the movie. The film contains a shorter version of "Vortex."

32. The movements performed that evening were: "The Spring," "The Meander," "The Giggling Rapids," "The Lake," "The Falls," "The Whirlpool," "The Village of the Virgins,"

and "The River." Their order does not respect the narration set out by Duke Ellington in *Music Is My Mistress*, which appears in the Private Collection CD. Most likely, Mercer decided to end the live performance with an upbeat piece. For further details about the audio and video recordings of this concert, see chapter 6, note 22.

33. The tapes have yet to be released.

34. The unreleased recording, which remained in the CJRT archives for a few years and then disappeared, was rediscovered in January 2005 by myself, thanks to the precious help of Ted O'Reilly. He contacted Cathy Collier, the widow of Ellington's orchestrator, who provided us with a few tapes, one of which turned out to be the recording of *Celebration*.

35. "Special CJRT Concert Celebrates Ellington's Birthday," *Toronto Star*, April 29, 1974, D6.

36. See note 6.

37. Ellington often used notepads from hotels to write memos to himself. I possess a photostatic copy of a note referring to "Chant for F.D. Roosevelt" scribbled on paper with the letterhead of the Hotel Excelsior in Montreux. The one for *Celebration* is conserved in the Ellington collection of the Smithsonian Institution in the box containing preparatory materials for *Music Is My Mistress*. On page 522 of this book, *Celebration* is dated 1973, the year it was copyrighted.

38. Stratemann, *Duke Ellington Day by Day*, 623.

39. Clifford A. Ridley wrote the article "The Orchestra Rose from the Grave." The center of the piece, which took up an entire page of the June 10, 1972, issue, is occupied by a photo of conductor Willis Page.

40. The history of the JSO is recounted by Betty B. Jean in the limited edition book *Fifty Years of Great Music: The Jacksonville Symphony Orchestra*, Sacramento, CA: Allied Printing, 1999.

41. Page's efforts to reinforce the orchestra were noted by Bob Phelps in "Turning a Page," an article commemorating the conductor's eightieth birthday, which appeared in the June 9, 1998, issue of the *Florida Times-Union*.

42. The quotation appears in the volume by Jean, *Fifty Years of Great Music*, 105.

43. An unreleased recording was made of that concert at the Kleinhans Music Hall in Buffalo, as mentioned in chapter 2, page 30, note 24.

44. "Symphony to Perform Ellington Composition," *Florida Times-Union*, January 28, 1972, B-17, col. 1.

45. "Symphony Season Ending—Almost," *Florida Times-Union*, April 25, 1972, B-1, col. 6. Ellington's recollections might date to September 21, 1935, when he played in this Florida city for the first time, performing at the Pythian Temple.

46. James Ward, "Singers Laud Jacksonville Symphony," *Florida Times-Union*, May 16, 1972, B-1, col. 1; Pope Haley, "Symphony's Present Is Good Music," *Florida Times-Union*, May 17, 1972, A-1, col. 3.

47. Stanley Dance noted this in the article "Celebration," which he wrote as a firsthand witness for the *Jazz Journal*, July 25, 1972, 4–5. He praised the orchestra's performance and the saxophonist and the percussionist in particular. Documentation about the key to the city is found at the Smithsonian Institution, box 4, folder 5, "Jacksonville (FL), Honorary Citizenship, May 16, 1972."

48. The private recording was made by Norman Vincent. A radio speaker in Jacksonville and the owner of a professional recording studio, Vincent told the *Florida Times-Union* that he owned what could be the only existing copy of that tape reel; "Radio Career Shows You Can't Go Wrong with Big Band Swing," *Florida Times-Union*, July 11, 2006.

49. This is what Ted O'Collier communicated to the Duke-LYM mailing list in 2013; one passage from the email is found on the site *The Duke—Where and When*, www.tdwaw.ellingtonweb.ca/TDWAW.html#Yr1974.

50. Maurice Peress, *Dvořák to Duke Ellington: A Conductor Explores America's Music and Its African American Roots*, New York: Oxford University Press, 2004, 168 and 234 n. 7.

51. I provided information on how this score was found at the Conference on Black Music Research 32nd Annual Conference (promoted by the Society for American Music), Chicago, March 15–19, 2006, as part of my presentation *La Scala, She Too Pretty to Be Neglected: History and Analysis of an Ellington Composition*.

52. This technique has been used since the ragtime era. "I Got the Blues" (1908), the first printed blues by New Orleans composer Antonio Maggio, is actually a two-step ragtime with four themes, the first of which is a blues in G major which then appears in G minor; see Luca Bragalini, "Il primo blues parlava italoamericano," *Musica Jazz*, March 1999, 56–8. Bubber Miley, who cowrote "Black and Tan Fantasy," improvised over a minor/major blues in the 1925 Kansas City Five recording of "St. Louis Blues" by Handy. This technique fell into disuse in modern jazz, but rare examples do exist; one of the most noteworthy is "Mr. Syms" by John Coltrane (1960), who loved Ellington and Johnny Hodges and recorded with both.

53. Stanley Dance informs us, in his article "Celebration," that Bernie Kaye's sound was similar to Johnny Hodges's. This saxophonist and surgeon is also mentioned in the volume by Jean, *Fifty Years of Great Music*. The Duke had implicitly suggested that improvisation is not a *sine qua non* for jazz in his poem "The Black Stick," which he used to recite when he wished to mock the commonplace way of thinking, according to which jazz is an instinctive and illiterate form of expression. Heard recited live by Ellington, as in the unreleased tape of an interview given to Carter Harman on October 13, 1964, this poem is highly amusing. Sincere thanks to the Smithsonian Institution for sending a digitalized version of the tape.

54. Many thanks to the Jacksonville University Library for providing the Jacksonville Sesquicentennial 1822–1972 program notes.

55. On the similarities between the text of "The Blues" and Eliot's *Ash Wednesday*, see David Schiff, *The Ellington Century*, Berkeley, CA: University of California Press, 2012, 212. John Latouche, taking inspiration from the poem by Yeats, wrote the text "Brown Penny" for the theater show *A Beggar's Holiday*, set to music by Ellington in 1946; the Duke recorded this ballad on more than one occasion in both vocal and instrumental versions.

56. Sector periodicals and newspapers covered this initiative, publishing articles with titles such as "Celebration, suite dimenticata di Ellington" ("Celebration, a Forgotten Suite by Ellington") (Franco Fayenz, *Il Giornale*, March 18, 2007) and "L'Ellington dimenticato rinasce grazie all'Italia" ("A Forgotten Ellington Is Reborn Thanks to Italy") (Claudio Sessa, *Corriere della Sera*, March 19, 2007). For the recording of *Celebration*, arranger Massimiliano Rocchetta, in addition to extracting the parts from the manuscript score, significantly adapted the instrumentation to suit the ensemble used on this occasion, giving the contrabassoon part to the second bassoon and, more rarely, the bass clarinet and tuba.

BIBLIOGRAPHY

QUOTED BIBLIOGRAPHICAL SOURCES

INTRODUCTION: FOR SYMPHONY ORCHESTRA AND JAZZ BAND

Anderson, Paul Allen. *Deep River: Music and Memory in Harlem Renaissance Thought*, Durham, NC: Duke University Press, 2001.

Baker, Houston A., Jr. *Modernism and the Harlem Renaissance*, Chicago, IL: University of Chicago Press, 1987.

Baskerville, David Ross. *Jazz Influence on Art Music to Mid-Century*, PhD dissertation, Los Angeles: University of California, Dept. of Music, 1965.

Bragalini, Luca. "Organizzare il suono: Dalla dodecafonia alle aree intervallari," Preface to D'Andrea, Franco, and Luigi Ranghino. *Aree Intervallari*, Milano: Volonté & Co., 2011.

Coady, Christopher. *John Lewis and the Challenge of "Real" Black Music*, Ann Arbor, MI: University of Michigan Press, 2016.

Dempsey, Peter. Liner notes for the CD *Paul Whiteman: Music for Moderns*, Naxos 8.120505.

Du Bois, W.E.B. *The Souls of Black Folk*, Chicago 1903; New York: W. W. Norton & Company, 1999.

Floyd, Samuel A., Jr. *The Power of Black Music: Interpreting Its History from Africa to the United States*, New York: Oxford University Press, 1995.

Gates, Henry Louis, Jr. *The Signifying Monkey: A Theory of African-American Literary Criticism*, New York: Oxford University Press, 1988.

Howland, John. *Ellington Uptown: Duke Ellington, James P. Johnson, and the Birth of Concert Jazz*, Ann Arbor, MI: University of Michigan Press, 2009.

Lambert, Eddie. *Duke Ellington: A Listener's Guide*, Lanham, MD/London: Scarecrow Press, 1999.

Levine, Lawrence. *Highbrow/Lowbrow: The Emergence of Cultural Hierarchy in America*, Cambridge. MA: Harvard University Press, 1988.

Levine, Lawrence. "Jazz and the American Culture," *Journal of American Folklore*, CII, 403 (January–March 1989).

Lewis, David. Liner notes for the CD *Skyscrapers Symphonic Jazz*, Naxos 8.120644.

Mintun, Peter. Liner notes for the CD *Jazz Nocturne—American Concertos of the Jazz Age*, Naxos 8.559647.

Rayno, Don. *Paul Whiteman: Pioneer in American Music*, Vol. I, 1890–1930, Lanham, MD: Scarecrow Press, 2003.
Smith Parsons, Catherine. *William Grant Still: A Study in Contradictions*, Los Angeles, CA: University of California Press, 2000.

1. LA SCALA, PART I: CONDEMNED TO OBLIVION

Candini, Pino. "Duke al Conservatorio," *La Notte*, February 20–21, 1963.
Candini, Pino. "Ellington non invecchia : Il trionfo del Duca al Conservatorio di Milano," *Musica Jazz*, March 1963, 12–6.
Cerri, Livio. "I concerti di Ellington a Milano," *Musica e dischi*, March 1963.
Cerri, Livio. *Mezzo secolo di jazz*, Pisa: Nistri-Lischi, 1981.
Chailly, Luciano. *À la manière de . . . Temi per lo studio della composizione*, Milano: Curci, 1978.
Chailly, Luciano. *Buzzati in Musica*, Torino: Ada Martello Editore, 1987.
"Ellington al Conservatorio," *Corriere della Sera*, February 21, 1963.
Franchini, Vittorio. "È arrivato il jazz coi calzoni lunghi: Il musicista negro suonerà nella sala grande del Conservatorio di musica intitolato a Giuseppe Verdi," *Corriere d'Informazione*, February 19–20, 1963.
Ionio, Daniele. "Duke e l'orchestra della Scala: La suite italiana," *Jazzland*, March–April 1963, 27.
Lettich, Furio. "Con Ellington al Conservatorio. Cootie Williams figliol prodigo," *Il Giorno*, February 21, 1963.
Massagli, Luciano, Liborio Pusateri, and Giovanni M. Volonté. *Duke Ellington's Story on Records 1963–1965*, self-published, 1979.
Mazzoletti, Adriano. *Il jazz in Italia dalle origini alle grandi orchestre*, Torino: EDT, 2004.
Montale, Eugenio. "Butterfly," *Corriere d'Informazione*, February 22, 1963.
Musica Jazz, May 1984 (issue devoted to the tenth anniversary of Ellington's death; enclosed the previously unreleased LP *Le suites sinfoniche*).
Musica Jazz, December 1991 (issue devoted to Ellington; enclosed the CD *The Great Duke Ellington* with the live recordings at the Conservatorio Verdi in Milan, February 20–21, 1963).

2. NEW WORLD A-COMIN': PROUD TO BE ON THE AIR

Collins, Al "Jazzbo." Liner notes for the CD, Don Shirley. *Tonal Expressions/Piano Perspective*, 2CD set, Collectables, col cd 2755.
Dance, Stanley. Liner notes for the CD *Duke Ellington's Concert of Sacred Music*, BMG-RCA 74321192542.
Dawson, Michael C. *Black Visions: The Roots of Contemporary African-American Political Ideologies*, Chicago, IL: University of Chicago Press, 2001.
Dawson, Michael C. *Blacks In and Out of the Left*, Cambridge, MA: Harvard University Press, 2013.

Denning, Michael. *The Cultural Front: The Laboring of American Culture in the Twentieth Century*, New York: Verso, 1997.
Dietrich, Kurt. *Duke's Bones: Ellington's Great Trombonists*, Rottenburg: Advance Music, 1996.
Edwards Hayes, Brent. "The Literary Ellington," in O'Meally, Robert G., Brent Edwards Hayes, and Farah Jasmine Griffin (eds.). *Uptown Conversation: The New Jazz Studies*, New York: Columbia University Press, 2004, 326–56.
Ellington, Duke. *Music Is My Mistress*, New York: Da Capo Press, 1973.
Ellington, Mercer. *Duke Ellington in Person: An Intimate Memoir*, Boston, MA: Houghton Mifflin Company, 1978.
FBI. "Edward (Duke) Kennedy Ellington 100-hq-434443," dossier.
Feather, Leonard. Liner notes for the CD *Duke Ellington, Live at Carnegie Hall Dec. 11, 1943*, Storyville 103 8341.
Franceschina, John. *Duke Ellington's Music for the Theatre*, Jefferson, NC: McFarland Company, 2001.
George, Don. *Sweet Man: The Real Duke Ellington*, New York: G. P. Putnam's Sons, 1981.
Hajdu, David. *Lush Life: A Biography of Billy Strayhorn*, New York: North Point Press, 1997.
Hasse, John Edward. *Beyond Category: The Life and Genius of Duke Ellington*, New York: Omnibus Press, 1993.
Henderson, Luther. *Luther Henderson Papers*, Schomburg Center for Research in Black Culture, 515 Malcolm X Boulevard, New York, NY 10037.
Hill, Wilbert Weldon. *The Sacred Concerts of Edward Kennedy "Duke" Ellington*, PhD dissertation, Washington, DC: Catholic University of America, 1994.
Howland, John. *Ellington Uptown: Duke Ellington, James P. Johnson, and the Birth of Concert Jazz*, Ann Arbor, MI: University of Michigan Press, 2009.
Huddle, Mark A. (ed.). *Roi Ottley's World War II: The Lost Diary of an African American Journalist*, Lawrence, KS: University Press of Kansas, 2011.
Ionio, Daniele. "La suite italiana," *Jazzland*, March–April 1963, 27.
James, Winston. *Holding Aloft the Banner of Ethiopia: Caribbean Radicalism in Early Twentieth-Century America*, New York: Verso, 1998.
Jewell, Derek. *Duke: A Portrait of Duke Ellington*, London: Elm Tree Books, 1977.
Johnson, Aaron J. "A Date with the Duke: Ellington on Radio," *Musical Quarterly*, XCVI, 3–4 (Fall–Winter 2013), 394.
Lambert, Eddie. *Duke Ellington: A Listener's Guide*, Lanham, MD: Scarecrow Press, 1999.
Lavezzoli, Peter. *The King of All, Sir Duke: Ellington and the Artistic Revolution*, New York: Continuum, 2001.
Liner notes for the CD, Luther Henderson. *Clap Hands!/The Greatest Sound Around*, Collectables Jazz Classics, col-cd-6895.
Lock, Graham. *Blutopia: Visions of the Future and Revisions of the Past in the Work of Sun Ra, Duke Ellington, and Anthony Braxton*, Durham, NC/London: Duke University Press, 1999.
Massagli, Luciano, and Giovanni M. Volonté. *The New DESOR: An Updated Edition of Duke Ellington's Story on Records 1924–1974*, 2 vols., self-published: Milan, 1999.
Monson, Ingrid. *Freedom Sounds: Civil Rights Call out to Jazz and Africa*, New York: Oxford University Press, 2007.

New World A-Comin' Arranged by Luther Henderson, Edited by Jeff Tyzik. Ellington Piano Transcription by John Nyerges, music score published by G. Schirmer.

Ottley, Roi. *New World A-Coming: Inside Black America*, Boston, MA: Houghton Mifflin Company, 1943.

Parker, Elliott. "African-American Correspondents during World War II," Conference paper, Association for Education in Journalism and Mass Communication Conference, Toronto, Canada, August 2004.

Pease, William, and Jane Pease. *Black Utopia: Negro Communal Experiments in America*, The State Historical Society of Wisconsin, 1963.

Rimondi, Giorgio. "Il jazz venuto da Saturno: Sun Ra e la science fiction afroamericana," *Jazzit*, 59 (July-August 2010), 154-63.

Robinson, Cedric J. *Black Marxism: The Making of the Black Radical Tradition*, Chapel Hill, NC: University of North Carolina Press, 1983.

Savage, Barbara Dianne. *Broadcasting Freedom: Radio War and the Politics of Race 1938-1948*, Chapel Hill, NC: University of North Carolina Press, 1999.

Schiff, David. "Symphonic Ellington? Rehearing New World A-Comin'," *Musical Quarterly*, XCVI, 3-4 (Fall/Winter 2013), 471-6.

Shawki, Ahmed. *Black Liberation and Socialism*, Chicago, IL: Haymarket Books, 2006.

Sisario, Ben. "Luther Henderson, 84; Arranged Broadway Music," *New York Times*, August 1, 2003.

Smith, Judith E. *Visions of Belonging: Family Stories, Popular Culture, and Postwar Democracy, 1940-1960*, New York: Columbia University Press, 2004.

Smith, Mona Z. *Becoming Something: The Story of Canada Lee: The Untold Tragedy of the Great Black Actor, Activist, and Athlete*, New York: Faber and Faber, 2004.

Steiner, Kenneth. Liner notes for the CD *Duke Ellington, Live at Carnegie Hall December 11, 1943*, Storyville 103 8341.

Stratemann, Klaus. *Duke Ellington, Day by Day and Film by Film*, Copenhagen: JazzMedia, 1992.

Tucker, Mark (ed.). *The Duke Ellington Reader*, New York: Oxford University Press, 1993.

Vail, Ken. *Duke's Diary: The Life of Duke Ellington, 1950-1974*, 2 vols., Lanham, MD: Scarecrow Press, 2002.

"Words of the Week," *Jet*, XXXI, 13, January 5, 1967.

3. HARLEM: SOUNDS FROM THE AIR SHAFT

Anderson, Jervis. *This Was Harlem 1900-1950*, New York: Noonday Press, 1981.

Anderson, Paul Allen. *Deep River: Music and Memory in Harlem Renaissance Thought*, Durham, NC: Duke University Press, 2001.

Baker, Houston A., Jr. *Modernism and the Harlem Renaissance*, Chicago, IL: University of Chicago Press, 1987.

Berish, Andrew S. *Lonesome Roads and Streets of Dreams: Place, Mobility, and Race in Jazz of the 1930s and '40s*, Chicago, IL: University of Chicago Press, 2012.

Berwick Sayers, W. C. *Samuel Coleridge-Taylor, Musician: His Life and Letters*, Whitefish, MT: Kessinger Publishing, 2008.

Bindman, David, and Henry Louis Gates (eds.). *The Image of the Black in Western Art*, vol. V: *The Twentieth Century*, part 2: "The Rise of Black Artists," Cambridge, MA: Howard University Press, 2014.

Blair, Sara. *Harlem Crossroads: Black Writers and the Photograph in the Twentieth Century*, Princeton, NJ: Princeton University Press, 2007.

Bloom, Harold (ed.). *The Harlem Renaissance*, Philadelphia, PA: Chelsea House Publishers, 2004.

Boyd, Herb (ed.). *The Harlem Reader*, New York: Three Rivers Press, 2003.

Cohen, Harvey G. *Duke Ellington's America*, Chicago, IL: University of Chicago Press, 2010.

Collier, James Lincoln. *Duke Ellington*, New York: Oxford University Press, 1987.

Cuney-Hare, Maud. *Negro Musicians and Their Music*, New York: G. K. Hall & Co., 1996; 1st ed. Washington, DC: Associated Publishers, 1936.

Davis, Frank Marshall. "Duke Ellington, Who Goes to the Movies Between the Shows, Wrote Song Hit 'Solitude' Three Years Ago," *Pittsburgh Courier*, January 26, 1935.

DeCarava, Roy, and Langston Hughes. *The Sweet Flypaper of Life*, New York: Hill & Wang, 1967.

Du Bois, W. E. B. *The Souls of Black Folk*, Chicago 1903; New York: W. W. Norton & Company, 1999.

"Duke's Book Will Explain His Carnegie Hall Symph," *Variety*, June 9, 1943.

Earle, Susan (ed.). *Aaron Douglas: African American Modernist*, New Haven (CT): Yale University Press, 2007.

Edwards Hayes, Brent. "The Literary Ellington," in O'Meally, Robert G., Brent Edwards Hayes, and Farah Jasmine Griffin (eds.). *Uptown Conversation: The New Jazz Studies*, New York: Columbia University Press, 2004, 343–5.

Ellington, Duke. "Beige," in *Black, Brown and Beige*, Ms. n.d. 8, Archives Center, Smithsonian Institution, Duke Ellington Collection, Series 4: Scripts, Box 3.

Ellington, Duke. *Music Is My Mistress*, New York: Da Capo Press, 1973.

Ellington, Mercer. *Duke Ellington in Person: An Intimate Memoir*, Boston, MA: Houghton Mifflin Company, 1978.

Faine, Edward Allan. *Ellington at the White House 1969*, Takoma Park, MD: IM Press, 2013.

Floyd, Samuel A., Jr. (ed.). *Black Music in the Harlem Renaissance*, New York: Greenwood Press, 1990.

Floyd, Samuel A., Jr. *The Power of Black Music: Interpreting Its History from Africa to the United States*, New York: Oxford University Press, 1995.

Galassi, Peter. *Roy DeCarava: A Retrospective*, New York: Museum of Modern Art, 1996.

Gardullo, Paul, Michelle Delaney, Jacquelyn D. Serwer, and Lonnie G. Bunch III (eds.). *The Scurlock Studio and Black Washington: Picturing the Promise*, Washington, DC: National Museum of African American History and Culture, Smithsonian Institution, 2009.

George, Don. *Sweet Man: The Real Duke Ellington*, New York: G. P. Putnam's Sons, 1981.

Gill, Jonathan. *Harlem: The Four Hundred Year History from Dutch Village to Capital of Black America*, New York: Grove Press, 2011.

Golden, Thelma, Deborah Willis, Cheryl Finley, and Elizabeth Alexander (eds.). *Harlem: A Century in Images*, New York: Skira Rizzoli, 2010.

Green, Edward. "Harlem Air Shaft: A True Programmatic Composition?" *Journal of Jazz Studies*, VII, 1 (Spring 2011).

Green, Jeffrey. *Samuel Coleridge-Taylor: A Musical Life*, London: Routledge, 2016.

Greenberg, Cheryl Lynn. *Or Does It Explode? Black Harlem in the Great Depression*, New York: Oxford University Press, 1991.

Groce, Nancy. *New York: Songs of the City*, New York: Watson-Guptill Publications, 1999.

Haskins, James. *The Cotton Club*, London: Robson Books, 1977.

Hasse, John Edward, *Beyond Category: The Life and Genius of Duke Ellington*, New York: Omnibus Press, 1993.

Haufman, Bo. "Konstnären Duke Ellington," Duke Ellington Society of Sweden, Bulletin No. 4, November 1914.

Haynes, George E. "The Church and the Negro Spirit," *Survey Graphic: Harlem Mecca of the New Negro*, March 1925, 695–7, 708–9.

Hebling, Edu. *Juan Tizol: Una rumba per l'uomo comune*, master's thesis, Adria Music Conservatory, Italy, 2013.

Henderson, Floyd. "The Image of New York City in American Popular Music: 1880–1970," *New York Folklore Quarterly*, XXX, 4 (December 1974), 267–78.

Henderson, Luther. *Harlem* (music score), arrangement by Maurice Peress, New York: G. Schirmer, 1950.

Hill, Wilbert Weldon. *The Sacred Concerts of Edward Kennedy "Duke" Ellington*, Washington, DC: Catholic University of America, 1994.

Hills, Patricia. *Painting Harlem Modern: The Art of Jacob Lawrence*, Berkeley, CA: University of California Press, 2009.

Hilmes, Michele. *NBC: America's Network*, Los Angeles, CA: University of California Press, 2007.

Howland, John. *Ellington Uptown: Duke Ellington, James P. Johnson, and the Birth of Concert Jazz*, Ann Arbor, MI: University of Michigan Press, 2009.

Hurst, Fannie. "The Other and Unknown Harlem," *New York Times Sunday Magazine*, August 4, 1946.

Hutchinson, George (ed.). *The Cambridge Companion to the Harlem Renaissance*, Cambridge, MA: Cambridge University Press, 2007.

Jaffe, Andy. "An Overview of Duke Ellington Compositions Techniques," *Jazz Research Papers*, XVI, 1996, 71–90.

James, Winston. *Holding Aloft the Banner of Ethiopia: Caribbean Radicals in Early Twentieth-Century America*, London: Verso, 1999.

Johnson, James Weldon. *God's Trombones: Seven Negro Sermons in Verse*, London: Penguin Books 2008; 1st ed. New York: Viking, 1927.

Johnson, James Weldon. *Black Manhattan*, New York: Alfred A. Knopf, 1930.

Johnson, James Weldon. *The Books of American Negro Spirituals*, Boston, MA: Da Capo Press, 2010.

Kirschke, Amy Helene. *Aaron Douglas: Art, Race, and the Harlem Renaissance*, Jackson, MS: University of Mississippi Press, 1995.

Kun, Josh. *Audiotopia: Music, Race, and America*, Los Angeles, CA: University of California Press, 2005.
Lane, Winthrop D. "Ambushed in the City: The Grim Side of Harlem," *Survey Graphic: Harlem Mecca of the New Negro*, March 1925, 692–4, 713–5.
Lasker, Steven. Liner notes for the CD set *Early Ellington: The Complete Brunswick and Vocalion Recordings of Duke Ellington, 1926–1931*, MCA - GRP 36402.
Lewis, David L. *When Harlem Was in Vogue*, New York: Penguin Books, 1977.
Lewis, David L. *W.E.B. Du Bois: A Biography*, New York: Henry Holt & Company, 2009.
Lock, Graham. *Blutopia: Visions of the Future and Revisions of the Past in the Work of Sun Ra, Duke Ellington, and Anthony Braxton*, Durham, NC/London: Duke University Press, 1999.
Lock, Graham, and David Murray (eds.). *The Hearing Eye: Jazz & Blues Influences in African American Visual Art*, New York: Oxford University Press, 2009.
Locke, Alain. *The Negro and His Music—Negro Art: Past and Present*, Salem, MA: Ayer Company Publishers, 1991.
Locke, Alain (ed.). *The New Negro*, New York: Simon & Schuster, 1997; 1st ed. New York: Albert and Charles Boni, 1925.
Lugon, Olivier. *Lo stile documentario in fotografia: Da August Sander a Walker Evans (1920–1945)*, Milano: Electa, 2008.
Marable, Manning, and Mullings, Leith. *Freedom: A Photographic History of the African American Struggle*, London: Phaidon, 2002.
Martin, Tony. *Literary Garveyism: Garvey, Black Arts, and the Harlem Renaissance*, Dover, MA: The Majority Press, 1983.
Massood, Paula J. *Making a Promised Land: Harlem in 20th Century Photography and Film*, New Brunswick, NJ: Rutgers University Press, 2013.
Meyer, Leonard B. *Emotion and Meaning in Music*, Chicago, IL: University of Chicago Press, 1961.
Molesworth, Charles (ed.). *The Works of Alain Locke*, New York: Oxford University Press, 2012.
Moon, Brian Alan. *The Old Songs Hymnal: Harry Burleigh and His Spirituals During the Harlem Renaissance*, Boulder, CO: University of Colorado, 2006.
Mooney, Amy M. *Archibald J. Motley Jr.: The David C. Driskell Series of African American Art, Volume IV*, San Francisco, CA: Pomegranate, 2004.
Morgan, John. Liner notes for the CD, Max Steiner. *The Son of Kong—The Most Dangerous Game*, Naxos 8.570183.
Ogbar, Jeffrey O. G. (ed.). *The Harlem Renaissance Revisited: Politics, Arts, and Letters*, Baltimore, MD: The Johns Hopkins University Press, 2010.
Osofsky, Gilbert. *Harlem: The Making of a Ghetto: Negro New York, 1890–1930*, Chicago, IL: Elephant Paperbacks, 1996.
Parks, Gordon. *Collected Works*, 6 vols., Göttingen: Steidl/Gordon Parks Foundation, 2012.
Pierce, Lemoine D. "Charles Alston: An Appreciation," *The International Review of African American Art*, XIX, 4, 2004, 28–42.
Piras, Marcello. "Duke and Descriptive Music," in Green, Edward (ed.). *The Cambridge Companion to Duke Ellington*, Cambridge, MA: Cambridge University Press, 2014, 221.

Petry, Ann. *The Street*, New York: Houghton Mifflin Company, 1974.
Platte, Nathan R. *Musical Collaboration in the Films of David O. Selznick, 1932–1957*, Ann Arbor, MI: University of Michigan Press, 2010.
Powell, Richard (ed.). *Rhapsody in Black: Art of the Harlem Renaissance*, Berkeley, CA: University of California Press, 1997.
Powell, Richard J. *Archibald J. Motley: Jazz Age Modernist*, Durham, NC: Duke University Press, 2014.
Powell, Richard J., and Virginia M. Mecklenburg (ed.). *African American Art: Harlem Renaissance Civil Rights Era and Beyond*, New York: Skira Rizzoli, 2012.
Williams, Ned E. "Six Composers to Collaborate on NYC Portrait," *DownBeat*, October 20, 1950, 3.
Roberts, John Storm. *The Latin Tinge: The Impact of Latin American Music on the United States*, New York: Oxford University Press, 1999.
Rosen, Aaron (ed.). *Religion and Art in the Heart of Modern Manhattan: St. Peter's Church and the Louise Nevelson Chapel*, Farnham: Ashgate, 2016.
Salazar, Max. *Mambo Kingdom: Latin Music in New York*, New York: Schirmer Trade Books, 2002.
Schoener, Allon (ed.). *Harlem on My Mind: Cultural Capital of Black America, 1900–1968*, New York: The New Press, 1995.
Serrano, Basilio. *Juan Tizol: His Caravan Through American Life and Culture*, Bloomington, IN: Xlibris, 2012.
Serrano, Basilio. *Puerto Rican Pioneers in Jazz 1900–1939: Bomba Beat to Latin Jazz*, Bloomington, IN: iUniverse, 2015.
Schiff, David. *The Ellington Century*, Berkeley, CA: University of California Press, 2012.
Shapiro, Nat, and Nat Hentoff. *Hear Me Talkin' to Ya: The Story of Jazz as Told by the Men Who Made It*, New York: Rinehart and Company Inc., 1955.
Shirley, Wayne D. "The Coming of Deep River," *American Music*, XV, 4 (Winter 1997), 493–534.
Siskind, Aaron. *Harlem Document: Photographs 1932–1940*, Providence, RI: Matrix, 1981.
Slome, Stanley. "Harlem, Duke and the Classical Connection," *Blue Light*, IV, 1 (March 1997), 1–14; *Blue Light*, IV, 2 (June 1997), 9–10.
Slowik, Michael. *After the Silents: Hollywood Film Music in the Early Sound Era 1926–1934*, New York: Columbia University Press, 2014.
Smith, Morgan, and Marvin Smith. *Harlem: The Vision of Morgan and Marvin Smith*, Lexington, KY: The University Press of Kentucky, 1998.
Smith, Shawn Michelle. *Photography on the Color Line: W.E.B. Du Bois, Race and Visual Culture*, Durham, NC: Duke University Press, 2004.
Spencer, Jon Michael. *The New Negroes and Their Music: The Success of the Harlem Renaissance*, Knoxville, TN: University of Tennessee Press, 1997.
Stratemann, Klaus. *Duke Ellington, Day by Day and Film by Film*, Copenhagen: JazzMedia, 1992.
Sublette, Ned. *Cuba and Its Music: From the First Drums to the Mambo*, Chicago, IL: Chicago Review Press, 2004.
Sullivan, Edward J. *Nueva York 1613–1945*, New York: Scala Publishers, 2010.

Thurman, Wallace. *The Blacker the Berry*, New York: The Macaulay Company, 1929.
Toomer, Jean. *Cane*, New York: Boni & Liveright, 1923.
Tortolano, William. *Samuel Coleridge-Taylor: Anglo-Black Composer, 1875–1912*, Lanham, MD: Scarecrow Press, 2002.
Trachtenberg, Alan. *Reading American Photographs: Images as History: Mathew Brady to Walker Evans*, New York: Hill & Wang, 1989.
Tucker, Mark (ed.). *The Duke Ellington Reader*, New York: Oxford University Press, 1993.
Tucker, Mark. "The Genesis of Black, Brown and Beige," *Black Music Research Journal*, XIII, 2 (Fall 1993), 67–86.
Tucker, Mark. *Ellington: The Early Years*, Chicago, IL: University of Illinois Press, 1995.
Tucker, Mark. Liner notes for the CD set *Duke Ellington, The Blanton-Webster Band*, Bluebird 74321-13181-2, 1986.
Tull Steed, Janna. *Duke Ellington: A Spiritual Biography*, New York: The Crossroad Publishing Company, 1999.
Ulanov, Barry. "The Ellington Programme," in O'Meally, Robert G. (ed.). *The Jazz Cadence of American Culture*, New York: Columbia University Press, 1998, 169.
Vail, Ken. *Duke's Diary: The Life of Duke Ellington, 1950–1974*, 2 vols., Lanham, MD: Scarecrow Press, 2002.
van de Leur, Walter. *Something to Live For: The Music of Billy Strayhorn*, New York: Oxford University Press, 2002.
Van Vechten, Carl. *Nigger Heaven*, New York: Alfred A. Knopf, 1926.
Vogel, Shane. *The Scene of Harlem Cabaret: Race, Sexuality, Performance*, Chicago, IL: University of Chicago Press, 2009.
Walker, Stanley. *The Night Club Era*, New York: Frederick A. Stokes Company, 1933.
Walther, Peter. *New Deal Photography: USA 1935–1943*, Köln: Taschen, 2016.
Wardlaw, Alvia J. *Charles Alston: The David C. Driskell Series of African American Art*, VI, San Francisco, CA: Pomegranate, 2007.
Willis, Deborah. *Reflections in Black: A History of Black Photographers, 1840 to the Present*, New York: W. W. Norton & Company, 2002.
Willis, Deborah, and Rodger C. Birt. *VanDerZee, Photographer 1886–1983*, New York: Harry N. Abrams, 1993.
Williams, Alwyn. "Jazz and the New Negro: Harlem's Intellectuals Wrestle with Art of the Age," *Australasian Journal of American Studies*, XXI, 1 (July 2002), 1–18.
Wright, Richard, and Russell Lee. *12 Million Black Voices*, New York: Basic Books, 2002.
Yanow, Scott. *Duke Ellington*, New York: Friedman/Fairfax Publishers, 1999.
Zinn, Howard. *A People's History of the United States*, New York: Harper & Row, 1980.

4. NIGHT CREATURE, THE GOLDEN BROOM AND THE GREEN APPLE: VISIONS IN BLUE

Berini, Antonio, and Giovanni M. Volonté. *Duke Ellington. Un genio, un mito*, Firenze: Ponte alle Grazie, 1994.
Bernstein, Leonard. *Young People's Concerts*, Jack Gottlieb (ed.), Pompton Plains, NJ: Amadeus Press, 2005.
Collier, James Lincoln. *Duke Ellington*, New York: Oxford University Press, 1987.

Cooper, Matthew J. *Duke Ellington as Pianist: A Study of Styles*, Missoula, MT: The College Music Society, 2013.
Dance, Stanley. *The World of Duke Ellington*, Boston, MA: Da Capo Press, 1970.
Delaunay, Charles. *Delaunay's Dilemma: De la peinture au jazz*, Mâcon: Editions W., 1985.
"Duke Captivates Audience; Gets N.Y. City's Highest Award," *Jet*, XXVIII, August 16 and 19, 1965.
Durieux, Jean. "Violini, consolate il vecchio negro," *Epoca*, XIV, 646, February 10, 1963.
Ellington, Duke. "The Jazz Fakers Can't Make It Now," *Negro Digest*, XII, 1, November 1961.
Ellington, Duke. *Music Is My Mistress*, New York: Da Capo Press, 1973.
Feather, Leonard. "The Night Creature at Carnegie," *Melody Maker*, April 2, 1955.
George, Don. *Sweet Man: The Real Duke Ellington*, New York: G. P. Putnam's Sons, 1981.
Green, Edward (ed.). *The Cambridge Companion to Duke Ellington*, Cambridge, MA: Cambridge University Press, 2014.
Harman, Carter. "The Duke Clicks in Squaresville: Ellington at the Philharmonic," *Life*, August 27, 1965.
Hasse, John Edward. *Beyond Category: The Life and Genius of Duke Ellington*, New York: Simon & Schuster, 1993.
Lambert, Eddie. *Duke Ellington: A Listener's Guide*, London: Scarecrow Press, 1999.
Lavezzoli, Peter. *The King of All, Sir Duke: Ellington and the Artistic Revolution*, New York: Continuum, 2001.
Mingus, Charles. "Duke Ellington, Carnegie Hall," *Metronome*, LXXI, 5, May 1955.
Nicholson, Stuart. *Reminiscing in Tempo: A Portrait of Duke Ellington*, Boston, MA: Northern University Press, 1999.
Peress, Maurice. *Dvořák to Duke Ellington: A Conductor Explores America's Music and Its African American Roots*, New York: Oxford University Press, 2004.
Roberts, John Storm. *The Latin Tinge: The Impact of Latin American Music on the United States*, New York: Oxford University Press, 1999.
Schiff, David. "Symphonic Ellington? Rehearing New World A-Comin'," *Musical Quarterly*, XCVI, 3–4 (Fall/Winter 2013).
Schuller, Gunther. *Night Creature* (score), critical edition, New York: G. Schirmer, 1992.
Scott, James W. "Duke Ellington Welcomes Long-Lost Jazzmen Back," *Kansas City Times*, November 24, 1962.
Shapiro, Nat, and Nat Hentoff. *Hear Me Talkin' to Ya: The Story of Jazz as Told by the Men Who Made It*, London: Peter Davies, 1966.
Stratemann, Klaus. *Duke Ellington, Day by Day and Film by Film*, Copenhagen: JazzMedia, 1992.
Tucker, Mark. Liner notes for the CD set *Duke Ellington, The Complete Reprise Studio Recordings*, Mosaic MD5-193.
Ulanov, Barry. "The Ellington Programme," in Williamson, Ken (ed.). *This Is Jazz*, London: George Newnes Ltd., 1960.
Vail, Ken. *Duke's Diary: The Life of Duke Ellington, 1950–1974*, 2 vols., Lanham, MD: Scarecrow Press, 2002.

5. LA SCALA, PART II. FATHERS, SONS, AND THE BLUES

Anderson, Paul Allen. *Deep River: Music and Memory in Harlem Renaissance Thought*, Durham, NC: Duke University Press, 2001.

Baker, Houston A., Jr. *Modernism and the Harlem Renaissance*, Chicago, IL: University of Chicago Press, 1987.

Bearden, Romare. *The Block*, New York: Viking, 1971.

Bernard, Emily (ed.). *Remember Me to Harlem: The Letters of Langston Hughes and Carl Van Vechten*, New York: Vintage Books, 2002.

Boyd, Herb (ed.). *The Harlem Reader*, New York: Three Rivers Press, 2003.

Bragalini, Luca. "Mexicanticipation e Latin American Suite: Metamorfosi nella fucina del Duca," *Musica Jazz*, March 2000.

Cohen, Harvey G. *Duke Ellington's America*, Chicago, IL: University of Chicago Press, 2010.

Crawford, Richard. *The American Musical Landscape: The Business of Musicianship from Billings to Gershwin*, Berkeley, CA: University of California Press, 1993.

Cuney-Hare, Maud. *Negro Musicians and Their Music*, New York: G. K. Hall & Co., 1996; 1st ed. 1936.

De Santis, Christopher C. (ed.). *The Collected Works of Langston Hughes*, 16 vols., IX: *Essays on Art, Race, Politics, and World Affairs*, Columbia, MO: University of Missouri Press, 2004.

Del Forno, Romano, "Sul sinfonismo di Ellington," *Musica Jazz*, July–August 1953.

Dunning, Jennifer. *Alvin Ailey: A Life in Dance*, Cambridge, MA: Da Capo Press, 1998.

Ellington, Duke. *Music Is My Mistress*, New York: Da Capo Press, 1973.

Feather, Leonard. Blindfold test on *La Scala* given to Woody Herman, *DownBeat*, April 23, 1964.

Feather, Leonard. Blindfold test on *La Scala* given to James Moody, *DownBeat*, February 22, 1968.

Franceschina, John. *Duke Ellington's Music for the Theatre*, Jefferson, NC: McFarland & Company, 2001.

Green, Edward (ed.). *The Cambridge Companion to Duke Ellington*, Cambridge, MA: Cambridge University Press, 2014.

Hawkins, Alfonso W., Jr. *The Jazz Trope: A Theory of African American Literary and Vernacular Culture*, Lanham, MD: Scarecrow Press, 2008.

Hughes, Langston. "The Negro Artist and the Racial Mountain," *The Nation*, June 23, 1926.

Hughes, Langston. *The Big Sea*, New York, Hill & Wang 1993; 1st ed. New York: Alfred A. Knopf, 1940.

Hughes, Langston. "The Twenties: Harlem and Its Negritude," *African Forum*, I, 4, 1966.

Hughes, Langston. *The Collected Works of Langston Hughes*, edited by Leslie Catherine Sanders, 3 vols., VI: *Gospel Plays, Operas, and Later Dramatic Works*, Columbia, MO: University of Missouri Press, 2004.

Hughes, Langston, and Milton Meltzer. *Black Magic: A Pictorial History of the African-American in the Performing Arts*, New York: Da Capo Press, 1967.

Johnson, James Weldon. *The Book of American Negro Poetry*, Champaign, IL: Book Jungle, 2008; 1st ed. New York: Harcourt, Brace and Company, 1922.

Johnson, James Weldon. *Black Manhattan*, New York: Alfred A. Knopf, 1930.

Kun, Josh. *Audiotopia: Music, Race, and America*, Los Angeles, CA: University of California Press, 2005.

Levine, Lawrence W. "Jazz and American Culture," *Journal of American Folklore*, XII, 403 (January–March 1989).

Locke, Alain (ed.). *The New Negro*, New York: Simon & Schuster, 1997; 1st ed. New York: Albert and Charles Boni, 1925.

Locke, Alain. *The Negro and His Music—Negro Art: Past and Present*, Salem, MA: Ayer Company Publishers, 1991.

McKay, Claude. *Selected Poems*, New York: Dover Publications, 1999.

Molesworth, Charles (ed.). The Works of Alain Locke, New York, Oxford University Press, 2012.

O'Meally Robert G. (ed.). *The Jazz Cadence of American Culture*, New York: Columbia University Press, 1998.

O'Meally, Robert G., Brent Hayes Edwards, and Farah Jasmine Griffin (eds.). *Uptown Conversation: The New Jazz Studies*, New York: Columbia University Press, 2004.

Polillo, Arrigo. "The Symphonic Ellington," *Musica Jazz*, February 1964.

Rampersad, Arnold. *The Art and Imagination of W.E.B. Du Bois*, New York: Schocken, 1990.

Rampersad, Arnold. *The Life of Langston Hughes*, 2 vols., I: *1902–1941: I, Too, Sing America*, New York: Oxford University Press, 2002.

Rampersad, Arnold. *The Life of Langston Hughes*, 2 vols., II: *1941–1967: I Dream a World*, New York: Oxford University Press, 2002.

Schuller, Gunther. *The Swing Era: The Development of Jazz 1930–1945*, New York: Oxford University Press, 1989.

Scivales, Riccardo. Transcription of the seven choruses of "Fugi," the first movement of Duke Ellington's Suite *Ad Lib on Nippon*, *Piano Today*, Winter 2000.

Simawe, Saadi. *Black Orpheus: Music in African American Fiction from the Harlem Renaissance to Toni Morrison*, New York: Garland Publishing, 2000.

Smith Parsons, Catherine. *William Grant Still: A Study in Contradictions*, Berkeley, CA: University of California Press, 2000.

Stratemann, Klaus. *Duke Ellington, Day by Day and Film by Film*, Copenhagen: JazzMedia, 1992.

Strother, Eric S. *The Development of Duke Ellington's Compositional Style: A Comparative Analysis of Three Selected Works*, master's thesis, University of Kentucky, 2001.

Tracy, Steven C. *Langston Hughes and the Blues*, Chicago, IL: University of Illinois Press, 2001.

Tucker, Mark (ed.). *The Duke Ellington Reader*, New York: Oxford University Press, 1993.

Waits, Sarah A. *"Listen to the Wild Discord": Jazz in the Chicago Defender and the Louisiana Weekly, 1925–1929*, master's thesis, University of New Orleans, 2013.

White, Lucien. "Decrying the Use of Spirituals as Companion Pieces to Blues and Jazz," *The New York Age*, November 29, 1924.

6. THREE BLACK KINGS: A TRIBUTE TO BLACK HISTORY

Alvin Ailey Talking with Harriett Milnes, tape transcript, Ailey Alvin OHIII 577 A-C, Yale University.

Bearden, Romare, Harry Henderson. *A History of African-American Artists: From 1792 to the Present*, New York: Pantheon, 1993.

Bindman, David, and Henry Louis Gates (eds.). *The Image of the Black in Western Art*, vol. II: *From the Early Christian Era to the "Age of Discovery,"* Part 1: "From the Demonic Threat to the Incarnation of Sainthood," and part 2: "Africans in the Christian Ordinance of the World," Cambridge, MA: Howard University Press, 2010.

Black Is Beautiful: Rubens to Dumas, Exhibit Catalog, Amsterdam: Waanders Publishers Zwolle, 2008.

Cardini, Franco. *I re magi: Storia e leggenda*, Venice: Marsilio, 2000.

Cohen, Harvey G. *Duke Ellington's America*, Chicago, IL: University of Chicago Press, 2010.

"Concert to Celebrate Duke Ellington Day on April 29," *New York Times*, April 20, 1976.

Dance, Stanley. Liner notes for the CD *Duke Ellington, The Private Collection*, Volume Nine: *Studio Sessions, New York 1968*, WEA 255 925-2.

DeFrantz, Thomas F. *Dancing Revelations: Alvin Ailey's Embodiment of African American Culture*, New York: Oxford University Press, 2004.

Dippie, Brian W. *Frederic Remington: The Frederic Remington Art Museum Collection*, New York: Harry N. Abrams, 2001.

"Duke Ellington Orchestra Concert to Benefit Cuttington College," *National Chairmen's Report*, April 1977.

Duke Ellington Society of Sweden. *Mercer Ellington*, Bulletin No. 2, May 2014.

Dunning, Jennifer. *Alvin Ailey: A Life in Dance*, Boston, MA: Da Capo Press, 1998.

Ellington, Duke. *Music Is My Mistress*, New York: Da Capo Press, 1973.

Ellington, Mercer. *Duke Ellington in Person: An Intimate Memoir*, Boston, MA: Houghton Mifflin Company, 1978.

Ellington, Mercer. Liner notes for the LP *Duke Ellington, Three Black Kings*, Frog Box TFB 100/2, 1980.

Félix, Madeleine. *I re magi*, Milan: Jaca Book, 2000.

Franceschina, John. *Duke Ellington's Music for the Theatre*, Jefferson, NC: McFarland Company, 2001.

Gardner, Jim. "Jazz Musicians Assemble to Benefit Ellington Scholarship," *Yale Daily News*, October 17, 1977.

Garrow, David J. *Bearing the Cross: Martin Luther King, Jr., and the Southern Christian Leadership Conference*, New York: William Morrow Paperbacks, 2004.

Gerald R. Ford Presidential Library. Box 1, Folder "1976/04/29—Duke Ellington Concert, New York City," Frances K. Pullen Papers.

International DEMS Bulletin, September–November 1996 (with a Mercer Ellington Discography compiled by Bjarne Busk).

Jennings, Kate F. *Remington & Russell and the Art of the American West*, Greenwich: Brompton, 1999.

Jewell, Derek. *Duke: A Portrait of Duke Ellington*, London: Elm Tree Books, 1977.
Karnath, Lorie. *Sam Shaw*, Ostfildern: Hatje Cantz, 2010.
Locke, Alain. *The Negro in Art: A Pictorial Record of the Negro Artist and of the Negro Theme in Art*, Washington, DC: Associates in Negro Folk Education, 1940.
Mazo, Joseph H. "Alvin Ailey's Dance Tribute to the Duke," *New York Times*, April 13, 1975.
McDonald, Anthony (ed.). *A Catalog of Music Written in Honor of Martin Luther King Jr.*, Lanham, MD: Scarecrow Press, 2012.
Peress, Maurice. *Dvořák to Duke Ellington: A Conductor Explores America's Music and Its African American Roots*, New York: Oxford University Press, 2004.
Smith, Arnold Jay. "Alvin Ailey Dance Company/Duke Ellington Orchestra," *DownBeat*, January 1977.
Stratemann, Klaus. *Duke Ellington, Day by Day and Film by Film*, Copenhagen: JazzMedia, 1992.
Troccoli, Carpenter (ed.). *The Masterworks of Charles M. Russell: A Retrospective of Paintings and Sculpture*, Norman, OK: University of Oklahoma Press, 2009.

7. *CELEBRATION*: THE SCORE FORGOTTEN ON THE BOTTOM OF THE RIVER

Bragalini, Luca. "Il primo blues parlava italoamericano," *Musica Jazz*, Marzo 1999.
Burford Mason, Roger. "Ron Collier: Memories of Duke," *Canadian Composer*, Spring 1991.
Chambers, Jack. "Bardland: Shakespeare in Ellington's World," *International DEMS Bulletin*, April–July 2005.
Collier, Ron. *The River*, music score, G. Schirmer, Tempo Music Inc., 1970.
Dance, Stanley. Liner notes for the LP *Duke Ellington, North of the Border*, ACDM 1425, 1967.
Dance, Stanley. "Celebration," *Jazz Journal*, July 25, 1972.
DeFrantz, Thomas F. *Dancing Revelations: Alvin Ailey's Embodiment of African American Culture*, New York: Oxford University Press, 2004.
Dunning, Jennifer. *Alvin Ailey: A Life in Dance*, Boston, MA: Da Capo Press, 1998.
Ellington, Duke. *Music Is My Mistress*, New York: Da Capo Press, 1973.
Fayenz, Franco. "*Celebration*, suite dimenticata di Ellington," *Il Giornale*, March 18, 2007.
Franceschina, John. *Duke Ellington's Music for the Theatre*, Jefferson, NC: McFarland Company, 2001.
Haley, Pope. "Symphony's Present Is Good Music," *Florida Times-Union*, May 17, 1972.
Homzy, Andrew. Liner notes for the LP *Live Performances by Duke Ellington and His Orchestra: 1956 Stratford, 1973 Winnipeg*; limited edition for the participants in the Duke Ellington Society Conference, Toronto 1987.
Jean, Betty B. *Fifty Years of Great Music: The Jacksonville Symphony Orchestra*, Sacramento, CA: Allied Printing, 1999.
Massagli, Luciano, and Giovanni M. Volonté, *The New DESOR: An Updated Edition of Duke Ellington's Story on Records 1924–1974*, 2 vols., self-published: Milan, 1999.
Miller, Mark. *The Miller Companion to Jazz in Canada*, Toronto: The Mercury Press, 2001.
Peress, Maurice. *Dvořák to Duke Ellington: A Conductor Explores America's Music and Its African American Roots*, New York: Oxford University Press, 2004.

Perlis, Vivian, and Libby Van Cleve. *Composers' Voices from Ives to Ellington: An Oral History of American Music*, New Haven, CT: Yale University Press, 2005.
Phelps, Bob. "Turning a Page," *Florida Times-Union*, June 9, 1998.
Pitman, Walter. *Louis Applebaum: A Passion for Culture*, Toronto: Dundurn, 2002.
Ridley, Clifford A. "The Orchestra Rose from the Grave," *National Observer*, June 10, 1972.
Robinson, Louie. "Ann of Mount Angel Abbey: Stricken Dancer Finds Success at Monastery," *Ebony*, XXVI, 4, February 1971.
Rose, Brian G. *Television and the Performing Arts: A Handbook and Reference Guide to American Cultural Programming*, Westport, CT: Greenwood, 1986.
Schiff, David. *The Ellington Century*, Berkeley, CA: University of California Press, 2012.
Sessa, Claudio. "L'Ellington dimenticato rinasce grazie all'Italia," *Corriere della Sera*, March 19, 2007.
Slome, Stanley. *The River*, Duke Ellington Society, Southern California Chapter, Newsletter, email January 7, 2004.
"Special CJRT Concert Celebrates Ellington's Birthday," *Toronto Star*, April 29, 1974.
Stratemann, Klaus. *Duke Ellington, Day by Day and Film by Film*, Copenhagen: JazzMedia, 1992.
"Symphony to Perform Ellington Composition," *Florida Times-Union*, January 28, 1972.
"Symphony Season Ending—Almost," *Florida Times-Union*, April 25, 1972.
Timner, W. E. *Ellingtonia: The Recorded Music of Duke Ellington and His Sidemen*, Lanham, MD: Scarecrow Press, 2007.
Vail, Ken. *Duke's Diary: The Life of Duke Ellington, 1950–1974*, 2 vols., Lanham, MD: Scarecrow Press, 2002.
Vincent, Norman. "Radio Career Shows You Can't Go Wrong with Big Band Swing," *Florida Times-Union*, July 11, 2006.
Ward, James. "Singers Laud Jacksonville Symphony," *Florida Times-Union*, May 16, 1972.

INDEX OF WORKS AND TITLES

"Across the Track Blues," 225n
Ad Lib on Nippon, 128, 224n
"Admiration" (Tyers), 119
"African Flower," 97, 227n
"African Jungle" (S. Williams), 206n
African Suite, 62
Afro-Bossa, 101, 119
"Afro-Bossa," 119
Afro-Eurasian Eclipse, 151
"Alabama" (Coltrane), 232n
American Ballet Theatre: A Close-Up in Time (WNET TV program), 175
"Angu," 93, 128–29
"Apes and Peacocks," 157
Ash Wednesday (T. S. Eliot), 184, 238n
"Asphalt Jungle," 205n
Aurora Borealis (Collier), 169–70, 182, 234n
"Azure," 214n

"Backward Country Blues," 125
"Backwater Blues" (Smith), 133
"Ballet of the Flying Saucers," 42, 94
"Baptist Mission" (Johnson), 64, 203n
Basso Profundo, 21
"Battle of Swing," 124
Beatitudines: Testimonianza per Martin Luther King (Petrassi), 159
Beggar's Holiday, A, 32, 47, 238n
"Biggest and Busiest Intersection, The," 97, 126
Bing Bang Bong (Gillis), 218n
"Birmingham Breakdown," 124
Black, Brown and Beige, xi–xii, 34–35, 40, 43, 62–63, 72, 84, 86, 88, 123, 137, 151, 202–3n, 206–7n, 213n, 217n, 232n

"Black and Tan Fantasy," 84, 124, 182, 238n
"Black Beauty," 24–25, 47, 89, 137, 193n, 205n
Black Nativity (Hughes), 155, 230n
Black No More (Schuyler), 41
"Blem," 235n
"Blind Bug," 96, 99–101, 103, 107, 110, 112, 220n
Block, The (Bearden), 214n, 227n
"Blue Bells of Harlem," 66, 68, 177, 206n
"Blue Harlem (Send Me)," 66–67
"Blue Light," 127, 200n
"Blue Mood," 70
"Blue Rose," 231n
"Blues, The," 123, 238n
"Blues for Miró," 218n
"Blues for New Orleans," 224n
Blues Has Got Me, The (Bearden), 139
Blues I'm Playing, The (Hughes), 135
"Blues in Blueprint," 113, 125, 224n
Blues in Orbit, 42
"Blues in the Night" (Arlen), 122
Blues Singer (Alston), 139
Blues Suite (Ailey), 151
"Blutopia," 41
"B.O. of Traffic, The," 97
Bobby Sox (Gillis), 218n
"Bojangles: A Portrait of Bill Robinson," 205n
Bolt, The (Šostakovič), 113
Boogie Bop Blue, 21, 192–93n
Boogie in Brass (Gillis), 218n
Boola, 62
"Bourbon Street Jingling Jollies," 119
"Boys from Harlem," 68
Brown Penny (Yeats), 184, 238n

Cabin in the Sky (Latouche), 32
"Caravan," 107, 220n, 230n
Caravan (Falco), 151
"Carnegie Blues," 127
Carneval, 170
"Carolina Shout" (Johnson), 63
Celebration, 43, 97, 167–85, 188n, 233–38n
"Central Park West" (Coltrane), 231n
Change of Mind (Stevens), 47
"Chant for F.D. Roosevelt," 26, 237n
"Christmas Bells of Harlem," 68
"Chromatic Love Affair," 37
City, The, 170
"C-Jam Blues," 123, 125
Classic Ellington, 196n
"Clothed Woman, The," 126
"Clouds in My Heart," 68
Cock of the World, 136
Collage #3 (Delamont), 169
"Come Sunday," 26, 63, 84, 207n
Concert for 5-String Banjo, 163
Concert of Sacred Music, 25, 193–94n
"Concerto for Cootie," 222n
Concerto for Horn and Orchestra No. 1 in D Major (Mozart), 222n
Concerto for Piano and Orchestra in D minor opus 23 (MacDowell), 222n
"Congo Love Song" (Dixie Rhythm Kings), 206n
Continuum, 229n
"Corta Jaca" (Gonzaga), 203n
"Cotton Club Stomp," 66–67
"Cotton Club Stomp 2," 67
"Cotton Tail," 217n
Cradle Will Rock, The (Blitzstein), 50
"Creole Love Call," 229n
"Creole Rhapsody," 58, 124, 187–88n
"Crescendo in Blue," 124, 214n
Crystal Tree, The (Henderson), 196n

Dance Symphony, A (Gillis), 218n
"Dancers in Love," 37, 58, 97
"David Danced Before the Lord," 94

"Dazzling Creature," 96–97, 103–7, 109–11, 218n, 220n
De Organizer (Johnson), 226n
"Deep River" (traditional), 87, 91, 216n
Deep South Suite, 47–48, 151
Degas Suite, 163, 233n
"Diamond Jubilee," 136, 226n
Dick Cavett Show (ABC TV program), 112
"Dicty Glide," 66–67
"Didjeridoo," 123
Dies Natalis (Hanson), 180
"Diminuendo in Blue," 123, 214n
"Do Nothin' Till You Hear from Me," 230n
"Dolce Vita, La" (arr. Henderson), 196n
"Don't Get Around Much Anymore," 29, 233n
Don't You Want to Be Free?, 137
Dorie Got a Medal (WMCA radio program), 52
"Drop Me Off in Harlem," 66, 68
Drum is a Woman, A, 41, 94, 97, 137, 151
Duke at Tanglewood, The, 222n
Duke Ellington, An Intimate Piano Session, 236n
Duke Ellington, Carnegie Hall, November 13, 1948, 217n
Duke Ellington, Cool Rock, 223n, 235n
Duke Ellington, Le Suites sinfoniche, 190n, 195n, 219n
Duke Ellington, Live and Rare, 221n, 234n
Duke Ellington, Live at Carnegie Hall, Dec. 11, 1943, 197n
Duke Ellington, 1951 at the Metropolitan Opera House, 210n
Duke Ellington, 1952 Seattle Concert, 210n
Duke Ellington, North of the Border, 169, 214n, 234n
Duke Ellington, Orchestral Works, 197n, 210n, 223n
Duke Ellington, The Blanton-Webster Band, 212n
Duke Ellington, The Complete Reprise Studio Recording, 219n

INDEX OF WORKS AND TITLES

Duke Ellington, *The Great London Concerts*, 210n
Duke Ellington, *The Piano Player*, 235n
Duke Ellington, *The Private Collection, Volume Five: The Suites, New York 1968 & 1970*, 174, 233n
Duke Ellington, *The Private Collection, Volume Six: Studio Sessions, New York 1968*, 236n
Duke Ellington, *The Private Collection, Volume Nine: Studio Sessions, New York 1968*, 233n, 236n
Duke Ellington, *Uptown*, 210n
Duke Ellington, *V-Disc: A Musical Contribution by America's Best for Our Armed Forces Overseas*, 197n
Duke Ellington *in Concerto, New York 1964*, 210
Duke Ellington *Live at the Whitney*, 26
Duke Ellington *Private Collection*, 233n
"Duke Tunes Up, The" (Baker), 57–58
"Duke's Back Again, The" (Baker), 57

Early Ellington: The Complete Brunswick and Vocalion Recordings of Duke Ellington, 1926–1931, 204n
"East St. Louis Toodle-Oo," 65, 67
Echoes in Blue (Myers), 151
"Echoes of Harlem," 66, 68–70, 124, 206n
"Echoes of the Jungle," 69, 124
Ed Sullivan Show (CBS TV program), 33
Electronic Sonata for Souls Loved by Nature (Russell), 159
Ellington '66 Reprise, 221n
Ellington Suites, The, 193n
"Elos," 163–65, 233n
Enchantment (Alexander), 89

Fair Wind (Symonds), 169
"Falls, The," 175, 235–36n
Fanfare for the Common Man (Copland), ix
Fantasy for Cello and Orchestra (Schuman), 222n
"Fantazm," 58, 218n

Far East Suite, 225n
Fighting Men (WMCA radio program), 52
"Fine and Mellow" (Holiday), 53
First Sacred Concert, 25–27, 41, 193–94n, 217n
"Fleurette Africaine," 137, 227n
"Flirtibird," 124, 224n
"For Ellington" (Lewis), 185
For My People (WMCA radio program), 52
Forty (Solomons Jr.), 151
Four Symphonic Works by Duke Ellington, 232n
From the Steeples and the Mountains (Ives), 222n
"Fugi," 128–29, 224–25n

Gershwiniana (Pistoni), 28, 194n
"Giant Steps" (Coltrane), 231n
"Giggling Rapids, The," 173–76, 235–36n
"Gimme a Pigfoot (And a Bottle of Beer)" (Wilson), 204n
Girl in a Red Dress (Alston), 89
Girl's Suite, The, 84
"Go Harlem" (Johnson), 69–70
"Golden Broom, The," 95, 118–20, 125, 223n
Golden Broom and the Green Apple, The, 43, 89, 93–97, 114–21, 125–26, 129, 138, 177, 185, 222n
"Goodbye Newport Blues" (Morganfield), 135
Goutelas Suite, 26, 193n
Grand Slam Jam, 21, 33, 194n
Great Duke Ellington, The, 189–90n
Great London Concerts, The, 210n
"Green Apple, The," 89, 95, 120, 129

"Handsome Traffic Policeman, The," 95, 120, 223–24n
"Happy Go Lucky Local," 123
"Happy Heaven of Harlem, The" (Porter), 69
Harlem, 5, 21, 32, 40, 43, 55–92, 94, 97–99, 101–2, 115, 121, 126, 170–71, 185, 188n, 194n, 200–203n, 210n, 214n, 220n
"Har-lem," 78
"Harlem Air Shaft," 66–68, 73, 207n

"Harlem Congo" (Webb), 206n
Harlem Family, A (WMCA radio program), 52
"Harlem Flat Blues," 66–67
"Harlem Hospitality" (Calloway), 69
"Harlem Mania" (Heywood), 205n
Harlem Night (Alston), 75
"Harlem Nights," 65
"Harlem Rhythm," 66, 68, 203n, 207n
"Harlem Serenade" (G. and I. Gershwin-Kahn), 206n
"Harlem Speaks," 66, 68
"Harlem Strut, The" (Johnson), 205n
Harlem Sweeties (Hughes), 71
Harlem Symphony (Johnson), 63–64, 203n
Harlem-Mania, 205n
"Harlemania" (Fields-McHugh), 205n
"Harlemania" (Rodgers-Hart), 205n
"Harmony in Harlem," 68
Hear Me Talkin' to Ya, 170, 217n
"Heart of Harlem, The," 136
"Hey, Cherie," 196n
Hiawatha (Coleridge-Taylor), 90
High to Low (Hughes), 204n
H.M.S. Times Square, 162
"Honey Song, The," 33
"Hymn of Sorrow," 84, 203n, 207n

"I Cover the Waterfront" (Green), 28
"I Got Rhythm" (Gershwin), 53
"I Got the Blues" (Maggio), 238n
"I Have a Dream" (M. L. Williams), 159
"I Let a Song Go Out of My Heart," 28–29
"I Remember Harlem" (Eldridge), 205n, 209n
I Too (Hughes), 89, 137
"I Want Jesus to Walk with Me (traditional), 64
"I Want to Hold Your Hand" (Beatles), 221n
"Igoo," 225n
"I'm Afraid," 58
"I'm Beginning to See the Light," 46
"I'm Slappin' Seventh Avenue with the Sole of My Shoe," 66, 68
"Immigration Blues," 65–67, 73, 204n, 206–7n

"In a Sentimental Mood," 131, 230n
In Memoriam Martin Luther King Jr. (Wilson), 159
"In the Beginning God," 217n
In the Uncommon Market, 189n
"Innovation" (Johnson), 63
Italian Suite, 9–10

Jaywalker, The, 97
Jazz Nocturne—American Concertos of the Jazz Age (various composers), 187n
"Jeep's Blues," 171
Jelly's Last Jam, 196n
Jerico Jim-Crow, 230n
"Joshua Fit the Battle of Jericho" (traditional), 159
Jump for Joy, 47–48, 50, 136, 198n, 227n
"Jumpin' Pumpkins," 217n
"Jungle Nights in Harlem," 67, 70

"Kansas City Stomp" (Morton), 221n
"King Fit the Battle of Alabam," 47, 159
King Kong (Cooper and Schoedsack), 59
"King of the Nativity," 153, 155–56, 160–61, 165
"King Solomon," 156, 158, 160–61
"Klop," 181
"Ko-Ko," 126, 224n
Konzertstück in F minor (Weber), 180

La Mer (Debussy), 172
La Scala, x, 7–23, 121, 122–40, 185, 188–91n, 193n, 225n, 228n
"Lady in Blue," 214n
"Lady is a Tramp, The" (Rodgers-Hart), 69
"Lady of the Lavender Mist," 214n
"Lake, The," 173, 175–76, 235–36n
Latin American Suite, 119, 224n
"Latin American Sunshine," 37
Lenox Avenue (Still), 228n
Les Indes Galantes (Rameau), 205n
Les Trois rois noirs (*Three Black Kings*), 149
"Let My People Go" (traditional), 64
Liberian Suite (Horton), 151
Lift Every Voice and Sing (Savage), 215n
Light Ahead for the Negro (E. Johnson), 41
"Light Blue," 214n

"Lightning Bugs and Frogs," 96
"Like Sonny" (Coltrane), 231n
Lincoln Portrait, A (Copland), ix
"Listen to the Lambs" (traditional/Dett), 87
"Little Purple Flower, The," 94, 97, 227n
Live Performances by Duke Ellington and His Orchestra: 1956 Stratford, 1973 Winnipeg, 234n
"Lover Come Back to Me," 33
Lullaby Tango (Gillis), 218n
Luther Henderson, Clap Hands!/The Greatest Sound Around, 33, 196n

Ma Rainey (Brown), 133, 226n
"Mad Scene from Woolworth's," 136
Madama Butterfly (Puccini), 20, 192n
"Magenta Haze," 214n
Magic of Music, The (CBC TV program), 178
"Mahalia," 84
"Main Steam," 123
Maker of the Blues (Hughes), 138
"Man I Love, The" (Gershwin), 28
"Manhã de Carnaval" (Bonfá-Maria), 169
Manhattan Street Scene, 63
"Marcia Regina," 173, 181
Martin (Parks), 232n
"Martin Luther King," 84, 159–61, 163, 165, 185
"Meander, The," 173–74, 176, 235–36n
Mechanic, The, 170
"Melancholia," 158
Memorial to Martin Luther King (Morawetz), 159
Men Behind the Gun (WMCA radio program), 52
"Merry Go-Round," 124
Mine Boy (Abrahams), 43
"Misty," 196n
"MLK" (U2), 159
Money Jungle, 125, 220n
"Monologue," 97
"Mooche, The," 125, 151, 182, 209n
"Mood Indigo," 54–55, 127, 136, 175, 200n, 214n, 233n, 235n
"Moon Maiden," 41
Moon Over Harlem (W. Johnson), 74
Morning After, The (CBLT TV program), 171

Most Dangerous Game, The (Schoedsack-Pichel film), 59–61, 202n
Most Dangerous Game, The (Steiner soundtrack), 59–60, 202n
"Mother, Her Majesty the Sea, The," 173, 235n
"Mr. Syms" (Coltrane), 238n
"My Funny Valentine" (Rodgers and Hart), 28
My People, 47, 51, 151, 159, 162, 177, 217n, 232n
"My People/The Blues Ain't," 217n
"Mystery Song, The," 58

"Nagoya," 225n
Nameless Hour (Symonds), 169, 234n
Native Son (Wright), 54
Negro Revue (Hughes), 136
Negro Spiritual (McKay), 227n
"Neo-Hip-Hot Cool-Kiddies Community, The," 173, 235n
New Orleans Junction (McDuffie), 152
New Orleans Suite, The, 84, 162, 234n
New World A-Comin', ix–x, 3, 5, 24–54, 76, 98–99, 101, 115, 118, 121, 153, 179, 185, 188n, 193–95n, 197n, 200n, 222n, 230n
"New York City Blues (An Urban Fantasy)," 205n
Nigger Heaven (Van Vechten), 69, 88, 204n, 215n
Night Creature, 21, 32, 93–114, 115–16, 121, 125, 151, 179, 185, 194n, 218–21n, 227n, 232n
"Night in Harlem, A," 67
1952 Seattle Concert, 210n
1962 MOMA Recital, The, 193n
"Nobody Knows the Trouble I've Seen" (traditional), 90
Non-Violent Integration, 21–22, 193n
North of the Border, 169, 214n, 234n
"Nude Young Dancer" (Hughes), 137

O King (Berio), 159
"Ocht O'Clock Rock," 123
"Oclupaca," 119, 124, 126, 224n
Octet for Sea Cliff (Mulligan), 4
"Oh! Well," 196n
"Old Man Harlem" (Carmichael), 69
"On a Turquoise Cloud," 214
On De No'thern Road (Douglas), 139

"On the Sunny Side of the Street," 33
"One Note Samba" (Henderson), 196n
Orchestral and Electronic Exchanges (Wuorinen), 222n
Orchestral Works, 31, 77, 197n, 210n, 212n, 223–24n
Original Sin (Lewis), 4
Othello (Shakespeare), 122

Paris Blues (Ritt), 162, 232n
"Park at 106th Street," 207n
"Parlor Social Stomp," 65–67
Pas de Duke (Ailey), 151
"Passage to Utopia" (Ottley), 42, 45
Paul Whiteman: Music for Moderns (Whiteman), 187n
"Peanut Vendor, The" (Simons), 80, 211n
"Pearls, The" (Morton), 221n
Perfume Suite, 97
Personnages dans la nuit (Miró), 85, 218n
Peter Grimes (Britten), 172
"Piano Pastel," 214n
Piano Perspective (Shirley), 28, 194n
Piegans (Russell), 163
Pins and Needles (Rome), 50
Play De Blues (Douglas), 139
"Portrait of a Lion," 204–5n
"Portrait of Bert Williams, A," 205n
"Portrait of Mahalia Jackson," 84, 124–25, 162
Portrait of New York (Henderson, Duke, Romberg, Gillis, Ellington), 56, 76
Preamble for a Solemn Occasion (Copland), 115, 222n
Prélude à l'après-midi d'un faune (Debussy), 38
"Prelude to a Kiss," 37
"P.S. 170," 120
"Purple Gazelle," 37, 214n

Queenie Pie, 149, 180, 228–29n
Queen's Suite, 97, 157

Race for Space, The, 42
Rape of Lucretia, The (Britten), 168

"Ray Charles' Place," 123
"Red Garter," 97
Reflections in D, 151
"Relaxing," 171, 182, 235n
Remembering Duke's World, 153, 230n
"Rent Party Blues," 66–67
Rhapsody in Blue (Gershwin), 4
"Rhumba," 203n
"Riba," 173, 236n
River, The, 151, 153, 171–77, 181, 230n, 235–36n
"River, The," 171, 176, 235–37n
Road of the Phoebe Snow, The (Beatty), 151
"Rockin' in Rhythm," 58, 136
Ron Collier Tentet (Collier), 235n
Rose-Colored Glasses (Strayhorn-Henderson), 32
"Run, The," 173, 181, 235n
"Russian Waltz" (Harling), 202n

Sacred Concerts, 126, 162
"Saddest Tale," 126–27
Salute to Canada Lee (MBS radio program), 54
"Satin Doll" (Strayhorn), 116, 222n, 230n, 234n
"Saturday Night Function," 66–67, 204n
"Savoy Strut," 66, 68, 206n
"Scenes in the City" (Mingus), 135
"Sea, The," 173
"Seabreeze" (Bearden), 87
"Second Line," 229n
"Second Portrait of the Lion, The," 205n, 269n
Second Sacred Concert, 84, 97, 218n
"Secret Love" (Shirley), 28
"Senegalese Stomp" (C. Williams), 206n
"Sepia Panorama," 124, 214n
Serenade to Sweden, 220n
Seven African Romances (Coleridge-Taylor), 90
"She Wouldn't Be Moved" (M. Ellington-Henderson), 196n
"Shepherd, The," 84, 218n
Shuffle Along (Blake), 87

INDEX OF WORKS AND TITLES

Silent Night, Lonely Night (Collier), 169, 182
"Sir Duke" (Wonder), 99, 153, 269n
Skyscrapers Symphonic Jazz (various composers), 187n
"Slip of the Lip, A" (M. Ellington-Henderson), 32, 196n, 200n
Soft Touch of Buddy Collette, The (Collette), 190n
Something About Joe (WMCA radio program), 52
"Something to Live for" (Strayhorn), 36
"Sometimes I'm Happy," 33
Son of Kong—The Most Dangerous Game, The (Steiner), 202n
Sonata for piano and jazz quintet (Collier), 170
Song and Dance (Delamont), 169, 234n
"Sonnet for Caesar," 42
"Sonnet for Sister Kate," 42
"Sonnet in Search of a Moor," 42
"Sonnet of the Apple," 97
"Sonnet to Hank Cinq," 42, 124
"Sophisticated Lady," 97, 213n
Southern Road (Brown), 133
"Spanish Flea" (Henderson), 196n
"Spring, The," 173–74, 176, 235–36n
"St. Louis Blues" (Handy), 238n
"Stalking Monster," 96, 100–101, 103–4, 107–8, 112–13, 121, 125, 219–21n, 224n
Star of Ethiopia, The (Cole, Coleridge-Taylor, Johnson, Verdi, Young), 91, 217n
Stars of Freedom Rally (Southern Christian Leadership Conference), 50
Stepping into Swing Society (M. Ellington), 33
Still Life (Lawson), 151
"Subtle Lament," 127
Such Sweet Thunder, 42, 168
"Such Sweet Thunder," 123, 229n
Sugar Hill (Johnson), 69
"Sugar Hill Penthouse," 63, 72
"Sugar Hill Shim Sham (You Ain't in Harlem Now)," 66, 68, 72
Suite Thursday, 42
"Sunswept Sunday," 84
Susannah (Floyd), 179
"Swampy River," 80, 119

Sweet Thursday (Steinbeck), 42
Swing Low, Sweet Chariot (Johnson), 215n
"Swingers Get the Blues, Too, The," 124
Symphonic Ellington, The, 3, 9, 17, 21, 30, 77, 99, 101, 107, 192n, 201n, 210n, 219–21n, 224n, 228n
Symphonic Ellington, The: Night Creature, 232n
Symphonic Portrait, The, 232n
Symphony in Black (Waller), 84, 203n, 207n
Symphony No. 1 "Afro-American" (Still), 139
Symphony No. 2 "Romantic" (Hanson), 36

"Take the 'A' Train" (Strayhorn), 112, 116, 171, 196, 222n, 230n, 234n
"Tarzan of Harlem" (Calloway), 206n
"Taste of Honey, A" (Scott-Marlow), 169–70
"Tatooed Bride, The," 94
Third Quartet in D Minor (Cerri), 190n
Three Black Kings, 32–33, 148–66, 185, 188n, 228n, 230–32n
Threesome, 170
"Timon of Athens March," 181
"Tina," 119
To a Brown Girl (Cullen), 89
"Tokyo," 225n
Tonal Expressions (Shirley), 28
Toot Suite, 97
"Traffic Cop," 97
"Traffic Extensions," 97
"Transblucency," 123–24, 127–28, 224n
"Triangle, A," 203n
Turcaret, 177
Turning Point, The (Ross), 175
"Two Cities," 173, 236n

Uhuru Afrika (Weston), 135
"Uptown Downbeat," 66, 68
UWIS Suite, 201n

"Vancouver Lights," 171, 235n
Victory Stride: The Symphonic Music of James P. Johnson (Johnson), 203n
"Village of the Virgins, The," 173, 175–76, 235–36n
"Vortex," 173, 175, 236n

Water Music (Händel), 172
Waterfront Night Thoughts, 170
"Way We Were, The" (Bergman), 152
We, Too, Sing America, 137
Weary Blues, The (Hughes), 135, 137
"When the Saints Go Marching In" (traditional), 54
"Whirlpool, The," 173, 175–76, 235–36n
Who Struck John?, 21
"Work Song," 63

INDEX OF NAMES

Abrahams, Peter, 43
Abruzzi, Angelo, 23
Ailey, Alvin, 122, 150–52, 155, 162, 172–73, 175, 218n, 227n, 229–30n, 235–36n
Aitken, Robert Baker, 170
Alexander, Lewis Grandison, 89
Ali, Muhammad (Cassius Clay), 150
Allen, Red (Henry James "Red" Allen Jr.), 135
Alston, Charles, 75, 86, 89, 139, 213n
Altman, Robert Bernard, 177
American Ballet Theatre, 151, 171–72, 175
American Ballet Theatre Orchestra, 173
American Negro Ballet, 63
Anderson, Jervis, 204n, 206–7n, 211n, 215n
Anderson, Marian, 27, 227n
Anderson, Paul Allen, 4, 188n, 215–16n, 225n
Andolina, Sal, 232n
Applebaum, Louis, 234n
Arlen, Harold, 122
Armstrong, Robert, 61
Arrau, Claudio, 27
Arrigoni, Arrigo, 189n
Ashby, Harold, 164
Azpiazú, Don (Justo Ángel Azpiazú), 79–80

Babs, Alice (Alice Nilson), 101, 219–20n
Bacchetta, Battistino, 23, 191n
Bailey, Pearl Mae, 152
Baker, Chet (Chesney Henry Baker), 98
Baker, Houston Alfred, Jr., 4, 188n, 213n, 226
Baker, Richard Evans ("Two Ton" Baker), 57–59, 201n
Balanchine, George (Georgij Balančivadze), 150

Baldwin, James, 48
Baltimore Symphony Orchestra, 116
Bancroft, Anne (Anna Maria Louise Italiano), 175
Banda Jazz Mediolana (Mediolana Jazz Band), 189n
Barbera, Karen S., x
Barboteu, Georges, 102, 220n
Bardi, Aloma, x
Barnet, Charlie (Charles Daly Barnet), 167
Barthé, Richmond, 86
Baryshnikov, Mikhail, 151
Basie, Count (William James "Count" Basie), 50, 112, 152, 229n
Bauzá, Mario, 80
Beame, Abraham, 150
Bearden, Bessye (Bessye Johnson Bearden), 86
Bearden, Harry, 86
Bearden, Romare, 86, 139, 162, 214n, 227n, 232–33n
Beatles, The, 169, 171, 221n
Beatty, Talley, 151
Belafonte, Harry (Harold Bellanfanti), 136
Bellson, Louie (Luigi Balassoni), 76, 115–16, 152, 168
Benjamin, Bea (Beatrice Benjamin), 219n
Benjamin, Joe (Joseph Benjamin), 115, 118, 120, 168, 221n
Beppato, Roberto, 191n
Bercovici, Konrad, 70, 206n
Berger, Arnold, 236n
Berger, David, 210n, 224n
Berio, Luciano, 159

Berlinghini, Gualtiero, 191n
Bernay, Eric, 50
Bernstein, Leonard, 56, 178, 220n
Berrino, Michele, 23
Bertozzi, Adriano, 23
Blair, Sara, 73, 208–9n
Blake, Eubie (James Hubert "Eubie" Blake), 29
Blitzstein, Marc (Marcus Samuel Blitzstein), 50
Bolden, James, 176
Bonds, Margaret, 216n, 232n
Bonfá, Luiz, 169
Borri Mottola, Lidia, 23
Bortoluzzi, Roberto, 23
Bosch, Hieronymus (Jeroen van Aken), 155
Boston Pops Orchestra, 115, 179, 221n
Boston Symphony Orchestra, 163, 179
Botticelli, Sandro (Alessandro di Mariano di Vanni Filipepi), 154
Boyer, Richard O., 35, 47, 197–98n, 205n
Bradford, Carmen, 229n
Brady, Mathew B., 208n
Bragalini, Luca, 187n, 238n
Braghiroli, Giovanni, 23
Brahms, Johannes, 60
Brand, Dollar (Adolph Johannes Brand/ Abdullah Ibrahim), 101
Breton, André, 96
Briggs, Bunny, 94
Britten, Benjamin, 168, 172
Brown, Anne, 27
Brown, Ethelred, 73
Brown, Lawrence, 15, 99, 109, 114, 127, 131, 219n
Brown, Sterling, 133–34, 139, 214n, 226n
Browne, Leslie (Lesley Brown), 175
Brubeck, Dave (David Warren Brubeck), 98, 152, 168
Bubley, Esther, 208n
Budini, Paolo, 191
Buffalo Philharmonic Orchestra, 30, 161, 179, 195n, 232n
Bukowski, Charles, 96

Burattin, Armando, 12, 15, 23, 190–91n
Burkhardt, Ernie, 168
Burleigh, Harry, 87, 91, 216n
Busetta, Giuseppe, 10, 189n
Busk, Bjarne, 229n
Butler, Octavia, 41
Buzzati, Dino, 12, 190n
Byard, Jaki (John Arthur "Jaki" Byard), 152

Caletti, Walter, 23
California Youth Symphony Orchestra, 116
Caliver, Ambrose, 52
Callas, Maria (Anna Maria Cecilia Kalogeropoulos), 190n
Calloway, Cab (Cabell "Cab" Calloway III), 50, 69, 80, 206n
Calvi, Gérard, 102
Cambursano, Glauco, 191n
Campbell, Elmer Simms, 81
Canadian Brass, 196n
Canarina, John, 178
Candini, Pino, 194n
Cane, Giampiero, 188n
Canfora, Bruno, 191n
Canfora, Oreste, 13, 23, 190–91n
Capriata, Carlo, 23
Carey, Hugh, 150
Carney, Harry Howell, 87, 99, 171
Carpana, Alcide, 23
Carrese, Vincenzo, 190n
Carrey, Jim (James Eugene Carrey), 167
Carroll, Diahann, 32, 136
Carter, Benny (Bennett Lester Carter), 152, 197n
Case, Russ, 28
Casey, Al (Alvin Casey), 53
Cavallo, Bruno, 12, 22, 189–91n
Cavern, Patti, 96, 218n
Cazzola, Mario, 191n
Cerri, Livio, 189–90n
Chailly, Floriana, 190n
Chailly, Luciano, 12, 190n
Chase, Lucia, 172, 175
Chesnutt, Charles W., 85

Chicago Symphony Orchestra, 91
Chopin, Fryderyk, 223n
Cincinnati Symphony Orchestra, 31, 77, 212n
City of Birmingham Symphony Orchestra, 196n
Civica Jazz Band, 161, 232n
CJRT Orchestra Toronto, 176–77
Clayton, Buck (Wilbur Dorsey "Buck" Clayton), 168
Cleveland Pops Orchestra, 100
Cleveland Symphony Orchestra, 116
Cliburn, Van (Harvey Lavan Cliburn Jr.), 222n
Clinkscales, Marietta, 91
Coady, Christopher, 5, 188n
Cole, Bob (Robert Allen Cole), 217n
Coleman, Ornette (Randolph D. Ornette Coleman), 112
Coleridge-Taylor, Samuel, 90–91, 216–17n
Coles, Johnny, 79
Collette, Buddy (William M. "Buddy" Collette), 190n
Collier, Cathy, 181, 237
Collier, James Lincoln, 48, 210n, 221n
Collier, Ron (Ronald W. Collier), 167–78, 180, 210n, 234–36n
Collins, Al Jazzbo (Albert R. "Jazzbo" Collins), 194n
Colliva, Tommaso, 14
Colombo, Gian Battista, 13, 190n
Colombo, Susanna, 13
Coltrane, John, 231–32n, 238n
Connors, Chuck, 195n
Cooper, Buster, 164, 202n
Cooper, Matthew J., 220n
Cooper, Merian C., 59
Copland, Aaron, ix, 56, 115, 222n
Corcella, Michele, 224n
Cornely, Henry, 178
Crosby, Bing (Harry Lillis "Bing" Crosby), 101
Cullen, Countee, 85, 89
Cuney-Hare, Maud, 87, 91, 132, 215–16n, 225n

Cuppini, Gil (Gilberto Cuppini), 194n
Curtin, Phyllis, 179

D'Amato, Bepi, 165
Dameron, Tadd (Tadley Ewing Peake Dameron), 233n
Dance, Stanley, 27, 94, 118, 157, 180, 192n, 194n, 217n, 222n, 231n, 233–34n, 237–38n
Davis, Benjamin J., 49–50
Davis, Frank Marshall, 61
Davis, Kay, 127–28
Davis, Miles (Miles Dewey Davis III), 190n
Davis, Sammy, Jr. (Samuel G. Davis Jr.), 47, 101, 136, 170
Davis, Wild Bill (William Strethen Davis), 125, 168–69
Dawson, Michael C., 199n
Dawson, William, 87, 91
De Paris, Wilbur, 168
De Poli, Ferruccio, 23
Debussy, Claude, 28, 38, 172
DeCarava, Roy, 74–75, 208–9n
DeFranco, Buddy (Boniface Ferdinand "Buddy" DeFranco), 165
Degas, Edgar, 162, 173, 233n
del Carmine, Luigi, 23
Del Pistoia, Paolo, 22
Delamont, Gordon Arthur, 169–70
Delano, Jack, 208n
Delany, Samuel, 41
Delaunay, Charles, 102–3, 220n
Delius, Frederick, 178
Desmond, Paul, 169
Dett, Nathaniel, 87, 91
Dexter, Dave (David Edwin Dexter Jr.), 101
Di Laura, Alfredo, 187n
Dickenson, Vic (Victor Dickenson), 53
Dietrich, Kurt, 195n
Dietrich, Marlene (Marie Magdalene Dietrich), 167
Ditson, Oliver, 91
Dixie Rhythm Kings, 206n
Dixon, Mildred, 207n

Douglas, Aaron, 71, 85–86, 139, 213n, 215n
Douglas Johnson, Georgia, 91
Draper, Paul, 168
Du Bois, W. E. B. (William Edward Burghardt Du Bois), 5, 71, 85–86, 88, 90–91, 133–34, 139, 188n, 208–9n, 213n, 215n, 217n, 225n, 227n
Duke, Vernon, 32, 56
Duke Ellington Orchestra, 58, 98, 101, 107, 149, 152–53, 167, 172, 180, 195n, 197n, 210n, 221n, 223n, 229–30n
Dunbar, Paul Laurence, 85, 90
Duncan, Todd, 27
Dürer, Albrecht, 155
Dylan, Bob (Robert Allen Zimmerman), 167

Eckstine, Billy (William Clarence Eckstine), 152
Edelstein, Hilly, 168
Edward, Brent Hayes, 198n, 203n
Elder, Lonne, 135
Eldridge, Roy, 53, 205n, 209n
Eliot, T. S. (Thomas Stearns Eliot), 184, 238n
Ellington, Mercer (Mercer Kennedy Ellington), 31, 94, 119, 153, 157, 195–96n, 200n, 204n, 229–31n
Ellington, Ruth, 32, 57, 86, 152, 196n, 201n, 207n, 213n
Ellis, Evie (Beatrice "Evie" Ellis), 207n
Ellison, Ralph, 44–45
Ernini, Vittorio, 23
Escudero Ralph (Rafael "Ralph" Escudero), 80
Evans, Walker, 208n

Falco, Louis, 150–51
Falcomer, Walter, 23
Falletta, JoAnn, 232n
Fantini, Franco, 12, 23, 190–91n
Farabola, Tullio, 190n
Father Divine (George Baker Jr.), 45
Fauset, Jessie, 85
Fax, Mark, 232n
Feather, Leonard, 78, 98, 100, 188n, 210n, 218–19n, 228n

Fededegni, Alfonso, 22
Ferrari, Defendente, 154
Ferreri, Albert, 102
Fiedler, Arthur, 115, 163, 179
Fields, Dorothy, 205n
Finkleman, Danny, 171
Fisk Jubilee Singers, 90
Floyd, Carlisle, 179–80
Floyd, Samuel A., 4, 188n, 193n, 213n, 215–16n
Focarino, Benedetto, 23
Fol, Raymond, 168
Ford, Betty (Elizabeth Ann Warren), 150, 152
Ford, Ricky, 158
Fracci, Carla, 28
Franchini, Vittorio, 9, 13, 189n
Franklin, John Hope, 45
Frigo, Mariano, 23
Fuller, Meta Vaux Warrick, 86
Fumagalli, Elena, 189n

Galassi, Peter, 209n
Galli, Umberto, 23
Garavini, Aldo, 22
Garrison, Margaret, 178
Garvey, Marcus, 45, 91, 216n
Gavazzeni, Gianandrea, 20
Gensel, John Garcia, 84, 176, 212n
George, Don, 46, 51, 58, 115, 198n, 214n, 221n
Gershwin, George, ix, 4, 27, 53, 194n, 206n
Gershwin, Ira, 206n
Ghetti, Genunzio, 23
Ghirlandaio (Domenico Bigordi), 154
Giancolombo Archive, 13
Giannini, Giuseppe, 13, 102, 191n
Giannuzzi Savelli, Oberto, 191n
Gillespie, Dizzy (John Birks "Dizzy" Gillespie), 50, 80, 87
Gillis, Don (Donald Eugene Gillis), 56, 98, 218n
Giuseppe Verdi Symphony Orchestra of Milan, 161, 232n
Gleason, Ralph, 114, 221n
Gonsalves, Paul, 15, 18, 109, 131, 164
Gonzaga, Chiquinha (Francisca Gonzaga), 203n

Goodman, Benny (Benjamin David Goodman), 50, 194n
Govi, Luigi, 23
Gramatica, Luigi, 23
Granz, Norman, 50, 101, 148, 218n
Greer, Sonny, 64
Gregory, Cynthia, 175
Gregory, Dick (Richard C. Gregory), 47
Grieder, Kurt, 14–15, 20, 191–92n
Griggs, Sutton, 41
Grünewald, Matthias, 155
Guard, John, 199n
Gusella, Mario, 23
Guy, Fred (Frederick Guy), 80
Gynt, Kaj, 136

Hall, Edmond, 53
Hall, Jim (James Stanley Hall), 14
Hamilton, Jimmy, 38, 128, 168
Hammond, John, ix, 49–51, 138, 199n
Hampton, Lionel Leo, 152
Händel, Georg Friedrich, 172
Handy, W. C. (William Christopher Handy), 53, 75, 138–39, 228n, 238n
Handy, W. C., Jr. (William Christopher Handy Jr.), 44
Haney, Carol, 32
Hanson, Howard, 36, 180
Hardwick, Otto (Otto J. "Toby" Hardwick), 64
Harling, W. Franke, 60, 202n
Harman, Carter, 42, 101, 116, 197n, 216n, 218n, 222n, 238n
Harper, Leonard, 65, 204n
Havana Casino Orchestra, 80
Hayden, Palmer, 86
Haydn, Franz Joseph, 112
Hayes, Roland, 87, 91, 134
Hayman, Richard, 115, 222n
Haynes, George E., 72, 207n
Hayton, Lennie (Leonard G. Hayton), 98
Heath, Jimmy (James Heath), 161, 232n
Hebling, Edu, 211n
Heifetz, Jascha, 27
Henderson, Fletcher, 50, 71, 225n

Henderson, Floyd, 68, 205n
Henderson, Harry, 162, 233n
Henderson, Luther, 5, 31–35, 38–39, 76, 84, 99, 112–13, 115, 149, 152, 161, 164, 168–69, 195–97n, 200–201n, 219
Henderson, Skitch (Lyle Russel "Skitch" Henderson), 56
Henderson Quartet, The, 31
Henry, Ann, 170, 234–35n
Hernández, Rafael, 79–80
Himes, Chester, 74
Hines, Earl "Fatha," 135
Hines, Gregory, 196n
Hines, Lewis, 208n
Hinton, Milt (Milton John Hinton), 152
Hodges, Johnny (John Cornelius Hodges), 21, 87, 99, 104, 108–10, 114, 164, 172, 219n, 222n, 238n
Holiday, Billie (Eleanora Fagan), 50, 53, 134, 226n
Hollywood Bowl Symphony Orchestra, 116
Hooker, John Lee, 135
Horne, Lena, 32, 47, 75, 98, 160
Horton, Lester, 151
Horton, Randall Keith, x
Howland, John, ix, 4, 187n, 193–94n, 196–97n, 203n, 216n
Hughes, Langston, 50, 63, 71, 85–86, 89, 134–39, 155, 204n, 208n, 215n, 226–28n, 230n
Hurston, Zora Neale, 134, 139, 226n

ICAMus-Centro di Documentazione sulla Musica Americana, x
ICAMus-The International Center for American Music, ix–x
Intra, Enrico, 161, 232n
Ionio, Daniele, 9, 15, 189n, 192n, 195n

Jackson, Calvin, 21, 33, 168, 196n
Jackson, Mahalia, 84, 124–25, 162
Jacksonville Symphony Orchestra, 178–79, 185, 237n
James, Harry, 196n
James, Stephen, 213–14n

James, Winston, 199n, 211n
Jannetta, Louis, 167
Jazz Vespers, 212n
Jenkins, Freddy, 140
Jiménez, Manuel, 79
Johnson, Aaron J., 199n
Johnson, Charles, 85
Johnson, Coffin Ed, 74
Johnson, Edward, 41
Johnson, James Price, 4, 29, 63–64, 70, 187n, 193–94n, 203n, 205n, 226n
Johnson, James Weldon, 44, 63, 72, 85, 89, 133–34, 203n, 207n, 213n, 215–16n, 225n
Johnson, Lyndon, 55, 175
Johnson, Malvin Gray, 86, 215n
Johnson, Martha, 172, 236n
Johnson, Rosamond, 217n
Johnson, Sargent Claude, 86, 89
Johnson, William, 74, 86
Jones, Gravedigger, 74
Jones, Jimmy (James Jones), 168
Jones, Sissieretta (Matilda Sissieretta Joyner Jones), 216n
Jordaens, Jacob, 156
Jungle Town Stompers, 206n

Kahn, Gus (Gustav Kahn), 206n
Kaye, Bernard L., 182, 238n
Kennedy, John Fitzgerald, 3
Kennedy, Robert, 47
Kenton, Stan (Stanley Newcomb Kenton), 190n
Kerr, Brooks, 201n
King, Martin Luther, Jr., 3, 47, 51, 152, 159, 162, 217n, 232n
Kirk, Roland (Rahsaan Roland Kirk), 9
Knight, Gladys, 122
Koger (Ira McKissick Koger), 179
Kubrick, Stanley, 214n
Kunzel, Erich, 31, 77, 117

La Scala String Quartet, 190n
Lamb, John, 115, 118
Lambert, Eddie, 26, 121, 188n, 193n, 223n
Lane, Louis, 100

Lane, Winthrop D., 70, 206n
Lange, Dorothea, 208n
Lanning, Van Lier, 178
Lasker, Steven, 60, 202n, 204n, 207n, 210n
Latouche, John (John Patrick Treville Latouche), 32, 238n
Lavezzoli, Peter, 99, 195n, 219n
Lawrence, Jacob, 74, 86, 209n
Lawson, Cristyne, 151
Lee, Canada (Leonard L. C. Canegata), 52–54, 200n
Lee, Russell, 208n
Lemoni, Lorenzo, 10
L'Engle Adams, Claudia, 178
Leonardo da Vinci, 154
Leur, Walter van de, 61, 202n, 207n
Levine, Lawrence, 4, 187n, 225n
Levins, Daniel, 236n
Levitt, Helen, 74
Lewis, David Levering, 85, 187n, 204n, 212–15n
Lewis, John, 4, 185
Liberace (Władziu Valentino Liberace), 167
Lincoln, Abraham, xii, 159
Lippi, Filippino (Filippo Lippi), 154
Liszt, Franz (Ferenc Liszt), 30
Lock, Graham, 48, 198n, 203n, 214n
Locke, Alain, 85–88, 91, 133–34, 155, 212n, 214–16n, 225n, 231n
Logan, Arthur, 86, 114, 160
Logan, Marian, 159, 232n
Lomax, Alan, 134, 226n
London Philharmonic Orchestra, 31, 116–17, 195n
Los Angeles Symphony Orchestra, 31, 116–17, 195n
Louis, Joe (Joseph Louis Barrow), 45, 54, 227n

Macchinizzi, Edgardo, 23
MacDowell, Edward, 222n
Machín, Antonio, 80
Machito (Francisco Raúl Grillo), 80
MacLaine, Shirley (Shirley MacLean Beaty), 175

INDEX OF NAMES

Maggio, Antonio, 238n
Mahler, Gustav, 60
Makowicz, Adam, 153, 195n
Maletto, Gian Mario, 188n
Mantegna, Andrea, 155
Marchesi, Fabio, 191n
Marshall, Thurgood, 71
Martin, Dean (Dino Crocetti), 101
Marx Brothers, 217n
Marzi, Marco, 192n
Massagli, Luciano, 189n, 191–93n, 195–96n, 222n, 234n
Massys, Quentin, 155
Matisse, Henri, 162
May, Billy (Edward William May Jr.), 167
Mayers, Lloyd, 149
Mazzoletti, Adriano, 189n, 192n
McCrea, Joel, 61
McDonald, Anthony, 232n
McDuffie, Alvin, 151
McGettigan, Betty, 149, 228n
McHugh, Jimmy (James McHugh), 205n
McIntyre, Dianne, 151
McKay, Claude, 44, 71, 86, 207n, 227n
McLaughlin, John, 14
McRae, Carmen, 32
Memling, Hans, 154
Meyer, Leonard B., 66, 204–5n
Miley, Bubber (James Wesley "Bubber" Miley), 238n
Miller, Mulgrew, 195n
Milnes, Harriett, 229, 235n
Minetti, Enrico, 191n
Mingus, Charles, 98, 112, 135, 138, 218n
Miori, Ennio, 11, 23, 189n, 191n
Miró (i Ferrà), Joan, 95, 218n
Mitchell-Ruff Trio, 9
Mitropoulos, Dimitri, 27
Modern Jazz Quartet, 5, 126, 168, 185, 189n
Mojoli, Franco, 12
Mojoli, Michelangelo, 12, 23, 190–91n
Montale, Eugenio, 20, 192n
Monti, Stefano, 23
Moody, James, 228n
Morawetz, Oskar, 159
Moretti, Alberto, 23

Moretti, Mario, 22
Moretto, Vanni, 191n
Morgan, John, 202n
Morgan, W. Astor, 87
Morgenstern, Dan, 223n
Morton, Benny, 54
Morton, Jelly Roll (Ferdinand Joseph LaMothe), 196n, 221n
Mosconi, Davide, 13
Mosconi, Ines, 190n
Motley, Archibald John, Jr., 86, 139, 213n
Mozart, Wolfgang Amadeus, 112, 222n
Mulligan, Gerry (Gerald Mulligan), 4, 98, 190n
Musi, Renato, 23
Myers, Milton, 151

Nance, Ray (Ray Willis Nance), 15–16, 18, 20, 32, 57, 77–78, 99, 104, 108–9, 114, 192n, 219n, 221n
Nardo, Aldo, 23
National Symphony Orchestra, 100, 218n, 221n
NBC Symphony Orchestra, 28, 56, 76, 98, 218n
New Haven Symphony Orchestra, 30, 77, 99, 218n
New York Negro Symphony Orchestra, 63
New York Philharmonic Orchestra, 115, 222n
Newborn, Phineas, Jr., 135
Newman, Paul, 162
Nimmons, Phil (Philip Rista Nimmons), 168
Nixon, Richard, 55, 200n, 228n
Norris, John, 169, 234n

O'Connor, Norman, 84, 212n
Oland, Warner, 86
O'Reilly, Ted, 119, 167, 176–77, 180, 182, 234n, 237n
Orlando, Ruggero, 114, 139, 187n
Ormandy, Eugene (Jenő Ormándy-Blau), 27
Orner, George, 178
O'Sullivan, Timothy, 208n
Ottley, Roi (Vincent Lushington "Roi" Ottley), x, 40–46, 49, 51–54, 74, 198–99n, 209n

Overton, Hall, 170
Owen, Robert, 198

Pagani, Mauro, 14
Page, Willis, 179, 195n, 237n
Palmquist, David, 57, 197n, 201–3n, 217n, 234n
Panciroli, Alfredo, 22
Paolillo, Tonino, 191
Paredes, Marcos, 175
Parker, Charlie (Charles Parker), 50, 80
Parker, Doug (Douglas Parker), 135
Parker, Elliott, 198n
Parker, Kay, 168
Parks, Gordon, 74–75, 208–9n, 232n
Parsons Smith, Catherine, 5
Peress, Maurice, 77, 117, 161, 178, 180, 201n, 221–22n, 228–29n, 232n, 238n
Pessani, Luigi, 234n
Peterson, Oscar, 168
Petrassi, Goffredo, 159
Petry, Ann Lane, 74, 209n
Peyton, Dave, 132, 225n
Pfohl, James Christian, 178
Philadelphia Orchestra, 21, 27, 33, 194n
Piccagliani, Erio, 189n
Pinkins, Tonya, 186n
Piras, Marcello, 207n, 220n
Poe, Edgar Allan, 96
Pogliani, Giacomo, 23
Poitier, Sidney, 47, 136, 162
Polillo, Arrigo, 139, 188n, 228n
Polish National Philharmonic Orchestra, 153, 175, 195n, 231n
Ponzoni, Tano, 9, 189n
Porta, Johnny, 191n
Porter, Cole, 69
Porzio, Gianni, 23
Post Wolcott, Marion, 208n
Powell, Adam Clayton, Jr., 43, 72–73, 207n, 227n
Powell, Adam Clayton, Sr., 73
Powell, Bud (Earl Rudolph Powell), 101, 190n
Powell, Richard, 213n
Pozo, Chano (Luciano Pozo González), 80

Price, Florence, 87, 216n
Procope, Russell, 15, 171
Profumo, John, 3
Prokofiev, Sergei, 112
Pullen, Frances Kaye, 229n, 251n
Pusateri, Liborio, 189n

Rachmaninov, Sergei Vasilyevich, 30
Raffaello (Raffaello Sanzio), 154
Rajski, Wojciech, 175, 153, 195n
Rameau, Jean-Philippe, 205n
Rampersad, Arnold, 133, 225–27n
Randolph, Asa Philip, x, 50
Ranzani, Francesco, 22
Rattle, Simon, 196n
Ravel, Maurice, 28, 130, 223n
Reich, Steve (Stephen Reich), 136
Reiner, Fritz (Frigyes Reiner), 27
Reiss, Winold, 85–86
Remington, Frederic, 163, 233n
Renzetti, Domenico, 23
Righetti, Domenico, 23
Riis, Jacob, 208n
Rivera, Angelina, 80
Rizza, Piero, 16, 192n
Roach, Max (Maxwell L. Roach), 138
Robbins, Jerome, 150
Roberts, John Storm, 211n, 223n
Roberts, Luckey (Charles Luckyth Roberts), 80
Robeson, Paul, 27, 46, 50, 52, 54, 71, 87, 134, 136
Robinson, Bill "Bojangles" (Luther Robinson), 54, 71, 205n
Robinson, Earl, 163
Robinson, Louie, 235n
Rocca, Giuseppe, 22
Rocchetta, Massimiliano, 238n
Roché, Betty (Mary Elizabeth Roché), 123
Rockefeller, John Davison, 71
Rollins, Sonny (Walter Theodore "Sonny" Rollins), 112
Romano, Renato, 23
Romberg, Sigmund, 56
Rome, Harold (Harold Jacob "Hecky" Rome), 50

Romero, Redentor (Redentor "Red" L. Romero), 221n
Ron Collier Orchestra, 169
Roosevelt, Franklin Delano, xii, 26, 194n
Roque, Julio, 79
Ross, Herbert, 175
Rostropovič, Mstislav, 159
Rothstein, Arthur, 208n
Rubinstein, Arthur, 27, 190n
Ruff, Willie, 152, 228n
Rulli, Aura, 235n
Rushing, Jimmy (James A. Rushing), 135
Russell, Bob (Sidney K. Rosenthal), 233n
Russell, Charles Marion, 163
Russell, George, 159, 170
Russotto, Giuseppe, 191n
Rutledge, Walter, 162, 232n

Saunders, Charles, 41
Savage, Augusta (Augusta C. Fells), 86, 215n
Savage, Barbara Dianne, 52, 199n
Sawyer, Raymond, 151
Schiff, David, 36, 50, 188n, 197n, 200n, 218n, 238n
Schiozzi, Bruno, 188n, 192n
Schoedsack, Ernest B., 59
Schubert, Franz, 25, 87
Schuller, Gunther, 100, 149, 170, 219n, 224n, 229n
Schuman, William, 222n
Schumann, Robert, 87
Schuyler, George, 41
Schwamenthal, Riccardo, 188n
Scivales, Riccardo, 225n
Scott, Bobby (Robert William Scott), 169
Scott, James W., 217n
Scott, Hazel Dorothy, 52, 194n
Scott, Tony (Anthony Joseph Sciacca), 165
Scott King, Coretta, 152
Scotto, Franco, 23
Screvane, Paul, 116
Seccia-Pesce, Michele, 23
Selassie, Haile (Hailé Selassié/Tafarì Maconnèn), 157
Senghor, Léopold Sédar, 137
Shahn, Ben, 208n
Shakespeare, William, 42–43, 122
Shavers, Charlie (Charles J. Shavers), 53
Shaw, Artie (Arthur J. Arshawsky), 50
Shaw, Edie, 163, 233n
Shaw, Sam (Samuel Shaw), 162–63, 232n
Shearing, George, 28
Shepard, Ernie (Ernest Shepard), 15, 18–19, 76
Shirley, Don (Donald Shirley), 28–30, 194–95n
Shirley, Wayne D., 216n
SIdMA Jazz Orchestra, 165, 185
Sigler, Vicente, 79
Sinatra, Frank (Francis Albert Sinatra), 101–2, 148, 167, 190n
Singleton, Willie, 158
Siskind, Aaron, 74
Smith, Arnold Jay, 152
Smith, Bessie, 66, 130, 134, 204n, 225n
Smith, Geoff, 223n
Smith, Judith E., 199n
Smith, Marvin, 209n
Smith, Mona Z., 200n
Smith, Morgan, 209n
Smith, Willie (Willie "the Lion" Smith), 66, 204n
Snowden, Elmer, 64
Socarrás, Alberto, 79–80
Solomons, Gus, Jr., 151
Sonny Price Trio, 135
Šostakovič, Dmitri, 113
Spencer, Jon Michael, 88
Spingarn, Arthur, 75
Steele, Frankie, 44
Steinbeck, John, 42
Steiner, Kenneth, 197n
Steiner, Max (Maximilian R. Steiner), 59–61, 201–2n
Stevenson Adlai, II, 116, 222n
Stewart, Rex, 71
Stewart, Slam (Leroy Eliot "Slam" Stewart), 53, 152
Still, William Grant, 87, 91, 138
Stockholm Symphony Orchestra, 104, 107, 110
Stokowski, Leopold, 27

Stone, Fred, 169, 171, 233–34n
Strappo, Adolfo, 23
Stratemann, Klaus, 178
Stravinsky, Igor, 11, 190n, 229n
Strayhorn, Billy (William Thomas Strayhorn), 16, 32, 36, 42, 61, 72, 108–11, 115, 160, 168, 196n, 202n, 212n, 214n, 221–22n
Studio Giancolombo, 13–14
Studio Zanibelli, 14–15, 191n
Stuttgart Radio Symphony Orchestra, 195n
Sun Ra (Herman Poole Blount), 41
Sweatman, Wilbur, 64
Symonds, Norman, 168–70, 234n
Symphony Foundation of America, 218n
Symphony of the Air, 28, 77, 98

Tabarelli, Franco, 11, 189–91n
Tatum, Art (Arthur Tatum Jr.), 53
Tavecchio, Louis, 223n
Teatro alla Scala Orchestra, 9, 12–13, 20, 22, 189n
Thomas, Norman, 205n
Thompson, Don (Donald Thompson), 171
Thurman, Wallace, 65–66, 86, 134, 204n
Timner, W. E., 20, 192n, 234n
Tizol, Juan, 34, 80, 211n
Tollara, Gianni, 189n, 192n
Tomelleri, Paolo, 191n
Tommaso, Bruno, 165, 185
Tonali, Luigi, 190n
Toomer, Jean, 215n
Toronto Symphony Orchestra, 170
Toscani, Fedele, 190n
Toscani, Oliviero, 190n
Toscanini, Arturo, 56–57, 98, 190n, 201n, 218n
Truman, Harry, 49, 55–56, 200n
Truman, Margaret, 56
Tucker, Earl "Snakehips," 207n
Tucker, Mark, 84, 86, 207n, 212n, 217n, 219n
Turio, Marcello, 23
Turner, Tina (Anna Mae Bullock), 167
Turney, Norris, 171
Turolla, Miles, 22

Ulanov, Barry, 34, 70, 94, 197n, 206n
Ulivieri, Filippo, 214n
United States Air Force Band, 232n
United States Coast Guard Quartet, 53
U2, 159

Vachon, John, 208n
Vail, Ken, 202n, 222n
Valdinoci, Alfredo, 191n
Van Der Zee, James, 74, 208–9n
Van Leyden, Lucas (Lucas Hugenszoon), 155
Van Vechten, Carl, 65, 69, 86, 88, 136, 204n, 213n, 215n, 230n
Vance, Dick (Richard Thomas Vance), 168
Vaughan, Sarah L., 28, 180
Veccia, Luigi, 23
Verdi, Giuseppe, 112, 223n
Vincent, Norman, 238n
Volpato, Giuseppe, 23

Walker, Alice, 134
Waller, Thomas "Fats," 44, 49
Ward, Samuel Ringgold, 216n
Washington, Booker T., 91
Waterhouse, Brent, x
Waters, Ethel, 75
Waters, Muddy (McKinley Morganfield), 135
Watts, André, 222n
Webb, Chick (William Henry "Chick" Webb), 50, 206n
Weber, Carl Maria von, 180
Webster, Ben (Benjamin Webster), 53, 135, 168
Weissberg, Eric, 163
Welch, Raquel (Jo Raquel Tejada), 167
Welles, Orson (George Orson Welles), 50
Wesley Krosnick, Mary Lou, 180
West, Dorothy, 44
Weston, Randy, 135, 196n
Weyden, Rogier van der (Rogier de la Pasture), 154
Whaley, Tom (Thomas Whaley), 35
White, Clarence Cameron, 71
White, Lucien, 132
White, Stanford, 71

White, Walter, 71
Whiteman, Paul Samuel, 4, 177, 187n, 194n, 206n
Willett, Chappie (Francis Willett), 168
Williams, Clarence, 80, 206n
Williams, Cootie (Charles M. "Cootie" Williams), 8, 15, 18, 70, 78, 99, 114, 170–71, 219n, 222n
Williams, Dudley, 162
Williams, Mary Lou (Mary E. Scruggs), 159, 168
Wilson, Gerald Stanley, 168
Wilson, Olly, 159
Wilson, Wesley, 204n
Wonder, Stevie (Stevland H. Morris), 153
Wood, Booty (Mitchell W. Wood), 176
Wooding, Sam, 16
Woodson, Carter G., 226n
Woodyard, Sam, 15, 18
Wright, Richard, 44, 50, 54, 208n

Yeats, William Butler, 184, 238n
Young, Charles, 217n
Young, David, 158
Young, Lester, 190n

Zanibelli, Carlo, 14
Zanibelli, Umberto, 14
Zoudenbalch, Evert, 157, 231n

ABOUT THE AUTHOR

Photo by Jonny Malavasi.

LUCA BRAGALINI is professor of history and analysis of jazz at the Music Conservatory Giuseppe Verdi of Milan. Bragalini was a distinguished scholar at Reed College, where he offered a series of lectures on Ellington. He has discovered unpublished works by Duke Ellington, Chet Baker, and Luciano Chailly and is the author of the Italian edition of this book, *Dalla Scala a Harlem: I sogni sinfonici di Duke Ellington*, named Best Musicological Book of 2018 by the Jazzit Awards.

www.ingramcontent.com/pod-product-compliance
Lightning Source LLC
Chambersburg PA
CBHW030611230426
43661CB00053B/1941